EARLY
AMERICAN
LITERATURE

EARLY AMERICAN LITERATURE

A COMPARATIST APPROACH

A. Owen Aldridge

PRINCETON UNIVERSITY PRESS
PRINCETON, NEW JERSEY

To

J. A. Leo Lemay
George Panichas
Kenneth Silverman

CONTENTS

PREFACE

AMERICAN LITERATURE as a separate entity in the university curriculum does not have a long history. Indeed, in a realistic sense, it can be said to have come of age as an academic discipline between the two World Wars almost concomitantly with comparative literature. The journal *Revue de littérature comparée* was founded in 1924; *American Literature*, in 1929. The consideration of the seventeenth and eighteenth centuries as a major segment or independent dimension of American letters represents an even later development.

Until very recently comparative literature as practiced both in Europe and the United States has been strongly oriented toward Europe. In the formative years of this discipline, comparatists paid scant attention to either Anglo-American or Ibero-American authors, and European literary historians made no effort to distinguish between the two groups. Even now this bias toward the European continent is revealed in a project of the International Comparative Literature Association for a series of volumes to represent a comparative history of literatures in European languages. It is not surprising that in projects of this kind the literatures of the Americas should be treated as mere appendages to European letters. History, however, indicates recurring relationships on a triangular basis; that is, the presence of various waves of influence and resemblance joining serious writing in Anglo-America, Ibero-America, and Europe. Even in the period before 1800, each of the Americas made substantial contributions to universal literature.

While comparatists, on one hand, have tended to overlook the Western Hemisphere, scholars of Anglo-American literature have exercised a related selectivity by concentrating upon American authors to the neglect of relationships with the rest of the world. Paradoxically, they have shown least interest in Latin America, particularly in regard to the period before 1800. My purpose in this book is twofold: to draw the attention of comparatists to the vitality of literary activity in the Western Hemisphere during the seventeenth and eighteenth centuries, an activity which in part borrowed from European sources and came to be reflected in subsequent European productions; and to suggest to specialists in early American literature that their subject matter does not represent an isolated, provincial phenomenon, but one that responded to the same influences, concerns, and idiosyncrasies affecting or accompanying other literatures of the period.

ACKNOWLEDGMENTS

OF THE ESSAYS in this book, three have never before been published in any form. The five others are based in varying degrees upon one or more of the following previously published articles: "Polly Baker and Boccaccio" in *Annali dell'Istituto Universitario Orientale*, Sezione Romanza, 14 (1971): 5-18; "Paine and Dickinson" in *Early American Literature* 11 (1976): 125-38; "Thomas Paine in Latin-America" in *Early American Literature* 3 (1969): 139-47; "The Vogue of Thomas Paine in Argentina," *Actes du VIème Congrès Internationale de Littérature Comparée* (Stuttgart, 1975), pp. 281-85; "The Concept of Ancients and Moderns in the Federal Period" in *Classical Traditions in Early America*, ed. John W. Eadie, pp. 99-118 (Ann Arbor, 1976); "The Enlightenment in the Americas" in *Proceedings of the 7th Congress of the International Comparative Literature Association*, 2 vols. (Stuttgart, 1979), 1: 59-67.

EARLY
AMERICAN
LITERATURE

ONE

INTRODUCTION

THE THEME of national consciousness, a concept that came into being immediately after the American Revolution, has been widely discussed in the literary history of North America. This patriotic spirit, as it flourished in the early years of the republic, may be interpreted as either the expression of a cultural identity distinct from that of England and, consequently, a salutary development, or, conversely, as an induced insensitivity to the rest of the world and, therefore, a deplorable example of intellectual insularity. Even before the period of 1776, the American people existed, according to Thomas Paine, "at a distance from, and unacquainted with the world." A staunch patriot at the turn of the eighteenth century, Jedidiah Morse, held the same opinion. "Before the Revolution," he maintained in the preface to his *American Universal Geography* (1793), "Americans seldom pretended to write or to think for themselves. We humbly received from Great Britain our laws, our manners, our books, and our modes of thinking; and our youth were educated as the subjects of the British king, rather than as the citizens of a free and independent republic." The accusations of insularity made during the colonial and federal periods have never been adequately investigated to determine whether they are true or false. The political part of Morse's statement must stand without contradiction, but the notions of complete literary dependence upon England cannot be supported. Ideas and styles of writing entered America from continental Europe as well as from Great Britain. Most historians of American literature, however, seem to be unaware that there is a problem to be clarified and are quite content indiscriminately to accept all works written in English in the Northern Hemisphere prior to Washington Irving as being products of Anglo-Saxon culture exclusively.

Two complementary, but, nevertheless, contrary explanations have been offered for the long-standing acceptance of this notion of British intellectual domination. First of all, both Europeans and Americans, during the seventeenth and eighteenth centuries, took for granted that any belletristic work produced in the American colonies (in either the English, Spanish or Portuguese languages) was an inherent part of the literature of the mother country. Although the colonial literatures were obviously outgrowths or transplants from the original stock, they were moreover regarded as integral parts of the culture of the nation from which they derived. A work produced, for example, in the English hegemony of America—that is, in the English literary zone, to borrow a term from Soviet literary criticism—would automatically be considered a part of English literature. Its nationality would be conferred by the same process as the birthright of its author.

From the perspective of colonial times, both nationality and birthright were indeed English, but the practice of classifying American writers as part of English literature continued in England and Europe after the American Revolution and throughout the nineteenth century. Major authors in the United States such as Whitman, Twain, and James, for example, were customarily classified under the rubric of English letters. It has been only since World War II that European universities have carved separate niches in their curricula for North American and Latin American literatures. Logically, geographical or political difference should not constitute a sufficient reason for separating the literature of the United States from that of England.

Only fundamental differences in language and culture warrant distinct categories. Swiss language and culture, for example, are so close to French on one side and German on the other that the Swiss authors Rousseau and Dürrenmatt are customarily treated as belonging to French literature and German literature respectively. Cultural differences between the United States and England justify the present method of setting apart the literatures of the two nations, but cultural differences have always been present and were perhaps even more pronounced in the seventeenth and eighteenth centuries than in our day. There is no question that political independence led Americans to proclaim their literary production as separate from English early in the nineteenth century, but the rest of the world had an insufficient knowledge of American writing to observe the distinction. At the present time when early American literature is being studied more seriously and more extensively than ever before, evidence is constantly being adduced to erode the opinion that the writing of the eastern seaboard in seventeenth- and eighteenth-century America was a product of British culture alone.

A second explanation, other than the colonial heritage, of why the relations between early American writers and Europe have been neglected may be found in a theory of ethnic roots. This is the view, based ultimately on a biological theory of the influence of climate upon human character, that the soil and other physical features of the American continent established the national identity or autonomy of its literature. The concept is exemplified in a passage from Paine's *Rights of Man* rhapsodically affirming his belief that the grandeur of the landscape inspires sublime concepts and promotes artistic creation. Other aspects of the landscape are presumed to impart specifically "American" characteristics to literature. The concept of topographical influence exists also in Europe, but it has not been taken seriously since the Romantic period. In Latin America, literary criticism is still dominated by notions of what is termed the telluric foundations of its literature, that is, effects of soil, climate, scenery, and, to some extent, racial strains.

Earth, blood and birthright are undoubtedly significant elements in the development of every national literature, but these elements are supplemented by the historical contribution of major writers from other literatures. However remote they may seem, Dante, Erasmus, Rabelais, and Cervantes as well as Chaucer, Shakespeare, and Milton constitute the heritage of the colonial and later literature of North America. Thomas Paine's comment in *Common Sense* about racial strains could be applied to literary production as well: "Europe and not England is the parent country." Obviously from the linguistic perspective, American and English literature are essentially a unit, but from the point of view of culture they are distinct. The circumstance that American and English literatures share the same language is no justification for failing to recognize, or for not investigating, similarities of a different kind between American and continental literatures. If English writers of the seventeenth and eighteenth centuries have been studied comparatively, that is, in relation to their counterparts on the continent, the same method might profitably be applied to American authors of the same chronological period. One may believe that the literature of the English colonies derived its basic materials from the mother country or that it acquired some of its distinct characteristics from the New World environment and still accept the premise that many American writings resemble those of other countries and that many American and European authors have come into contact with each other's works.

As early as 1830, pioneer literary critic William Ellery Channing advocated study of relationships of this kind.

In an essay "On National Literature" in the *Christian Examiner*, Channing earnestly recommended "a more extensive acquaintance with the intellectual labors of continental Europe." The reading of his countrymen, Channing felt, was "confined too much to English books, and especially to the more recent publications of Great Britain." Channing urged, moreover, that "we ought to know the different modes of viewing and discussing great subjects in different nations" and we "should be able to compare the writings of the highest minds in a great variety of circumstances." This awareness of European letters he specifically proposed as a means of fostering "our own intellectual independence and activity." In other words, Channing actually prescribed what is now known as the comparative method of literary study as a means of promoting American letters. At the same time he considered that it "would be better to admit no books from abroad than to make them substitutes for our own intellectual activity." The America of his time, he felt, needed a literature of its own both to counteract and to appreciate imported ones. The reverse is just as applicable in the twentieth century—that students of American literature need a knowledge of relevant foreign works as an aid for the understanding of domestic ones.

The major omission from Channing's prescription for literary study is any reference to parallel developments in Latin America. This deficiency is excusable in Channing's essay since at the time he was writing, technology had not sufficiently advanced to permit general awareness in either Anglo-America or Latin America of literary activity in the other hemisphere. Today, however, readers of book reviews in any major newspaper of the United States are regularly apprised of literary activities in Mexico, Brazil, and Argentina. Unfortunately the process has not worked retrospectively. Even though the literature of the United States in many ways has more in common with the lit-

eratures of other American nations than with those in
Europe, few scholars have taken the trouble to investigate
parallels, influences, and other relationships. Linguistic
and cultural resemblances cause the literatures of Latin
America ordinarily to be associated with those of Spain
and Portugal, and the literature of the United States to be
associated with that of England. Belletristic connections
among the various American nations, however, are just
as close as those between any American and any European
literature. The periods of conquest, colonization, revolution, expansion, and national consciousness draw the
writings of the American nations together in a historical
framework just as movements of greater esthetic intensity
such as neoclassicism, Romanticism, and realism provide
them with links of another kind with each other and with
their European forebears.

One of the major topics treated by comparatists has
been the problem of tracing and defining the various literary movements and periods, five of which touched both
North and South America between 1635 and 1810: The
Renaissance, the baroque, neoclassicism, the Enlightenment, and Romanticism. Students of national literatures
have relatively little difficulty in assigning chronological
limits to these movements or periods, merely placing them
in consecutive order and allowing for overlapping on either
side. When several literatures are considered together,
however, the chronological limits of a movement in one
literature do not necessarily coincide with those in another. The Renaissance, for example, began in Italy in the
thirteenth century, but did not have a major influence in
England until the sixteenth. Neoclassicism also had its
origins in Italy (in the sixteenth century), reached its ze-
nith in France in the seventeenth century, but did not
dominate in England until the eighteenth. Until very recently, scholars have paid scant attention to the effect of
any of these movements on American literature except

for Romanticism. Even then the emphasis has been on the quest for American nationality, which neoclassicism is "supposed to have hindered" and Romanticism "to have promoted."[1] The conscious efforts in America at the turn of the eighteenth century to promote independence from European literary traditions parallel those of Herder and other Europeans to glorify folklore and ethnic writing. The great difference is that in Europe critics looked almost reverently to the past; in America they looked rhapsodically toward the future.

Paradoxically, scholars of American literature have given more attention to the European antecedents of New World Romanticism and to parallels between European and American manifestations of Romanticism, a movement that presumably encouraged independence and individualism, than to the origins and manifestations of the Renaissance, the baroque, and neoclassicism, movements that placed a premium upon convention and imitation. In actuality, all of these European movements had repercussions in America. The effects of some critical theories that originated in Italy and Spain may be discernible in poetry written in colonial Virginia or Massachusetts, and certain elements of colonial neoclassicism have as much in common with French as with English traditions. Eighteenth-century American literature represents much more than the infiltration of the rhetorical art of Pope and Johnson into the milieu of New England Puritanism. Neoclassicism and the Enlightenment were not exclusively Anglo-Saxon, and they embraced much of European culture before being felt in America. Neoclassicism, moreover, did not reach its apex in the New World until after the creation of the United States, when it had been completely superseded by Romanticism in England, France,

---

[1] William L. Hedges, "Toward a Theory of American Literature, 1765-1800," *Early American Literature* 4 (1969): 5.

and Germany. Indeed, neoclassicism flourished so late in the United States that it coexisted with many elements of Romanticism, sometimes in the work of a single author.

The theory that Colonial American literature was an outgrowth of English, or even of English and continental together, suggests not only an intellectual dependence of the colony upon the metropole but also a colonial cultural lag. A major critic of early American poetry, Harold Jantz, accepts these assumptions for the eighteenth century, but not the seventeenth. He argues that "American literature was to an unusual degree independent during its first hundred years" and that "only after the 1720's or '30's does it become a more fully dependent, a genuinely colonial literature, imitating the approved homeland models."[2] Jantz establishes this hypothesis upon the purely political grounds that the early settlers of Massachusetts and Connecticut created model societies based on Puritan ideals and that many of their leaders were later recalled to England to serve in the Cromwellian government. Because of their political experience, the colonies could be considered temporarily ahead of the mother country instead of lagging behind. A weakness of this theory is that it applies only to the New England colonies. An even greater weakness is that it fails to account for the disparity in literary production between the English colonies and those of Spain. The latter in the first half of the seventeenth century boasted a brilliant concentration of poets, chroniclers, and diarists far exceeding the modest talents of those to the north. It is hard to see, moreover, why there should have been a greater degree of literary independence in the early years of the North American colonies than a century later when they had accumulated a larger and more diverse

---

[2] "American Baroque," in *Discoveries & Considerations*, ed. Calvin Israel (Albany, 1976), p. 8.

population, established newspapers, created educational institutions, and developed native traditions. Some literary historians have accepted the notion of an "Anglo-American cultural lag,"[3] that is, the notion of late American awareness and imitation of English literary fashion, but one never hears even the suggestion that America may have trailed behind the continent.

One way of avoiding the question of cultural lag—with its connotations of superiority in the originating or emitting body and inferiority in the receiving one—is to think in terms of an universal literature rather than a national one. In the broadest sense, universal literature represents the sum total of all texts or works throughout the world. The concept assumes that all writing in all geographical areas and in all chronological periods has equal historical validity—and that any particular work may profitably be considered in relation to any other that is relevant through subject matter, style, or historical circumstances. The perspective of universal literature has been adopted primarily by critics in small or emerging countries in order to promote international attention to minor literatures. Otherwise world attention would be monopolized by the great writers of Europe, the United States, China, and Japan. Since there is a real conflict between concentration on world masterpieces and concentration on national literatures, those nations without a claim to recognized masterpieces naturally support the universal perspective. This method of study brings minor literatures and minor writings into contact with major movements and even with world masterpieces. It enables specialists in minor literatures to deal with matters of universal rather than merely local concern or significance. America before 1800 was, in regard to literary production, in much the same position

[3] Robert D. Arner, "The Connecticut Wits," in *American Literature, 1764-1789*, ed. Everett Emerson (Madison, Wis., 1977), p. 242.

as that of the emerging nations in the second half of the twentieth century. In the words of Samuel Miller's *Brief Retrospect of the Eighteenth Century*, published in 1803, America belonged at that time among the "nations lately become literary." It would seem, therefore, that the universal perspective would be ideally suited for the modern study of early American literature.

The adoption of this perspective does not by any means invalidate or rule out studies of local or provincial literatures. Serious investigation of the literary output of each of the colonies in North America will obviously add to the store of knowledge concerning the continent as a whole. Each of the British colonies had its own population center, produced its own intellectually dominant individuals, and fostered its own literary circles.[4] It is just as important to know how each writer reflects the particular conditions of his local environment as it is to perceive how he fits into the international literary mosaic of his own and earlier times. As Henry F. May has said of the eighteenth century, "The American Enlightenment, like American Romanticism or for that matter American Christianity can be at once American, Anglo-American, and European."[5]

The universal perspective shares with the local perspective the assumption that all literary works have equal historical validity, but this assumption does not by any means imply that all works are equal in esthetic or intellectual importance. In other words, all works may be legitimately considered as documents in the history of culture or the history of ideas, but the literary merits of individual texts differ widely, and it is the obligation of scholarship to notice and to comment upon these varia-

[4] J. A. Leo Lemay, *Men of Letters in Colonial Maryland* (Knoxville, Tenn., 1972), p. x.

[5] "The Problem of the American Enlightenment," *New Literary History* 1 (1969): 204.

tions. Notions of who and what are important, moreover, change with the times. An outstanding example is the tremendous interest in the black poetess Phillis Wheatley that developed after World War II.

Literary merit does not necessarily coincide with the esthetic criteria that happen to be in vogue at a given period of time. The critical standards of neoclassicism and of Romanticism, for example, are quite at variance with each other. Much of the scholarship devoted to early American literature during the past twenty years consists of elaborate formalistic analysis, despite the fact that nearly all of the significant writing of the seventeenth and eighteenth centuries was pragmatic rather than belletristic. World critical opinion undoubtedly considers Franklin's autobiography to be the major literary work of the entire period, but Verner W. Crane (a professional historian, but, nevertheless, the outstanding authority on Franklin's style) is quite correct in affirming that Franklin was "not a literary artist of the first order." Paine, Edwards, and Jefferson were even less gifted as stylists. Of the four, Franklin is the only one to have made a substantial contribution to imaginative literature. He successfully used genres in which the manner of expression shared importance with the ideas or information being conveyed or in which the subject matter was personal rather than utilitarian. *The Way to Wealth*, a compendium of proverbs taken from several cultural traditions, and "The Speech of Polly Baker," a satirical hoax, belong to the first of these categories, and his *Memoirs* belongs to the second. The major literary genres in vogue throughout America before 1800, however, were singularly uncomplicated—the sermon, the essay, the treatise, the didactic poem—and their subject matter was primarily political and theological. It can hardly be questioned that both the most extensive and the most readable part of this literature is a literature of ideas. As such, it would seem to lend itself particularly well not

INTRODUCTION

only to intellectual analysis, but also to the type of literary history that is international in outlook. It is a paradox that most scholars have slighted the technique best adapted for colonial and Federal literature—that of the history of ideas—and have concentrated instead upon formalistic analysis, which requires almost no reference to the mainstreams of thought and expression.

A second paradox has been noticed by Henry F. May, that much of the eighteenth century in North America as well as in Europe was the Age of Enlightenment, but scholars have neglected American writings of the period that stress the Enlightenment themes of reason, scientific progress, toleration, and the dissemination of knowledge in order to concentrate on the milieu of Puritan religion and anti-Enlightenment figures such as Cotton Mather, Jonathan Edwards, and Edward Taylor.[6] One reason for this emphasis on Puritanism may be the same that, according to Leo Lemay, accounts for the predominance of New England writers as subjects of scholarly study, that is, that the earliest compilers of histories of American literature were natives of the New England states. To restore the balance, new attention needs to be given to the Enlightenment as a literary movement in North America. The attitude of progressive eighteenth-century writers that they belonged to a republic of letters transcending political boundaries is based on essentially the same suppositions as the modern concept of international literature.

A third paradox is that the writers regarded most highly in American universities are, with the exception of Franklin, not those who have acquired an international reputation. This is probably in large measure a result of the emphasis of esthetic criteria over ideas and historical relationships. The only true objective measure of a writer's

[6] Ibid., pp. 201-2.

importance is the number of editions of his works published at home and of translations done in other parts of the world. This measure indicates that only Franklin, Paine, and Jefferson among Americans before 1800 have achieved a noticeable degree of international recognition. This objective evidence is confirmed by Rudolph Haus, a professor from the University of Hamburg, who delivered a lecture commemorating the American Bicentennial at three American institutions in which he attempted to assess the American contribution to world literature. He summarized the colonial period as furnishing "interesting and significant impulses to the field of religious poetry, of homiletics, books of edification and diaries," but the only writers before Cooper whom he named were Franklin, Paine, and Jefferson. It is possible that a visiting professor from France speaking on the same subject would have added Crèvecoeur.[7] The American editor of a recent collection of essays on the period 1764-1789, however, confidently affirms that Edward Taylor, Benjamin Franklin, and Jonathan Edwards are "the three greatest writers of early America."[8] Yet Taylor is recognized only by a narrow clique even in the United States. Edwards, except for the Anglo-American world and a small number of Dutch Puritans, was completely unknown in his own time, and even today his works are published only in the United States. Actually the Quakers William Penn and John Woolman have had more European translations than Edwards or any other American Puritan. It is not Edwards's philosophical works which have been translated, moreover, but merely two or three minor pietistic ones.

At the end of the eighteenth century three of the greatest works of the American post-Revolutionary period were printed for the first time in Paris in the French language:

[7] "Some American Contributions to World Literature," *Yearbook of Comparative and General Literature* 26 (1977): 17-23.

[8] Everett Emerson, ed., *American Literature, 1764-1789*, p. 15.

Franklin's *Memoirs*, Paine's *Age of Reason*, and Jefferson's *Notes on Virginia*. All three, moreover, were published in part to influence French public opinion. Franklin sent a manuscript copy of his autobiography to his Paris friends Le Veillard and La Rochefoucauld, and as a result the story of his life became known and appreciated in France before being printed anywhere else. The first collected edition of Franklin's works was printed in 1773 in Paris in French translation. Paine published his *Age of Reason* partly to dissuade the French people from adopting atheism as an official belief, and Jefferson wrote his description of Virginia to counteract fallacious notions concerning his native country that had been spread by various French *philosophes*.

The problem of how authors should be ranked hierarchically is almost unsolvable. Should they be placed according to their reputation in their own culture or according to their reception in the world at large? The problem is, of course, not limited to early American literature, but is endemic. Writers in eighteenth-century England such as Shaftesbury and Young can be adduced whose reputation in other major literatures is far greater than in their own. From the opposite perspective, other British writers such as Johnson and Boswell are considered of major importance in the Anglo-Saxon milieu, but remain unknown elsewhere in the world. The best solution may be to reserve the designation of masterpiece for works that show bibliographical strength in both the culture of origin and abroad. No serious scholar would advocate as criteria for excellence his personal feelings, inclinations, or prejudices—even though cliques or vogues based on little else than shared prejudices sometimes dominate academic criticism. There is much to be said for the attitude of sociologists of literature: that the test of a great book is its being widely read with approval and pleasure by a public different from that for which it was originally intended.

If the principle of public acceptance is taken as the dominant standard for evaluating early American writers, they may be classified according to at least four categories or degrees of recognition.

1) There are those who attained a fair amount of celebrity in their own times in the Anglo-Saxon world, but are now forgotten. An example is Richard Lewis, the author of "A Journey from Patapsco to Annapolis," the first poem by an American author to be widely reprinted in England and considered by Leo Lemay to be "the best neoclassical poem of colonial America."

2) There are writers who were completely unknown in their time, but have been brought into prominence by modern American scholarship. The obvious example is Edward Taylor.

3) There are writers who were known in the Anglo-Saxon world in their own time, are equally recognized at present in England and America, but are unknown elsewhere. An example is Jonathan Edwards.

4) There are writers who attained international recognition in their own time and who have maintained an international reputation until the present. Franklin, of course, is a prime example.

Purely esthetic criteria would not justify Franklin's high reputation as a literary figure, based as it is on the reflection of his ideas and personality, even though his prose style compares favorably with Addison's. Critics who accept the doctrines of the New Criticism of the 1940s and 1950s would consider it appropriate to rank Edward Taylor as a major author. These criteria might also confirm Lemay's judgment concerning "A Journey from Patapsco to Annapolis." The doctrines of New Criticism, however, have absolutely no relevance to the works of Edwards and

Paine and very little to those of Franklin. If taken as the standard of judgment, these criteria would effectively reduce these literary giants to dwarves.

A viable compromise might be to classify writers in both the first and second of the above categories as minor and those in both the third and fourth as major. The perspective of universal literature offers a further escape from the dilemma. From this vantage, all authors may be valued for their ideas, historical significance, ability to reflect personality or social milieu, or even for antiquarian charm.

The purpose of comparative literature is not, however, to erect a universal hierarchy of literary merit or to place authors of one culture in competition with those of another, even though it provides an important service by portraying various national literatures in a proper perspective. The comparative method seeks to increase the understanding and enjoyment of the works of two or more cultures by bringing them into contact with each other. Also it discriminates between the elements of each culture that are truly unique and those that are shared with one or more similar cultures.

The chapters that follow represent an effort to show that the study of American literature before 1800 need not (and perhaps should not) be confined exclusively to the American continent. They illustrate the principles that some aspects of movements, trends, and themes in early American literature parallel previous developments in Europe; that some well-known American texts have sources or analogues in other literatures; and that some American works have had a significant influence upon writers in other traditions. Even though in these introductory remarks I have maintained that the scholarly method of the history of ideas has in general more relevance to early American literature than the method of esthetic analysis, I do not wish to suggest that the latter should be abandoned. The chapters on Anne Bradstreet and Edward Taylor that come first in this collection treat matters of style and structure primarily. The others stress themes and ideas. I am treating Bradstreet because of her undeniable historic importance as the first American poet, and Taylor because much criticism has decreed him to be preeminent among American poets before 1800.

ferences may be noted in the poetry of the colonies from that of the homeland, although in prose the straightforward approach of Addison almost instantaneously found imitators in America, of whom the most illustrious was Franklin. The Spanish colonies experienced almost no intellectual retardation in either the sixteenth or seventeenth centuries, during which literary centers flourished in Mexico and Peru that rivaled those of Spain itself. No reason has been advanced to explain this literary fecundity, but it may have been due to the frequent movement back and forth from the New World and Spain, at least among the higher levels of society. A cultural lag does not become evident in Latin America until the period of the Enlightenment, and even then the disparity was not between the colonies and Spain, but between Spain and her colonies as a unit and the enlightened parts of Europe and North America.

The two chapters that follow concern two products of the seventeenth century, Anne Bradstreet, a representative of the Renaissance, and Edward Taylor, a practitioner of the style known as the baroque. I compare Bradstreet to Sor Juana Inés de la Cruz, a Spanish-American contemporary poetess. Although one was a wife and mother in rural New England and the other a nun, a symbolic bride of Christ, in a rich and thriving Mexican city, they both reflected the literary standards of the times in which they lived. Sor Juana is considered to be one of the major poets of all Spanish literature, but Bradstreet is minor even in the limited scope of the British colonies. Yet Bradstreet conforms to the literary conventions of her time equally as well as Sor Juana, even though she may not have adorned them with the same brilliance.

Edward Taylor, however, was an anomaly in the period in which he lived, and he remains a puzzle today. Although he was born about 1642 and died in 1729, his poetry was not published until the third decade of the

PART I

STYLE
AND
STRUCTURE

WHEN SETTLERS go from one country to another they naturally carry with them their cultural traditions, including the predominant literary style of their period. This is true whether they are emigrating to a new world, which has never before been settled, or to an area with well-established communities. When Spanish colonization occurred early in the sixteenth century and English colonization followed over a century later, both Spain and England were in the midst of the Renaissance. This literary movement had traveled to Spain from Italy early in the fifteenth century and to England in the sixteenth. The English colonies at first suffered little or no cultural lag since their settlers continued to write in the manner to which they had been accustomed in England. By the turn of the eighteenth century, however, distinct dif-

twentieth century. He has been regarded by one admirer as "the initiator of a great tradition"[1] and by another as one of the three greatest writers of early America.[2] On the other extreme, he has been considered "at best a mediocre poet."[3] A critic who has devoted to Taylor a book of over 300 pages nevertheless admits that "on the conventional scale of canonization, Taylor is a second-string poet, perhaps even a poor poet."[4] Whatever his merits, the three elements upon which he must be judged are his subject matter, his personality as reflected in his work, and his style. Taylor's subject matter is for the most part Calvinistic doctrine, material that not even a genius could successfully render poetical. Milton is no exception, for *Paradise Lost* stands out because of its epic, not its didactic features, and it is neither Calvinistic nor doctrinal. Wordsworth's *Ecclesiastical Sonnets* is a good example of what may be expected of doctrinal verse, and on comparison Taylor appears to advantage. Some of his human characteristics do indeed shine out in his poetry. Even though consisting primarily of a wry delight in the perplexities of religion, his personality grants to his verse a certain individual charm. Taylor's style is the single element critics have admired, and it is true that his linguistic tricks and intricacies set him apart from fellow Puritan versifiers. He is individual, however, only within the New England frame of reference. When placed in contact with his predecessors in the European baroque, his uniqueness

[1] H. H. Waggoner, *American Poets: From the Puritans to the Present* (Boston, 1968), p. 22.

[2] Everett Emerson, "The Cultural Context of the American Revolution," introduction to volume edited by Emerson, *American Literature, 1764-1789* (Madison, Wis., 1977), p. 15.

[3] Sidney E. Lind, "Edward Taylor: A Reevaluation," *New England Quarterly* 21 (1948): 519-30.

[4] Karl Keller, *The Example of Edward Taylor* (Amherst, Mass., 1975), p. 3.

completely disappears. Instead he becomes an example of the cultural lag from which Bradstreet had escaped.

The baroque style flourished in Italy, Spain, France, and England during the first half of the seventeenth century, after which it was replaced nearly everywhere by neoclassicism. Apart from the inevitable overlapping on both sides, the change was about as abrupt as any in major styles that has ever been recorded. The duration of the baroque in England was so short that with the exception of Taylor it does not seem to have crossed to the English colonies of America. Anagrams and acrostics in which Puritan verse abounds are not touchstones of the baroque.

Taylor was presumably introduced to the baroque while he was a student at Cambridge University. At least he acquired no books by baroque authors for his personal library in America. He came to the New World in 1668, and by the time that he began writing poetry, apparently around 1671, not only metaphysical style but also devotional subject matter had given way in England to John Dryden's neoclassical innovations. In the colonies, late Renaissance style still prevailed and would continue to do so until the introduction of neoclassicism early in the eighteenth century.

The following pages will demonstrate how Bradstreet is related to the Renaissance in other countries and how Taylor is related to the baroque. The process will not make either American poet seem less important, but, if anything, elevate their stature by bringing them into contact with poets in other cultures of international significance.

TWO

ANNE BRADSTREET: SOME THOUGHTS ON THE TENTH MUSE

THE PHILOSOPHER PLATO, according to legend, bestowed the flattering appelation "the Tenth Muse" upon Sappho, the female poet of Lesbos in ancient Greece. The phrase was subsequently applied in the seventeenth century to two poets of North America, one writing in English, the other in Spanish. In 1650, there appeared in London a book of over 200 pages with the title, *The Tenth Muse Lately Sprung up in AMERICA, or Severall Poems, Compiled with great Variety of Wit and Learning, full of Delight.* The author, according to the title page was "a Gentlewoman in those parts," but she was several times identified in the book itself as Anne Bradstreet, a married lady of New England. Thirty-nine years later (1689) a similar title introduced a collection of Spanish poems published in another European capital, Madrid. In English translation, the title page proclaimed *The Muses' Inundation of the Unique Poetess, Tenth Muse, Sister Juana Inés of the Cross, Professed Nun of the Monastery of Saint Jerome of the Imperial City of Mexico. Who in Various Metres, Idioms, and Styles, Fertilizes Various Subjects, with Elegant, Subtle, Clear, Witty, Useful Verses.*[1]

---

[1] The original Spanish reads: *Inundación Castálida de la única poetisa, musa décima, soror Juana Inés de la Cruz, religiosa profesa en el monasterio de San-Jerónimo de la Imperial ciudad de México. Que en varios metros, idiomas, y estilos, fertiliza varios asuntos, con elegantes, sutiles, claros, ingeniosos, útiles versos.* In the remainder of this chapter,

Titles of the second editions of both collections were rendered less flamboyant; that of Anne Bradstreet deleted the appellation *Tenth Muse* and that of Sor Juana discarded *The Muses' Inundation*. The latter metaphor implies that the Castalian springs in Greek mythology had descended upon the author in a flood of poetic inspiration. The Peninsular poet Quevedo had previously said of himself, "Inundación será la de mi canto," and in both contexts "inundación" suggests a torrent or an extraordinary force, a hyperbole typical of the baroque style. The word "wit" in Anne Bradstreet's title also has strong overtones of the baroque even though in her work itself there are few of the verbal eccentricities her contemporaries would have recognized as wit.

Bradstreet is the founder of the literature of English America, and one of its most respectable early poets. Sor Juana ranks with Cervantes, Calderón, Lope de Vega, and Quevedo as a luminary of the Golden Age of Spanish literature.

Although the exact birth date of neither Tenth Muse is known, it would appear that each poet was thirty-eight years old at the time of the publication of the first edition of her book. Both of the collections of poems, moreover, were taken in manuscript from the New World to a metropolis of the Old, there to be published, and each author wrote a verse prologue for her volume.

Apart from these bibliographical and biographical coincidences, it is possible to trace several intellectual and literary parallels between these representatives of separate American literatures. Both Anne Bradstreet and Sor Juana were acutely aware of their double identities as writers and women; both revealed a compulsion to compose serious verse; both were deeply religious, but developed sec-

---

it will be understood that quotations from Sor Juana translated by me into English were originally composed in Spanish.

ular as well as pious themes; both experienced a period of skepticism before crystallizing their religious seeking into firm faith; both echoed major linguistic conventions of their times, and both incorporated metaphors and subject matter from the world of science. Perhaps most significant of all, both introduced a catalog of the nine muses into a poem, naming each of the Greek allegorical sisters and indicating the genre personified by each.[2]

Naturally there exist many differences, both biographical and literary, separating these representatives of two opposing cultures, and the major ones should be noted before a detailed exposition of parallels or similarities. The private life of Anne Bradstreet was essentially conventional, despite the rigors of the frontier community in which she passed her adult years. The second of several children born to a solid English family with connections to the Puritan aristocracy, she was married before emigrating at the age of seventeen with the first contingent of settlers to Massachusetts Bay in 1630. There she lived for the rest of a long life as a devoted wife and mother of eight children. During her English girlhood as a member of the household of the Earl of Lincoln, she had enjoyed the amenities of a well-stocked library, but in the pioneer environment of Massachusetts she was able to draw upon only a limited number of texts in history and theology.

Not only the actual birth date, but also the antecedents of Bradstreet's Hispanic counterpart Sor Juana are obscure, but it appears that she was one of six children born in the extreme southern tip of Mexico to an unmarried mother. Showing prodigious intellectual talents as a child, she persuaded her mother to send her at the age of eight to Mexico City, a thriving capital of 50,000 Spanish colonists and twice that number of Indians. Here she avidly read

[2] Bradstreet: "Elegy upon ... Sir Philip Sidney"; Sor Juana: "Romance" no. XI. All titles and quotations from Sor Juana are taken from Sor Juana Inés de la Cruz, *Obras escogidas*, ed. Juan Carlos Merlo (Barcelona, 1968).

the classic Spanish and Latin authors. Her physical beauty kept pace with her intellectual maturity, and in her early teens she attracted not only the glances of a number of young male admirers but also the notice of the wife of the Viceroy, who invited her to the court and made available rare books vital to her studies. The young girl's brilliance was so extraordinary that during her sixteenth year forty experts in theology and the humanities were summoned to the palace for the purpose of conducting a public oral examination, at which she astounded the audience by the extent and profundity of her knowledge. Her later poetry has given rise to the theory that she suffered disillusionment over a romantic attachment at this time, but this is only speculation. A few months after her intellectual triumph at court, she took religious vows and entered a convent for life—the same age at which Anne Bradstreet entered upon matrimony. Although subject to strict cloistral rules, Sor Juana still received visitors from the outside, had the services of a Negro slave, possessed a personal library as vast as any in the territory, and had ample free time for study and writing.

In brief, Anne Bradstreet, after a placid childhood in a conventional English family, dedicated her life to the domestic duties of wife and mother in a harsh pioneer environment, responding in all social and intellectual situations in the approved austere manner of Puritanism. Sor Juana, overcoming the stigma of illegitimacy, emerged as a child prodigy in the bustling capital of New Spain and spent her mature life as a cloistered nun, dominated intellectually by Roman Catholic religion and culture.

Fundamental as these differences may be, they are overshadowed by resemblances in the writings of the two women, one of the most important of which in the present climate of opinion is the repudiation of prejudices against women poets. Both insisted on the right of women to be taken seriously as literary artists, each using the arguments most appropriate to her own circumstances.

Bradstreet, for example, had to contend with the opinion of Thomas Hooker's *Ecclesiastical Polity*, widely accepted in her milieu, that the judgments of women are "commonly weakest by reason of their sex" [Preface, chap. III, sec. 13]. She characterized herself, therefore, in the "Prologue" to her poems as "obnoxious to each carping tongue" who "says my hand a needle better fits." Critics such as these she branded as so prejudiced against "female wits" that they would say of anything good in her work that it was either copied or the result of chance. On the contrary side she cited the ancient Greeks as proponents of women since they conceived of the nine muses as feminine and ranked poetry as the child of one of them, Calliope. Apparently she was not aware that Calliope was considered to be the muse of specifically epic or heroic poetry. After this relatively strong defense, however, Bradstreet retreated by admitting that "men have precedency" and "women know it well." In the end she asked merely that masculine fellow poets allow her humble efforts to exist as a foil to their superior achievements. It must be remembered, however, that in the seventeenth century the prologue to a collection of verse, like the prologue to a play, was intended to show the author in a favorable light, and male authors also conventionally displayed an attitude of respectful humility such as Bradstreet's. Her conclusion should, therefore, not be considered as a complete surrender to the claim of masculine superiority. Her only forthright concession to the preeminence of male poets appears in a line from another poem in which she apologizes for not having completed an encyclopedic project of versifying the history of the ancient world. "This task," she laments, "befits not women like to men." In various other references to the deficiencies or inadequacies of her poetry, however, she does not attribute them to her sex, but rather to lack of time, poor health, and other difficulties that beset men as well as women.

Bradstreet rises to militancy in defending the record of women as rulers of great nations in an elegy on Queen Elizabeth, who "hath wiped off the aspersion of her sex / That women wisdom lack to play the rex." She further remarks that the "personal perfections" of Elizabeth were so extraordinary that in order to record them one

> Must dip his pen in the Heliconian well,
> Which I may not; my pride doth but aspire
> To read what others write, and so admire.

These self-deprecatory lines are intentionally ironical since Bradstreet is obviously doing that which she says is forbidden to her—extolling the queen's perfections in verse.

Sor Juana also professed humility concerning her intellectual accomplishments. Indeed, after confounding her forty interlocutors, she claimed to have felt no more satisfaction than if she had demonstrated needlework in the schoolroom, almost the same metaphor previously used by Bradstreet, but turned in a contrary sense.[3] She displayed a similar indifference in the prologue to the second edition of her works, and later in the volume dispraised her own poems as idle pastimes or mere exercises in penmanship.[4]

In a completely different frame of mind, however, she defended herself in a sonnet against those who had objected to her poetic vocation. By means of a technically superb series of paradoxes, she inquired how her dedication to poetry could possibly give offense to anyone. She pointed out that her intention was to weigh beauty by her understanding, not understanding by beautiful things; that she esteemed neither wealth nor riches and was, therefore,

---

[3] *Obras escogidas*, p. 18.
[4] "Romance" no. XI, p. 53.

much happier to weigh riches by her understanding than her understanding by riches; and that she considered it preferable to spend time with the vanities of life than to spend her life in vain [Soneto II].

Sor Juana's most brilliant defense of the female sex in general appears in a lyric poem rejecting as stupid and irrational the common complaints of men against women. Primarily literary in inspiration and reflecting the atmosphere of the court rather than the convent, it still mirrors the battle of the sexes in common walks of life. Sor Juana charges men with inconsistency in expecting women to be virtuous while inciting them to vice; in attributing to feminine looseness the result of masculine persistence; in wanting their amorous conquests to be like Thais before possession and like Lucretia after; in complaining of those women who reject their addresses and ridiculing those who accept them; in blaming one for being cruel and another for being easy. Which has greater responsibility for a guilty passion, she asks, the one who succumbs to entreaties or the one who entreats to succumb; the one who sins for payment or the one who pays for sin?[5]

The sentiments of these poems, although sincere, are somewhat conventional and abstract. The work in which Sor Juana expresses an intensely personal defense of the rights of women to intellectual freedom and development and to literary creation is an extensive argument in prose entitled *Reply of the Poetess* [*Respuesta de la poetisa*], a vindication of some critical remarks she had previously published on a theological matter. As much intellectual autobiography as polemical theology, *Reply of the Poetess* combines an impassioned recital of the author's artistic career with a justification of the claims of women to education and culture. It ranks with Milton's *Areopagitica* as one of the major seventeenth-century documents in

---

[5] *Obras escogidas*, pp. 177-78.

the history of the assertion of human rights. Among the topics relevant to the work of Anne Bradstreet are the interconnection of all academic disciplines; the example of the metrical parts of the Scriptures as a justification for poetry itself; the vindication of secular rather than religious themes; a catalog of eminent women, including biblical characters, saints, rulers, and writers; and an interpretation of the various passages of St. Paul and the Church Fathers that seem to deny intellectual functions to women. Sor Juana admits that it is forbidden for women to read publicly in cathedrals or to preach in pulpits, but insists that it is by no means improper for women to study any and all subjects and to write, or to teach in private. She herself, she maintains, did not study to write or to teach, but in order to minimize her ignorance.

She asks whether the Church in any of its principles requires that she believe with closed eyes. She suggests that there is no harm in her being free to dissent from her antagonist, a Jesuit father, provided that everyone else have the same freedom to disagree with her. After giving an example of free speech which the ancient Romans derived from natural law, she argues that Catholics, who have been given a positive command to love their enemies, are equally obliged to tolerate them. To justify her secular studies, Sor Juana cites two nuns of her acquaintance. One had memorized her breviary so thoroughly that she could recall any part of it in perfect order at any time; the other had familiarized herself with the style of St. Jerome so that she could apply it to the exposition of scientific principles. Sor Juana concludes that the talent of one is as valuable as that of the other.

Sor Juana also devoted herself to the study of the sciences and used them as poetic material, one of the major parallels with Anne Bradstreet. Indeed she declared in her *Reply* that the only work she had written to satisfy her own taste without external considerations was a long poem,

Primero sueño, The First Dream, part imaginative, part descriptive, which combines scientific observation, mythology, and private fancy. As such, it has much in common with Bradstreet's cosmic poems, "The Four Elements," "The Four Humours," "The Four Ages," and "The Four Seasons." Sor Juana describes the physiological details of dreaming and sleeping, classifies the phenomena of the earth, both organic and inorganic, in a hierarchical grouping, and explains the circulatory and recuperative processes of the human body with appropriate attention to the four humors.

Some of the physiology in Anne Bradstreet's poems is directly paraphrased from Dr. Helkiah Crooke's treatise, *Microcosmographia, or a Description of the Body of Man* (1618).[6] Sor Juana for her vast scientific lore in physics, astronomy, and mathematics depended chiefly upon the famous German Jesuit Athanasius Kircher, whose works included *Magnes sive de arte magnetica* (1634), *Ars combinatoria* (1640), *Ars magna lucis et umbrae* (1646), and *Mundus subterraneus* (1664). Indeed Sor Juana drew so extensively from Kircher that she invented the verb *kirkerizo*, the present indicative of "to Kircherize."

Bradstreet's biographer, E. W. White, has indicated that the notion of the Great Chain of Being is implicit in her cosmological poetry.[7] In Sor Juana, the concept is explicit, expressed in her *Primero sueño* as a hierarchical ladder and in her *Respuesta* as a universal chain, which was imagined originally by the ancients and developed in modern times by scientific investigations of magnetism.[8] It is not clear from Sor Juana's citation whether she is referring to William Gilbert's *De magneto* (1600) or to Kircher's *Magnes sive de arte magnetica*.

[6] Helen McMahon, "Anne Bradstreet, Jean Bertault, and Dr. Crooke," *Early American Literature* 3 (1968): 118-23.

[7] *Anne Bradstreet, "The Tenth Muse,"* (New York, 1971), p. 183.

[8] *Obras escogidas*, p. 532.

Hispanic scholars have concluded from the *Primero sueño* that Sor Juana had read Harvey's *De motu cordis* (1628), and from a reference in another poem to the sun making the tour of the world that she was not aware of the heliocentric theories of Copernicus.[9] The method of comparative literature suggests that a similar inquiry be made concerning Anne Bradstreet. No evidence can be found to show whether she placed the sun or the earth at the center of her cosmic system, but it appears from the following passage from "The Four Humours" that she understood the circulation of the blood.

> I am the fountain which thy cistern fills
> Through warm blue conduits of my venial rills.
> What hath the heart but what's sent from the liver?

The speaker in this passage, the personification of blood addressing choler, seems to give an accurate picture of the flow of blood through veins from the liver to the heart. The meaning of "thy cistern" is ambiguous, however, but it probably refers to the brain. In an earlier passage, choler affirms that she heats the blood in the liver.

> What comes from thence my heart refines the same,
> And through the arteries sends it o'er the frame;
> The vital spirits they're called, . . .

This resembles a passage in which Sor Juana describes the heart as the human clock (*Reloj humano*) as well as the King of the parts of the body and center of the vital spirits. Sor Juana also incorporates the four humors in her *Primero sueño*. It may be that the notion of the four humors is incompatible with the theory of the circulation of the blood, but neither Sor Juana nor Bradstreet apparently saw any contradiction.

[9] *Obras escogidas*, pp. 199, 29.

Este, pues, miembro Rey y centro vivo de espíritu vi-
tales.

[ll. 210-11]

One may point to an individual poem by Bradstreet
which, taken as a whole, has an extraordinary resemblance in theme and feeling to one by her southern counterpart. In "Before the Birth of One of Her Children,"
Bradstreet describes her distress at the thought that she
might die and be separated from her husband. Sor Juana
similarly describes the anguished love that a woman feels
for her deceased husband in a poem that differs from Bradstreet's mainly by depicting an imaginary rather than a
real situation.[10] The wife depicted by Sor Juana is mourn-
ing a husband who is actually dead rather than anticipating the feelings that a husband might experience after her
own death. To be sure, the lamenting of a wife for her
dead partner is not a common theme for a cloistered nun,
but Sor Juana's techniques for expressing grief are as appropriate and convincing as those of the New England
mother—even though differences in culture and temperament give their poems an individual tone. Bradstreet,
reflecting Christian fortitude and acceptance of the mor-
tality of existence, reveals greatest concern for her husband and children who will survive. Her tone is placid,
and the only conceit in the poem consists in the reflection
that by writing her verse she will belong to him even
though being taken away.

I may seem thine who in effect am none.

Sor Juana's persona, to the contrary, is passionate and
inconsolable, but conveys her emotion by means of in-

---

[10] *Obras escogidas*, "Que expresan el sentimiento que padece una
mujer amante de su marido muerto," p. 211. Sor Juana has another poem
on the same theme to which has been assigned an almost identical title,
"Expresa, aún con expresiones más vivas, el sentimiento que padece una
mujer amante de su marido muerto," p. 143.

tricate verse patterns and brilliant conceits. She argues
that it is justifiable for her to complain to heaven, which
has robbed her of her precious loved one, but at the same
time admits that heaven with deaf and righteous ears would
account her complaint as blasphemy. In another stanza
she affirms that she does not envy the happiness of others;
the eternal suffering she goes through is so great that all
she can envy is the misery of other people, which, no
matter how great, is less than hers. Bradstreet does not
use this kind of hyperbole in the poem written during her
pregnancy but something less extreme appears in "A Letter to Her Husband, Absent Upon Public Employment."
Here she maintains that only the person who numbers
the stars, the grains of sand, the leaves of grass or the
drops of rain may count her sighs or teardrops, certainly
not a startling or an original trope, but one of the few
passages in her work related to the general tradition of
baroque style to which Sor Juana belongs.

Sor Juana's complex hyperboles have little in common
with the simple and unpretentious style of the New England Puritan, but the feeling of deep sorrow is genuine in
both poems. Critics have not felt the need to certify Bradstreet's sincerity, which has been taken for granted since
her poems concern her actual husband and children. Sor
Juana, as a cloistered nun, however, had neither spouse
nor issue, and her poetic expressions of love and grief are,
therefore, subject to the charge of being imaginary and
contrived. Spanish critics, including one of the most distinguished, Menéndez y Pelayo, have consequently taken
pains to affirm that the profane poems of Sor Juana are
spontaneous and from the heart.[11] Other critics have even
suggested a strain of lesbianism and argued that her poems
about husbands or lovers may, like the sonnets of Shake-

[11] *Obras escogidas*, p. 66.

speare, be ostensibly devoted to a member of one sex, but in actuality refer to the other.

In fact, it is no more possible for a reader to determine the sincerity of any literary passage that an author intends to be taken as genuine than it is for him to know whether a person is lying or telling the truth. All that can be said about a literary passage is that it appears to be sincere or that its portrayal of emotion is effective—in other words, that it communicates sincerity. From this perspective of the communication of feeling and the parallelism of situation, Bradstreet's lines to her husband have much more in common with Sor Juana's portrayal of a grieving wife than with Bishop Henry King's *Exequy* to his dead wife, the English work to which these lines have several times been compared.

Some American scholars have complained that Bradstreet's poetry does very little to portray indigenous New England life, that all of her allusions, metaphors, and illustrations are taken from English sources, and that none of her descriptions reflects the American landscape. The culture and topography of the New World are equally absent from the work of Juana Inés de la Cruz, but Hispanic critics do not consider this a shortcoming. They realize that she was working in a recognized poetic tradition combining artificial style with ideological substance, allowing for a high degree of personal emotion, but not local color or topography. Essentially the same is true for Bradstreet.

In the scholarship that has grown up around these two New World representatives of established literary traditions, a controversy has developed over the indebtedness of each one to a European forerunner. Spanish scholars have debated the influence on Sor Juana of the greatest exponent of the baroque in Spanish poetry, Góngora, and Americanists have sought to estimate the influence on Anne Bradstreet of an outstanding Renaissance poet of France, Du Bartas. The link between Sor Juana and Góngora was first established by the editor of the second edition of her poems in 1692, who added to the title of her *First Dream* a phrase affirming that it was composed in imitation of Góngora. From then until modern times, both when Góngora was in critical favor and when he was not, it has been assumed that Sor Juana should be considered a faithful disciple of the Spanish stylist. In 1939, a member of the Modern Language Association published a study arguing that the supposed imitation of Góngora consisted in little more than reminiscences of some metaphors, allegories, and special constructions, but other scholars still adhere to the view that a close relationship exists between the two poets.[12]

Most Americans who know Du Bartas at all know him only by name and as the author of a biblically inspired epic about the Creation of the world, *La Semaine* (1578), which is supposed to have influenced Milton and perhaps Anne Bradstreet as well. The view that Bradstreet derives inspiration directly from Du Bartas is based upon a number of references to the French poet in *The Tenth Muse* and upon a line in a commendatory poem by Nathaniel Ward indicating that "The Authoress was a right Du Bartas girl," a parallel to Sor Juana's editor adding to her *First Dream* the phrase "imitating Góngora." Almost everyone who has written about Bradstreet has quoted Ward's line or some part of it. The anti-Bartas position did not come into prominence until 1941 when Austin Warren affirmed: "Save for their pentameter couplets and their panoramic scope, Anne Bradstreet's long poems have nothing in common with Du Bartas; she does not or cannot imitate his conceits. . . . The humbler ingenuities were what the New Englanders could reproduce."[13] The expression "Du Bartas girl" is an exact parallel to the appelation "Bartas

[12] *Obras escogidas*, p. 67.
[13] *Rage for Order. Essays in Criticism* (Chicago, 1948), p. 8.

Junior," which Edward Cooke used in 1631 as part of the title to a poem which, like that of his French predecessor, deals with the Creation. The full title of Cooke's work, which appeared in London the year after Bradford sailed for Massachusetts, is *Bartas Iunior: or, The World's Epitome. Man. Set Forth in his 1. Generation, 2. Degeneration, 3. Regeneration.* Bradstreet also treats man as an epitome of the universe by means of her parallel exposition of the four elements (earth, air, fire, and water), the four humors, the four ages of man, and the seasons.

A German scholar, Hans Galinsky, has superbly traced and analyzed all the external evidence that has so far come to light concerning Bradstreet's allegiance to Du Bartas and all of the substantive stylistic resemblances between the two poets.[14] His conclusion places him somewhat closer to Nathaniel Ward than to Austin Warren, but it does not really settle the question for future writers of literary history. According to the paraphrase that E. W. White has made available for Americans who do not read German, Galinsky has shown that Bradstreet followed various suggestions derived from the works of Du Bartas and Shakespeare, but that "there was a 'transformation,' as well as a 'transplatation,' of whatever they contributed to her work."[15] Galinsky has treated the subject so thoroughly that there is no need whatsoever of reexamining his evidence or that of previous scholars. His method is impeccable and his conclusion completely warranted.

It is still possible, however, to demonstrate remarkable similarities between the work of Bartas and Bradstreet in

---

[14] "Anne Bradstreet, Du Bartas und Shakespeare im Zusammenhang kolonialer Verpflanzung und Umformung europäischer Literatur," in *Festschrift für Walther Fischer* (Heidelberg, 1959), pp. 145-80. I am following Galinsky in my depiction of the history of Bradstreet scholarship. In future references to the French poet, I shall follow the seventeenth-century English form of Bartas rather than Du Bartas.

[15] *Anne Bradstreet*, p. 65.

areas other than those elements of literary style upon which previous scholars have concentrated, chiefly the use of conceits, metaphors, and the compound epithet. A good starting point is the title itself of Bradstreet's collection, *The Tenth Muse, Lately Sprung up in America*. There is reason to believe that contemporary readers of this title would associate it with the English translation of Bartas's major work, *Les Semaines*, by Joshua Sylvester and published in London in 1605 under the title *Bartas: His Devine Weekes and Workes*, with other editions appearing in 1608, 1620, and 1641, the last one, nine years before the publication of *The Tenth Muse*. Eleven pages of the introductory material to Sylvester's work are devoted exclusively to the muses—one complete page to each of the individual muses, one to their mother Mnemosyne, and one to "Sylvestres: nove musae," that is, Sylvester of the nine muses. All of this material as a unit is entitled "Corona Dedicatoria." This repeated association of Sylvester with the nine muses would seem to indicate that a subsequent title referring to an American poet as representing the Tenth Muse would immediately remind English readers of its predecessor. On the page in Sylvester devoted to Mnemosyne, the muses crown James I as laureate and present him their coat of arms,

> *Thrice Three Pennes Sun-like in a Cinthian field.*
> Sign'd by THEM-SELVES, and their High Treasurer
> BARTAS, the great; In-gross'd by SYLVESTER.

A line by J. Rogers to one of the dedicatory pieces in the second edition of Bradstreet's poems seems to refer directly to the *Thrice Three Pennes* in the first line. Rogers declares,

> I saw the Muses treble trine.

An even closer link between Bartas and Bradstreet may be seen in the general structure of their published volumes. Sylvester's translation comprises two works of Bartas, originally published as separate volumes, *The First Week* and *The Second Week*. The latter is divided into four days, each of which is subdivided into four internal divisions, and there are also two separate poems at the end, not directly related to the four days. Exactly the same arrangement exists in *The Tenth Muse*: that is, four main divisions internally compartmentalized into four sections, comprising "The Four Humours in Man's Constitution," "The Four Ages of Man," "The Four Seasons of the Year," and "The Four Monarchies." At the end there are added, as in Sylvester's volume, a group of miscellaneous poems. In the original work of Bartas, *The Second Week* does not limit itself to the literal events of the second seven days of creation, but treats the history of the world after the fall of man, even including the discovery of the Western Hemisphere. A later French poet, J. Gailhard, wrote an addition of 630 lines, calling it part of the fifth day, which he published in 1659.[16] The four divisions of Bradstreet's *Tenth Muse* would also qualify as additional days in the scheme of Bartas, even to their internal separation into four parts. Indeed the precise subject matter of three of Bradstreet's sections is set forth in outline form in Bartas's "Second Day." In the effects of the wind, he enumerates and describes

> . . . fower Tempraments,
> Foure Times, foure Ages, and foure Elements.[17]

These are, in other words, the four humors, the four seasons, the four ages of man, and the four elements (air, earth, fire, and water). The first three obviously corre-

---

[16] *The Works of Guillaume de Salluste, sieur Du Bartas, a Critical Edition*, ed. Urban Tigner Holmes, Jr. et al., 3 vols. (Chapel Hill, N.C., 1935-1940), 1: 96.

[17] *Bartas His Devine Weekes and Workes (1605). Translated by Joshua Sylvester*. Facsimile edition (Gainesville, Fla., 1965), p. 52.

spond to Bradstreet's "The Four Humours of Man's Constitution," "The Four Seasons of the Year," and "The Four Ages of Man"; the material of the fourth topic, the four elements of the universe, moreover, is interspersed throughout all three sections.

Bradstreet's second group of four major poems, "The Four Monarchies" is suggested in Bartas's "Fourth Booke, of the first Day, of the second Weeke," entitled "The Handie-Crafts" in which the history of the world is divided into six ages between Adam and Christ. Bradstreet's poem continues the record into later ages. Bartas himself sketches the development of subsequent history in "The Colonies," but indicates that he will not undertake the topic in depth because of the obscurity of historical records. An actual parade of monarchs, something like Bradstreet's, appears, moreover, in "The Triumph of Faith," a separate poem also present in the Sylvester edition.

Bartas even provides a metaphysical explanation for the significance of the number four.

> The (*Cubes*-Base) *Foure*; a full and perfect summe,
> Whose added parts just unto Tenne doo come;
> Nomber of Gods great Name, Seasons, Complexions,
> Windes, Elements, and cardinall Perfections.[18]

To be sure, Bartas also gives the metaphysical significance of the other primary numbers, but it is the number four that is the basis of his own poetic structure. He describes the Hebrew tongue, for example, as being figuratively upheld by four pillars, that is, by Moses, David, Solomon, and Isaiah. He enumerates as well the four major writers in each of the other major Western languages: Greek, Latin, Italian, Arabic, German, Spanish, French, and English. In Bartas's original, the French authors come last, immedi-

---

[18] Ibid., p. 473. The Hebrew name for God with the vowels eliminated, as in Hebrew practice, is J-h-w-h. The number 4 when added to each of its parts produces 10: $4 + 3 + 2 + 1 = 10$.

ately preceded by the English, but in Sylvester's translation the order is reversed. The same poets, however, are included in each roster.

Bradstreet seems to have been the first to apply the mathematical term quaternion to the poetic structure of "four times four." Her own four-part division has usually been attributed to the example of her father, Thomas Dudley, on the basis of a dedicatory poem in which she refers to his "four sisters, deckt in black & white," glossed by a marginal note, "T D on the four parts of the world." Further in her poem she says that in order that her lowly pen might wait upon those four,

> I bring my four; and four, now meanly clad.

No other trace of Dudley's work on the four parts of the world has ever come to light, however, but if it were indeed a work written in verse, it could very well have been, like his daughter's, after the manner of Bartas-Sylvester. No matter what the form or substance of Dudley's work may have been, it cannot detract from the obvious structural similarity between Bartas and Bradstreet.

There is another passage in the dedication to Bradstreet's father that has been interpreted as a declaration of freedom from the influence of Bartas.

> Something of all (though mean) I did intend,
> But fear'd you'ld judge, one *Bartas* was my friend,
> I honour him, but dare not wear his wealth,
> My goods are true (though poor) I love no stealth,
> But if I did, I durst not send them you;
> Who must reward a theife, but with his due.

Here Bradstreet is unequivocally repudiating the charge of plagarism, but she is certainly not disclaiming strong resemblance to Bartas or denying that she has taken him as her model. The mere fact that she recognizes that her father, or any one else, would conclude Bartas to be her friend indicates that the similarities between her work and his are apparent. The passage quoted above is preceded by a summary of her method of dealing with the four elements, air, water, earth, and fire. In its context, therefore, Bradstreet's declaration means that she is using material already handled by Bartas, but treating it in an original manner.

In recent years, two students of *The Tenth Muse* have discussed its internal organization. One of these, E. W. White, affirms that "there is both chronological and textual confusion" in the order in which its constituent poems were printed. She adds that "if Anne Bradstreet had been in a position to supervise their publication she would undoubtedly have arranged them differently."[19] This scholar then rearranges the various poems in a chronological order, according to date of composing, as "their most logical form of presentation."

More recently an article on "The Structure of Anne Bradstreet's *Tenth Muse*" has maintained that the published arrangement was that which Bradstreet herself preferred and that her book "is far more impressive, finally, when it is considered as a unit than when we isolate individual poems for analysis."[20] After arguing for a considerable degree of thematic unity and structural complexity in *The Tenth Muse*, this article suggests that Anne Bradstreet herself was aware of the principles upon which it is organized and published. It makes the valid point that the fact that the poems were supposedly printed without her knowledge is no argument against their incorporating a deliberate structural design, for "she had evidently given her father a complete manuscript" and there are no signs of editorial work by anyone else. The article, therefore,

[19] *Anne Bradstreet*, p. 253.

[20] By Robert D. Arner in *Discoveries & Considerations*, ed. Calvin Israel (Albany, 1976), p. 47.

comes to the conclusion that "the careful attention Bradstreet paid to the structure of her book ought to be immediately evident to anyone who considers" its "pat-
terned arrangement."[21] Anyone who goes a step further
by comparing the thematic and structural unity of *The
Tenth Muse* in its original format with the same features
of Sylvester's *Devine Weekes* would realize almost at a
glance that Bradstreet's volume contains a conscious pattern of organization deriving from its forerunner.

The Sylvester-Bartas edition provides an explanation of
why Bradstreet selected three of the four subjects included
among her elegies and epitaphs. One of these consists of
a paraphrase of King David's lamentation for Saul. The
other three are dedicated to near-contemporary figures,
Bartas himself, Sir Philip Sidney, and Queen Elizabeth.
There is no mystery over why Bradstreet should conse-
crate an elegy to her model, Bartas, but one may wonder,
perhaps, at the choice of such unlikely heroes as Sidney
and Elizabeth in the climate of opinion of Puritan Massachusetts in 1650. E. W. White reports, for example, that
so far as she has been able to discover, the elegy to Sidney
is the only seventeenth-century New England tribute to
him ever written.[22]

Bradstreet may have decided to honor Sidney because
he was one of her family ancestors,[23] but she may also,
or otherwise, have been impelled to write in his praise by
a page in Sylvester's translation of Bartas addressed to the
reader, "Lectoribus," following the table of contents, a
page entirely devoted to Sidney and thus serving as a kind
of secondary dedication, the primary one having been offered to James I. In keeping with one aspect of the English
baroque style, shaped verse, Sylvester's verses to Sidney
are printed in the form of a pencil, and Sidney is described

[21] Ibid., p. 63.
[22] *Anne Bradstreet*, p. 141.
[23] Ibid., p. 11.

as England's Apelles and the world's wonder. Bradstreet
specifically refers to these verses in her lines

> How to persist, my muse is more in doubt,
> Which makes me now with Sylvester confess
> But Sidney's muse can sing his worthiness.

Bartas himself in the second day of *La Seconde Semaine*
or "Babylone" treats Sidney as one of the four major writers of England, a passage to which Bradstreet alludes in
her own verses on Sidney:

> Noble Bartas, this to thy praise adds more,
> In sad, sweet verse, thou didst his death deplore.

This is a reference to the Sylvester translation, not to the
original French text, as E. W. White observes, since Sidney's death had not yet taken place when Bartas himself
was writing.

Bartas also provided a precedent for saluting Queen Elizabeth, for he devotes twenty-three lines to her immediately following his lines on Sidney. Sylvester, moreover,
interpolates a two-page tribute to Elizabeth in "The Third
Day of the First Weeke," in which she is compared to a
lotus flower, to the daughter of the sun, and to a phoenix.
The latter metaphor was, of course, one of the most common in the Renaissance, used by almost every poet in
every language. Anne Bradstreet also applied it to Queen
Elizabeth, and Sor Juana Inés de la Cruz was called the
Phoenix of Mexico in the title of a posthumous edition
of her works. In her elegy of Bartas, Bradstreet suggests
that she had wished at one time to imitate the French
poet, but had given up in despair of achieving her ambition. She further reveals that more recently she had achieved
her purpose in a modest way. According to her metaphoric
terms, while she was rereading his lines, the rays that
they emitted enabled her to produce a homely daisy in
her "later spring." If she should produce a richer harvest

in her summer and autumn years, she promises, this mature production will be dedicated to Bartas.

The tone of all of Bradstreet's poetic references to Bartas is that of deep humility. She speaks of herself disparagingly, for example, "Thus weake brain'd I, reading thy lofty stile." This artistic self-abasement is not necessarily representative of Puritanical mortification or of feminine submission, however; it may just as well be the reflection of a purely literary device that can be traced back to Sylvester and Bartas himself. The latter in the fourth day of the first week repudiated the notion that poets attain everlasting glory through their efforts. In other terms, he rejected a common topos in Renaissance verse, the "proud conceit" or the poet's boast that his own lines will last through future ages or eternity. Bartas, in direct contrast to this poetic convention, after admitting that his verses had caused him great pains, declared that he expected no glory from them, but hoped merely that they would inspire more gifted poets to undertake his theme in the future. Sylvester paraphrased these lines in such a way as to apply them to himself. Repudiating the practice of the "best English wits," whose verses revealed flattery, courtship, sycophancy, and affectation, he dedicated his works to God's glory, not his own, until posterity may find more dextrous poets to record the same events

> And foot by foot with far more life and grace,
> follow Great BARTAS admirable pace.

Rather convincing evidence that Sylvester's modesty was merely a literary reflection of Bartas's delineation of the humble conceit may be found in his dedication of another translation, "The Triumph of Faith," to his deceased uncle. His "Toombe of Words," he affirms,

> . . . shall out-last
> The proud cloud-threatning Battlements,

> Th' aspiring Spires by NILUS plac't,
> And Hell-deepe-founded Monuments.

Bradstreet, however, was following Sylvester in his modest rather than his proud attitude. It is probably not through mere coincidence that she addresses her model as "Great, deare, sweet *Bartas*" or that she concludes with a reference to those who will excel her efforts in the future:

> Ile leave thy praise, to those shall doe thee right,
> Good will, not skill, did cause me bring my mite.

If it is true that Bradstreet followed the Bartas-Sylvester model closely and consecutively rather than casually and sporadically, it would follow that she possessed more than elementary acquaintance with French culture and history. It would also follow that her poems should not necessarily be interpreted exclusively in the light of an Anglo-American background. With these conclusions in mind, I should like to suggest alternate interpretations of two passages from the quaternions.

In the first of these, "Old Age" is reporting historical and political events that he has witnessed.

> I've seen one stabbed, and some to lose their heads,
> And others flee, struck both with guilt and dread.
> I've seen, and so have you, for 'tis but late,
> The desolation of a goodly state
> Plotted and acted so that none can tell
> Who gave the counsel but the prince of hell—
> Three hundred thousand slaughtered innocents
> By bloody popish, hellish miscreants.

The "one stabbed" would seem to be Henry IV of France, who was assassinated by Ravaillac in 1610, and the "three hundred thousand slaughtered innocents" the victims of the St. Bartholomew's Day massacre in Paris. Whether or not Bradstreet could read French, it is almost certain that she knew of these events. Sylvester, for example, interpolated in his translation a reference to St. Bartholomew's Day "when SEIN did swell with blood."[24] White assumes that two English noblemen, Buckingham and Strafford, were alluded to as the victims of stabbing and beheading, which is also plausible, but her explanation that "three hundred thousand slaughtered innocents" were victims of the Irish Rebellion of 1641 is most unlikely.[25] Even if that many English soldiers had died in Ireland, they could hardly be considered "slaughtered innocents" as were the Huguenot citizens of Paris and other parts of France. The number "three hundred thousand" is, of course, a gross exaggeration in regard also to the St. Bartholomew's massacre.

Bradstreet had many anti-Catholic prejudices, as was natural for one in her environment, but she sometimes had misgivings about her biased conceptions and once even wondered, as she confided to her children, "why may not the Popish religion be the right?"[26] Caution should be used, therefore, in reading anti-Catholic sentiments into her poetry. The following lines of the "Apology" appended to "The Four Monarchies" in her second edition, for example, have been misinterpreted.

> Although my Monarchies their legs do lack:
> No matter is it this last, the world now sees,
> Hath many ages been upon his knees.

According to White, the final line represents "a pleasant example of Anne Bradstreet's individual turn of humor, that deftly twists a punning dig at popery out of her own

[24] *Bartas*, trans. Sylvester, p. 95.

[25] *Anne Bradstreet*, p. 214.

[26] *The Works of Anne Bradstreet*, ed. Jeannine Hensley (Cambridge, Mass., 1967), p. 244.

misfortune.''[27] Bradstreet's humor is there well enough, but the reference is not to the Catholic religion, but to the commonplace Renaissance doctrine that the world was degenerating or running down and, so to speak, in its dotage. Bradstreet could have acquired this notion from many sources. The most obvious is Sir Walter Raleigh, who wrote in his *History of the World*, "We have neither giants such as the elder world had; nor mighty men such as the elder world had; but all things in general are reputed of less virtue, which from the heavens receive virtue.''[28]

White's criticism suffers at another point from underestimating the influence of the European literary milieu. After labelling the subject matter of "The Four Monarchies" as "grim and unfeminine," she observes that there is not in Bradford's poem "a sin of the flesh or the spirit that is not described, often with revolting detail, in her account of the ambitions, conquests, cruelties, and licentious self-indulgences of the monarchs of antiquity.''[29] Whether or not Bradstreet's historical poetry reveals a masculine cast to her mind and personality, there are few of her alleged grisly or ferocious elements that cannot be

[27] *Anne Bradstreet*, p. 235.

[28] (Edinburgh, 1820), p. 1. Not only did Bradstreet know this work, but she paraphrased large sections of it in "The Four Monarchies." Ann Stanford, *Anne Bradstreet: The Worldly Puritan* (New York, 1974), p. 137. Critics have been willing to acknowledge the humor in Bradstreet, but have ignored it in Du Bartas, which to me seems an injustice. He compares, for example, the sheets of water in the seas to the floods of words in his poem [*Première Semaine. Troisième Jour*, 1. 217]. And as an illustration of the effects of lightning, he describes having often seen in his youth a flash sear off in an instant the pubic hair from a woman and do no other harm whatsoever [*Première Semaine. Second Jour*, 11. 705-5]. Du Bartas's humorless American editors seriously maintain that the poet is here recording an incident of his youth when his mother was knocked unconscious by a bolt of lightning. *Works*, ed. Holmes et al., 1: 17.

[29] *Anne Bradstreet*, p. 237.

observed in Bartas as well. If Bradstreet acknowledged a literary model, she can hardly be faulted for following it.

As Hans Galinsky has shown, there is absolutely no agreement among critics about the merits of Bradstreet's poetry; one speaks disparagingly of the "Bartas disease" and another suggests that she is inferior precisely because she does not reproduce ingenious conceits. Most commentators now feel that her occasional poems written to and about members of her family are the ones with greatest poetic merit. Paradoxically the same critical climate of opinion that has rejected Anne Bradstreet's *The Tenth Muse* as contrived and artificial has at the same time highly applauded Edward Taylor's poems, charged as they are with bizarre imagery and conceits. Regardless of the prevailing attitude toward artificiality in verse, it must be recognized that Bradstreet, like Taylor, was the product of a literary period as well as of a geographical environment. Also it must not be forgotten that she originally acquired her place in literary history through the published edition of *The Tenth Muse*, while her personal verse remained in manuscript, and that the book that introduced her to her seventeenth-century contemporaries will always retain its significance as a register of colonial taste and a reminder of literary internationalism. The more *The Tenth Muse* resembles *La Semaine*, the closer it approaches the mainstream of literature. Both those who patronize Bradstreet as a victim of the "Bartas disease" and those who maintain that she had little to do with her French predecessor mistakenly look for significant signs of their relationship in "a contrived metaphor, a stilted image, or an overelaborate descriptive passage," to use the words of her biographer.[30] Far more significant resemblances are to be found in two major aspects of the Renaissance style, that is, the maintaining and extending of

---

[30] Ibid., p. 270.

a complex structure and the development of the theme of the grandeur and magnificence of the universe. In this regard, Bradstreet shares the poetic vision not only of her French predecessor Bartas, but also of her Mexican successor Sor Juana Inés de la Cruz.

THREE

EDWARD TAYLOR AND THE AMERICAN BAROQUE

ANNE BRADSTREET and Edward Taylor are ordinarily considered as by far the two best poets of colonial America. Few links other than religious and geographical can be discerned between them, however, even though it appears that the only book of English poetry discovered in Taylor's library after his death was a copy of *The Tenth Muse*.[1] The subject matter of Taylor's verse is almost exclusively devotional, whereas Bradstreet's covers a variety of human concerns, including domestic relationships. Her simple diction and clear syntax contrast sharply with Taylor's elaborate verbal techniques. Although Taylor's artificial language may seem to be almost unique when compared with the plain style of his contemporary poets in the English colonies of America, his mannerisms seem less extravagant when seen as part of the widespread esthetic tradition throughout the major European literatures of the seventeenth century known as the baroque.

Critics have accepted the notion that the baroque style passed from Europe to Spanish America, and as a result the term a "Spanish-American baroque" is widespread. The designation in the Spanish language is either "El barroco de Indias" or "Barroco literario de Indias."[2] The cor-

[1] *The Poems of Edward Taylor*, ed. Donald E. Stanford (New Haven, 1960), p. xxvi.

[2] Mariano Picón-Salas, *De la conquista a la independencia* (México, 1944), pp. 99-109.

responding concept of an artificial style passing from Europe to English America has so far gained only moderate acceptance. It was formulated originally, appropriately enough, by a Czechoslovakian scholar, Zdeněk Vančura, who spoke in 1933 of "Baroque prose in America."[3] Eight years later Austin Warren used the phrase "Colonial Baroque" and a Japanese scholar, Ken Akiyama, more recently appropriated "belated baroque prose" to explain the phenomenon to the Orient.[4] Warren based his definition on the strictures of unfriendly critics: " 'Baroque' shall name such English poetry and prose antedating the neoclassical movement as would, by neoclassical standards, be judged 'false wit.' "[5] Warren's notion of an "American Baroque" was taken up and extended by Harold Jantz, an authority on German baroque literature and the pioneer anthologist of seventeenth-century American poetry.[6] Jantz also does not provide a comprehensive definition, but accepts with reservations a pejorative description by Moses Coit Tyler delivered over a century ago—not of baroque as such, but of one kind of English poetry fashionable early in the seventeenth century, "the degenerate euphuism of Donne, of Wither, of Quarles, of George Herbert." The advantage of these definitions is that they depart from conventional expositions of the baroque in Europe by eliminating all reference to art and architecture or to themes and ideologies and limit themselves entirely to linguistic and rhetorical characteristics.

There is no question that the concept of baroque de-

[3] René Wellek, *Concepts of Criticism* (New Haven, 1963), p. 88.

[4] Hans Galinsky, " 'Colonial Baroque,' A Concept Illustrating Dependence, Germinal Independence and New World Interdependence of Early American Literature" [a beautiful baroque title], in *Actes du VIIe Congrès de l'Association Internationale de Littérature Comparée* (Stuttgart, 1979), 1: 44.

[5] *Rage for Order. Essays in Criticism* (Chicago, 1948), p. 2.

[6] In *Discoveries & Considerations*, ed. Calvin Israel (Albany, 1976), pp. 7-10.

veloped originally in the history of art and that criteria previously applied to painting, sculpture, and above all architecture came to be transferred to the literature of the seventeenth century. If there is a baroque presence in the Anglo-Saxon part of America, it is obviously exclusively literary, for New England and the other British colonies of America, unlike the Spanish colonies covering the territory of the present Mexico and Peru, produced very little before 1700 in the way of art and architecture except for the utilitarian and primitive. The Spanish colonies, on the other hand, not only erected magnificent cathedrals and splendid palaces, but created masterpieces in the decorative arts, which today are among the world's outstanding examples of intricacy and embellishment.

Another reason why the concept of baroque seems somewhat alien to the English colonies is that the earliest critics to establish its standards or criteria were German and Italian art historians. When the concept was first applied to literature, it was Italian, Spanish, and German writers who were considered relevant, and even now they are the ones to whom the designation seems most applicable. Many critics of French and English literature seem uncomfortable with baroque as a period concept, and it has certainly not been accepted in these literatures on an equal level with other terms such as Renaissance, neoclassicism, Enlightenment, or Romanticism. Indeed, during most of the nineteenth century, the term baroque, in its application to literature at least, was used as a synonym for bad taste.

Even contemporary critics who deal primarily with Spanish and Italian texts are by no means unanimous in identifying the particular elements that constitute the baroque, and few have attempted to apply any but the most general criteria in seeking common ground in all the literatures of Europe. Some major differences in philosophy or cosmic attitudes may be perceived, however, that distinguish the baroque from the Renaissance that preceded or in some instances coexisted with it. The Renaissance was the period of humanism, when man felt proud of his humanity, believed that each individual could excel in every form of knowledge and endeavor, tried to extend the limits of science and philosophy, and considered art to be inferior to nature as its mirror and servant. In literature, the Renaissance expressed the notion of ideal beauty, frequently associating it with Platonic philosophy. In the period of the baroque, however, man emphasized his limitations, both physical and mental; abandoned the notion of attaining competency in many disciplines; and looked to the spiritual rather than the natural world for knowledge and inspiration. Paradoxically, he placed art on an equal level with nature and even in some senses on a superior plane. Beauty was considered as something illusory or relative, and its physical manifestations were frequently described in crude and earthy language. In literature, content was subordinated to language, and words were frequently used for words' sake. Having abandoned the quest for new knowledge, the writer sought novelty in expression, not in content. The product of this activity, when successful, was known as *wit* in English, *ingegno* in Italian, *agudeza* in Spanish, and *esprit* in French. A famous English poem by Abraham Cowley, "Of Wit" (1656), defines and illustrates this elusive intellectual quality and also warns against its excesses, subsequently known as "false wit." Whether Taylor's wit is true or false or whether it is appropriate to consider his poetry under the heading baroque, he was certainly the leading exponent in the English colonies of the exuberant style. Indeed, the poets who resemble him most in the devising of verbal intricacies are not from either England or the English colonies of America, but from Italy, Spain, and Spanish America.

The outstanding Italian practitioner of the baroque style, Giambattista Marino, expressed his esthetic creed in one of his verses, "The aim of the poet is to create wonder" [È del poeta il fin la meraviglia]. By this, Marino meant that poetry should evoke a feeling of astonishment or amazement by means of its novelty, daring, or intricacy. For Marino as for other writers in the baroque tradition, the essence of good poetry is wit or acuity; its effectiveness depends upon the degree of wonder it produces; and its chief instruments are rhetorical figures and tropes, the most important of which is the metaphor.[7]

Marino's favorite metaphors are geological (jewels and precious metals such as rubies, pearls, crystal, silver, and gold), botanical (flowers, and the effects of the seasons and the elements), and biological (the natural functions of birth, death, and regeneration). He piles up nouns and adjectives in heaps or assembles them in clusters and uses structural devices such as the chiasmus, and balance and antithesis. He frequently uses carnal metaphors for spiritual themes, for example, describing the drops of blood exuding from Christ's wounds as tongues of love that work for the poet's benefit [Tanto son per mio ben lingue amorose].

The chief ingredient of the Marinistic style, however, is elaborate conceit. The more numerous the conceits, according to Marino, the better the poem. In one of his prose works, he accumulates the following expressions for the human tongue: "midwife of souls, forge of words, key of memory, bell of wit, hand of reason, curb of prudence, helmsman of the will, the stamp that presses conceits in others' ears, the pen that writes the letters of thought; brush that paints the images of the intellect, the battering ram assaulting the strongest hearts; trumpet making public the internal affections; arrow that wounds and heals; spear that kills and revives."[8]

[7] James Mirollo, *The Poet of the Marvelous, Giambattista Marino* (New York, 1963), p. 120.

[8] Ibid., pp. 153, 134-35, 148, 131, 33. Richard Crashaw, the English poet, translated a section of one of Marino's religious poems, *The Massacre of the Innocents [La Strage degl' Innocenti (1632)]*, and it was

EDWARD TAYLOR

Although Marino and his Spanish contemporary Luis de Góngora were acquainted with each other's works, there is no evidence that either borrowed from the other. In other words, they arrived independently at remarkably similar poetic styles, a statement that can be broadened to include Taylor as well. The poetry of Góngora and his school is commonly labelled Góngorism, and there are two other terms widely used in Spanish criticism to describe its primary elements. The first of these is *culteranismo* or "cultism," derived from the adjective *culto*, referring to people who are cultured or cultivated. Cultism designates esoteric language, consisting of such elements as recondite vocabulary, complicated syntax, and extravagant figures of speech. The second Spanish term, *conceptismo* or "conceptism," which derives from the noun *concepto*, designates intellectual formulations such as conceits, paradoxes, and ingenious antitheses. Although one term theoretically concerns words and the other ideas, it is almost impossible in practice to separate the two. A conceit, for example, may both create images and stimulate ideas. The terms cultism and conceptism are useful primarily in attributing a preponderance of one quality or another; that is, a poet who depends largely on vocabulary and verbal effects is considered cultist; one who regularly establishes intellectual relationships is considered conceptist. Both tendencies exist in Góngora, but it might be fair to say that he is less cultist than Marino and less conceptist than Sor Juana Inés de la Cruz. In the same way, Taylor is highly cultist, and hardly conceptist at all.

---

published as the longest piece in Crashaw's verse collection *Steps to the Temple* (1646), a matter of some significance to students of Taylor since the English poet whom he resembles most is considered to be Crashaw. L. C. Martin, the editor of Crashaw's *Poems*, gives 1610 rather than 1642 as the date of *La Strage*, and this error has been perpetuated by many critics of Crashaw. Other works of Crashaw showing indebtedness to Marino are treated by Mirollo, *Poet of the Marvelous*, pp. 248-49.

Like Marino, Góngora is noted for elaborate conceits and for using carnal metaphors to express spiritual themes. He also uses balance and antithesis, paradox, repetition, oxymoron, allegory and personification, and he alludes liberally to the *topoi* of Greek and Latin authors. Several other characteristics, all tending to make his work obscure, are so widespread in Góngora's work that they set him apart from other writers. His vocabulary is loaded with neologisms, slang, and foreign words. His analogies are often not only far-fetched, but almost unintelligible; he is, in other words, guilty of catachresis or recondite analogy. Spanish critics in the past have condemned him particularly for his *hipérbaton*, a word that may be translated as "hyperbate" or "hyperbaton," but which is almost never encountered in English. It refers to innovations in syntax, usually inversions in word order, which are considered a blemish in Spanish prosody, but which in English have been made respectable by the blank verse tradition.

A British scholar, fully cognizant of the parallel to Marino, argues that one of Góngora's major aims is the evocation of wonder through the description of nature and that this element in his poetry is inherently related to his verbal techniques of intricacy and novelty. The wonder that seventeenth-century poets perceived in nature does not resemble that associated with the sublime in the eighteenth century, which is more familiar to modern students. The Augustans felt that the sublime was inspired by the infinitude of the universe as reflected in such vast works as the ocean, the skies, and the mountains, but the wonder in Góngora stems from the perception of artistic arrangements in nature. According to one of Góngora's contemporaries, "What is most marvellous about the world is not the immensity of these Heavens, nor the number of stars there, nor the sheer bulk of essences, but its wit, its design, its framework, its order, its correspondences."[9]

Sor Juana Inés de la Cruz, although obviously affected by the techniques of Góngora, developed a unique and independent style. She shares with both Marino and Góngora the use of puns, paradox, and parallelism and antithesis, but uses conceits sparingly. Like Góngora, she derives her metaphors from the crudest parts of nature as well as from the pleasurable and the picturesque, attaining, in the words of a Spanish critic, "almost a preciosity of the gross."[10] In structure, her favorite device is the chiasmus, and she developed the art of the hyperbole to a height beyond that attained by any of her predecessors.

The English metaphysical poets obviously belong to the same tradition as these Italian and Hispanic writers, but there are important differences among them. Marino and Góngora may be considered as "practitioners of a style marked by sensuous imagery, exclamatory syntax, and an attempt to achieve the stupefying and the marvelous."[11] Donne, Crashaw, and other exponents of the metaphysical style, on the other hand, specialize in conceits that communicate intellectually rather than astonish or overwhelm. Equally important, their works are pervaded by a sense of irony and cosmic paradox.[12] Austin Warren has pointed out major characteristics of Taylor's poetry that are alien to the baroque style in England, "his downright coinages, his inversions and other awkward, sometimes unconstruable constructions."[13]

[9] Juan Eusebio Nieremberg, *Curiosa y oculta filosofía* (Madrid, 1643), p. 300. Cited by M. J. Woods, *The Poet and the Natural World in the Age of Góngora* (Oxford, 1978), p. 188.

[10] Picón-Salas, *De la conquista*, p. 100.

[11] Frank J. Warnke, *European Metaphysical Poetry* (New Haven, 1974), p. 3.

[12] Ibid., pp. 6-7.

[13] *Rage for Order*, p. 13.

These characteristics are part and parcel of the style of Góngora as well, indeed his distinguishing ones. Since the poetry of Taylor is sensuous and stupefying rather than intellectual and ironical, and since scholars have already pointed out the major resemblances between Taylor and the two English poets with whom he has greatest affinity, Herbert and Crashaw, the following pages will concentrate on analogies between Taylor and his Italian and Hispanic counterparts.

In one of Taylor's unpublished manuscripts appears the phrase, "I wrote these . . . not for the Wit sake nor for the Verse sake but for the History sake."[14] This sentence reveals that Taylor conceived of three separate elements in poetry, its substance or subject matter, "the History," and its two separate rhetorical adornments, "the wit" and "the verse." The latter can be considered as equivalent to the conceptism and cultism of Spanish criticism, both of which, in most of Taylor's poetry, take precedence over the history or subject matter.

One of Taylor's major aims, if not the primary one, is, like Marino's, to evoke wonder. Not only are nearly all of his verbal artifices directed toward this purpose, but he several times expressly evokes objects and sensations associated with the marvelous. In one poem of sixty-six lines, he uses some form of the word *wonder* six times together with *amazed* and *marvels* [125-126]. In other poems he cites "A Clew of Wonders!" together with "Big belli'd Wonders" [67]. He introduces another poem with the exclamation, "Stupendious Love! All Saints Astonishment!" [20]. And he celebrates the sacrament of communion because of its imparting "To mee to wonderment" [240].

In temporal affairs, the kind of wonder that intrigued

---

[14] *Poems*, p. 507. Future references to this edition will consist of page numbers within brackets after particular quotations.

Taylor was that derived from the mechanical, labeled in an Italian treatise on wit as *mirabili per arte*. He cites a number of wonders of the ancient and the modern worlds, including the hanging gardens of Babylon, the pyramids, the military engines of Archimedes, the clock with moving figures at Strasburg, and the artificial man of Albertus Magnus that could walk and speak [180]. Taylor's interest in the mechanical arts links him with two representatives of the Romantic movement who were also fascinated by mechanical creatures, E.T.A. Hoffmann and Nathaniel Hawthorne. In the dichotomy of Art-Nature, the baroque tradition accorded respect to art in greater measure than did preceding or subsequent historical periods. Taylor comes close to placing the two on an equal plane in his statements: "Nature doth better work than Art," and "Art, nature's Ape, hath many brave things done" [181, 179]. He even affirms, "An heap of Pearls is precious: but they shall / When set by Art Excell" [456]. He consistently proclaims, of course, that for him everything in both art and nature is inferior to the glories of God. In reference to Christ's redemption, therefore, he admonishes himself, "Wonder, my Soule, at this great Wonder bright" [157]. Spiritual phenomena he regards as a kind of artifice, superior to nature; he describes, for example, bread and wine turned into the flesh and blood of Christ as "not fram'd by natures acting, but by Art" [270]. As Austin Warren has pointed out, Taylor analogizes nature to the crafts,[15] exactly the reverse process associated with the Romantics. In a typical poem, he conceives the earth as laced and girded by rivers like green emerald ribbons, and compares it to "a Quilt Ball within a Silver Box." The stars he describes as "twinckling Lanthorns in the Sky."

It has been argued that Taylor's poetical theory bears an intimate relationship to his theology—that his view

---

[15] *Rage for Order*, p. 8.

of language, while consistent with Puritan literary theory in general, is at the same time based on "a close analogy between words and the Word."[16] Two German seventeenth-century philosophers, Böhme and Leibniz, did indeed develop such a theory of language as a manifestation of the Deity, viewing Hebrew as the language closest to that spoken in the Garden of Eden, but Taylor cannot be said to belong to their tradition, for he nowhere directly alludes to any kind of inherent relationship between language and the Divine Being except for quoting John 1:14, "The Word was made Flesh." Indeed, his practice indicates that, like Marino, he saw no special connection between words and metaphysics, but believed that the poet seeks to attain wonder, primarily through verbal effects that by their brilliance and novelty dazzle the reader's mind.

Kindred themes repeated consistently throughout Taylor's verses are the difficulties of poetic composition and his personal deficiencies as a writer of verse. These themes are united in a "Prologue" in which he asks whether a mere "Crumb of Dust" may have the power to outshine the earth, the mountains, and the sky by means of poetic creation. He then identifies himself as this crumb of dust and admits the dullness of his fancy, but concludes in a submerged proud conceit that if granted divine inspiration he could make the Lord's works shine like flowers or precious jewels. The phrase "Crumb of Dust" has been seen as a link between Taylor and George Herbert, who also uses the metaphor, but it could equally illustrate resemblance to any number of French and Spanish writers in the biblical tradition, who refer to man as *"poca tierra"* or *"dépouille de bou."*

In various poems, Taylor speaks about the inadequacy

---

[16] William J. Scheick, *The Will and the Word* (Athens, Ga., 1974), p. 103.

of "Quaint Metaphors" in general and terms his own "Quaintest Metaphors" as better fitted to criticize his own shortcomings than to praise God [25, 37]. His "tatter'd Fancy" and "Ragged Rymes," he affirms "Teeme leaden Metaphors" [233] which "are but dull Tacklings tag'd / With ragged Non-Sense" [149]. On other occasions, however, he seems content with his "sparkling Metaphors" [146] and admits the possibility of "Rich Metaphors" [267]. In one of these "rich" metaphors, he compares the travail of composing under divine inspiration to the agonies of a victim in a torture chamber being put to the question [51]. Sor Juana also treats the mental torments of the poet by comparing wit to fire, which the more matter it consumes, the more it flares up.[17] In lines which might be compared to Góngora's for their ambiguity, Taylor proposes,

> . . . Glory as a Metaphor, Il 'tende
> And lay it all on thee, my Lord!
> [262]

His meaning can be discerned only by the aid of a further poem in which he portrays a metaphor as a medium of communicating sensual as well as intellectual stimuli. Here he describes the glories of nature as themselves being a metaphor for God. In other words, he uses the word "metaphor" as itself a metaphor.

> . . . Lord . . . thou dost use
> This Metaphor to make thyself appeare.
> [263]

Superficially these lines seem to support the hypothesis that Taylor believed that language is inherently connected with divinity, but he is actually saying that the glories of

---

[17] *Obras escogidas*, ed. Juan Carlos Merlo (Barcelona, 1968), p. 111.

nature, not metaphor or any other aspect of language, reveal the Divine Presence.

In his commentary on the biblical verse, "The Word was made Flesh," he affirms,

> The Orator from Rhetorick gardens picks
> His Spangld Flowers of sweet-breathed Eloquence.

And in extending the metaphor, he suggests that the flowers are converted into earrings, the identical coupling of flowers with precious jewels that he introduced in his prologue. This blending of the animate and the inanimate and giving equal emphasis to the beauty of art and that of nature is also one of the chief characteristics of the style of both Góngora and Marino. Góngora, for example, devotes an entire stanza to a description of Dawn scattering red roses over a woman, embodying a carefully contrived balance between art and nature. He wonders whether snowy crimson or scarlet snow suits her best, suggests that the Abyssinian pearl enters into competition with her natural beauty, and portrays Cupid, whose anger is aroused by the presumption of the pearl, as condemning it for its brilliance and sentencing it to hang in gold from the mother-of-pearl of the woman's ear.[18] In a single one of his sonnets, Góngora introduces ivory, marble, ebony, amber, gold, silver, crystal, pearl, sapphire, and ruby. Equally significant in Marino, as we have already seen, is the basing of metaphors upon gems and precious metals, particularly "ruby, pearl, amber, sapphire, crystal, silver and gold."[19]

Taylor's favorite jewels are pearl, jasper, ruby, diamond (which he usually names carbuncle), and emerald (which he also names smaragdine). Pearl appears most frequently because of its biblical meanings of wisdom and experi-

---

[18] Lowry Nelson, *Baroque Lyric Poetry* (New Haven, 1963), p. 186.
[19] Mirollo, *Poet of the Marvelous*, p. 153.

EDWARD TAYLOR

ence, and other theological associations. Taylor uses the pearl as a symbol for Christ, grace, and life. In addition to specifying particular gems, Taylor employs general terms such as "precious stones" and "rich jewels." He also alludes frequently to crystal, silver, and gold. In his various poems over sixty different objects are described as golden, including gutters, bread, feathers, anvils, and rivets. Perfumes and aromatic spices are frequently introduced to represent the qualities of luxury and splendor as well as to embody the exotic flavor of the Old Testament. In one of his meditations, Taylor portrays Christ's garden as comprising beds of flowers beset with pearl, opal, gold, and silver, another example of the play between animate and inanimate [194]. In a further poem using jasper, ruby, and sapphire to represent the divine perfection and resplendence, Taylor refers to Christ as "Grace's chiefe Flower pot." In a separate reference to Christ and his "Deare Spouse," the Christian Church, Christ is her Flower, and "she thy flower pot" [148]. Elsewhere Taylor calls upon Christ, "Be thou my Flowers, I'le be thy Flower Pot" [15].

The use of carnal metaphors in a religious context represents another major link between Taylor and Marino. The latter, for example, describes the mouth of Mary Magdalen as the dwelling place of nectar between vivid pearls and fervid rubies and of pungent thorns in the midst of vermilion and odorous roses.[20] Innumerable parallels may be discerned in Taylor. His theological subject matter is based on analogies between the physical and the spiritual worlds. The largest part of his published work consists of over two hundred poetic *Meditations* on the Lord's Supper, and almost a quarter of these are based on passages from the Song of Solomon. The theology of the Lord's Supper obviously rests upon the metaphor of bread and wine as flesh and blood, and the Song of Solomon is in-

[20] Ibid., p. 291.

terpreted in Calvinistic theology as a metaphorical representation of the Christian Church as the Bride of Christ. Taylor's poetry, which is also metaphorical rather than ideological, does not reveal his personal interpretation of the doctrine of the Lord's Supper, although he specifically rejects transubstantiation and consubstantiation, and one would assume that he accepted the Calvinist concept of merely spiritual transference. This knotty theological question is dealt with by Ursula Brumm, but Taylor's verse is too cryptic to make a complete resolution possible even for this fine scholar. According to Brumm, Taylor draws on the notion of types and antitypes to explain the sacrament. "He is able to account for Christ's flesh and blood being bread and wine by establishing a typological connection of them with manna and the Paschal lamb."[21]

Taylor calls upon his soul to "Purge out and Vomit by Repentance" all ill humors [269]. He terms the human veins of Christ golden gutters and golden pipes which pour forth nectar or red wine into crystal vessels (divine ordinances) with sapphire taps [21]. He drinks Christ's health in his own blood-wine [46] and even proposes to use Christ's blood as a writing fluid [182]. He portrays God's flesh as a feast laid out on a banquet table [22] and suggests that human blood runs through the veins of Christ to extinguish the fires of Hell [5]. The latter conceit is based upon the doctrine of mystical union with Christ, who has "Marri'de our Manhood, making it its Bride." Taylor also emblemizes Christ as a vine that produces a wine to make things clear in contrast to ordinary wine that makes people drunk [258]. In elaborating a verse from the Song of Solomon, he asks why Christ bestowing "his lovely Love" should, nevertheless, mask his face, "allowing not a kiss?"

[21] *American Thought and Religious Typology* (New Brunswick, N.J., 1970), p. 75.

[254]. He also portrays Christ hugging him within his bosom [73], and asks his body

> Why hast thou done so ill
> To Court, and kiss my Soule, yet kissing kill?

This is very close to a paradox in one of Marino's erotic poems, "The Song of the Kisses" in which kissing, by depriving the poet of life, revives him.

> Quel bacio, che mi priva
> Di vita, mi raviva.

A good deal of Taylor's imagery is coarse and crude in the extreme, as in the above references to purging and vomiting. Elsewhere he refers to his "Members Dung-Carts that bedung at pleasure" [73], "Puddle Water Boyld by Sunn beams" [77], and "drops dropt in a Closestool pan" [78]. He lists loathsome diseases, including "Bad Stomach, Iliak, Colick Fever, . . . Scurvy, Dropsy, Gout, and Leprosy. . . . Itch, Botch Scab" [206]. Vocabulary such as this is not completely alien to Anglo-Saxon literature of Taylor's century, as witness Thomas Coryate's *Crudities* (1611), but it is not to be found in the English metaphysical poets, not even in Donne. There is none of it in Marino although parallels are to be found in Góngora and Sor Juana Inés de la Cruz. Góngora describes a native of Esgueva drinking that which has been emptied into the river from the toilet Cabinet "according to the laws of digestion,"[22] and Sor Juana ends single lines of a group of five burlesque sonnets with words describing biological functions, for example, offal [*caca*], coitional pleasure [*refocilo, regodeo, regüilo*], and bad breath [*tufo*], fine illustrations of the preciosity of grossness.[23]

Taylor goes further than any of his contemporaries in phallic and other sexual imagery. In reference to the erotic

---

[22] "Letrilla" No. 4, f. 68. *Obras en verso del Homero español, 1627,* facsimile edition (Madrid, 1963), folio 68.

[23] Picón-Salas, *De la conquista,* p. 106.

element in life, he asks his soul why it dwells in such "sensual Organs" which make it stray from its "noble end" [430]. Then he pursues the subject

> My nobler part, why dost thou laquy to
> The Carnal Whynings of my senses so.

"Nobler part" is a pun on high ideals and the male organ. In his most daring image, he describes the phallus of God as "thy royall Pipe" [88]. In one of his longer poems, "A Fig for Thee Oh! Death," he works out an elaborate sexual analogy describing his body as "my vile harlot" and "my strumpet" and looking forward to the General Resurrection when "The Soule and Body now, as two true Lovers / Every night . . . do hug and kiss each other." Although his body has sought to seduce him into sin, Taylor never has "Surprised been nor tumbled in such grave." This means in a general sense that he has never been victim to sensuality, but it also refers to tumbling as a sexual activity. A similar double meaning exists in the subsequent line, "Hence for my strumpet I'le ne'er draw my Sword." The sword has both theological and phallic connotations. Subsequently Taylor challenges Death to capture and rape the body (portrayed as a woman) "And grinde [her] to power in thy Mill the grave."[24]

Taylor's most distinctive feature, one that separates him from the English metaphysical poets, is the vast number of his deliberate innovations in language. He invents new words, resurrects obsolete ones, interweaves dialect and standard forms, and interchanges parts of speech. Al-

---

[24] This sexual imagery has been brought to light by Thomas M. Davies and Arthur Forslater in "Edward Taylor's 'A Fig for Thee Oh! Death,' " in *Discoveries & Considerations*, ed. Calvin Israel, pp. 67-77. They go too far, however, in interpreting the last line of the poem, "I still am where I was, a Fig for thee," as equivalent to making the sign of the *fica*, the thumb between two closed fingers. Although I am alert to all evidence of transatlantic relationships, I doubt that Taylor meant to suggest this Italian gesture. In my opinion, he was using *fig* merely in the biblical sense of the unproductive life.

though these linguistic techniques are typical of the baroque style, they are also associated with burlesque poetry, which flourished in England and on the continent during the sixteenth and seventeenth centuries, particularly in travesties of the classics. They are obvious adornments, moreover, of Samuel Butler's now neglected comic masterpiece *Hudibras* (1663). Taylor, however, has much more in common with Góngora, whose characteristic vocabulary has been extensively analyzed by Spanish critics. They have noted particularly neologisms, archaisms, erudite terms, vulgarisms, slang, colloquialisms, and foreign words. Góngora describes his verse style as "learned although bucolic" [culta sí, aunque bucólica],[25] a description that has equal application to Taylor's. Typical of Taylor are such colloquial expressions as Kerfe [99], saddlebackt [134], puking [137], fuddled [149], bedotcht [149], tittle-tattle [150], Bloomery [159], thrum [179], and muck [8]; such pedantic or esoteric ones as osculated [95], Conjues [157], Quintessenced [172], evigorate [177], Visive [203], Dicotomy [400], Secundine [448], facete [478], and verbous [478]; and such exotic ones as Spicknard [22], Citterns [135], Al-tashcketh Mictam [152], and Garzia Horti [12].

During the seventeenth century, esoteric and abstruse terms were commonly known as "hard words," Butler, for example ridiculing them as

> Words so debas'd and hard, no stone
> Was hard enough to touch them on.
> [*Hudibras*, Part I, Canto i.]

Sylvester's translation of Du Bartas conveniently supplied "An Index of the Hardest Words" or a "briefe explanation of most of the most-difficulties through the whole worke." If Taylor's poetry had been published early in the seven-

[25] "Al excelentisimo Señor Conde de Niebla," dedicatory poem to *Polifemo*, in *Obras en verso del Homero español*, folio 113.

teenth century, his learned and exotic vocabulary would have been considered as a fashionable display of hard words and accepted by the reading public in about the same way in which it viewed the pedantic affectations of the French *précieux*. A modern critic must, therefore, exercise considerable caution in attempting to determine how much of Taylor's strange diction should be interpreted as individual idiosyncrasy and how much as merely conforming to a literary convention—outmoded though the convention may have been while Taylor was writing.

One type of colloquial language to be found in Góngora is the proverb or folk saying in such forms as the following:

Como estaba flaco,
parecía cencerro.
[f 109][26]

cantaba mis aleluyas
[f 105]

pues conoce un galgo
entre cien gallinas
[f 106]

La vida es corta, y la esperança larga,
[f 86]

Que se nos va la Pascua, mozas, que se nos va la Pascua.
[f 110]

One finds in Taylor a correspondingly large variety of popular idioms:

---

[26] The citation in brackets refers to a folio page (either recto or verso) in the facsimile edition of *Obras en verso del Homero español*. The same system of citation will be used in subsequent references to this work.

EDWARD TAYLOR

> a Bird in hand
> [21]
> full as is an Egg of meate
> [40]
> Out of the Frying Pan
> [482]
> Beggar upon horseback
> [394]
> Whosoever trust doth to his golden deed
> Doth rob a barren Garden for a Weed.
> [396][27]

Another trait of Taylor's verse which closely resembles that of Góngora is the extensive use of hyperbate or inversion. As previously indicated, Spanish critics are particularly attentive to this element in Góngora, and most consider it a blemish. A single example will suffice,

> Nuevos conoce oy día
> Troncos el bosque i piedras la montaña.[28]

Literally translated, this means: "New knows today / Trunks the thicket and stones the mountain"; the normal word order would, of course, be, "The thicket knows new trunks today; the mountain, stones." In English poetry, little attention is ordinarily paid to inversion, perhaps because of the influence of Milton, who used it exten-

----

[27] Benjamin Franklin remembered so well the latter "good old verse" in popular speech that he teased his sister by means of a mildly scatological paraphrase,

> A man of deeds and not of words
> Is like a garden full of . . .

Papers of Benjamin Franklin, ed. Leonard W. Labaree et al. (New Haven, 1965), 8: 155.

[28] Elisha Kent Kane, *Gongorism and the Golden Age* (Chapel Hill, N.C., 1928), p. 75.

sively both in *Paradise Lost* and in his sonnets. Inversion is coupled with syntactical confusion in the following typical lines by Taylor.

> I kening through Astronomy Divine
>   The Worlds bright Battlement, wherein I spy
> A Golden Path my Pensill cannot line,
>   From that bright Throne unto my Threshold ly.

Although the meaning of these lines cannot be completely unraveled, the normal word order would be the following: "I [am] kening through the world's bright battlement, divine astronomy, wherein I spy a golden path ly[ing] from that bright throne unto my threshold, [which] my pencil cannot line." This passage illustrates another characteristic of Taylor's poetry, its obscurity. Recondite metaphors such as "the World's bright Battlement" are common in Góngora, where they are classified according to formal rhetoric as catachresis. They also are in large measure responsible for the labeling of his poetry as cultist or intelligible only to the elite.

The only innovation in language developed by Góngora that Taylor does not also practice is the introduction of foreign words. Taylor favors colloquialisms, archaisms, and unusual forms of standard words, but only sparingly interjects Greek and Latin phrases. Among Anglo-Saxon poets, Butler in *Hudibras* excels in adapting foreign words to English, but the best single example of a parallel to Góngora's multilingual proclivities among contemporary English poets is the last four lines of Donne's "Upon Mr. Thomas Coryat's Crudities," which contains Latin, Old French, modern French, Spanish, and Italian and is printed in Black Letter as well as ordinary type. It may be compared to a sonnet of Góngora's utilizing Spanish, Latin, Italian, and Portuguese, and to a much earlier English poem of twenty-one lines by John Skelton, "Speke Parrot," containing phrases in Latin, Greek, French, Italian, and Dutch as well as English.

Taylor shares another essential element of Gongorism, a fondness for extravagant conceits. The Spanish poet typically makes comparisons or draws analogies between disparate objects and brings the pure, the noble, and the refined into contact with the base, the vulgar, and the crude. As a result, his conceits are often labeled grotesque, bizarre, or ludicrous.

Taylor's method is exactly the same, and most of his conceits are just as far-fetched. Whereas Góngora describes a cliff as urinating,[29] Taylor tells his readers that "the heavens in rain shed / Their Excrements upon our lofty heads" [471]. Taylor describes himself as God's "well-tuned instrument" [11], as a coin "new minted" by God's stamp [16], and as a sundial reflecting God's sunshine [140]. In a single poem, he compares himself to a bran, a chaff, a grain of barley, a husk, a shell, a thistle, a briar prickle, a thorn, a lump of lewdness, a pouch of sin, and a purse of naughtiness; he also compares his heart to a park and his head to a bowling alley [111]. He suggests that God is a coconut the size of the earth and then retracts the comparison as debasing [140], in effect convicting himself of false wit.

One of the elements in Góngora's style most difficult to define is that of word arrangement—the use of a variety of verbal tricks designed to amuse or to astonish. One of his sacred poems begins with the nursery rhyme:

A la dina dana dina, la dina dana
[f. 74]

In a sonnet composed of a single sentence, he uses the interrogative *qual* eleven times in seven lines [f. 16]. In

---

[29] Ibid., p. 79.

another he associates the similar sounds of *libros* and *libres* and the forms *passo* and *paseo*. "Con pocos libros libres . . . / . . . passo, y me paseo" [f. 26]. In like manner, he couples *con grasa buena* and *con buen gracia* [f. 26].

Taylor's word games are similar, but not identical. He plays, for example, on "form" in the couplet,

> Thou dost it Form, Inform, Reform, and Try
> Conform to thee, marre her Deformity.
>
> [150]

In four stanzas of one poem he uses some form of the word *crown* twelve times [70-71]. In six lines from another poem he combines repetition with punning [448].

> The'Uncharitable Soul oft thus reflects,
> After each Birth a second birth doth Come.
> Your Second Birth no Second Birth ejects,
> The Babe of Grace then's strangld in the Womb.
> There's no new Birth born in thy Soul thou'lt find
> If that the after Birth abide behinde.

Taylor plays elsewhere with "mite" and "might," using some form of the homonym thirty-seven times [167-69]. In another segment of fifteen lines, he uses some form of the verb "do" twenty-two times [147]. I could cite innumerable other examples. Taylor was obviously conscious of the artificiality of these verbal effects, once referring to his poetry as "Acrostick Rhimes" [473].

Other easily recognizable rhetorical devices in Taylor's style are hyperbole, oxymoron, pun, alliteration, and the chiasmus. These techniques can be found in several literary periods or styles, but they are so widespread in seventeenth-century verse that they have come to be associated with the baroque, particularly when two or three of them together appear in the same poem.

Góngora, in a hyperbole, states that a nightingale sings

with such force that the sound of a hundred thousand birds issues from her throat ("que tiene otros cien mil dentro del pecho" [Soneto LXIX]). Taylor has the same hyperbole, but draws it out over thirty lines. In treating the inadequacy of human praise of God, he imagines the entire world broken up into its constituent atoms, then each atom as a world populated by as many men as the world can hold, and finally each of these men praising God with as many tongues as there are men in the world [451-52]. In another place, he affirms that the glory of Christ's apparel darkens by contrast "Ten thousand suns at once ten thousand wayes" [24]. This type of contrast Sor Juana treats in one of her poems as in itself a rhetorical device. Things are seen better by means of their extreme opposites, she maintains, and whiteness shines more brightly when placed next to blackness.

> Las cosas se ven mejor
> por sus contrarios extremos,
> y lo blanco luce más,
> si se pone junto al negro.[30]

Naturally this doctrine of contraries is applied pragmatically throughout Sor Juana's works. There are many instances in Taylor as well. Christ's glory, for example, makes a shine that benights the sun [25], and the "glory seen, to that unseen's a Smut" [21].

Oxymoron, or the juxtaposing of opposites, another way of presenting contraries, is illustrated in Góngora by the phrase "rhetoric of silence" ("retórico silencio" [1. 259, Polifemo]) and in Marino by "loquacious silence" ("silenzio loquace" [Poesie varie, p. 135]).[31] Taylor speaks of "Fireless Flame" and "Chilly Love" [5] and declares, "Hell

---

[30] Obras escogidas, p. 120.
[31] Mirollo, Poet of the Marvelous, p. 136.

Heaven is, Heaven hell, yea Bitter Sweet" [50]. The lowly pun appears in various poems by Góngora, including one on money in which he brings out the second meaning of each of the following coins: *cruzados* (crosses), *escudos* (nobles), *dados* (earls), *ducados* (dukes) and *coronas* (crowns).[32] Taylor represents Christ saying "Fight not for prey, but Pray and Fight" [405]. In a funeral elegy for a minister named Hooker, he writes, "That thou callst home thy Hooker with his Hook" [482].

Alliteration is so common in all baroque poets that a single line will serve as illustration, one from Sor Juana Inés de la Cruz, "que a cada cual tocarle considera."[33] In Taylor, we find "The Girths of Griefe alone / Do gird my heart till Gust of Sorrows groan" [472]. As well as:

> What shall Mote up to a Monarch rise?
> An Emmet match an Emperor in might?
> [252]

The chiasmus is a structural device used sparingly by Góngora, moderately by Marino, and lavishly by Sor Juana Inés de la Cruz. Twelve of the fourteen lines of one of her sonnets, for example, contain a chiasmus, and in another the chiasmus is present in ten out of fourteen.[34] The intellectual crossing from one word to another which is called chiasmus may take place in a single line, but it more frequently occurs in two consecutive lines. Both types are illustrated in a single poem by Sor Juana.

> Amo a Dios y siento en Dios;
> [I love God and feel well in God]
> que si son penas las culpas
> que no sean culpas las penas

---

[32] Kane, *Gongorism*, p. 78.
[33] *Obras escogidas*, p. 271.
[34] Ibid., pp. 190-91.

EDWARD TAYLOR

> [That if the penalties are sins
> That the sins are not penalties][35]

In the single line, *amo* crosses with *siento* and *Dios* with *Dios*. In the doublet, *penas* crosses with *penas* and *culpas* with *culpas*. Another of Sor Juana's single lines has a striking resemblance to one of Taylor's, not only in the use of the chiasmus, but also in its concept.

> muerto a la vida y a la muerte vivo[36]

> [I am dead toward life and toward death I live]

Taylor expresses it as

> A Dying Life, and Living Death by
> Sin.
> [390]

Since Taylor's lines are regularly longer than Sor Juana's, his crossings are less compressed.

> Oh! that thou wast on Earth below with mee!
> Or that I was in Heaven above with thee.
> [10]

> Such as are Gracious grow in Grace therefore
> Such as have Grace, are Gracious evermore.
> [438]

> Thy Grace will Grace unto a Poem bee
> Although a Poem be no grace to thee.
> [473]

The only one of all the major characteristics uniting Marino, Góngora, and Sor Juana Inés de la Cruz that Taylor does not share is that of constant allusion to the literary traditions of Greek and Latin antiquity. All three of

[35] Ibid., pp. 131-32.
[36] Ibid., p. 270.

Taylor's forerunners were immersed in the classics, and their works incorporate on almost every page either a verbal echo of some celebrated passage or some reference to the ancients, whether to an author, literary personage, or mythological situation. Even though Taylor was a "learned man who kept his Theocritus and Origen, his Augustine and Horace, with him in the wilderness,"[37] he makes no effort to display this classical background in his poetry. Out of thousands of lines of verse, one may discover hardly a dozen classical allusions, and these are the most rudimentary such as "Mercury" [207], "promethius' filching" [226], "Pandora's box" [226], and "Sapphick Slippers" [488].

Submerged under the surface of Taylor's verse, however, exists a classical mode that he shares with Marino and Góngora, that of the pastoral. Marino's most important poem *Adone* is an idyllic treatment of the myth of Adonis, and one of his most delightful short works is *La Pastorella* [*The Shepherdess*], both a pastoral and an erotic masterpiece. Góngora describes his most popular work *Polifemo*, which treats the love between the shepherd Acis and the nymph Galatea, as bucolic rhymes sung to the sound of a rustic flute [stanza 1]. Taylor similarly describes his *Meditations* in terms of the pastoral, but his symbols are those of the Hebrew Old Testament rather

---

[37] *Poems*, ed. Stanford, p. xviii. A manuscript translation of the Daedalus-Icarus story in Ovid's *Art of Love* written about 1700 has recently been attributed to Taylor. Mukhtar Ali Isari, "Edward Taylor and Ovid's *Art of Love*: The Text of a Newly-Discovered Manuscript," *Early American Literature* 10 (1975): 67-74. If indeed from his hand, this fragment not only reveals a connection between Taylor's poetic vocation and the Latin classics, but also indicates that his earliest experiments were in the neoclassical vein. The diction of this translation has more resemblance to Dryden's *Virgil* or Pope's *Homer* than to the devotional works of Herbert or Crashaw. In other words, Taylor seems anachronistically to have explored the neoclassical vein before specializing in the baroque.

than those of Theocritus and Virgil. He accompanies himself on a harp, described in one poem as "brassy wire" and
"jews trump" [177], and in another as "my Shoshannim's
sweetest Well tun'de string" [209]. He calls upon God to
"blow this Oaten Straw of mine" [162], and apologizes,
in the tradition of scores of other literary shepherds, for
his "unskilfull ditty" "piped through my sorry quill" [175].

Certain other differences may be noted between Taylor
and his Italian and Hispanic predecessors. Taylor sets forth
his various tropes in rapid succession, producing a kind
of cornucopia effect; whereas Marino and Góngora inter-
sperse their conceits between passages of narrative or description. The conceits of Marino and Góngora are rich
and subtle, the most sophisticated of which are double in
the sense of combining linguistically almost incompatible
elements, a process that one of Marino's contemporaries
described as a "supermarvelous" product of human wit.[38]
An example from Marino cited by James Mirollo is *Donna
che cuce*, literally "woman who sews," which refers in
its context to the beams of contact between a woman's
eyes and her lover; the doubling consists in converting
the sight beams to a thread that binds the two together.[39]
Essentially the same figure may be noticed in Donne's
well-known "The Ecstasy":

> Our eye-beames twisted, and did thread
> Our eyes upon one double string.

Milton, in one of his Italian sonnets, "Diodati, e te'l diro,"
develops a similar metaphor, portraying the fire that darts
from the eyes of his mistress as so powerful that filling
his ears with wax has little efficacy in blunting the effect.

---

[38] E. Tesauro, *Il Cannocchiale Aristotelico* (Torino, 1670), p. 446.
[39] *Poet of the Marvelous*, p. 155.

E dagli occhi suoi avventa si'gran fuoco,
Che l'incernar gli orecchi mi fia poco.

The doubling here consists in transferring the sensation
of sight to hearing. The same process takes place in a
phrase of merely two words in Milton's *Lycidas*, "Blind
mouths" [l. 118]. An English scholar, M. J. Woods, gives
a number of examples from Góngora of the transference
from one element to another.[40] "Winds of crystal" refers
to showers of water; "a Libya of waves" portrays the ocean
in terms of desert sands; "feathery fishing" represents
falconry; and "nautical venery" describes girls engaged in
hunting seals, the latter metaphor incorporating in addition a play on the two senses of venery—hunting and
sexual desire. Taylor's metaphors, in contrast, are for the
most part single-edged rather than double, and his conceits rarely involve intricate patterns of antithesis and
paradox such as are found in Marino, Góngora, and Sor
Juana. As Austin Warren has said in another context, the
humbler ingenuities were what the New Englanders could
reproduce.[41]

Taylor's eighth meditation, which Warren considers one
of his best, has an example of multiple meanings, although
not metaphorical doubling. Here Taylor compares his soul
to a bird of paradise that has been put into a wicker cage,
his body, and suggests that the bird also represents Adam
in the cage of the Garden of Eden. This metaphor might
be considered a double one only if the bird of paradise
were taken in the Renaissance sense as a representation
of Venus or carnal love. There is no reason for assuming
that Taylor intended this connection, but if he did, the

[40] *The Poet and the Natural World in the Age of Góngora*, pp. 124-
27.
[41] *Rage for Order*, p. 5.

metaphor could be taken also as a major baroque symbol in which the peacock represents ostentatious profusion.[42]

Taylor should certainly not be considered to be a poet of ideas, even though he makes considerable intellectual demands upon his readers. His *Determinations* touches upon a few basic points of theology and doctrine, but his *Meditations* consists primarily of word play, sensuous description, and emotion. The debate which various critics have carried on over the relative merits of the *Determinations* and the *Meditations* depends largely on whether the function of poetry is to convey meaning, which would place the *Determinations* ahead, or to dazzle by verbal effects, which would give the preference to the *Meditations*. Although individual poems in both collections involve a complex theology, Taylor never treats ideas systematically, but at most implies them or introduces them in fragments. The following typical lines, for example, are said to delineate the concept of the Great Chain of Being.[43]

> Life Vegetative now hatcht in the Egge,
>   Flourishing some things nobler than the rest.
> Life sensitive gives some of these its Head,
>   Inspiring them with honour next the best.
> And some of which Life Rationall Enfires,
>   Cloathd with a Spiritualizing Life, aspires.
>
> This Life thy Fingers freely dropt into
>   The Humane shaped Elements and made
> The same Excell the Rest and nobler goe
>   Enspirited with Heavenizing trade.
>   [*Meditations* 2.89. 13-22]

[42] A Swiss scholar, Jean Rousset, argues that the two major symbols of the French baroque are Circe and the peacock, representing respectively metamorphosis and ostentation or "domination du décor." *La Littérature de l'âge baroque en France. Circé et le paon* (Paris, 1954).

[43] Scheick, *The Will and the Word*, pp. 13-14.

Glory lin'de out a Paradise in Power
  Where e'ry seed a Royall Coach became
For Life to ride in, to each shining Flower.
And made mans Flower with glory all ore flame
                  [*Meditations* 1.33 19-22]

These lines indubitably depict four stages of existence, the vegetative, the sensitive, the rational, and the spiritual, but they do not imply that the four are related to each other in any kind of hierarchical system. They are taken from two unconnected poems and do not portray the notions of gradation, continuity, and plenitude that represent the essence of the doctrine of the Chain of Being as set forth by A. O. Lovejoy and found in such poetic representations as Alexander Pope's *An Essay on Man*.

One of the few extended ideological passages in Taylor's works appears in a funeral elegy on his wife. The second of its three parts takes up the question of whether true grief may be expressed through the artificiality of measured verses and whether poetry is an appropriate medium for the display of such grief, a theme common to other elegies, including Tennyson's *In Memoriam*. On the negative side, Taylor suggests that work and music suit each other better than do sorrow and music, that deep emotion cannot be expressed in contrived verbal patterns ("Frisk in Acrostick Rimes"), that ostentation of grief reduces its sincerity ("Break a salt tear to pieces as it drops"), that David's lamentation for Jonathan had provoked no poetic display, and that many heads of state are buried without poetic tributes. He observes, on the other side, that his duty requires him to memorialize his wife's virtues, that otherwise her progeny will remain ignorant of her excellence, that the enumeration of her qualities will lend distinction to his poem, that she may in heaven learn of his poem and derive pleasure from it, and that the act of writing may help to assuage his deep sorrow. This poem is notable also for three paradoxes, rhetorical devices that are elsewhere rare in Taylor's poetry. Death is ordinarily considered as the untying of the knot of true love, but Taylor finds his love increased: "Oh strange Untying! it ti'th harder." He is reconciled to his wife's passing since he expects that she will join the Lord in heaven: "thou tookst her into thine / Out of my bosom, yet she dwells in mine." His wife contributes to his poem although it does nothing for her: "Thy Grace will Grace unto a Poem be / Although a Poem be no grace to thee."

In subject matter, Taylor's lament for his deceased wife resembles Sor Juana's portrayal of the grief of a wife for her departed husband, which we have commented upon in the preceding chapter. Paradoxically the tone of neither poem conforms to its rhetorical devices. Sor Juana's diction is restrained, apart from a series of extreme hyperboles, but she, nevertheless, gives rein to her emotions or to what she calls "the rhetoric of tears."[44] Taylor's poem, on the other hand, is a melange of conceit, paradox, alliteration, chiasmus, hyperbole, and bizarre vocabulary; yet his feelings are held in check. Sor Juana communicates bitterness and inconsolable grief; Taylor, Christian resignation.

It has been said that poetry like Taylor's could not have been written in England because the cultural milieu of that intimate island would impose itself upon the artist's creativeness, thus stifling his individuality. Taylor's poems, according to this view, could have been produced only in a frontier wilderness where no curbs existed on the poet's imagination. It would seem to the contrary, however, that the baroque elements of Taylor's style which we have been examining are the products of an artificial society, no matter what the conditions of the poet's daily life.

[44] Picón-Salas, *De la conquista*, p. 120.

Taylor's poetry, moreover, is just as barren of allusions to things typically American as is Bradstreet's. The qualities that make his verse seem un-English are primarily the exotic ones derived from the Old Testament—such elements as an alien vocabulary (for instance, smaragdine for emerald, carbuncle for diamond) and references to the birds and rare products of the East. There is an English poet also embodying these qualities who resembles Taylor strongly, but he is not Herbert, Crashaw, or any other of the metaphysicals, but a product of the eighteenth century—the partly mad Christopher Smart, whose highly sensuous *Song of David* (1763) draws on many of the exotic biblical images and symbols that are typical of Taylor.

Both Smart and Taylor were anachronistic. Smart's poetry found its way into print because he lived in the second half of the eighteenth century, when various precursors of romantic attitudes made other deviations from neo-classical standards acceptable. Taylor, however, was writing in the age of Pope and Swift when Herbert was ridiculed and even Donne looked down upon. Since his poems were conceived in New England, an environment in which the baroque had not only never flourished, but had come to be regarded with hostility, it is not strange that his verse had to wait until the twentieth century for its initial printing. In German literature, anachronistically delayed writers in the baroque style are sometimes classified under the rubric late or high baroque, but such terms would make no sense in reference to Taylor since the baroque presence in North America is not extensive enough to justify chronological subdivisions.

The literary career of Sor Juana Inés de la Cruz helps explain the fortunes or misfortunes of Taylor. He was born a few years prior to Sor Juana near the midpoint of the seventeenth century, but survived her for more than thirty years into the second quarter of the eighteenth. This chronology is significant when considered in relation to publishing history. Sor Juana's poems were written and published while the taste for linguistic exuberance was still fashionable in her literary milieu. There were nineteen editions of her works under various titles between 1689 and 1725, but not a single one after 1725 until 1865, almost a century and a half later. During the period prior to 1725, Sor Juana was more widely read than any other poet of Spain or Spanish America,[45] but the penetration of neoclassicism and French critical standards into Hispanic culture during the eighteenth century brought her style of poetry into disfavor and caused her works to be almost completely forgotten. Neoclassicism arrived much earlier in England—concomitant with the Restoration in 1660—and as a result Taylor's poems were out of date before they were written. Early in the twentieth century a myth arose that Taylor had given instructions in his will forbidding the publication of his poetry, and a critical debate ensued concerning the nature of his motives for doing so. One of the most imaginative embroideries on the topic appeared in a thick book published as late as 1977, ornately, but falsely, informing its readers of the "pastor-physician of the frontier village of Westfield having left orders with his heirs that his four hundred pages of poetry not be published, lest their rich, sensuous warmth corrupt his brethren or his own reputation."[46] Some myths die hard or never. A clear-headed scholar has investigated the source of the myth and discovered that no will exists which mentions Taylor's poetry.[47] It would seem, therefore, that the only reason why Taylor's works remained in manuscript is the same that explains why Sor Juana's

[45] *Obras escogidas,* p. 63.

[46] Arthur Bernon Tourtellot, *Benjamin Franklin The Shaping of Genius* (Garden City, N.Y., 1977), p. 306.

[47] Francis Murphy, "Edward Taylor's Attitude toward Publication: A Question concerning Authority," *American Literature* 34 (1962): 393-94.

fell into obscurity after 1725—that they were completely alien to prevailing neoclassical standards and consequently had no appeal in the marketplace. When Taylor's works were finally published and hailed in the twentieth century, it was because the baroque had by then gained new understanding and a new generation of adherents.[48]

[48] The latest development in the study of comparative literature consists in showing relationships between works of the West [Europe and America] and those of the East [Asia and Africa]. Convincing parallels have been established between sartorial imagery or the "clothing conceit" in Taylor and similar rhetoric in Indian and Persian devotional poetry. Mohan Lai Sharma, "Of Spinning, Weaving and Mystical Poetry: The Fine Yarn of Taylor, Indian Yogis, and Persian Sufis," *Mahfil* 6 (1970): 51-61.

PART II

THEME
AND
IDEOLOGY

ONE OF THE MAJOR concerns of comparative literature is the tracing of themes in the thought, folklore, and imaginative literature of various nations, in the process of which both major and minor writers are taken into consideration. The two best known of the themes in Western literature derive from purely imaginary characters, Faust and Don Juan. Both of these are far more important to Latin American than to North American letters, perhaps because the story of Don Juan originated in Spain and is closely linked to that of Faust, each having at its core the problem of evil. North American literature touches on the Faust theme in the works of Increase Mather and his grandson Thomas Walter. The latter published a theological pamphlet in Boston in 1720, *A Choice Dialogue between John Faustus, a Conjurer, and Jack*

Tory, His Friend.[1] A century later Washington Irving introduced the Hispanic symbol of sexual exploitation in his sketch "Don Juan: A Spectral Research." The classical theme of the Golden Age was also transplanted to the New World. Adventurers such as Gonzalo Jiménez de Queseda and Sir Walter Raleigh located the utopian land of Eldorado in South America, and it later acquired universal recognition through Voltaire's ironical portrayal in *Candide*. William Byrd of Westover sought a "Land of Eden" and Thomas Morton of Merrymount a "New Canaan" in North America.

Purely North American themes that originated before 1800 include those featuring three heroines, embodying typically American virtues, Pocahontas, Polly Baker, and Jane McCrae. The dramatic episodes with which they are associated arose from the historical periods of exploration, colonization, and revolution respectively. Pocahontas and Jane McCrae were actual living figures, but Polly Baker, so far as can be determined, was a pure invention by Franklin, even though she eventually came to be accepted in both Europe and the United States as an actual historical personage.

The most widely known of the three heroines is Pocahontas, probably because her story has become part of the mythology regularly imparted to American schoolchildren. She is essentially the literary creation of Captain John Smith, one of the early explorers of the Virginia territory. In his early reports, he mentions Pocahontas only casually, and it was not until many years after his return to England that he portrayed her as his rescuer. According to his *Generall Historie of Virginia* (1624) he was captured by a group of Powhatan Indians while seeking food on a journey up the James River. After being exhibited to sev-

---

[1] André Dabezies, "The First American *Faust* (1720)," *Comparative Literature Studies* 8 (1971): 303-9.

eral camps of Indians over a period of several days, he was prepared for a ceremony of execution. Suddenly the daughter of the Indian chieftain emerged from the crowd of onlookers, took his "head in her armes and laid her owne upon his to save him from death" [*Historie*, 3: 46-49]. The original Pocahontas eventually married one of Smith's subordinates and was taken to London. As a literary legend, the story of her gallant rescue of Smith, apart from its intrinsic drama, served to vindicate the conquest of the Indians by portraying a native princess as the benefactor of an English adventurer.

The third of the three archetypes of feminine initiative, Jane McCrae, is the least known even though she is the only one whose story can be authenticated by contemporary documents. Her tragic tale figures in several English and American poems and in a French historical novel, *Mis Mac Rae*, by Hilliard d'Auberteuil, published in 1784. The author was an acquaintance of Franklin and fellow member of the Masonic lodge of the Seven Sisters in Paris. Jane McCrae also appears as Lucinda in Joel Barlow's *The Columbiad*. A Loyalist sympathizer during the American Revolution, she was engaged to be married to an American soldier fighting on the Loyalist side. En route to an army camp where the marriage ceremony was to be performed, she was abducted by a group of Indians, who shot and scalped her and then demanded payment for her scalp from the British General Burgoyne, who had offered a bounty on American scalps. The story of Jane McCrae made Burgoyne's policy seem inhuman and barbaric and was useful in stirring American patriotic sentiments against the enemy.

The stories of Pocahontas and Jane McCrae, however, lack the universal human elements and ideological overtones that have elevated the European themes of Faust and Don Juan to the preeminence that they have enjoyed for at least three centuries. Faust epitomizes the spirit of

Western man in his quest for knowledge, power, and technological prowess and Don Juan explores the fundamental problems involving the sexual nature of mankind. Both themes raise questions about the existence of God, the nature of good and evil, and the possibility of salvation or damnation. Franklin's apparently artless comic anecdote of the speech of Polly Baker does not invoke quite such an extensive range of philosophical problems and notions, but her simple narrative has important ramifications in theology and theories of human rights.

The transition from the study of themes to the study of the history of ideas is almost imperceptible. Ideologies, in contrast to separate ideas, represent combinations of notions that are joined together in a pattern or sequence leading to particular conclusions. The first person to go through the process is an original thinker; anyone who later repeats the same system is reflecting an ideology. Organized groups, or individuals in common with other individuals, may reflect ideologies, and there may even be personal ideologies or systems of belief held by single individuals.

During the eighteenth century, among the major concepts inspired by political developments there were two of particular consequence to the American colonies, those of natural rights and those of the state of nature. Both concepts were fundamental in the writings of Paine, Dickinson, and Franklin. Indeed, the speech of Polly Baker represents a combination discourse-apologue on the doctrine of natural rights. The earliest literary manifestation of the notion that the individual has rights that transcend the body politic appears in Sophocles' play *Antigone* in the fifth century B.C., in which Antigone defies Creon's edict forbidding the burial of her brother. Her justification of her action may be interpreted as either a vindication of the law of nature over positive law or as a placing of a moral imperative over obedience to the civil power. Polly

Baker's defense of her breaking the laws against adultery may be interpreted in exactly the same manner, and as a person she may be compared to Antigone as an exponent of human rights and, secondarily, women's rights.

One of the major Enlightenment statements of the doctrine of human rights was that of Diderot in the article "Natural Law" of the *Encyclopédie*. In essence, according to Diderot, "You have the most sacred *natural right* to everything which is not challenged by the entire race. . . . Everything which you shall conceive, everything which you shall meditate, will be good, great, elevated and sublime if it is to the general and common interest." In the key passage of the article, Diderot exhorts his readers: "Say to yourselves often, I am a human being, and I have no other *natural rights* truly inalienable except those of humanity." The importance of Diderot's argument is that he defines rights in terms of humanity, establishing their human, not divine, origins. The weakness of his argument is that the notion of a general will upon which rights are supposed to depend is an abstraction of little value to the average man. Diderot's affirmation, moreover, is severely limited to merely generic rights (those belonging to all humanity in the aggregate). Paine later attempted to transcend these limitations. He not only defined rights in concrete terms, but also distinguished between civil and individual rights. In contrast to Diderot, he not only stressed those rights belonging to single persons, but maintained that the rights of physical liberty and liberty of conscience are held immediately from God rather than being granted by a human leader or even acknowledged by common assent.

Throughout the eighteenth century, many theorists had speculated about a period in the history of mankind known as the state of nature, a period before the institution of social life. Classical literature, by means of the pastoral idyll and the legend of the Golden Age, had celebrated the age of innocence when man lived close to nature, eating nuts and drinking pure water, sharing all things in common, and knowing neither anger nor war. The notion was revived in the eighteenth century and applied to political theory by various European writers, including Rousseau. In their theories, the crucial moment was when man left the state of nature for organized relationships. According to Rousseau's *Discours sur l'origine et les fondements de l'inégalité* (1755), the period just at the brink of entering society, that period "of the development of human faculties, maintaining a golden mean between the indolence of the primitive state and the petulant activity of our vanity," must have been "the happiest and most durable epoch" of human existence. Rousseau does not make clear whether in the transition from the state of nature to society the process involves the domination of a leader or whether the social order is decided by an agreement among equals. Paine does not refer to the state of nature, but he uses another expression for the same concept, the "state of natural liberty." He opens *Common Sense* with the complaint that "some writers have so confounded government with society as to leave little or no distinction between them." In addition to characterizing society as good and government as bad, he suggests that the earliest societies were formed by the association of equals.

Writers who cherished nostalgic feelings for the lost state of nature were likely to accept a cluster of ideas now known as primitivism. Essentially this is the view that the earliest stage of human history was better than any following ones and that whatever developments have occurred after the state of nature have been pernicious. Linked with this view in art and literary criticism is the opinion that the earliest specimens of any artistic genre are the models for later ones and, therefore, superior to later productions. A passionate dispute over this opinion developed in the Renaissance and flared up again in the eighteenth century. Those who maintained the preeminence of past traditions were designated symbolically as the ancients, in contrast to the defenders of the present known as the moderns. The main arguments on both sides were reproduced in the Western Hemisphere in discussions on the nature of epic poetry and on the truth of the doctrine of progress. A closely related theme of even more venerable lineage is that of *translatio studii*, the passage of the arts and sciences from one place or milieu to another. This theme is to be found in America throughout the entire eighteenth century. The American version of the Golden Age was nearly always located in the future. In the patriotic euphoria that followed political independence, writers who adopted the opinion that no place or culture in the past could be compared to America in the present were enlisting themselves on the side of the moderns, whether consciously or not.

It was certainly consistent for partisans of the moderns and advocates of the doctrine of progress to join in celebrating the glories of the newly proclaimed national literature of the United States, but logically the defenders of the ancients might have been expected to be somewhat more reticent. Apparently aware of the risk of contradiction, most of the latter praised the classical heritage in such a way as to enlist it as one of the elements contributing to the luster of emerging American letters. In similar fashion, the European tradition of republican government was commonly regarded as a major component of the new American state, but nevertheless overshadowed by the modern superstructure. The self-congratulatory attitude of many literary voices of the period anticipated an attitude that Goethe epitomized for his own purposes in 1827, "Amerika du hast es besser."

Few of the authors who expounded the theme of American superiority were known outside the United States, but earlier ones such as Franklin, Dickinson, and Paine,

who espoused natural rights and reported democratic political aspirations, were read and taken seriously in Europe. The study of literary relations involving these later
figures registers actual contact, not merely analogies and
resemblances.

FOUR

THE MANY VERSIONS OF POLLY BAKER: DEISM AND HUMAN RIGHTS

RANKLIN has been called "a greater and more influential writer than Dr. Samuel Johnson."[1] The comparison is certainly provocative, and there is no question about its truth from the perspective of comparative literature. Dr. Johnson was a scholar trained in the classics, who progressed through journalism to become a professional man of letters. Dr. Franklin, who was almost entirely self-taught, took up journalism as an adjunct to the printing trade, and developed his literary talents as an aid in his careers in science, politics, and statesmanship. Johnson wrote poetry and literary criticism vastly superior to Franklin's; Franklin drew upon the proverbial wisdom of all the literatures of Europe for his *Way to Wealth*; he wrote an autobiography that is one of the world's masterpieces in the genre, and a literary hoax "Polly Baker" to which the greatest authors in the French Enlightenment paid tribute. Most students of English literature, who call the second half of the eighteenth century the Age of Johnson, know Franklin merely as one of the Founding Fathers of the American nation and have never read a page of his work. But outside of the Anglo-Saxon hegemony, where few readers would even recognize Johnson's name, Franklin is still being studied at all levels

[1] J. A. Leo Lemay, "Franklin and the Autobiography. An Essay on Recent Scholarship," *Eighteenth-Century Studies* 1 (1968): 185.

from secondary school to the seminar. In the realm of universal literature, comprising the masterpieces known and admired throughout the world, Johnson has no place at all, but Franklin is securely represented by his autobiography, his *Way to Wealth*, and his story of Polly Baker.

As early as 1762 David Hume remarked that Franklin was "the first Philosopher, and indeed the first Great Man of Letters" in the English part of the Western Hemisphere.[2] At this time Franklin's major literary works had either not been published or were not known to be Franklin's, and Hume was, therefore, basing his highly flattering estimate of Franklin's literary distinction upon his personal and political letters and upon his descriptions of scientific experiments, particularly the famous electrical ones. Franklin had not even embarked upon his autobiography, and although *The Way to Wealth* was already widely known, it was not associated with Franklin. It was nowhere attributed to him in print until 1773, when it was included in a French edition of his works under the title of "Father Abraham's Speech." A version in English bearing Franklin's name did not appear until 1779. French sources, as we shall see later in this chapter, were also the first to associate Franklin with Polly Baker, but not until the period of the American Revolution. Hume, therefore, appears to have been gifted with extraordinary prescience or intuition.

Of Franklin's three masterpieces, we shall be concerned only with his "Speech of Polly Baker." When considered as the prototype of a literary genre in which semiserious courtroom rhetoric invests unconventional sexual behavior with comic overtones, Polly's speech is unique in American letters, but it has one illustrious European predecessor and several equally distinguished progeny. As every

---

[2] *Papers of Benjamin Franklin*, ed. Leonard W. Labaree et al. (New Haven, 1966), 10: 82.

student of Franklin knows, Polly is accused of bearing five bastard children. She defends herself in an impassioned protest that she has always been ready to marry the man who had betrayed her and that in bearing children she has been carrying out the religious and civic duty of replenishing the population. Several ideological themes animate her discourse, varying in importance according to the printed text in which it is presented (Franklin's original not being extant) or to the interpretation of editors and commentators.

The archetype of Franklin's serio-comical legal plea is a tale from the Italian Renaissance in Boccaccio's *Decameron*. In a story entitled "Lady Filippa against the Statute of Prato," a dynamic and intelligent young woman charged with a sex offense defends herself by attacking the injustice of the law. This lady, Filippa de Pugliese, having been discovered in bed with her lover, has been charged with violating a strict law that every woman found by her husband in the act of adultery should be put to death by fire. Against the advice of her family and friends, Filippa refuses to save her life by denying the charge, but prefers to appear in court to answer it. She admits to her judge without shame and hesitation that she has many times slept with her lover, but argues against the validity of the law by which she is condemned. She maintains that laws should apply to all citizens equally and be enacted by common consent, but the law by which she is accused applies only to women, not to men, and no women, furthermore, had been involved in forming it. She then asks her husband whether she had ever declined to gratify his physical needs or been the least reluctant to do so, and the husband admits that she has always been willing to indulge him, indeed more often than he had himself desired. Filippa then asks the judge what release she should be expected to find for her sexual needs that still remain after her husband has been fully satisfied. Is it not more fitting, she asks, for her to share her pleasures with a worthy gentleman who loves her exceedingly than to let them be wasted or to be lost entirely? The judge and au- dience are convinced by her arguments, and after much laughter the edict is modified to concern henceforth only those women who disgrace their husbands by accepting money from their lovers.

Exactly the same primary elements exist in the speeches of Filippa and Polly Baker: 1) the situation of a resourceful woman addressing a bar of justice in her own behalf; 2) the defense of women's rights as equally valid as men's; 3) the palliation of sexual indulgence; and 4) the appeal to good sense over tradition, or natural law over civil law. Both speeches illustrate equally the principle supplied as a heading in the 1620 English translation of *Il Decameron*, but not present in Boccaccio's original text, "What worth it is to confesse a trueth, with a facetious and witty ex- cuse."[3] To be sure, the two ladies are accused of different crimes, Filippa of adultery and Polly of bearing illegiti- mate children, but both defendants are impelled to satisfy overpowering physical needs, and are in the end vindi- cated on the grounds of natural law. The two ladies have the same termperament or personality; that is, they are lusty, enterprising, audacious, spirited, and candid. Even physically they seem to be alike, although here the evi- dence is scant. Filippa is described as *bellissima*, trans- lated in 1620 as of "singular beautie and praise-worthy parts." One might suspect that Polly, after bearing five bastard children, would have but a faded beauty at best. The first known text is completely silent concerning Pol- ly's physical features, but in later printings in both *The Gentleman's Magazine* and the *Irish London Magazine* she is described as "the beautiful Polly Baker." The pri-

---

[3] *The Decameron . . . Translated into English Anno 1620 with an Introduction by Edward Hutton* (London, 1909), III: 131.

mary link between the two narratives, however, is the formal one—the courtroom setting, a beautiful woman on trial, and a speech delivered by the accused in her own defense.

Franklin had an opportunity of reading the *Decameron* during his youthful sojourn in England for a period of nearly two full years in 1725 and 1726. Here he worked in a printing house, and, in addition to consorting with other press hands and minor poets, enjoyed in his leisure hours the company of an alehouse coterie presided over by the cynical and jovial Dr. Bernard Mandeville, author of *The Fable of the Bees*. In this society, it is possible that Franklin had access to an English translation of *The Decameron*, or that during one of his drinking sessions he heard the story of the beautiful and audacious Filippa narrated as a good story by some tavern companion.

Although the connection between Boccaccio and Franklin is merely conjectural, that between Franklin and the next contributor to the genre of the salacious legal memoir, Voltaire, is clear, direct, and specific. In 1774 Voltaire published two closely parallel fictitious courtroom speeches, one by a husband, the other by a wife, but both complaining that the laws and customs of their times permitted them no redress of the sexual injustices that they had respectively suffered. That Polly Baker provided Voltaire the inspiration for the wife's speech has already been suggested by a writer in the French newspaper *Le Figaro* (1 June 1976). Polly's speech had appeared in French as early as 1770 in a celebrated work that Voltaire read and discussed immediately after its appearance, the abbé Raynal's *Histoire philosophique et politique des deux Indes* (1770). Not only does it seem probable that Voltaire became acquainted with Polly's speech in 1770, but it is clear that he eventually learned the secret of its authorship, for the collected edition of his works published posthumously at Kehl in 1785-1786 provides the first attribution of Polly's speech to Franklin to appear anywhere in print. In the article "Ana, Anecdotes," originally published in *Questions sur l'Encyclopédie* in 1774, but now included as part of the *Dictionnaire philosophique*, appears the statement that the story of Polly Baker "is a pleasantry, a pamphlet of the illustrious Franklin." This statement did not appear in the original publication of "Ana, Anecdotes" in the *Questions*, but was added sometime between 1774 and 1785 either by Voltaire himself or by the editors of the Kehl edition. It is highly unlikely that the Kehl editors would have tampered with Voltaire's text, for in the notes to their edition they make a scrupulous distinction between those of Voltaire and their own. Voltaire himself probably added the information concerning Franklin's authorship, acquiring it from one of his longstanding admirers, the abbé Morellet, who was intimately associated with Franklin during his residence in Paris during the American Revolution. Morellet's "Ana" manuscript, which is now in the British Museum, includes an interesting section on Polly Baker in which Franklin is identified as her creator.

Voltaire's two courtroom speeches in the tradition of Boccaccio and Franklin also appeared in the original *Questions sur l'Encyclopédie*, but in a separate article, that on "Adultère." Both were as fictitious as the speech of Polly Baker, and both were designed to protest against the irrationality and inflexibility of marriage laws in Catholic countries. One was presumably delivered by a French magistrate to the ecclesiastical authorities of his city, complaining that the laws prevented him from divorcing a wife who had repeatedly made him a cuckold; the other was allegedly delivered by a Portuguese countess to the municipal council of Lisbon protesting against the rigorous penalties she faced for a single indiscretion despite her husband having gone unpunished for scores of them.

In the speech of the injured husband, whose wife has

created a public scandal by her promiscuity, Voltaire typically attributes to a priest her original loss of chastity
before marriage. The aggrieved husband, only forty years
old and still handsome and vigorous, has separated in disgust from his wife, but is kept by scruples from seducing
the wife of another man, or from consorting with willing
girls or pliant widows. He wishes a second marriage, the
only honorable solution to his plight, but precisely the
one that is forbidden him by his Church and its dominance over French society. He affirms then in a formal
plea to the Church authorities that his wife is the crim-
inal, but that he is the one who is being punished. Just
as Polly has "debauched no other Woman's Husband," he
is "too scrupulous to seek to seduce the spouse of another." His sense of virtue and propriety requires that he
continue to satisfy his sexual needs, but the Church pro-
hibits him from marriage with an honorable woman. In
his words, "Today's civil laws, unfortunately founded upon
canon law, deprive me of the rights of humanity." This
recourse to human rights, which in the eighteenth century
were identical with natural rights, is parallel to Polly's
complaint that the laws of New England go contrary to
natural law in that they keep her from performing "the
Duty of the first and great Command of Nature, and of
Nature's God, *Encrease and Multiply*." Voltaire's aggrieved husband also suggests the principle more clearly
affirmed by Polly that Church and state be kept separate,
that if hers is a religious offense, it should be left to religious punishments. Voltaire's husband, moreover, observes that social customs based upon theology go contrary to the teaching of the Scriptures; as Polly appeals to
natural law or the command of nature's God, the aggrieved
husband cites the verse in Matthew (14:9) in which Christ
sanctions divorce on the grounds of adultery. In his words,
"God allows me to remarry, but the Bishop of Rome does
not allow it." After a brief summary of historical episodes

in which divorce has been allowed in Europe, he returns in his peroration to a stronger wording of his principle: "the Church does not have the right to deprive me of a blessing which God grants to me."

Voltaire's second address, that of the adulterous wife, has even stronger formal resemblances to the speeches of Lady Filippa and Miss Baker. The complainant, a Portuguese countess accused of adultery, admits her guilt, but argues in extenuation that her husband has carried on with impunity with the lowest sluts of the court and the town whereas she has imitated him only a single time and then with the handsomest young man of Lisbon. Like Polly, the countess argues that theology is irrelevant. Polly says to her accusers "You believe I have offended Heaven, and must suffer eternal Fire." Significantly she refers to the belief of her judges, but does not say that she shares this belief. The countess also refers to a religious belief, but is equally careful not to say that she accepts it. She makes the additional point that whatever punishment religion places upon her must also be her husband's lot: "The Scriptures have forbidden adultery to my husband as well as to me: he will be damned like me, nothing is more clear." Polly also adduces the sharing of guilt by affirming that all of the members of the court are acquainted with "that very Person," her seducer. He has in the meantime become advanced to honor and power in the government whereas she has been punished "with Stripes and Infamy." She complains of their contrary situations as being "unjust and unequal." The countess similarly affirms that "in matters of justice, things must be equal." Yet her husband goes unchallenged by the civil authorities for his host of infidelities, while she for her single one is liable to have her head shaved, to be shut up in a convent, and to have her dowry taken away and given to her husband. She asks, therefore, whether these things are just and whether it is not evident that cuckolds have made the laws.

Voltaire's speeches were in their own way as humorous as Franklin's and their purpose was equally serious, for they broached three of the major topics prohibited by French censorship of the time, and they took the unorthodox side. These fundamental topics were the right of reason, the limits of authority and Revelation, and the foundation of Christianity and its relationship to the state.[4]

Voltaire's heroine in one way is closer to Boccaccio's Lady Filippa than to Polly Baker, for the Portuguese and the Italian ladies are both on trial for committing adultery, whereas the crime of the unmarried Polly is merely fornication aggravated by the offense of giving birth to children out of wedlock. The Portuguese and the Italian ladies are, of course, not accused of producing illegitimate children. All three admit committing the act for which they are condemned, but deny that they are guilty of any crime. And all three criticize the laws under which they are brought to trial as unjust. Boccaccio's heroine commits adultery because her husband does not provide her sexual satisfaction; Voltaire's does so because her husband is promiscuous in pursuing other women. Although neither Voltaire nor Franklin was an outstanding advocate of women's rights, both used the argument that a double standard is unjust—that women should not be condemned for behavior that is condoned in men. In this sense, therefore, Voltaire's Portuguese countess is more closely related to Polly Baker than to Lady Filippa.

One further example of the influence of Polly Baker upon a major French author of the eighteenth century is a speech in the written text of Beaumarchais's famous play, *Le Mariage de Figaro* (1776), the source, of course,

---

[4] Ira O. Wade, *The Clandestine Organization and Diffusion of Philosophic Ideas in France from 1700 to 1750* (Princeton, 1938), *passim*.

of the opera of that name by Mozart.[5] This speech even
in our day is omitted from staged versions of the play,
presumably for the reason given by Beaumarchais in his
preface, that the actors feared that its severe philosophical
outlook would darken the gaiety of the action.

In the speech, Marceline, the mother of Figaro, appears
before a tribunal presided over by a judge and the Count
Almaviva in order to defend herself for all of the faults of
her youth, including a single illegitimate birth, a somewhat modest score in contrast to Polly's five offspring.
Here there is no comedy, no deism, and no philoprogenitiveness, but in place of them a passionate statement of
the principle that men are to blame for the lapses of the
women they pursue and that it is men and not women
who should be punished. Marceline's words advocate the
cause of all women who have ever been accused of lapses
from virtue.

> In the age of illusions, of inexperience, and of physical
> necessities, when seducers besiege us while poverty
> wounds us what weapons can a child wield against so
> many united enemies? Such a one judges us here se-
> verely who perhaps in his life has been responsible for
> the loss of ten unfortunate ones. . . . Men, worse than
> ungrateful, who brand with scorn your victims, the
> playthings of your passions! It is you who should be
> punished for the errors of our youth; you and your mag-
> istrates, so vain of the right to condemn us, those who
> through their guilty negligence allow all honest means
> of subsistence to be taken away from us. . . . Even among
> the highest ranks women obtain from you only a de-
> risive respect; trapped [as they are] with superficial es-
> teem into a real servitude; considered as minors with

[5] I am basing my account of Beaumarchais on Agnes G. Raymond,
"Figaro, fils naturel de Polly Baker? ou la Réhabilitation de Marceline,"
Comparative Literature Studies 12 (1975): 34-43.

regard to our property, punished as adults in regard to our faults, your conduct toward us inspires horror or pity.

This is, of course, not a translation of Polly Baker's speech, but a parallel to her situation, and the reference to property also suggests Voltaire's countess. Marceline's reproach to her accusers and to her judge, who may himself have corrupted ten women, is, nevertheless, essentially the same as Polly's. The latter complains of injustice and inequality in that her "Betrayer and Undoer," the first cause of all her "Faults and Miscarriages . . . should be advanced to Honour and Power, in the same Government that punishes" her "Misfortunes with Stripes and Infamy." Beaumarchais, like Boccaccio, appears as an outspoken feminist and presents the male sex as the persecutor of the female. Franklin never went this far in his own ideology, perhaps because he was not completely free from offenses against women in his own life.

Beaumarchais's Marceline may be linked to Polly Baker through Voltaire's twin discourses in his article "Adultère," published two years before *Le Mariage de Figaro*. Beaumarchais, moreover, was the major entrepreneur and joint editor with Condorcet of the notable Kehl edition of Voltaire's works, which, as we have indicated above, first attributed the story of Polly Baker to Franklin. To be sure, this proves merely that Beaumarchais was aware of Polly's history in 1785, not in 1775 or 1776 when he wrote the speech of Marceline, but the parallels indicate his awareness at the earlier date.

The legend of Polly Baker grew and shaped itself not only by means of imitations and adaptations of the story, but also by translations and interpretations of its earliest known printing. Two years after its publication in the London newspaper *The General Advertiser* in April 1747, an annotated text was reprinted in a London tract by Peter

Annet entitled *Social Bliss Considered: In Marriage and Divorce; Cohabiting unmarried, and Public Whoring*. The author used the example of Polly to underscore his disapproval of divorce and premarital sex together with his advocacy of the social benefits of public prostitution.

Full-scale ideological development of the Polly Baker theme took place, however, in an expanded French translation, which we have already indicated appeared in the abbé Raynal's *Histoire philosophique et politique des deux Indes*, one of the most famous contemporary books about the American continent. Raynal incorporated the speech in his book under the impression that it was a genuine historical document, and he was later amazed to learn, on a visit to Franklin's apartments in Paris when Franklin was serving as commissioner from the United States, that his host had written the speech as a hoax. Upon hearing this from Franklin's own lips, the French philosophe replied, "My word, . . . I am more pleased to have included your tales in my work than the truths of others."[6]

The great liberties that Raynal takes with Franklin's original text are all the more remarkable considering that he at first believed he was reporting an actual speech. He completely rewrote entire sections of his alleged translation in order to strengthen the deism of the original and to add principles of feminine equalitarianism, which are certainly not dominant in Franklin's version. Raynal shifts the emphasis from the duty of augmenting population to the pleasure in the sexual act itself, in a sense combining the arguments of Polly with those of Boccaccio's Filippa. Raynal's heroine complains, therefore, of masculine injustice in condemning the female partner from whom the male derives pleasure and companionship. "Let him," she says, "not crush with opprobrium a sex which he has

---

[6] A. O. Aldridge, *Franklin and His French Contemporaries* (New York, 1957), p. 96. Subsequent remarks on abbé Raynal are based on this book.

himself corrupted; let him not infuse shame and misery into the pleasure which thou hast given him as the consolation of his affliction; let him not be ungrateful and cruel to the very seat of happiness in delivering to torture the victim of his voluptuousness." Polly's speech is incorporated into the chapter of Raynal's work bearing the title, "Severity which still exists in the laws of New England," ostensibly an attack on the excesses of Puritanism.

By and large Raynal transforms Franklin's basically comic discourse into a deistic sermon. Raynal's heroine, for example, in her introductory remarks, independently acknowledges reason as her guide and arbiter. "I am going to make Reason speak. As she alone has the right to dictate the laws, she can examine them all." In speaking of the education she has given to her illegitimate offspring, an extention of the situation that had not occurred to Franklin, she again praises reason as her moving principle. "I have formed them to virtue, which is merely reason. They will be citizens as yourselves unless you take away from them by new fines the basis of their maintenance and force them to flee a region which has spurned them from the cradle."

Franklin's Polly complains of the severity of the laws, but argues merely that their rigidity should sometimes be relaxed in particular circumstances, that "there is left a power somewhere to dispense with the execution of them." Raynal's Polly unequivocally sets forth the Rousseauean precept of the supremacy of conscience over law. "I defy my enemies, if I have any which I have not merited, to accuse me of the least injustice. I examine my conscience and my conduct; the one and the other, I say it boldly, both appear pure as the day which gives me light, and when I look for my crime, I find it only in the law."

Franklin's Polly is not a prude; yet she justifies her cohabitation solely on the grounds of procreation. Raynal's Polly, as we have seen, frankly admits the force of carnal urges, and, perhaps because of the tolerant attitude toward gallantry in the French milieu, justifies these urges as part of the nature of things.

> In order not to betray nature, [she says,] I do not fear to expose myself to unjust dishonor, to shameful punishments. I should prefer to suffer everything than to foreswear the vows of propagation, than to suppress my children either before or after conceiving them. I have not been able, I admit it, after losing my virginity, to remain celibate in a secret and sterile prostitution, and I ask for the punishment which awaits me rather than to hide the fruits of the fecundity which heaven has given to man and woman as its principal benediction.

Raynal's alterations are not limited to the intellectual content of the original text; they embrace also a fundamental change in the integral form or structure of the narrative. Where Franklin's original piece consists entirely of Polly's speech directed to her judges and accusers, Raynal's version contains an additional dramatic peroration addressed to the Divine Being Himself. After repeating Franklin's argument that God could not be angry at her deed since He had endowed her progeny with immortal souls, she turns from her accusers to address God directly.

After Raynal, Polly appeared in another major work of the French Enlightenment, Diderot's *Supplément au voyage de Bougainville [Supplement to the Voyage of Bougainville]*, which was written soon after Raynal's *Histoire* but not published until 1796. Diderot made an independent translation of Polly's speech, following his original somewhat more closely than had Raynal. After Polly admits bringing five handsome children into the world, Diderot has her affirm that "I have nourished them with my milk." This reference to the then popular practice in France of breast-feeding may have been due to the influence of

Rousseau.[7] Diderot also echoed Peter Annet by adding a denunciation of unmarried men who seduce virtuous women and start them on the road to prostitution. Diderot excluded, on the other hand, Polly's view that failing to have children is a crime of the same nature as assassination, her proposal to tax bachelors, and her claim to have deserved a monument for her procreative activities.

Franklin's motive in writing "Polly Baker" may still be obscure; although it is obvious that he was interested in both an entertaining situation and a platform for his ideas, we cannot tell which was of primary importance. Also we cannot be sure which of the ideas incorporated in the story he considered to be the most vital. With Diderot no such doubts exist. He used the situation to illustrate the philosophical principle which had been introduced into Raynal's 1780 edition, perhaps by Diderot himself, and which Diderot later adapted as the subtitle of his *Voyage*: that is, "On the Inconvenience of attaching moral considerations to certain physical actions to which they are not appropriate." As a principle it is actually not far removed from Polly's objection to laws which "turn natural and useful Actions into Crimes." Nearly everything in Diderot's *Voyage* concerns the natives of Tahiti, who were handsome and gracious in physique and completely free and uninhibited in their sexual behavior. They illustrated, therefore, for Diderot, living proof that the puritanical notions of jealousy, fidelity, chastity, and modesty associated in Europe with sexual gratification represent moral concepts improperly attached to a physical act. He rebuked his European compatriots, therefore: "Busy yourself, if you wish, in the dark forest with the perverse companion of your pleasures, but allow the good and simple Tahitians to reproduce without shame in the sight of heaven in broad daylight." Diderot's idyllic portrayal of the un-

[7] Raymond, "Figaro, fils naturel," p. 40.

inhibited sexual behavior of the inhabitants of the South Seas represents an Enlightenment refurbishing of the classical pastoral tradition in which Arcadia and the Golden Age represented the myth of the ideal society.[8] Franklin's Polly Baker may seem quite remote from ancient Arcadia or eighteenth-century Tahiti, but she certainly illustrates Diderot's (and Raynal's) principle that moral considerations are artificially attached to physical actions. The law under which she is condemned she repudiates as unreasonable in itself; the entire body of laws of this kind she condemns as turning natural and useful actions into crimes; and the particular law which she has been accused of violating, she affirms, contradicts the first and great command of nature, to increase and multiply.

No reference to Polly Baker in German literature has hitherto been noted prior to the twentieth century. Eleven years before Franklin's death, however, Polly was cited by a German philosopher, August Hennings, in a treatise published in Copenhagen, *August Hennings Philosophische Versuche.*[9] The author occupies a respected place in the annals of American-European comparative literature because of a poem in the epic genre (also published in Copenhagen in 1799) entitled *Olavides,* devoted to the trials and victories of a Peruvian hero of the Enlightenment, Pablo de Olavide.[10] Hennings is also important in Franklin scholarship as probably the first writer in Germany to draw attention to Franklin's "Standing Queries for the Junto," which, several years before Herder, he published in both English and German in his *Philosophische Versuche.*[11] He indicates that the Junto papers are to be

[8] Renato Poggioli, *The Oaten Flute* (Cambridge, Mass., 1975), p. 60.

[9] 2 vols. (Copenhagen, 1779), 2: 205. A second edition was published in the following year.

[10] Estuardo Nuñez, *El nuevo Olavide* (Lima, 1970), p. 28.

[11] 1: 355-361. Information on Herder's use of Franklin is found in *Papers,* ed. Labaree (1959), 1: 259.

found in Franklin's *Political, Miscellaneous and Philosophical Pieces* (London, 1779) and that they are extracted in the *Monthly Review* for March 1780. The latter rather than the printed volume was probably Hennings's source as well as Herder's later on. Hennings treats Polly in connection with the emotional effect of the experiences of other people, presenting her as an illustration of the manner in which the distress of others operates upon one's feelings. "Who can read the story of Polly Baker," he writes, "one of these unfortunates in New England without emotion? Who would not consider her innocent and admire the gentleman who recognized virtue in her offence?" According to Hennings, the perverted view of female honor in the case of Polly Baker was almost as horrible as that which required widows in Indostan to immolate themselves upon the funeral pyres of their husbands. No doubt Hennings had read about Polly in the sentimentalized version of Raynal because he echoes Raynal's implied praise of the judge who marries her, by that action illustrating the primacy of reason over the courts of law.

After this survey of the European metamorphoses of Polly Baker, we are in a position to analyze the ideological and literary elements in Franklin's original creation. We may hope to decide, for example, to what degree Franklin was attempting to convey a serious message and to what degree he was being facetious. On the serious side we may investigate the ideas he was seeking to present. We may inquire whether he felt that women were being discriminated against in the society of his day, that the stigma against bastard children should be removed, or that maximum population was so desirable in a "new country" such as America that any means to obtain it was legitimate? It is self-evident that Franklin's purpose was both comical and serious and that he was concerned with all of the forementioned ideas.

The basic elements of "Polly Baker" that elevated it

above its provincial colonial milieu and led to its international renown may be considered under the headings
of eroticism and ideology. Eroticism is used in the sense
of deriving pleasure from contemplation of the human
sexual act and its accompaniments. In "The Speech of
Polly Baker" this type of pleasure blends with the comic
as it does in the tradition of bawdy tales from the period
of Boccaccio and Chaucer to the present. In the Puritanical
setting of colonial New England the notion of a woman
being tried in public five times consecutively for having
an illegitimate child creates a comic shock in the ludi-
crousness of the situation. J. A. Leo Lemay has recently
pointed out the scattering of a number of salacious puns
throughout Polly's speech.[12] She remarks, for example, "I
cannot conceive . . . what the Nature of my Offense is"
and refers to "the first Cause of all my Faults and Miscarriages," deliberately emphasizing the words "conceive" and "Miscarriages," by inserting parenthetical
phrases immediately after them. The man who originally
seduced her, she declares, is "now a Magistrate of this
Country," recalling the anatomical overtones in Hamlet's
phrase "country matters." To be sure, these puns are not
as obvious in the present day as they would have been to
many of Franklin's contemporary readers. The scholar who
first noted these double meanings vindicated his perceptions by observing that Franklin at the age of sixteen printed
in his brother's newspaper, *The New-England Courant*,
the bland statement that "Women are prime Causes of a
great many Male Enormities." One might also suggest
that Franklin discerned sexual overtones in one of his
favorite proverbs, which he put forward conspicuously in
his autobiography and elsewhere: "it is hard for an empty
Sack to stand upright." He indulged in the openly sca-

---

[12] "The Text, Rhetorical Strategies, and Themes of 'The Speech of
Miss Polly Baker,' " in *The Oldest Revolutionary. Essays on Benjamin
Franklin*, ed. J. A. Leo Lemay (Philadelphia, 1976), p. 109.

tological, moreover, in his surreptitious *To the Royal Academy of Brussels*, a parody of Enlightenment academia in which he proposes research into converting to perfume the noxious effluvia caused by breaking wind.[13] Whatever puns exist in "Polly Baker," therefore, are probably intentional.

Franklin, like Polly, was not a prude in any sense of the word, and he believed that the sexual act is a good in itself, not only as a means to procreate. In a famous letter to Joseph Priestley, written toward the close of the Revolutionary War, he dramatically elaborated the modern philosophy of "Make Love, Not War." With supreme disgust he condemned the human race, "for without a Blush they assemble in great armies at Noon Day to destroy, and when they have kill'd as many as they can, they exaggerate the Number to augment the fancied Glory; but they creep into Corners, or cover themselves with the Darkness of night, when they mean to beget, as being asham'd of a virtuous Action." Modern scholarship has discovered that Franklin is here paraphrasing the great Renaissance skeptic Montaigne,[14] but the sentiments were nonetheless his own. They were repeated by Diderot, in the remark already quoted, "Busy yourself, if you wish, in the dark forest with the perverse companion of your pleasures, but allow the good and simple Tahitians to reproduce without shame in the sight of heaven in broad daylight."

During all periods of his life, Franklin believed that a healthy eroticism was superior to Puritanical morality that stressed the subduing of sexual impulses. This is one of the themes of "Polly Baker." To show that Franklin was presenting Polly sympathetically in order to condone

[13] Richard E. Amacher, *Franklin's Wit and Folly. The Bagatelles* (New Brunswick, N.J., 1953), pp. 66-69.

[14] Robert Newcomb, "Benjamin Franklin and Montaigne," *Modern Language Notes* 72 (1957): 489-91.

her breaches of the traditional sexual code rather than to condemn her, it is sufficient to point to parallel treatments of the theme in his other works. Carl Van Doren associates Polly Baker with his surreptitious "Advice to a Young Man on the Choice of a Mistress," both presumably written when he was entering his fortieth year, and suggests that Franklin's acute sexual awareness at this time was the result of the normal life cycle.[15] With Franklin, however, there is no need to isolate a particular "salty year," for eroticism may be found in his works in all periods. During his sojourn in Paris during his seventies, for example, he composed several libidinous *jeux d'esprit* for Mme Catherine Helvétius, widow of the noted *philosophe*. Two of them were printed on his private press, and one was soon afterward reprinted in the famous *Correspondance littéraire* of Melchior Grimm.[16] In the first, entitled *The Flies*, Franklin converts the buzzing sounds of the insects in his apartment into a plea for the separate households of Franklin and Mme Helvétius to merge into a single one. The second bagatelle, entitled *The Elysian Fields*, ventures on a theme which is called in our day wife-swapping. Here Franklin reports a dream that he has been transported to paradise, where he meets Helvétius, now married to Franklin's late wife. Franklin thereupon returns to the good Earth, reports his adventure to Mme Helvétius, and challenges her, "Let us take our revenge." The nineteenth-century French critic Sainte-Beuve, writing at the height of the French Romantic movement, felt that in the *Elysian Fields* "one can sense a deep emotion underlying the playful surface,"[17] but seen as a companion piece to Polly Baker, the facetiousness is more apparent. After Franklin's return to America, Mme Helvétius wrote a reminiscing letter about Franklin's dream of the Elysian

---

[15] *Benjamin Franklin* (New York, 1938), pp. 150-54.

[16] Ed. Maurice Tourneux, 16 vols. (Paris, 1877-1882), 12: 385-86.

[17] Claude-Anne Lopez, *Mon Cher Papa* (New Haven, 1966), p. 268.

Fields and remarked, "I believe you have been a rascal and will find more than one wife up there!"[18]

When Franklin wrote the *Elysian Fields*, Mrs. Franklin had been dead for several years, but even during her lifetime he had treated the same theme of marital exchanges. He once reported that one of the young ladies in his English social circle whom he described as an "amiable and delectable Companion" had vowed to marry either Franklin or his friend John Hawkesworth, depending on "whose Wife should first depart this Life." As a consequence both Franklin and Hawkesworth "sincerely wished Health & long Life to the other's Wife."[19]

The explicit theme of these bagatelles is that constancy or fidelity to a single mate is a questionable virtue. This is implicit also in "Polly Baker," and it seems to have been a reflection of Franklin's own personality. One of his French friends, in commentary on his popularity with the ladies of Paris, remarked that he treated all of them with an amiable coquettishness that they loved. "When one particular lady, eager for his preference, asked him if he did not care for her more than for the others, he would answer: 'Yes, when you are closest to me, because of the force of attraction.' "

In all of Franklin's bagatelles in which eroticism appears, the situation being described usually has some unrealistic element, for example, talking flies, a visit to the Elysian Fields, and five consecutive trials for bearing bastard children. It is hard to discern a serious purpose in the bagatelles for Mme Helvétius, but there are a number of them in Polly Baker.

The theme of the equality of the sexes, or at least equal justice, may be discerned in Franklin's "Polly Baker" text as distinguished from adapters such as Hennings, Diderot,

[18] Ibid.

[19] A. O. Aldridge, *Benjamin Franklin Philosopher and Man* (New York, 1965), p. 212.

and Peter Annet, who emphasized other notions. Even in Franklin, feminism is not as dominant as it is in Voltaire and Beaumarchais, for Franklin's Polly merely complains that for her to be prosecuted while her partner in crime becomes a magistrate is "unjust and unequal." Probably Franklin himself believed that men and women should not be treated disproportionately for the same transgression of the law, which is essentially all that Polly is saying, but at no time in his life did he ever suggest women's equality in any other sense. When one considers Polly's speech in conjunction with the briefs of Boccaccio's Filippa and Voltaire's countess, however, it becomes difficult not to read feminist ideology into it. Boccaccio's Filippa is forthright in her demand for sexual equality. She declares as a universally acknowledged principle "that the Lawes enacted in any Country, ought to be common, and made with consent of them whom they concerne." The edict under which she is accused, however, "is rigorous against none, but poore women onely." It is unjust, moreover, since when it was made, "there was not any woman that gave consent to it, neither were they called to like or allow thereof." Voltaire's countess echoes this principle in inquiring "whether it is not evident that it is cuckolds who have made the laws." Polly's speech was overtly associated with feminism in March 1778, when it was incorporated in one of the earliest French feminist periodicals, the *Journal des Dames*.[20]

[20] Evelyne Sullerot, *Histoire de la presse féminine en France, des origines à 1848* (Paris, 1966), pp. 24-25. This author explains in a footnote that she had completed her description of the Polly Baker text as found in the *Journal des Dames* with no knowledge whatsoever of its source or previous history when she mentioned it by chance to an acquaintance who was writing a thesis on Diderot and who then explained that it had been included in the *Supplément au Voyage de Bougainville*. After comparing the two texts, Mme Sullerot concluded that without being word for word, the two versions are identical in facts, arguments, and entire phrases.

Another serious topic that Franklin's Polly Baker embraces is religion. Her speech serves the double purpose of holding up to ridicule the Puritan morality associated with New England and presenting for approval the rational deism that Franklin embraced as his personal religion throughout his entire life. He had previously derided the Puritan spirit in print, condemning particularly its dismal outlook. In 1734, for example, he published in the *Pennsylvania Gazette* a ribald parody of the clerical style of contemplative ascetic gloom, concluding that we should "rejoice and bless God, that we are neither Oysters, Hogs, nor Dray-Horses; and not stand repining that He has not made us Angels."[21] A few years later Franklin wrote for his *Gazette* a series of essays defending a liberal Presbyterian minister against the other clergymen of his synod who had accused the minister of heterodoxy because of his preaching morality and good works instead of salvation by faith alone.[22] To be sure, Polly Baker in her speech says nothing about the clergy, since she is being judged by civil lawyers and magistrates. She cleverly blends or equates the religious and the secular, however, by suggesting that both base their dedication to the sacredness of the marriage ceremony upon its usefulness as a source of income. In her words, only "the Minister, or the Justice" could have any complaint "because I have had Children without being Married, by which they have miss'd a Wedding Fee." Also she remarks parenthetically, "I am no Divine." She argues convincingly for the principle that eventually became a pillar of the American Revolution, the separation of church and state. "If mine, then, is a religious Offence," she states, "leave it, Gentlemen, to religious Punishments." She also directly attacks the laws that turn what she considers normal sexual behavior

[21] A. O. Aldridge, "A Religious Hoax by Benjamin Franklin," *American Literature* 36 (1964): 204-9.

[22] *Papers*, ed. Labaree (1960), 2: 27-33, 37-126.

into crime. "Abstracted from the Law," she says, "I cannot
... conceive what the Nature of my Offence is." Franklin
is here hitting at all of the laws in New England regulating
private morality, not only those against fornication. Since
Franklin draws particular attention to the circumstance
that her speech was uttered "before a Court of Judicature,
at Connecticut near Boston in New England," we can be
sure that it is the rigorous morality of Puritanism associated with this region of America that is his target.

Along with the ridicule of Puritan theology, Franklin
blended into Polly's speech one or two elements of deism.
A modern scholar has suggested that "the satire of the
speech was directed both at the orthodox religionists who
wished to impose their own moral ideas on others and
the unorthodox who were forever appealing to Nature."[23]
If this is true, Franklin was indulging in self-satire, for the
deistical strains are to be found duplicated with utter seriousness in many other passages in Franklin's works.
These deistic elements are so important that subsequent
writers, such as Peter Annet in England and the abbé Raynal
in France, revised the speech in such a way as to eliminate
its comedy altogether and present it as a document of
deist propaganda.

In her speech Polly refers to "the Nature of Things" as
an absolute standard, and in the same manner in which
a clergyman would cite a biblical text, she points to "the
first and great Command of Nature, and of Nature's God,
Increase and multiply." Polly's reference to the "Command of Nature, and of Nature's God" is the second most
famous use of the phrase in all American letters. It is more
widely known only in the version "Laws of Nature and
of Nature's God," which appears in the Declaration of
Independence. Before the publication of Polly's speech,

[23] Max Hall, *Benjamin Franklin and Polly Baker* (Chapel Hill, N.C.,
1960), p. 111.

Pope in *An Essay on Man* had praised the independent spirit who "looks through Nature up to Nature's God" [IV. 331] and Bolingbroke echoed that "one follows Nature and Nature's God" [*Letter to Mr. Pope*, 1753].

Polly also uses the teleological argument for the existence of God; that is, the view that a creator may be discerned in the regularity and order of the universe. In a lecture "On the Providence of God in the Government of the World," which he had delivered in his youth, Franklin had marveled at "the admirable Structure of Animal Bodies of such infinite Variety, and yet every one adapted to its Nature, and the Way of Life it is to be placed in, Whether on Earth, in the Air or in the Waters, and so exactly that the highest and most exquisite human Reason, cannot find a fault and say this would have been better so or in another Manner."[24] Polly is falling back on this mode of reasoning when she asks, "How can it be believed that Heaven is angry at my having Children, when to the little done by me towards it, God has been pleased to add his divine skill and admirable Workmanship in the Formation of their Bodies, and crown'd it by furnishing them with rational and immortal souls." Polly adds an element that has nothing to do with the teleological argument or with Franklin's religious opinions expressed elsewhere in his works—immortal souls. There is no evidence whatsoever in Franklin's works to show that he ever believed that human beings have souls, although he often expressed the hope of immortality.

Another dominant theme in Polly's speech is the attempt to erase in some measure the stigma from unwed mothers and illegitimate children, a theme that was first noted in 1926 by one of Franklin's biographers, Phillips Russell. Alluding to Franklin's own illegitimate son, William Franklin, Russell interpreted Polly's defense of her-

---

[24] *Papers*, ed. Labaree, 1: 264-69.

self as the mother of natural children as "in reality Franklin's own defense of himself made for the benefit of those critics in Philadelphia who had been saying nasty things about him."[25] Although this opinion has been challenged by the argument that "such an attempt might boomerang by simply calling attention to a painful situation,"[26] there can be no question that Franklin felt that being born out of wedlock should not be considered a disgrace. He once confided to the physician-philosopher Cabanis that he attached very little importance to the wedding ceremony. "To the contrary, he regarded it, especially in countries where divorce has not been established, as an institution equally immoral and absurd. He also considered as extremely unjust those laws which placed in a special category children born outside of marriage."[27] Franklin, by the way, was not alone in the eighteenth century in this opinion. The prime minister of Denmark, Struensee, worked persistently to rehabilitate the image of illegitimate offspring and before his execution in 1772 for treason succeeded in forcing the repeal of laws in his country making it a crime to have a bastard child.

Franklin introduces two other ideological topics by means of Polly's question, "Can it be a Crime (in the Nature of Things I mean) to add to the Number of the King's Subjects in a new Country that really wants People?" Here she makes a distinction between positive and natural law, that is, between the standards of artificial society and those of nature, and the necessity of maximum population for the political benefit of a nation. The distinction between positive and natural law is the basis of the later Raynal-Diderot principle concerning "the Inconvenience of attaching moral considerations to certain physical ac-

[25] Cited by Hall, *Franklin and Polly Baker*, p. 109.
[26] Ibid.
[27] Jean P. G. Cabanis, *Oeuvres philosophiques*. Edited by Claude Lehec and Jean Cazaneuve. 2 vols. (Paris, 1956), 1: 348.

tions to which they are not appropriate." The conviction
of the economic benefits of a growing population comprises one of the elements of philoprogenitiveness (or love
of progeny), along with erotic pleasure and participation
in the joys of family life, which may also be traced in
Franklin's private ideology. Hundreds of novels, like Richardson's *Pamela*, stressed the personal pleasure to be derived from pregnant wives and healthy babies; sermons
invoked the divine imperative implicit in Proverbs 14:28,
"In the multitude of people, is the king's honor"; and
treatises on political and economic theory upheld the
maxim that "in proportion to the numbers of useful subjects, will be the strength and riches of a state." Nobody
revealed a greater fondness than Franklin for fecundity
and procreation as such. In 1755 he published, for example, *Observations concerning the Increase of Mankind, Peopling of Countries*, a tract that was reprinted and
widely circulated throughout America and Europe and
gained for Franklin the reputation of being the outstanding demographer in the British colonies. His argument
runs: People increase in proportion to the ease and con-
venience of supporting a family. This economic facility
exists to a high degree in unsettled countries like America.
Whatever increases production increases population, and
those citizens who aid in the process deserve to be called
"Fathers of their Nation." In the American colonies the
population doubles in twenty to twenty-five years, but
the process requires about 350 years in Europe. In another
century, the colonies will outstrip the mother country.
All of the presuppositions of this argument are found in
Polly Baker's speech. Voltaire shared Franklin's notions
concerning the advantages to a state of maximum population, and in the speech of his cuckolded husband he
inserted one of his perpetual complaints against the clergy,
that its mandatory celibacy was an affront against population.

After the abbé Raynal's adaptation of Polly's speech, it became for Franklin a symbol of the unreliability of history. In a conversation with one of his intimate associates in Paris, abbé André Morellet, Franklin cited his hoax as an example of the short time in which a contrived tale could be converted into historical fact. The literary genre in which Morellet places Polly's speech—"un petit roman politique et moral" [a short political and moral piece of fiction]—provides a clue toward Franklin's own interpretation of the work. Franklin related to Morellet the chief circumstances of the circulation of the speech—that it was composed around 1740, inserted into the newspapers of the time, its authenticity debated until public interest declined, revived by Raynal, and since then firmly believed. "Thirty years had been sufficient to convert the tale into history."[28] While still in France, Franklin cited as an example of the errors in Raynal's *Histoire philosophique* the charge that "the people of Massachusetts Bay preserve their Fanaticism," a strong indication that he felt either that fanatical Puritanism no longer existed in New England or that this aspect of Polly's speech had been distorted.[29]

In a sense, Franklin's objections to the converting of Polly's speech into a historical document show that he considered it as a work of the imagination, as a revelation of human character and behavior as well as a vehicle for moral and political ideas. When the analogies between Franklin's Polly and Boccaccio's Filippa are perceived, Polly's character transcends the New England setting. Her speech becomes less important for its portrayal of Puritanical rigor and the quaintness of some colonial customs than for its exposition of psychological attitudes and a social situation of universal application, of equal rele-

[28] A. O. Aldridge, *Benjamin Franklin et ses contemporains français* (Paris, 1963), p. 92.
[29] Hall, *Franklin and Polly Baker*, p. 125.

vance to Renaissance Italy as to Colonial America. Probably the elements of broad application in the story of Polly Baker had as much to do with the decision of Diderot and abbé Raynal to repeat and embellish it as had the elements of deism and primitivism, which are generally considered to have had primary appeal to the French *philosophes*. This consideration points to an important paradox in their portrayals of Polly. By translating her speech into French they seem to lift her from provincial boundaries, but at the same time, by associating her with primitivism, they put her back again. Diderot in particular seems to place Polly apart from the stream of advanced civilization by associating her with the natives of Tahiti as outstanding examples of nonconformity to a characteristic of social development that Diderot condemns, the attaching of "moral concepts to physical actions which do not correspond with them." The example of Filippa would have suited Diderot's purpose just as well, but the connotations of ribaldry and bawdiness associated with *Il Decameron* would have made the Italian heroine inappropriate for his serious purpose.

Franklin's achievement in the indirect portrayal of character may also be given greater recognition than it has received in the past by comparing his method with Boccaccio's. If literary characters are considered on a scale, with wooden types like the personae of fables and fairy tales at one end and sophisticated and complex personalities like those in *Les Liaisons dangereuses* and *Anna Karenina* on the other, Boccaccio occupies a position close to the middle. Thanks to his artistic skill, Filippa is a vital and realistic character. The reader has no difficulties in imagining her either in the arms of her lover or pleading her case before her judge. Polly Baker has equally apparent human dimensions despite the fact that her speech lacks any kind of narrative framework. Polly lives as a real personage because of the psychological acuity and credibility of her reasoning, which portrays a personality as well as an ideology.

Despite the ready acceptance by Franklin's contemporaries of the authenticity of Polly's speech, some twentieth-century critics have condemned the basic human situation on which it is predicated as far-fetched or even ludicrous. They cannot accept the coincidence of a man who has been responsible for the ruin of a young virgin recognizing her many years later when he is a judge at her trial and then proposing marriage to her. This situation, whether presented by Franklin with adequate literary verisimilitude or not, actually happened at least once in real life and provided the basis for a full-length novel by one of the masters of world fiction—a writer in the class of Goethe, Dickens, and Stendhal. The novel, published at the very end of the nineteenth century, is *Resurrection* (1899), and its author is Tolstoy. Its plot was suggested by an incident in Russian society—the plight of a girl of sixteen, who was seduced and then deserted by her lover, forced into prostitution, and eventually rescued by her seducer, who recognized her while acting as a juryman at her trial on a charge of prostitution. In the novel, Tolstoy deviates from the circumstances of the real incident, thereby bringing the story of the unfortunate victim, Katúsha Máslova, even closer to that of Polly Baker. The seducer is the protagonist of the novel, a member of the aristocracy, Prince Dmítri Neklúdoff, and Katúsha is a servant girl at his aunt's estate. On a brief visit, he takes advantage of her in a moment of delirious passion, thrusts a bank note upon her, and then disappears. Ten years afterwards, during which time she has completely vanished from his mind, he is summoned for jury duty and recognizes her in the prisoner's dock. She has spent the intervening years in a brothel and is on trial for poisoning a patron of the establishment. She does not recognize Neklúdoff as her seducer, but the latter is so overwhelmed by the encounter that he determines to secure her legal vindication and to marry her in order to atone for the great wrong he has committed against her. He later learns that Katúsha had carried his child, but that it died at birth. He succeeds in having the judgment against her modified, but in the end she refuses his offer of marriage. *Resurrection* is an ideological vehicle for the presentation of Tolstoy's religion (based on Christian socialism) and of his economic theories (based on Henry George's single tax) in the same way that the "Speech of Polly Baker" is designed to portray Franklin's principles of deism and philoprogenitiveness. But the plot elements in the two narratives are essentially the same.

I had already written the above section on Tolstoy when my attention was drawn to an article, also treating the subject of the relations between "Polly Baker" and *Resurrection*, in a Festschrift for a Soviet comparatist. The author, G. M. Fridlender, surveys Tolstoy's interest in the Enlightenment, provides documentary evidence of Tolstoy's acquaintance with Franklin's autobiography, and underscores the similarity of plot lines in *Resurrection* and the novella-pastiche of Franklin, Raynal, and Diderot.[30] Fridlender is unable to prove any more than I, however, that Tolstoy had read the story of Polly Baker in any of its multitudinous versions. I mention his article primarily to indicate that he and I independently arrived at a similar conclusion. According to Fridlender's interpretation, the *philosophes* of the eighteenth century emphasized Polly's maternal role in presenting to the government five useful new citizens; whereas Tolstoy stressed the theme of the seducer-judge (or juryman in *Resurrection*) from the ruling class confronting the girl of the common people who had been abandoned by him. A polemic

---

[30] " 'Voskresenie' L'va Tolstogo i 'Reč Polli Beker' B. Franklina," in *Sravnitel'noe izučenie literatur [The Comparative Study of Literatures]*, ed. E. A. Smirnova (Leningrad, 1976), pp. 304-8.

has developed in American scholarship over whether Tolstoy had ever read Franklin's works, even his autobiography, and whether the latter work had exercised a significant influence upon the Russian novelist.[31] Fridlender seems to have settled the question by reporting that Tolstoy recommended the publishing of an edition for the common reader of Franklin's autobiography, Swift's *Gulliver's Travels*, and Lessing's *Nathan der Weise*.

From the perspective of bare plot or the theme of the seducer-judge, Polly's basic situation is identical to that of the protagonist of a major American novel of the nineteenth century, Hawthorne's *Scarlet Letter*. Both Polly and Hester Prynne are accused of a sexual offense, both are brought to judgment before a tribunal of which the partner in the offense is a member, and both remain silent instead of revealing their identities.

Comparison of Polly Baker with other fictional heroines brings up the question of whether the Polly who is on trial in Connecticut should be considered an actual prostitute or merely an oversexed or normally sexed woman. One must decide whether she earns her living through selling her favors, or whether she provides for her economic existence through ordinary means and satisfies overwhelming erotic needs in her leisure moments as best she can. I have always held the latter interpretation, which is both the more plausible and the more comical, and I know of only one critic who calls Polly a whore.[32] The latter designation gives her a greater resemblance to Tolstoy's Katúsha, but at the same time makes her, like Katúsha, a tragic figure and, therefore, not the comic personality that Franklin probably intended. If she is merely an ordinary woman whose sexual drive has driven her to

[31] Henry Hill Walsh, "On the Putative Influence of Benjamin Franklin on Tolstoi," *Canadian-American Slavic Studies* 13 (1979): 306-9.

[32] Leo Lemay, *Oldest Revolutionary*, p. 109, remarks "we see a direct reference to her livelihood, gained by soliciting the men."

throw caution to the winds, she is entirely comic—almost a caricature. If she is a prostitute she cannot be regarded, like Boccaccio's Filippa, as a crusading opponent of the double standard in sexual relations, an attitude that she certainly expresses.

Leo Lemay believes that "Franklin has deliberately created an ironic obtuse persona in Polly Baker,"[33] but such an opinion can hardly be reconciled with the view that Polly is Franklin's spokesman on serious points of ideology, as she certainly is. If she were vulgar and stupid, moreover, her speech would not have obtained the international celebrity with which it was almost immediately rewarded. The novelist Balzac was so impressed with Polly Baker that he gave Franklin credit for inventing the literary genre of the canard along with the lightning rod and republican government. This is exaggerated praise in reference to both literature and politics—Swift and Voltaire had previously perpetrated equally successful journalistic hoaxes.[34] That which distinguishes the Polly Baker story from other masterpieces of the kind is its extraordinary degree of verisimilitude. Other hoaxes were soon exposed and moved from the realm of actuality to that of fiction. Polly Baker, however, not only kept her credibility throughout the entire eighteenth century, but even in the twentieth continued to be cited as an actual historical figure, for example, in *A Social History of the American Family* published during World War I.[35]

Polly's fame depends upon three separate elements: the

[33] Ibid., p. 103.

[34] *Les Illusions perdues*, Pt. II, chap. 23. Balzac was off the mark, moreover, in attributing to Franklin at the same time another anecdote from Raynal's *Histoire*, that of an "Englishman who sold a negress who had saved his life, but first . . . got with child in order to make more money out of the sale." Voltaire correctly pointed out that this tale is no other than the famous story of Inkle and Jarico, originally told by Steele in *Spectator* no. 11.

[35] Hall, *Franklin and Polly Baker*, p. 153.

verisimilitude of Franklin's style, the eroticism associated with Polly's situation, and her forthright character. It is probably the last that has contributed most to her universal appeal. Because of the seriousness of attention given to her character and predicament by eminent European writers, Polly Baker transcends the genre of the canard of literary hoax and attains the rank of a literary theme, joining the company of such celebrated fictional legends as Faust, Don Juan, and Dracula.

FIVE

PAINE AND DICKINSON: POLITICS AND LITERATURE

BALZAC in one of his novels establishes a parallel in French letters between conservative political philosophy and Romanticism on one side and between liberal philosophy and classicism on the other.[1] "By a strange anomaly," he observes, "the romantic royalists call for literary freedom and the abrogation of laws which provide our literature with its conventional forms; while the liberals cling to the unities, regular rhythms in the alexandrine line and classical themes." It would be difficult to establish for the American Revolutionary and Federal periods a similar relationship between political philosophy and literary theory and practice although ethical ideals obviously contributed to political ideologies of all shades. Among classicists, Joseph Dennie believed that government should be in the hands of an aristocratic elite and Joel Barlow believed that it should be controlled by the people; among Romanticists, James Fenimore Cooper took the conservative side in politics and William Cullen Bryant the liberal.

The two men who have generally been considered to be the foremost propagandists of the American Revolution, John Dickinson and Thomas Paine, seem on the surface to illustrate the contrary of Balzac's paradox. Paine's literary style embodies many Romantic characteristics with its irregularity, impulsiveness, and flamboyance, and his

---

[1] *Les Illusions perdues*, Pt. II, chap. 8.

political opinions were certainly in the vanguard of the radicalism of his time, combining as they do the ideals of republicanism and natural rights. Dickinson's literary style, on the other hand, embodies neoclassical standards of careful organization, restraint, and decorum. To this extent there does exist a substantial difference between the two propagandists, but this contrast cannot be extended to comprise political attitudes as well. Dickinson has traditionally been portrayed as highly conservative, but in actuality he and Paine shared the same fundamental ideology. Indeed the only major intellectual difference separating the two men is their attitude toward the Greek and Roman classics, Dickinson establishing them as models for almost his entire way of life, and Paine rejecting them in favor of the languages and cultural ideals of the modern world.

My primary concern in this chapter will be with American political ideas rather than universal literature, but I shall retain the comparative method in treating the manner in which the works of Dickinson and Paine were received in France.

Although Dickinson and Paine knew each other personally and both ended their political careers as staunch defenders of the administration of their mutual friend Thomas Jefferson, they are practically never considered as kindred figures in political or intellectual history. Biographers of either man uniformly ignore the other. The notable exception is Moncure D. Conway, a graduate of Dickinson College and the author of the first biography of Paine to be based on extensive original research. Conway told how "honest John Dickinson" helped obtain a financial grant for Paine from the state of Pennsylvania. Most modern historical works that make any comparisons between Paine and Dickinson, however, erroneously suggest that their political systems were antithetical.

It cannot be denied that historical figures frequently

become symbols of economic and political ideologies. Franklin and Jefferson on one side, Hamilton and Adams on the other, do represent concrete political attitudes, and their followers in political life have magnified their differences by forming opposing factions. These are not dichotomies artificially imposed by historians many years after the events in which these figures participated. To their contemporaries and near-contemporaries, these men stood for separate political philosophies as different from each other as the systems of Thomas Paine and Edmund Burke. On the American scene, Paine may without much discussion be ranked on the side of Franklin and Jefferson. Historians have had difficulty in correctly placing Dickinson because of one major event in his life, his decision not to support the Declaration of Independence in the Second Continental Congress. This decision, Dickinson later maintained, was based primarily on timing, on his personal appraisal of the wretched state of unpreparedness of the colonies.[2] By voting against independence, Dickinson indeed temporarily enrolled himself in a camp opposite from that of Thomas Paine. Because of the cautious legalism of much of his writing, moreover, Dickinson has frequently been compared to Burke, and it is easy to understand what created the impression that his thought is inimical to Paine's. The related belief has grown up that throughout his career Dickinson habitually appealed to history and legal precedent rather than to natural law and natural rights. This interpretation is not supported by the facts. Not only was Dickinson not the American Burke, but his mature political philosophy was essentially the same as that of Thomas Paine. Dickinson himself recognized the similarity in their fundamental views, and he declared it emphatically.

[2] "Vindication" in Charles J. Stillé, *The Life and Times of John Dickinson* (Philadelphia, 1891), p. 367.

PAINE AND DICKINSON

At first glance the two men seem to have resembled each other only in their life span. Dickinson was born in 1732, Paine five years later. Dickinson died in 1808 and Paine the following year. But Dickinson saw the light in surroundings of ease and affluence, Paine amid poverty and proletarian strife. Dickinson during most of his life held high political office and his prestige was never challenged. Even his political opponents treated him with the utmost deference. Paine, however, was as much reviled as respected throughout his entire public career. Although he exerted considerable political influence at various times and places, he worked almost invariably behind the scenes, and he never held an elected office in America. Early in the Revolution he served as the paid secretary of the committee of foreign affairs of the Congress and later as clerk of the Assembly of Pennsylvania. Dickinson held any number of elected offices including that of president of the Supreme Executive Council of Pennsylvania. Paine was on close enough terms to be invited to dine at the President's table at least once when the question of the recompense for his services during the Revolution was being considered. Dickinson reported to the Council of the state that he and Washington had discussed Paine's financial status and that both desired that provision be made for him. On another occasion both Paine and Dickinson were present at a spectacular fête in Philadelphia to celebrate the birth of the Dauphin of France. Benjamin Rush, who reported their presence, added that Paine "retired frequently from company to analyze his thoughts and to enjoy the repast of his own original ideas."[3]

A minor episode involving the return of Congress from Princeton to Philadelphia in 1783 reveals Paine's support of Dickinson in local politics. In a letter to Rush con-

[3] *Letters of Benjamin Rush*, ed. L. H. Butterfield, 2 vols. (Princeton, 1951), 1: 280.

cerning rival addresses to the citizens of Philadelphia, Paine described one that he had himself drawn up as initiated by "those whom Mr. Dickinson have very good reason to believe his friends, and who intend it as a softening healing measure to all sides."[4] In 1805 after Paine returned to the United States from France, he paid a merited tribute to Dickinson. In the midst of his attacks on the politicans "who once figured as leaders under the assumed and fraudulent name of *federalism*," he particularly complimented those who had since gone "into honorable and peaceable retirement, like *John Dickinson* and *Charles Thomson*."[5]

Both Paine and Dickinson were at one time associated with a Quaker environment, and in mature life both questioned conventional Christian doctrine. Paine's religion is a complicated subject, but one may certainly say that during most of his adult years he accepted deist principles. Dickinson late in his career expressed belief in Christianity, but also admitted, "I am not, and probably never shall be, united to any religious Society, because each of them, as a society, holds principles which I cannot adopt."[6]

As early as 1765 in his writings on the Stamp Act, Dickinson revealed traces of the political ideology that would make him comfortable with the system of Paine and Jefferson at the end of the century. A recent scholar has pointed out that in opposing the Stamp Act, Dickinson did not, as most historians maintain, depend upon legalistic logic or appeals to precedent, but offered instead "a clearly articulated theory of natural rights—to be happy,

---

[4] *Complete Writings of Thomas Paine*, ed. Philip S. Foner, 2 vols. (New York, 1945), 2: 1219.

[5] Ibid., p. 949.

[6] Samuel Miller Papers, Princeton University Library, cited by David L. Jacobson in *John Dickinson and the Revolution in Pennsylvania 1764-1776*. University of California Publications in History (Berkeley and Los Angeles, 1965), p. 2.

to be free, and to be secure in one's property."[7] His various defenses of American rights were not based upon charters or compacts, but upon "immutable maxims of reason and justice." In a work of 1766 written under the pseudonym of a "North American," Dickinson described rights in the following terms: "They are created in us by the decrees of Providence, which establish the laws of our nature. They are born with us; exist within us; and cannot be taken away from us by any human power."[8] One could readily accept these words as being taken from the works of Thomas Paine.

Exactly the same presuppositions figure in Dickinson's *Letters from a Farmer in Pennsylvania* of 1768, and many of the phrases in this, his most popular work, recall his arguments of the preceding years. "The colonists, and men everywhere, enjoyed a basic right to be happy, they could not 'be happy, without being free,' and they could not be free unless secure in their property. Dickinson argued, as he had three years before, that American rights had been 'created . . . by the decrees of Providence, which establish the laws of our nature.' "[9] Despite many recent interpretations which see very little in the Farmer's *Letters* except resistance to Parliamentary taxation for the purpose of revenue rather than for the control of trade, the *Letters* actually stress freedom and natural rights. They make use of standard Whig themes such as the threat to liberty by executive control over assemblies, the danger of losing the right of voluntary taxation, the evils inherent in establishing the precedent of a revenue tax, the record of ministerial injustice, and the horrors of bureaucracy, corruption, and a standing army. Dickinson states his argument forthrightly and does not hedge it with legalistic refinements, and whenever he cites precedents he does so in order to show that traditions may be wrong and per-

---

[7] Ibid., p. 39.

[8] *An Address . . . Barbadoes*, 1776, cited by Jacobson, ibid., p. 262.

[9] Jacobson, *John Dickinson*, p. 55.

nicious. In other words, Dickinson even in the 1760s shows little resemblance to Edmund Burke of the 1790s. So forceful was Dickinson's style that the Tory *Critical Review* in England "accused the Farmer of inciting the colonies to independence."[10]

Although the Farmer's *Letters* and *Common Sense* are based on similar presuppositions and are rightly considered as the two most successful propaganda pieces of the American Revolution, their stylistic techniques reveal important differences. Dickinson writes in the vein of an Addisonian essay; Paine in that of a Swiftian tract. Dickinson adopts the device of an invented character as the presumed author; in the words of his opening sentence, he is "a farmer settled after a variety of fortunes, near the banks of the river Delaware, in the province of Pennsylvania." Paine in contrary fashion bluntly asserts, "Who the Author of this Production is, is wholly unnecessary to the Public, as the Object for Attention is the *Doctrine itself*, not the *Man*."

As Dickinson introduces himself in the character of the Pennsylvania farmer, he seems to be a colonial Montesquieu. He casually reveals that his servants are few and that he spends most of his time in his library, which is the most valuable part of his small estate. These details put his readers at ease by explaining, as he subsequently indicates, how it is that he has acquired more knowledge in history, law, and the constitution of his country than most men of his class. Paine keeps his personality as the author completely submerged, but he uses a style and vocabulary to suggest that he is a common man as well as an exponent of common sense.

Dickinson's style is in its way as forceful as Paine's, but it incorporates a different manner of insistence. Dickinson announces his themes, states them, and comes back

[10] Carl F. Kaestle, "The Public Reaction to John Dickinson's *Farmer's Letters*," *Proceedings of the American Antiquarian Society* 78 (1968): 345.

to them repeatedly. Paine relies on single presentations, occasionally drawn out, but usually short and self-contained. He makes one point and then passes on rapidly to another.

Without question Paine's subject matter is more philosophical and of more universal interest than Dickinson's. Much of *Common Sense* represents pure ideology, based on theoretical reasoning and abstract principles. The Farmer's *Letters*, on the other hand, are entirely pragmatic, treating issues, conditions, and personalities of the immediate time and specific place. Paine probes such basic concepts as the presumed state of nature, the origin of government, and the basic principles of monarchy, hereditary succession, and republicanism. Dickinson confines himself to such particular and specific issues as taxation without representation, the authority of Parliament to regulate trade but not to raise revenue, the distinction between external and internal taxes, and the relationship between virtue and liberty. Dickinson's letters have exclusive and continuous reference to the thirteen British colonies in America. Paine's pamphlet interprets the situation of the colonies as an illustration of principles that relate to the fundamental interests of all mankind. The two writers touch common ground mainly in attempting to rouse their countrymen to contemplate the imminent ruin confronting them; to take immediate action, not wait for the future; and to recognize the common bond of unity joining the thirteen colonies. The major example of verbal similarity between the Farmer's *Letters* and *Common Sense* exists in their common expression of the principle of solidarity. Dickinson says of the colonies, "the cause of one is the cause of all" [Letter I]. Paine enlarges the prospect, declaring "the cause of America is in a great measure the cause of all mankind."[11]

[11] *Complete Writings*, 1: 3.

Most hortatory works published in colonial America were oriented toward either the Greek and Roman classics or the Christian Scriptures, and many authors leaned alternately in both directions. Since Dickinson was one of the most dedicated classicists on the American continent, it is not strange that he should embellish his letters with appropriate allusions to the ancients. Indeed, every one of his twelve letters concludes with a Latin phrase or sentence, followed by an elegant translation into English. Dickinson also adorns his text with quotations from Plutarch, Tacitus, Sallust, Cicero, Demosthenes, and Virgil. These quotations are overweighed, however, by others from European and English authors, including Machiavelli, Rapin, Montesquieu, Locke, Pitt, Cambden, Hume, Pope, and Shakespeare. In his footnotes, Dickinson learnedly cites relevant legal decisions, but he keeps his main text completely free of these documentary authorities.

Even though historians associate Dickinson with the religious sect to which his wife belonged, the Quakers, he was, as we have already seen, not a particularly religious man. He nevertheless incorporates a fair number of biblical quotations in his *Letters*, and he particularly praises "the beautiful and emphatic language of the sacred scriptures" [Letter V]. Here and elsewhere when he cites biblical passages, however, he does not imply any authority in his texts, but uses them, as he does his classical sources, entirely for their language or their meaning. Paine, who had close associations with Quakers in early life, is usually considered by critics as anticlerical in all his writings, but in *Common Sense* he cites Scripture passages much more extensively than does Dickinson, and he appeals to these texts, moreover, as representing divine authority. He several times refers to "the will of the Almighty" and speaks of "the King of America" who "reigns above." In comparison to his scriptural quotations, Paine's references to secular literature are sparse indeed. They are limited to Milton; to three English political writers, Sir William Meredith, James Burgh, and Sir John Dalrymple; to a naval historian, John Entick; to a Quaker pamphleteer, Richard Barclay; and to an Italian moralist, Dragonetti.

Dickinson flatters his readers and countrymen, actually describing the inhabitants of the colonies as in general "more intelligent than any other people whatever" [Letter VII]. Paine in some of his other works writes in a similar ingratiating strain, but in *Common Sense* he limits himself to praising the material strength of the colonies and the advantages inherent on the American continent. Dickinson's style, which has reconciliation as its aim, is appropriate for urging resistance to oppression and injustice, but it remains squarely within the limits of propriety and decorum. Dickinson does indeed make such appeals as "my dear countrymen, ROUSE yourselves, and behold the ruin hanging over your heads," but he advises these same countrymen to "exert themselves in the most firm, but most peaceable manner, for obtaining relief" [Letters II and III]. Paine unequivocally places independence over reconciliation, and he adopts an extreme style to suit his message. As Dickinson's words are appropriate for resistance, Paine's are keyed to revolution. Paine does not seek merely to incite sporadic riots and tumults, but rather to turn every citizen of America against British rule. He castigates all Crown officials as murderers and colonists friendly to them as cowards and sycophants. He affirms that "thousands are already ruined by British barbarity," and denounces George III as "the Royal Brute." Paine's free use of invective is completely alien to Dickinson's sober restraint. Both propagandists, however, appeal to feeling. After Dickinson reviles those colonists who attempted to enforce the Stamp Act as "base-spirited wretches," the closest he comes to personal abuse, he remarks that "every honest bosom, on their being mentioned, will feel what cannot be *expressed*." Paine subjects the record of British atrocities to "those feelings and affections which nature justifies, and without which, we should be incapable of discharging the social duties of life." Parenthetically, Dickinson's style in private correspondence is much less reticent than it is in his public writings. In reference to the fall in public esteem which he suffered consequent to his voting against independence, he affirmed in a personal letter, "no youthfull Lover ever stript off his Clothes to step into Bed to his blooming beautiful Bride with more delight than I have cast off my Popularity."[12]

The publishing histories of the Farmer's *Letters* and *Common Sense* are completely different. Dickinson wrote the entire series of letters as a unit, but divided his material into twelve parts as a promotional device, assuming that they would obtain greater circulation and visibility if put out as twelve installments in newspapers rather than a single pamphlet. He carefully orchestrated the serial publication, fabricating objections to previous letters by fictitious readers and then providing his own answers.[13] Paine adopted the contrary method of publishing his entire work at one time as a pamphlet. His material is even less unified or homogeneous than that of the Farmer's *Letters* and would have been equally suited to serial publication. No one knows why he chose the pamphlet form, but it may be that he was dissatisfied with the results he had obtained from previous contributions to Philadelphia newspapers. Dickinson's *Letters* appeared in "nineteen of the twenty-three English-language newspapers published in the colonies in early 1768," and seven American pam-

---

[12] To Charles Thompson, 7 August 1776, in New York Historical Society, *Collections* 11 (187): 29.
[13] Kaestle, "Public Reaction," p. 339.

phlet editions followed in two years.[14] A modern scholar has estimated that the various newspaper printings had 75,000 readers and the pamphlets an additional 27,000.[15] *Common Sense* appeared in at least twenty-nine issues in the colonies during the single year of 1776, and Paine himself estimated that 120,000 copies were printed within three months.

In August 1776, Silas Deane reported from Paris to the American Committee of Secret Correspondence that "Common Sense has been translated, and has a greater run, if possible, here than in America." Deane also quotes from a letter to a French official which affirms that the author of *Common Sense* "is one of the greatest legislators [political experts] among the millions of writers whom we know; without question if the Americans follow the fine program which their compatriot has outlined for them, they will become the most flourishing and happy nation that has ever existed."[16] Paine's pamphlet was indeed well received in France, but Deane may have exaggerated the degree of its popularity. It originally appeared in translation in a periodical devoted to furthering the American cause, *Affaires de l'Angleterre et de l'Amérique*. It was mentioned there first in May 1776 in a letter from a mythical London banker, which included scattered sections in paraphrase. In the next month, large extracts were given, interwoven with commentary. Since *Common Sense* had appeared anonymously in Philadelphia and Paine was totally unknown anywhere else in the world, the *Affaires* mentioned Dickinson, Franklin and John Adams as possible authors. A complete translation—the only one in French to appear during the American Revolution—was published in Rotterdam in 1776. It was based on an Eng-

[14] Ibid, pp. 325-26.
[15] Ibid., p. 353.
[16] Francis Wharton, ed., *Revolutionary Diplomatic Correspondence*, 6 vols. (Washington, 1889), 2: 124.

lish edition and, therefore, had blank spaces wherever the original text refers to the British monarch.

Paine did not become personally known in France until after the publication of his *Rights of Man*, which defended the French Revolution against the attacks of Burke. He took up temporary residence in Paris in the spring of 1791, where he collaborated with Condorcet in editing an incendiary journal *Le Républicain*. Another of his associates, François Xavier Lanthenas, translated *Common Sense* in this year along with *Rights of Man*. A second edition came out in the same year and a third in 1793-94. Another publisher, Buisson, the same who published the first edition of Franklin's *Mémoires*, brought out in 1793 a new translation by A. G. Griffet de la Baume, but unfortunately based upon an English edition in which the most energetic passages of the original had been replaced by asterisks. Hence it was inferior to the translation of Lanthenas, which was based on a presentation copy to Turgot in which Paine himself had filled in all the blank spaces. A fourth translation, anonymous, was brought out by a later publisher, Poulet, in 1822.[17]

Although *Common Sense* was thus more widely known in France than were the Farmer's *Letters*, Dickinson's pamphlet was reviewed by one of the most eminent representatives of the French Enlightenment, an honor not accorded to *Common Sense*, although Brissot praised Paine's *Rights of Man* in a discourse on the floor of the French Convention and Condorcet also eulogized it in print.[18] The eminent French *philosophe* who reviewed the

[17] Further details may be found in A. O. Aldridge, "The Influence of Thomas Paine in the United States, England, France, Germany and South America," in *Proceedings of the Second Congress of the International Comparative Literature Association*, ed. W. P. Friederich (Chapel Hill, N.C., 1959), 2: 369-83.

[18] *Bibliothèque de l'homme publique . . . par M. Condorcet*, Seconde Année, Tome Neuvième (Paris, 1791), p. 3n.

Farmer's *Letters* was Diderot. Before treating his review, I shall summarize the antecedents of the French translation.

Dickinson owed this distinction entirely to the influence of Benjamin Franklin, who had also been responsible for the publication of a London edition of the *Letters*. Franklin sent a copy of the English edition to one of his most ardent French disciples, a deistic physician, Dr. Jacques Barbeu Dubourg, an associate of Turgot, Mirabeau, and other physiocrats, who immediately began turning it into French. While engaged in this task in his apartment in Saint Germain de Prés, he was visited by Benjamin Rush, carrying a letter of introduction from Franklin.[19] The first question Dubourg asked was whether Rush knew the author of the *Letters*, and when he learned that Rush was indeed acquainted with Dickinson, Dubourg broke into warm praise, saying "that in his opinion the Roman Orator Cicero was less eloquent than the Pennsylvania Farmer," a remark that Dubourg subsequently included in the preface to his translation. Dubourg later introduced Rush to his physiocratic associates and arranged for him to attend the weekly gatherings of the Marquis de Mirabeau. Rush reported that at his first visit to the Marquis's salon, one of the subjects of conversation was the recent translation of the Farmer's *Letters*. "They were praised with enthusiasm by all the company." Rush was then able to answer many questions about their author. He told Dubourg that Dickinson had been called the Demosthenes of America and that in consideration of his patriotic zeal a generous ecclesiastic of Virginia, whose name he had forgotten, had made Dickinson a present of ten thousand pounds sterling. Rush was probably also re-

[19] For documentation on the relations between Rush and Dubourg see A. O. Aldridge, "Jacques Barbeu-Dubourg, a French Disciple of Benjamin Franklin," *Proceedings of the American Philosophical Society* 5 (1951): 344-47.

sponsible for the equally unreliable statement in Dubourg's preface that the *Letters* had had thirty editions in America in six months, a number larger than the combined newspaper and pamphlet printings during two years.

As soon as Dubourg's translation appeared, the physiocrats published lengthy extracts in their literary organ, *Ephémérides du citoyen, ou bibliothèque raisonnée des sciences morales et politiques*.[20] Their comments represent Dickinson's most substantial influence in France. The editors cited the writings of Franklin and Dickinson as evidence to refute the popular European theory of biological degeneration, the notion that all species—including the human—tend to deteriorate in the American climate. Noble works such as those of Franklin and Dickinson, they argued, can be developed and can flourish only among a courageous, moderate, and wise people. The editors presented a summary of each of Dickinson's twelve letters supplemented with generous extracts, but then devoted most attention to the ninth concerning the problem of taxation. In their discussion they disagreed completely with Dickinson's fundamental tenet—which he shared with English Whigs—that a free people must hold the government purse-strings in their own hands.

Other published references to Dickinson in France are few indeed. In the last decade of the century, a Swiss writer on the American Revolution, although making no mention of the Farmer's *Letters*, gave Dickinson credit for being the single voice in America that brought about the independence of the United States. Jefferson, in France when the Swiss writer's book was being reviewed, actually wrote a letter to the editor of a literary periodical protesting against this gross misinterpretation, but he never

---

[20] The extracts from Dickinson, which appeared throughout the year 1769, were translated by Dubourg.

sent the letter and, presumably, the error was never corrected.[21]

Diderot read Dubourg's translation of the Farmer's *Letters* as soon at it appeared and immediately wrote a review, which he intended for the *Correspondance littéraire*. Grimm, the editor of the *Correspondance*, mentioned Diderot's review in November 1769, but did not publish it, considering it perhaps, as Diderot's modern editors suggest, too libertarian (*éleuthéromane*). It remained in manuscript until after Diderot's death, when it was published in 1798 by his friend and associate Naigeon. In contrast to most modern historians, Diderot considered the *Letters* to be bold and outspoken. He believed that even though Dickinson was speakng to Americans, his principles were addressed to all men. Diderot was particularly impressed by the last letter, summarized in the French edition by the phrase "Assoupissement, avant-coureur de l'esclavage," a rendering of Dickinson's maxim, "SLAVERY IS EVER PRECEDED BY SLEEP." Diderot quoted two paragraphs that he found bold and inspiring and suggested that they contained the potential for a tremendous impact upon French society. In his words:

> We are allowed to read such things as this, and then people are amazed to find us at the end of a dozen years become other men. Can it be that they do not understand how easily spirits with a little generosity must imbibe these principles and be intoxicated by them? Oh, my friend, happily the tyrants are still more stupid than they are wicked; they will disappear; the lessons of great men will bear fruit, and the spirit of a nation will expand.

If Diderot was right about the boldness and inspirational potential of the Farmer's *Letters*, Dickinson's words prob-

[21] Saul K. Padover, ed., *The Complete Jefferson* (New York, 1943), p. 74.

ably had more to do than modern historians are willing to admit with preparing public opinion in America for the somewhat more inflammatory message of *Common Sense*, which appeared, in Diderot's phrase, precisely "at the end of a dozen years."

No American historians or literary critics have hitherto pointed out the significance of Diderot's comments, but there has been, nevertheless, considerable attention to the alleged vogue in France of the Farmer's *Letters*, a vogue that has been greatly exaggerated. The *Literary History of the United States*, edited by Robert E. Spiller, states that "in France . . . two editions were published" [p. 136]. The *Literature of the American People*, edited by Arthur Hobson Quinn, remarks that "In Europe the 'essays . . . became, for a time, the fashion,' 'Voltaire praised them,' 'they were talked of in the salons of Paris,' and 'the Farmer himself was likened to Cicero' " [p. 147]. I would not recommend that anyone spend much time looking for the second French edition or for praise of the *Letters* in the works of Voltaire. Both are completely fictitious. Except for Franklin, the only American author whom Voltaire is known to have commented upon is Phillis Wheatley. In a letter to Constant Rebeque, 11 April 1774, shortly after the London publication of her *Poems on Various Subjects* (1773), Voltaire affirmed: "Fontenelle was wrong in saying there could never be poets among the Negroes. There is at this time a Negress who writes very good verses in English."[22] Incidentally, a contemporary French tribute to Wheatley appeared in *De la littérature des Nègres* (Paris, 1808) by the legislator and former Bishop of Blois, Henri Grégoire. Grégoire's work, the world's first study of black literature, was later translated by D. B. Warden and published in Brooklyn in 1810 under the title *An Enquiry*

---

[22] *Complete Works of Voltaire*, ed. Theodore Besterman et al. (Geneva, Banbury, and Toronto, 1968-   ), Correspondence D. 17781.

concerning the Intellectual and Moral Faculties and Literature of Negroes. Grégoire refutes Jefferson's disparaging opinion of Wheatley, stresses her knowledge of Horace and praise her sentimental melancholy. While serving in the French Convention, Grégoire had ordered the translation of Joel Barlow's *Letter to the National Convention* (1792) and had proposed that Barlow, like Paine, be accorded the title and rights of French citizenship. After the publication of *The Columbiad*, however, he wrote a pamphlet against its anticlerical bias, which was translated as *Critical Observations on the poem of Mr. Joel Barlow* (Washington, 1809).

Responsibility for introducing Voltaire into the bibliographical history of John Dickinson may be traced to Charles J. Stillé, author of the only full-length biography of Dickinson, which was published almost a century ago. Stillé quoted a passage from George Bancroft's *History of the United States*, concluding with the statement: "Translated into French, they [the Farmer's letters] were much read in Parisian saloons [*sic*]; and their author was compared with Cicero." This comment is based entirely on Dubourg's preface to the single French edition of the letters, and in this sense it is accurate. But Dickinson's biographer engrafted upon this passage an additional sentence of his own, enclosing it within the same quotation marks which surround the previous one: "Voltaire joined the praise of the farmer of Pennsylvania and that of the Russians who aspired to liberate Greece." This sentence is embellishment, not quotation—and its only source is the author's imagination. Moses C. Tyler quoted Stillé in his famous *Literary History of the American Revolution*, and our twentieth-century literary historian quoted Tyler.

A period of over twenty years and the stirring events of the American Revolution intervened between Dickinson's Farmer's *Letters* and the first series of his *Letters of Fabius*. The latter reveal extensive and basic resemblances to Paine's *Rights of Man*. In these later essays, Dickinson abandoned his pose of a gentleman farmer alerting his neighbors to the pressing issues of the moment and in its place adopted the character of a moralist and philosopher. As such he incorporated the method of reasoning that Paine had introduced in *Common Sense* and developed in *Rights of Man*. The resemblance goes much further than similarity of method; not only are the essential principles of the *Letters of Fabius* the same as those of *Rights of Man*, but the two authors expressed themselves in language remarkable for its affinity.

Dickinson wrote two series of Fabius letters, one in 1788 advocating the adoption of the Federal Constitution and the other in 1797, defending the pro-French position of the Democrats against the anti-French attitudes of the Federalists. The first series was published originally in a Wilmington newspaper and was later combined with the second series in book form in 1797. The collected edition contains a number of footnotes, pointing out parallels between Dickinson's letters on the Constitution and Paine's *Rights of Man*. The editor, moreover, specifically draws attention to the close ideological and linguistic relationship between Paine and Dickinson. He explains that he has added

> some notes . . . of extracts from "The Rights of Man," published about three years after these Letters, containing similar sentiments, expressed with a remarkable resemblance of language, especially on the two great subjects—the *organization* of a CONSTITUTION from *original* rights, and the FORMATION of GOVERNMENT from *contributed* rights, both of so much importance in laying regular FOUNDATIONS of civil society, and consequently in securing the advancement of HUMAN HAPPINESS.

Dickinson himself almost certainly added these extracts as well as some others that are included from Joel Barlow and miscellaneous sources. But even if someone other than Dickinson may have been responsible for these editorial comments, Dickinson himself indicated his recognition of their appropriateness by allowing them to be reprinted in his *Political Writings* in 1801.

Many of the appended quotations from *Rights of Man* concern the necessity of a constitution—and it is not strange that Dickinson would use similar arguments in supporting the ratification of the document drawn up by the American Constitutional Convention. Before we may affirm that Dickinson was in the same camp with Paine, however, we need to decide exactly what each meant by the term "constitution."

Paine meant a drafted document or written code setting forth in detail the principles upon which a particular political society was to be governed. Edmund Burke, as is well known, maintained on the other hand that a constitution comprises the complex of laws, charters, and precedents that the members of the political society accept as a standard for the regulation of conduct which had grown up gradually rather than being adopted at a precise moment in history. Practically everyone in the eighteenth century admitted the value of some kind of constitution, with the notable exception of William Godwin, who regarded Paine's assertion that England possessed no constitution as an unmerited eulogium. Godwin believed that England did have a constitution, and as an opponent of government as such he felt that to say that it had not was undeserved praise.

More important than the form of a constitution is its spirit. The basic issues, as formulated by Paine and Burke, were the purposes for which a constitution exists. Is its main function to regulate those rights and privileges of individual men and classes of society, which have been acquired by tradition; or is it to protect the rights of all men, which were acquired at birth? The debate between Paine and Burke concerned precedent versus natural rights. Dickinson declared himself forthrightly with Paine on the side of natural rights against Burke and historical precedent. In a stirring passage, he proclaimed,

> Trial by jury, and the dependence of taxation upon representation, those corner stones of liberty, were not obtained by *a bill of rights* or any other RECORDS, and have not been and cannot be preserved by them. They and all other rights must be preserved, by *soundness* of *sense* and *honesty of heart*.—Compared with *these*, what are a bill of rights or any characters drawn upon PAPER or PARCHMENT, those frail remembrancers? Do we want to be reminded, that the sun enlightens, warms, invigorates, and cheers? or how horrid it would be, to have his rays intercepted by our being thrust for life, into mines or dungeons? Liberty is the sun of society. Rights are the rays.

The 1797 edition of Dickinson points out a parallel passage in *Rights of Man*—Paine's encomium of Lafayette's address to the French National Assembly. "Instead of referring to musty RECORDS and mouldy PARCHMENTS to prove that the rights of the living are lost, 'renounced, and abdicated for ever,' by those who are now no more," the French hero "applies to the living world, and says—'Call to mind the sentiments which *nature* has engraved in the heart of every citizen, and which take a new face when they are solemnly *recognized by all*. For a nation to love *liberty*, it is sufficient that she knows it; and to be free, it is sufficient that she wills it.' " A fundamental step in Paine's argument was to trace the process by which man evolved from an individual in the state of nature to a member of civil society. Dickinson went over the same process. In his words, "Each individual—

must contribute such a share of his rights, as is necessary for attaining that *security* that is essential to freedom; and he is bound to make this contribution by the law of his nature, which prompts him to *a participated happiness*; that is, by the command of his *Creator*; therefore, *he must submit his will in what concerns all, to the will of all, that is of the whole society.*" This passage is footnoted in the 1797 edition with Paine's remark that after the transformation of man from a natural individual to a member of society, "civil power, properly considered as such, is made up of the aggregate of that class of the natural rights of man, which becomes defective in the individual in point of power, and answers not his purpose, but when collected to a focus, becomes competent to the purpose of every one."

Other passages, not indicated by footnotes, reveal even closer verbal parallels. Paine distinguished between "that class of natural rights which man retains after entering into society, and those which he throws into the common stock as a member of society." Dickinson remarks that "in forming a political society, each individual contributes some of his rights, in order that he may, from a *common stock* of rights, derive *greater benefits*, than he would from merely his own." In supporting the Constitution, Dickinson compared the federated states to individual men forming a society. Constantly Dickinson emphasized the individual. "A confederation is but an assemblage of *individuals*. The auspicious influence of that *law* of his nature, upon which the happiness of MAN depends in society, must attend him in confederation, or he becomes unhappy; for confederation should promote the happiness of *individuals*, or it does not *answer the intended purpose.*" The footnote refers us to Paine's observation that "*individuals, themselves,* each in his own personal and sovereign right, *entered into a compact with each other* to produce a government: and this is the only mode in which governments have a right to arise, and the only principle on which they have a right to exist."

In this letter, Dickinson quotes a verse from the Old Testament which he had formerly used to good effect in the Farmer's *Letters*. When the individual realizes that his own happiness comes through submitting himself to the will of the whole society, he gains a perfect repose. Figuratively this state exists "When every man shall sit under his vine, and under his fig tree, and none shall make him afraid." In the Farmer's letters Dickinson had emphasized a somewhat different sentiment [Letter V]. Man could sit in repose under his fig tree when assured of the rights inherent in the relationship of the mother country to the colonies, particularly that great one, "the foundation of all the rest—that their property acquired with so much pain and hazard, should be disposed of by none but themselves." Paine in his last *Crisis* was much less materialistic. He depicted America "Descending to the scenes of quiet and domestic life . . . to enjoy in her own land, and under her own vine, the sweet of her labors."

In his Fabius letters Dickinson stressed the necessity of tracing every social right to its ultimate source as a natural right. Even citizenship in the federal union could be so traced.

> As MAN, he becomes a *citizen*; as a citizen, he becomes a *federalist*. The generation of one, *is not the destruction* of the other. He *carries* into society the naked rights received from nature. *These* thereby improved, he *carries* still forward into confederation. If that sacred law before mentioned, is not here observed, the confederation would not be *real*, but *pretended*. He would confide, and be deceived.

This principle is supported in the footnotes by three separate passages from Paine. The first is a famous denunciation of "the error of those who reason by precedent, drawn from antiquity, respecting the rights of man." They "do not go far enough into antiquity. They do not go the whole way. They stop in some of the intermediate stages of an hundred or a thousand years." In showing how civil rights originated from natural rights, Paine declared that "Man did not enter into society to become worse than he was before, nor to have fewer rights than he had before, but to have those rights better secured. His natural rights are the foundation of all his civil rights."

Dickinson in his fourth letter turned to the subject of the relationship of a constitution to civil rights. This is the most fundamental point in Paine's debate with Burke. Dickinson declared that a constitution possesses its grave and sacred character because it is a rational creation of man, designed to preserve his natural and civil rights. According to Dickinson,

A *constitution* is the *organization of the contributed rights* in society. GOVERNMENT is the EXERCISE of them. It is intended for the benefit of *the governed*; of course [it] can have no just powers but what conduce to *that end*; and the awfulness of the *trust* is demonstrated in this—that it is founded on the nature of man, that is, on the will of his MAKER, and is *therefore* sacred. It is then an offence against heaven, to violate that *trust*.

The footnotes cite Paine's insistence that

A constitution is not a thing in name only, but in fact. It has not an ideal, but a real existence; and wherever it cannot be produced in a visible form, there is none. A constitution is a thing ANTECEDENT to a government, and a government is only the creature of a constitution. The constitution of a country is not the act of its government, but of the people constituting a government.

In principle, if not in language, Dickinson's *Letters of Fabius* were just as revolutionary as Paine's *Rights of Man*. Paine is famous in history for advocating revolution in America, England, and France. Dickinson, by placing final authority in the people, recognized the right of revolution as firmly and openly as ever Paine did. If the organization of a constitution were defective, he argued, it could be amended. "A good constitution promotes, but not always produces a good administration." But in the event that despite everything, a bad administration should come into control, Dickinson's answer was unequivocal: "Let the *fasces* be *lowered* before—the *supreme sovereignty* of the people. It *is their duty to watch, and their right to take care, that the constitution be preserved*; or in the Roman phrase on perilous occasions—*to provide, that the republic receive no damage*." This is buttressed in the notes by a quotation from Locke as well as one from the second part of *Rights of Man*. According to Paine, when the controlling power is vested in a constitution, "it has the nation for its support, and the natural and controlling powers are together. The laws which are enacted by governments, control men only as individuals, but the nation, through its constitution, controls the whole government, and has a natural ability so to do. The final controlling power, therefore, and the original constituting power, are one and the same power."

In addition to these similarities in ideas, the language of Paine and Dickinson reveals a strong resemblance in treating the subject of the origin of political union. Both speak of it as a natural process of cohesion and both use the somewhat unusual verb (in this sense) "to condense." In speaking of the coming into being of modern republics, Dickinson remarked that

> their institutions consist of old errors tissued with hasty inventions, somewhat excusable, as the will of the Ro-

mans, made with arms in their hands. Some of them were *condensed*, by dangers. They are still compressed by them into a sort of union. Their well-known transactions witness, that *their connection is not enough compact and arranged*. They have all suffered, or *are suffering* through *that defect*. Their existence seems to depend more upon others, than upon themselves.

Paine used the same imagery: "If we consider what the principles are that first *condense* man into society, and what the motive is that regulates their mutual intercourse afterward, we shall find, by the time we arrive at what is called government, that nearly the whole of the business is performed by the natural operation of the parts upon each other."[23]

Previous writers on Dickinson, assuming that the first series of Fabius letters represents a conservative Federalist point of view, have been at a loss to understand Dickinson's presumed conversion to Jeffersonian liberalism in the second series written in 1797. One cannot doubt that when the Constitution was presented for ratification, Dickinson was indeed a pronounced Federalist. But he was a Federalist in Paine's sense of one who believed in "cementing the Union by a general government operating equally over all the States, in all matters that embraced the common interest." In this sense, Paine declared that he himself "ought to stand first on the list of Federalists." Even though frontier farmers in western Pennsylvania condemned the Constitution and its advocates as "the pillars of slavery, tyranny and despotism," other citizens of the state such as Paine, equally concerned for the wel-

[23] Even though Dickinson's first series of letters was originally printed before *Rights of Man*, the publishing of parallel passages in 1797 was not intended to suggest that Paine had written in any way under the influence of Dickinson. Paine left for France in April 1787, and there is little likelihood that Dickinson's letters, written in the following year, were known anywhere in Europe.

fare of the common man, saw the necessity of the Constitution and campaigned energetically in its behalf. Dickinson and Paine based their support of the Constitution
on identical grounds. There is no contradiction, therefore,
between Dickinson supporting the principles of federalism in 1788 and enlisting himself nine years later among
the proponents of Jeffersonian philosophy. The parallels
with the *Rights of Man* in the first series of Fabius letters
show that Dickinson did not go through a drastic conversion between 1788 and 1797. Indeed, there was little
change in his essential political philosophy ever since the
publication of his *Letters from a Pennsylvania Farmer* in
1767-68. Paine and Dickinson, therefore, were philosophical allies and joint campaigners for the humanitarian ideals of the Enlightenment.

SIX

THE CONCEPT OF ANCIENTS AND MODERNS IN AMERICAN POETRY OF THE FEDERAL PERIOD

ORDINARILY the expression Augustan Age when applied to the modern world comprises English literature during the first half of the eighteenth century, but an essayist under the name of the Meddler in a Connecticut newspaper of 1791 remarked that "the Augustan age bears greater resemblance to the present, than to any intermediate period."[1] In reference to what is now called the Federal period of American literature, the Meddler observed, "Under a similarity of circumstances, America has at length become the seat of science, and the great mirror of freedom and politics. Her Attica has produced a Homer, who leads the way; a Virgil, who was the pupil of that great master, and a Horace, who resides at the seat of Augustus."[2] The American Homer here referred to is Timothy Dwight, author of a Biblical epic *The Conquest of Canaan* (1785); the American Virgil is Joel Barlow, author of a patriotic epic, *The Vision of Columbus* (1787); and the American Horace is Philip Freneau, author

---

[1] The English background is fully explored by James William Johnson, "The Meaning of 'Augustan,'" *Journal of the History of Ideas* 19 (1958): 507-22. Charles Perrault in 1687 drew the parallel with France in the seventeenth century in a poem "Le Siècle de Louis-le-Grand."

Et l'on peut comparer, sans crainte d'être injuste,
Le siècle de Louis au beau siècle d'Auguste.

[2] *New Haven Gazette* (26 January 1791).

of miscellaneous lyrics and satires.³ These three are generally considered to be the outstanding poets of the Federal period, a roster completed with the addition of two other New England names, David Humphreys and Robert Treat Paine.

A similar description of American letters in terms of the ancients appeared in a Massachusetts poem of 1789 entitled *Anticipation of the Literary Fame of America.* The anonymous author predicted the rising in the near future of "Columbian *Livies*," "countless *Cicero's*," "another Plato," "another Stagyrite," "some new Euripides," "some future *Virgil*," and "some modern Ovid." As a consequence of this emergence of counterparts of Greek and Latin authors, the anonymous poet forecast that

> The brilliant treasure of the Attick mine,
> Shall glow refulgent in our western clime.⁴

Although Dwight, Barlow, and Freneau were the outstanding American poets of their time, they are read today less for esthetic pleasure than for the ideological and social riches they contain. Their relative lack of emotional and esthetic appeal has been attributed in large measure to the tradition of classical rhetoric to which they belong. According to one modern critic, they tended in practice to obscure the dichotomy in the adage "Poeta nascitur, orator fit," and classical forms and figures became their stock in trade. One is hard put to decide today, therefore, "whether the works of such men as Robert Treat Paine are more properly described as declamatory poems or poetic orations."⁵ Other critics have charged that most of

---

³ *Rising Glory of America* (1772), had made the same connection between American literature and the ancients, "I see a Homer and a Milton rise."

⁴ *Massachusetts Magazine* 1 (February 1789): 117-18.

⁵ Gordon E. Bigelow, *Rhetoric and American Poetry of the Early National Period*, University of Florida Monographs, Humanities No. 4, 1960, Gainesville, Fla., p. 28.

the American poets of the Federal period slavishly imitated the neoclassical rhetoric of Pope and the Augustan
English poets. Sometimes the classical and the neoclassical traditions are indistinguishable in their work, as are
the images and symbols associated with one or the other
style. Frequently a reference to a neoclassical author could
be substituted for a classical one without changing the
fundamental meaning. An example is the following line
from a lyric by Freneau.

> To such wild scenes as Plato lov'd.

In a later version of the poem, Freneau simply inserted
Shenstone for Plato.

It is not my purpose, however, to discuss the quality of
Federal poetry or to affirm or deny the thesis that either
classical or neoclassical rhetoric is responsible for its alleged deficiencies. I intend rather to investigate the literary traditions affirmed by these poets and to attempt to
ascertain whether their outward subservience to classical
models was accompanied by the kind of ideological commitment to the ancient world which is associated with
the Augustan Age of English literature at the beginning
of the eighteenth century. A definite pattern may be discerned among these poets, consisting of superficial discipleship combined with fundamental rejection. They imitated the style of the ancients and conformed to
Aristotelian notions of genre, but repudiated many of the
intellectual traditions associated with antiquity. This is
the first principle that I hope to establish. The second is
that the verse and critical writings of these poets contain
close parallels with concepts in the European quarrel between the ancients and moderns.

The formal stage of this famous polemic belongs to the
seventeenth and eighteenth centuries and concerns French
literature primarily, but the attempt to decide the relative
merits of the intellectual achievements of the ancient

world and those of later ages goes back at least as far as the Renaissance. The question is one part of the idea of progress, and treatments of it exist in all Western European literatures. A parallel to one of the esthetic aspects of the question—consideration of the degree to which literary works should conform to critical standards of the past—has even been shown to exist in the thought of ancient China.

American writers in the Federal period, in common with almost all authors in Western culture after the Renaissance, drew upon both a generally accepted literary tradition from the past and a less orthodox but nonetheless familiar body of writings from their own century. Insofar as America is concerned, these connections may be represented graphically by horizontal and vertical lines, the horizontal one going back to the Greek and Latin classics, and the vertical extending across the Atlantic to the European continent. Nobody doubts the influence in eighteenth-century America of the social theories of Montesquieu, the sentimental psychology of Richardson, or the poetic structure of Pope. It seems logical to assume that many of the issues in the quarrel of the ancients and moderns should also be debated in the New World even though the French treatises of La Motte, Fontenelle, and Perrault may not have been available in American libraries. It is true that none of the poets I mention refers to the ancients-moderns quarrel as such or cites its main protagonists, but the relevant passages in the works of such English combatants as Sir William Temple, Jonathan Swift, Joseph Addison, and Oliver Goldsmith were probably as well known to the American literati of the eighteenth century as they are today.

A striking illustration may be found in the critical theories of the so-called American Homer, Timothy Dwight, and the American Virgil, Joel Barlow. Both wrote prose essays attempting to dislodge Homer from his pedestal and using arguments strongly resembling those of the moderns in the French phase of the quarrel of the ancients and moderns. Dwight in a *Dissertation on the History, Eloquence, and Poetry of the Bible* (1772), published thirteen years before his *The Conquest of Canaan*, argued that the beauties of the Bible are at least equal to those of the greatest classical writers and in many passages greatly superior to them. After observing that Homer has been praised for giving life to every object which he attempts to describe, Dwight maintains that he is excelled by the Old and New Testaments. There, according to Dwight, "objects are not barely endued with life; they breathe, they think, they speak, love, hate, fear, adore, & exercise all the most extraordinary emotions of rational beings. *Homer* or *Virgil* can make the mountains tremble, or the sea shake, at the appearance of a God; in the *Bible* the mountains melt like wax, or flee away; the Deep utters his voice, and lifts up his hands on high, at the presence of the LORD of the whole earth" [p. 5].

Admitting that the Scriptures would be found wanting were they to be judged by the rules associated with classical criticism, Dwight had no hesitation in disparaging these rules. Confronting an imaginary critic, Dwight replied: "When you can convince me that *Homer* and *Virgil* . . . were sent into the world to give Laws to all other authors; when you can convince me that every beauty of fine writing is to be found, in its highest perfection, in their works, I will allow the beauties of the divine writers to be faults. 'Till that can be demonstrated, I must continue to admire the most shining instances of Genius, unparallel'd in force, or sublimity" [p. 5]. Sentiments such as this explain why Dwight selected as the subject matter of his own epic, not a secular theme such as Camoëns and Voltaire had exploited, but one based on the Old Testament account of the gory victory of Joshua over the Canaanites. In the structure of his poem, Dwight prided himself on giving unity to the entire action, but in doing so he grossly garbled the facts of his historical source. He tended as a consequence "to dilute, to render garrulous, and to cheapen, the noble reticence, the graphic simplicity, of the antique chronicle"—the model that he had taken pains to exalt above the Greek and Roman epics precisely because of its noble sublimity of style.[6] But we are not concerned with esthetic achievement, but with ideas, the reasons for Dwight's choosing biblical subject matter over pagan and historical themes. He was following not only the example of Milton, but also the arguments of a French champion of the moderns, Desmarets de Saint-Sorlin, in a prose *Discourse to Prove that Only Christian Subjects are Appropriate to Heroic Poetry* (1673). [*Discours pour prouver que les sujets chrétiens sont seuls propres à la poésie héroïque*].

Joel Barlow also adopted the form of the classical epic while rejecting the authority of Homer and Virgil, but his objections to the ancient poets were based not on subject matter, but on political ideology. Barlow published his *Vision of Columbus* in 1787 and twenty years later brought out a revised and greatly expanded version under the more Virgilian title of *The Columbiad*. In the preface to the latter, Barlow drew a distinction between the poetical object of an epic and its moral object, the first representing the fictitious design of the action; the latter, the real design or ideological purpose. Since the poetical object of the *Iliad*, which is to portray the anger of Achilles, excites a high degree of interest, it is extremely important, according to Barlow, that the real design should be beneficial to society. In reality, however, the real design has just the reverse effect. "Its obvious tendency was to inflame the minds of young readers with an enthusiastic ardor for

---

[6] Moses Coit Tyler, *Three Men of Letters* (1895), quoted in *Major Poems of Timothy Dwight*, ed. William J. McTaggart and William K. Bottorff (Gainesville, Fla., 1969), p. vii.

military fame; to inculcate the pernicious doctrine of the divine right of kings; to teach both prince and people that military plunder was the most honorable mode of acquiring property; and that conquest, violence and war were the best employment of nations, the most glorious prerogative of bodily strength and of cultivated mind" [p. ix]. Barlow found the moral tendency of the *Aeneid* to be "nearly as pernicious." Virgil's real design, in Barlow's opinion, "was to increase the veneration of the people for a master, whoever he might be, and to encourage like Homer the great system of military depredation" [p. x]. The only ancient epic poet whom Barlow would accept as a republican was Lucan. The ancients in general, and the Greeks in particular, were widely appealed to throughout the eighteenth century in both Europe and America as noble examples of republican virtues. The Whig historian Catherine Macaulay, for example, attributed her liberal political philosophy to the spirit of liberty in classical literature. It is somewhat unusual to see an American poet condemning both Homer and Virgil for inculcating political sentiments which allegedly enforce subjection and constraint. In judging the ancients by modern moral and sociological standards, Barlow was following the practice of the *Discourse on Homer* [*Discours sur Homère* (1714)] of abbé La Motte, who, as a leading exponent of the moderns, insisted that criticism had the right to condemn the barbarous conditions portrayed in the *Iliad*.

One of the subsidiary questions discussed in the quarrel of ancients and moderns was that of the comparative beauty of the classical and modern languages and their relative fitness for poetry. On this question, Barlow affirmed that when writing *The Vision of Columbus* he had labored under "the error of supposing that the ancients had a poetical advantage over us in respect to the dignity of the names of the weapons used in war," but that he became convinced that the advantage is actually on the side of the moderns. "There are better sounding names and more variety in the instruments, works, strategems and other artifices employed in our war system than in theirs. In short, the modern military dictionary is more copious than the ancient, and the words at least as poetical" [p. xv]. The circumstances of battle in ancient times, Barlow admitted, gave the ancients an advantage in the description of single combats, but in "a general engagement, the shock of modern armies is, beyond comparison, more magnificent, more sonorous and more discoloring to the face of nature, than the ancient could have been; it is consequently susceptible of more pomp and variety of description" [p. xvi].

In keeping with his dichotomy of the narrative design and the real design of an epic, Barlow indicated that the superficial object of *The Columbiad* was to survey the labors and achievements of Columbus and to portray him as "the author of the greatest benefits to the human race" [p. xii]. The real object of the poem, however, was "to inculcate the love of rational liberty," to "discountenance the deleterious passion for violence and war," to show that all good morals as well as all good government must be founded on republican principles, and to persuade that "the theoretical question of the future advancement of human society" remains unsettled only because of the lack of experience of organized liberty in the government of nations [p. xii]. In other words, *The Columbiad* was designed to teach the doctrine of progress, an essential notion of the moderns. In his notes to the poem, Barlow particularly rejected the notion of a Golden Age "or the idea that men were more perfect, more moral and more happy in some early stage of their intercourse," as well as the related doctrine that the world has been perpetually degenerating or growing worse [no. 50]. Both doctrines were widely used by the ancients in their quarrel with the moderns. In another note connected with the controversy, Barlow admits that the ancients may perhaps claim to be unrivalled in some of the arts which depend upon the imagination, those such as architecture, statuary, painting, eloquence, and poetry, but he points out that these are not the arts which "tend the most to the general improvement of society" [no. 47]. In particular reference to Homer, Barlow repeated the accusation of his preface that the *Iliad* was filled with the pernicious doctrine of the divine right of kings [no. 42].

Even stronger evidence of Barlow's adherence to the moderns may be found in his earlier *Vision of Columbus* (1787), but this evidence requires interpretation. Barlow followed as one of the models for this poem a modern rather than a classical epic—a sixteenth-century work in Spanish, *La Araucana* by Alonso de Ercilla—and he did so because of reading a description of it in an essay by Voltaire, the author of another modern epic, *La Henriade*. In order to prepare advance publicity for a London edition of *La Henriade*, Voltaire published in English an essay, *Epick Poetry of the European Nations from Homer down to Milton* (1727), a pioneer treatment of the study of literary genres. Barlow explained in the notes to his *Vision* that it was entirely due to Voltaire's essay (probably in a later French version) that his mind had been opened to "a new field of Poetry, rich with uncommon elements." In treating the preliminary section of *La Araucana*, a description of the geography, manners, and customs of Chile, Voltaire had argued that the strangeness of the American continent to European readers made the introduction of this type of material necessary, although otherwise it would have been quite out of place. This justification inspired Barlow to include geographical and sociological passages in his own epic, as well as a treatment of South America and its native population. In his notes Barlow also complained bitterly about not being able to procure a copy of either *La Araucana* or the parallel Portuguese epic, *Os Lusiadas* by Luis de Camoëns, considering the lack of materials one of the "disadvantages that an Author, in a new country, and in moderate circumstances, must have to encounter."

Besides its indebtedness to Voltaire and Ercilla, *The Vision of Columbus* is important internationally because of a dedication to Louis XVI of France, who returned the compliment by subscribing for twenty-five copies.

In a sense, Voltaire, in acquainting Barlow with Ercilla and Camoëns, was posthumously repaying a debt to Anglo-Saxon letters. The English poet William Collins told Joseph Warton that the former's uncle, Col. Martin Bladen, "had given to Voltaire, all that account of Camoëns inserted in his essay on the Epic Poets of all Nations, and that Voltaire seemed before entirely ignorant of the name and character of Camoëns" [*Works of Alexander Pope*, ed. W. L. Bowles, 10 vols. (London, 1806), 5: 322]. Nothing is known about Voltaire's first acquaintance with Ercilla, but it may equally have been through the agency of Colonel Bladen, who had served as an officer in Spain.

On the surface there seems to be a close relationship, ideological if not historical, between the doctrine of progress and the poetic themes of *translatio studii* and *translatio empirii*, which flourished in classical times and in the Middle Ages and have been widely recognized by scholars of early American literature. The most famous English version is, of course, Bishop George Berkeley's "Verses on the Prospect of Planting Arts and Learning in America," written in 1726, but not published until 1752. Joining *translatio studii* with the imagery of the stage and the theological doctrine of the millennium, he predicted that the fifth act of the human drama would take place in the West and affirmed that "Time's noblest offspring is the last." Later in the century the theme of *translatio studii* was joined to that of the rising glory of America, but it flourished in the colonies long before either the Revolution or the publication of Berkeley's verses. A single example will suffice, one taken from a Pennsylvania almanac of 1729 and reprinted in the *Gentleman's Magazine*.

> Rome shall lament her ancient Fame declin'd
> And Philadelphia be the Athens of mankind.[7]

Other examples from the Federal period are given in a later chapter on nationalistic fervor.

Superficially it would appear that the *translatio* theme represents evidence of the dedication of early American literature to its classical heritage, but analysis reveals that classical antecedents are consistently portrayed as inferior to contemporary manifestations. The *translatio* theme is one aspect of the idea of progress and as such weighs on the side of the moderns rather than the ancients. In other words, whatever salutary concept is considered as originating in Greece and Rome, it is always improved or brought to perfection in the West. Indeed, if the theme were carried to the extreme, future development could be envisaged as even transcending the European settlements of America. The same author who compared Dwight, Barlow and Freneau to their classical counterparts reminded his readers that the descendants of the barbarians who had overturned the Roman Empire had become the modern cherishers of the arts and sciences. The Americans, he observed, are the posterity of "those whom the Romans once held in as little esteem, as that in which we at present hold the [Indian] nations of the West." While considering the likelihood extremely remote, he nevertheless expressed the possibility that America, like the Roman Empire, might in the future "be again re-peopled and governed by her

---

[7] J. A. Leo Lemay, *A Calendar of American Poetry* (Worcester, Mass., 1972), p. 162.

native inhabitants" [Meddler no. II]. The only aspect of the *translatio* theme which may be effectively counted as a tribute to the ancients is that which treats political liberty as their contribution to civilization. There existed another widespread notion throughout the Enlightenment that liberty, as manifested in European thought, had not emerged from the Greeks at all, but had developed instead from the nations of northern Europe.[8] Any motif, such as *translatio*, that would restore liberty to the ancients could in this sense legitimately be considered as supporting the prestige of the Greeks and Romans. A pseudonymous poem in the *Pennsylvania Gazette*, 30 May 1778, neatly resolved the question by assuming an autochthonous origin.

> Even Liberty herself from Heaven shall come,
> And fair America shall rival Rome.

One of the most extreme statements against the Old World came from the pen of the lexicographer Noah Webster, who instead of treating *translatio studii* in the conventional sense, suggested in the preface to his *Spelling Book* (1783) that it would be better to reject everything from the past and make a completely new beginning. In his words, "Europe is grown old in folly, corruption and tyranny—in that country laws are perverted, manners are licentious, literature is declining and human nature debased. For America in her infancy to adopt the present maxims of the Old World, would be to stamp the wrinkles of decrepit age upon the bloom of youth and to plant the seeds of decay in a vigorous constitution."[9] In a sense,

---

[8] The concept of the superiority of northern or Germanic culture to that of the Mediterranean is treated from different perspectives in two excellent surveys: Thor J. Beck, *Northern Antiquities in French Learning and Literature (1755-1855)*, 2 vols. (New York, 1934-1935); J.G.A. Pocock, *The Ancient Constitution and the Feudal Law* (New York, 1967).

[9] Harry R. Warfel, *Noah Webster, Schoolmaster to America* (New York, 1936), pp. 59-60.

this repudiation of the past is a logical extension of Paine's metaphor in *Common Sense* that "youth is the seed time of good habits, as well as in nations as in individuals" and his amazing statement "we have it in our power to begin the world over again."[10]

In addition to abstract notions such as liberty and freedom, the idea of progress incorporated scientific discoveries and the material advances of civilization such as mechanical inventions. The printing press symbolized the combination of enlightenment and technology. As such, it represented one of the milestones in human advancement. The theme was introduced into America thirty years before the Federal period, specifically by James Sterling in a poem dedicated to Samuel Richardson, author of *Pamela*, entitled "On the Invention of Letters and the Art of Printing" (1757). The poem particularly describes the triumph in philosophical thought of the moderns over the ancients as well as the progress in science and technology, symbolized by the printing press. The same theme was developed in 1795 by Robert Treat Paine in a poem with an almost identical title, *The Invention of Letters*. The work, like Sterling's, does not concern polite or belles lettres, but the process of printing, without which, according to Paine, scarcely any scientific discoveries or political reforms would have been possible. That Paine should have written on such a theme is remarkable since he was probably the most dedicated to classical traditions of all American poets of the time. Paine was so gifted that when he was assigned a Greek oration at Harvard, instead of following the general practice of reciting a passage from Demosthenes, Isocrates, or Plutarch, he "chose to write his own in Greek, without first preparing in English."[11]

[10] *Complete Writings of Thomas Paine*, ed. Philip S. Foner, 2 vols. (New York, 1945), 1: 36, 45.

[11] *Works in Verse and Prose of the Late Robert Treat Paine* (Boston, 1812), pp. xix-xx.

Despite his dedication to classical civilization, he clearly espoused in *The Invention of Letters* the side of the moderns in the polemic between the two factions.

No more presume with bigot zeal to raise,
O'er modern worth, the palm of ancient days.
No more let Athens to the world proclaim,
Her classick phalanx holds the field of fame.

[p. 164]

In subsequent lines, Paine elevated Gutenberg to a position of universal eminence.

The barbarous Rhine now blends its classick name,
With Rome's, Phoenicia's, and Achaia's fame.

[p. 165]

The major writers in the French Enlightenment tended to recognize the preeminence of the ancients in the realm of eloquence, but otherwise considered the moderns superior. Following this tradition, David Humphreys in the "Advertisement" to a *Poem on the Death of General Washington* (1800), reflects the tendency to grant to the ancients superiority in the area of rhetoric, even though he leaves the question open without settling it unequivocally. "It is not intended to be decided here," he observes, "that the Greek and Latin poets possess no advantage over the moderns in the copiousness or melody of their languages; or that poesy in those languages does not admit of more boldness in the figures, pomp in the diction, music in the cadences, variety in the numbers, or greater facility for imitative beauty in making the sound an echo to the sense, than in most of the languages." Instead of asserting the supremacy of the moderns in such areas as science or the plastic arts, however, he turns to the examples of illustrious men and finds more inspiring ones in America, the most sublime of whom is, of course, George Washington.

In a shorter poem "On the Love of Country," Humphreys even impugns the patriotism which had throughout the century been accorded to the Romans as one of their outstanding virtues.

> Perish the Roman pride a world that braves,
> To make for one free state all nations slaves;
> Their boasted patriotism at once exprest,
> Love for themselves and hate for all the rest.

Exactly the same disparaging description of classical patriotism appears in Barlow's *Columbiad*.

> Where Grecian states in even balance hung
> And warm'd with jealous fires the patriot's tongue,
> The exclusive ardor cherisht in the breast
> Love to one land and hatred to the rest.
> And where the flames of civil discord rage,
> And Roman arms with Roman arms engage,
> The mime of virtues rises still the same
> To build a Caesar's as a Pompey's name.
>
> [Book X, l. 321-28]

So far as I know, this argument appeared first in Thomas Paine's *American Crisis* no. V (1778). "The Grecians and Romans were strongly possessed of the *spirit* of liberty," Paine remarked, "but *not the principle*, for at the time that they were determined not to be slaves themselves, they employed their power to enslave the rest of mankind."

Madison in *The Federalist* [no. 14] similarly considered it to the glory of the American people that "whilst they have paid a decent regard to the opinions of former times and other nations, they have not suffered a blind veneration for antiquity, for custom, or for names, to overrule the suggestions of their own good sense." Hamilton in the ninth *Federalist* reacted with "horror and disgust" to "the history of the petty republics of Greece and Italy" because of the "distractions with which they were continually agitated" and "the rapid succession of revolutions, by which they were kept perpetually vibrating."

The pattern of superficial obeisance to the classic tradition combined with a rejection of it ideologically is highlighted in an anonymous biblical poem in the *New Haven Gazette* (21 September 1786) entitled "The Trial of Faith." The poem itself does not concern us, but its epigraph from Virgil reveals the paradoxical ambivalence toward the classics which we have been discussing.

Sicelides Musae, paulo majora canamus!

The paraphrase of this line supplied by the author announces that "American Muses aim at higher subjects than those commonly sung in the Eastern continent."

A similar ambivalence is shown by Philip Freneau in regard to the value of studying the classical languages. He was trained at Princeton in both Latin and Greek, filled his poems with classical allusions, wrote an imitation of Horace, and embellished his works with quotations from Virgil, second in number only to those from Shakespeare. At the commencement exercises, 25 September 1771, when Freneau himself was graduated, there was featured on the program "An English forensic dispute on this question, 'Does ancient poetry excel the modern?'" Freneau had been chosen as affirmative "respondent," but was absent from the ceremonies. His remarks were read by another student and answered by a second, who was in turn refuted by a third.

Despite this academic flourish, Freneau later unequivocally disparaged the role of ancient languages in the educational system. In a poem entitled "Expedition of Timothy Taurus, Astrologer" (1775?), he affirms:

This age may decay, and another may rise,
Before it is fully revealed to our eyes,

ANCIENTS AND MODERNS

> That Latin and Hebrew, Chaldaic, and Greek,
> To the shades of oblivion must certainly sneak;
> Too much of our time is employed on such trash
> When we ought to be taught to accumulate cash.

Although these lines are intended to be humorous, they are not meant ironically. Freneau expresses an even stronger antagonism in another of his poems, "Epistle to a Student of Dead Languages."[12]

In France, the relative merits of the classical and modern languages had been treated as part of the battle of ancients and moderns. As early as 1683, for example, François Charpentier published his treatise *On the Excellence of the French Language*, making among other points the practical one that French rather than Latin should be used for inscriptions on public monuments. An essayist in the *New Haven Gazette* (DECIUS, 2 and 16 March 1791) applied the controversy to the subjects of study at Yale University. In his opinion, the traditional curriculum was outmoded in Europe, but still entrenched in America and, therefore, all the more absurd in a new environment. His main point was not that the classical languages were objectionable in themselves, but that the candidate was required to spend two years "in getting a useless smattering of latin and greek" at the end of which he could not even translate a single page of a single book. This author considered Latin and French "desirable, and even necessary," but he felt that knowledge of our own language and literature was indispensable. The worst abuse of the system was the teaching of New Testament Greek by rote. In his

---

[12] See also his prose essay *Pilgrim* no. XII in *The Freeman's Journal*, 13 February 1782, reprinted in *The Prose of Philip Freneau*, ed. Philip M. Marsh (New Brunswick, N.J., 1955), pp. 55-58. Freneau, in politics a radical and in religion a deist, thought that Dwight's epic was ridiculous and superstitious and condemned it for giving the preference of "the dreams and nonsense of antiquity" to "modern rationality" (*Prose*, ed. Marsh, p. 265).

words, "The time for education is short. From twelve years of age to twenty-one, is a period of nine years, and two of these should be employed, by almost every one, in obtaining professional knowledge.—Seven remain. If part of these must be spent in acquiring words, the English and French, are decidedly, the most learned ever spoken by man; nor can I make exception, even of the *Hebrew* or *Mohegan*."

In treating essays in the *New Haven Gazette*, we have digressed from the poets of the time, but the newspaper background is relevant as exposing the climate of opinion in which these poets developed. The sentiments expressed by the *Gazette* essayist are mild, moreover, compared with those previously set forth in satirical verse by John Trumbull in *The Progress of Dulness* (1772). The latter affirms that half of classical learning merely displays the follies of former days and denies that knowledge must be conveyed to the brain in "ancient strains." At the same time he calls for criticism to accord to "ancient arts" their "real due" and "explain their faults, and beauties too." Another essay in the *New Haven Gazette*, one in the same issue with the criticism of the Yale curriculum, contrasts ancient learning with the doctrine of progress in the precise terms in which the debate had been carried on in Europe [Meddler no. VIII, 16 March 1791]. According to the essayist, "The sophistical reasoning of the ancient schools, served only to lead the minds of men into continued mazes of error and absurdity. . . . The improvements made in the arts and sciences, in the course of the last century, have been more rapid than they ever were at any former period; and if we were to reason from analogy, we should conclude that future improvements will be in an inverse ratio, with the time at which they are distant. . . . The moderns have a manifest superiority over the ancients, in most of the arts and sciences."

The particular American cachet which is placed upon

this essay is a reference to developments in political theory, a consciousness of which grew out of the pamphleteering in the American Revolution. The essayist proceeds imperceptibly from the Baconian theme of the deficiencies of Aristotelian philosophy to the millennial one of international harmony which concludes many of the poems of the Federal period, including Dwight's "America: or, a Poem on the Settlement of the British Colonies" (1780) and Barlow's *The Columbiad*.[13] The essayist concludes, "We are so far enlightened in the present age, as to discard most of the fictions of the ancient schools and render the unknown abstrata [*sic*] by which Aristotle and his followers solved the knotty points of philosophy, into a mere object of ridicule. Should our successors continue to make improvements upon our knowledge, as we have upon that of our *predecessors*, they will become so thoroughly acquainted with the true nature and principles of government, as to form institutions of society, which will promote the internal prosperity of nations, and by shewing the blessings of peace, bring on a universal harmony among the different nations of the earth."

The last sentence could almost serve as a paraphrase of the concluding book of *The Columbiad*, which portrays the future progress of society in all areas including government and reveals, in the words of the "Argument," a "general Congress from all nations assembled to establish the political harmony of mankind." Thomas Paine in *Rights of Man* even used the political argument to support one of the earliest positions of the moderns in the European phase of the ancients-moderns debate, Bacon's paradox

---

[13] The following couplets illustrate the theme in Dwight:
EUROPE and ASIA with surprize behold
Thy temples starr'd with gems and roof'd with gold.
. . .

No more on earth shall Rage and Discord dwell,
But sink with Envy to their native hell.

Antiquitas saeculi juventus mundi, "ancient times are the youth of the world." According to Paine, the only value in studying governments in ancient times is "to make a proper use of the errors or the improvements which the history of it presents. Those who lived a hundred or a thousand years ago, were then moderns as we are now."[14] Paine in an earlier essay also touches on the millennial theme and joins it with disparagement of the ancients for their vanity and ignorance. "Improvement and the world will expire together," he remarks. "And till that period arrives, we may plunder the mine, but can never exhaust it! That *'We have found out everything,'* has been the motto of every age. Let our ideas travel a little into antiquity, and we shall find larger portions of it than now; and so unwilling were our ancestors to descend from this mountain of perfection, that when any new discovery exceeded the common standard, the discoverer was believed to be in alliance with the devil" [*Writings,* 2: 1111].

One cannot solely on the evidence of the foregoing passages maintain that the European quarrel of the ancients and the moderns extended itself in a kind of *translatio studii* to the Western world, but there can be no doubt, on the other hand, that many of the same principles of that debate were seriously discussed in the Anglophone areas of America throughout the second half of the eighteenth century. Certainly the debate reached university circles in America, for John Witherspoon of Princeton in an essay "Of Eloquence" summarized the European background of the "controversy . . . upon the preference being due to ancient or modern writers." Although taking an eclectic position by recognizing good in both camps, Witherspoon seemed to join Dwight and Barlow in feeling that Homer had been overpraised. "Now the beauties of Homer we are easily capable of perceiving," he wrote, "though

[14] *Complete Writings,* ed. Foner, 1: 273.

perhaps not his faults. The beauty of a description, the force of a similitude, we can plainly see; but whether he always adhered to truth and nature, we cannot tell, because we have no other way of knowing the manners and customs of his times but from what he has written."

Even though most of the evidence consists of parallel themes, there certainly exists a strong possibility that most of the Americans who expressed themselves in regard to the amount of subservence due to the ancients were fully aware of the ramifications of the ideas they expressed. It is hard to believe, for example, that most of them had not read Swift's *Tale of the Tub* and *Battle of the Books* in which the battle lines were clearly drawn. The poets in question were in a sense products of two cultures—the classical and the modern—and they sought to identify themselves with both.

The painter John Trumbull, who flourished during the period with which we are concerned, recalls in his *Autobiography* a discussion in his youth with his father over his desire to embrace the pictorial arts as his life's work. His father listened gravely to the aspiring painter dwelling rhapsodically upon "the honours paid to artists in the glorious days of Greece and Athens." The senior Trumbull then rejoined, "You appear to forget, sir, that *Connecticut is not Athens*" [New York, 1841, p. 49]. This is a cryptic remark, and, like the young Trumbull, we cannot be sure whether preference was meant to be accorded to ancient Greece or to eighteenth-century America. My discussion of the five major poets of the Federal period in American literature reveals that they shared a similar ambivalence.

By suggesting that American poets were aware of the European quarrel between ancients and moderns and that they consciously espoused the modern side, I am by no means attempting to diminish the stature of the Greek and Latin traditions in early American letters or to portray these poets as unequivocally opposed to classical learning. It could even be maintained that to engage in the debate at all on either side one had to possess both an appreciation and a knowledge of classical culture. Certainly every one of the European critics who espoused the moderns was at the same time skilled in at least the Latin language and possessed more than a rudimentary knowledge of Greek and Latin masterpieces. Boileau, for example, who cherished the ancients with an informed devotion, fought valiantly in their behalf for most of his career until eventually forced to admit with great reluctance that "the Age of Louis XIV is not only comparable but superior to the most famous ages of antiquity, even the Age of Augustus." Voltaire likewise derived more pleasure from being known as the French Sophocles than from any other of his literary distinctions; yet he insisted on the preeminence of the French stage over that of the ancients with the same vigor with which he defended Newton in the realm of science. In England, the best informed classical scholar in the controversy was Richard Bentley, the Royal librarian. It was precisely his classical learning which proved to be most damaging to the position of the British defenders of the ancients.

The classical training of the five American poets with whom I am concerned is impressive to say the least. Dwight, Barlow, and Humphreys were graduates of Yale; Freneau of Princeton, and Paine of Harvard. Even though, according to one of the adverse critics whom I cite, the teaching methods may have depended too greatly on rote learning, graduates of these institutions in the late eighteenth century must inevitably have attained both linguistic and literary competence in both Latin and Greek. Graduates in Barlow's class at Yale, for example, were at the end of their course of studies examined on Cicero and on the Greek Testament.[15] These poets were also living in times of intense nationalism and patriotic fervor, however, times

[15] Theodore Albert Zunder, *The Early Days of Joel Barlow* (New Haven, 1934), p. 54.

in which in any expression of the superiority of former societies would have seemed a betrayal of the ideals of the Revolution. It was acceptable for poets to praise their classical heritage, but they were careful to do so in a manner which made this heritage contributory to American glory and subservient to it. David Humphreys in a poem entitled "On the Happiness of America" written in 1780 during the midst of the Revolutionary War went so far as to portray every society previous to that of America as inferior.

> All former empires rose, the work of guilt,
> On conquest, blood or usupation built:
> But we, taught wisdom by their woes and crimes,
> Fraught with their lore, and born to better times;
> Our constitutions form'd on freedom's base,
> Which all the blessings of all lands embrace;
> Embrace humanity's extended cause,
> A world our empire, for a world our laws.

The strongest evidence of the pervasiveness of classical influences is that found in the poem "Anticipation of the Literary Fame of America," which recasts the appearance of an American masterpiece in many of the classical genres and which describes them in terms of Greek or Latin prototypes.

> Columbian *Livies* throng the historick field,
> A brighter band than ever Greece could yield.
> The morn of eloquence again shall dawn,
> And courtless *Cicero's* our courts adorn.
> Another Plato utter truths divine,
> Another Stagyrite our taste refine.
> Some new Euripides, with tragick art,
> Shall calm the passions, and shall touch the heart,
> Describe with energy *Orestes'* rage,
> And prompt to virtue from the moral stage.

Some future *Virgil* shall our wars rehearse
In all the dignity of epic verse.
Some modern *Ovid* paint his fair one's charms,
Her eyes bright sparkling and her twining arms;
The panting bosom and the ambrosial kiss,
The dying languor and the heavenly bliss.
In ——'s bowers new porticoes shall rise,
And fairer *Lyceums* glad our wondering eyes.
Groves academic grace the sylvan scene,
And Tully's Tusculum again be seen.
The brilliant treasure of the Attick mine,
Shall glow refulgent in our western clime,
Till the Archangel's trump thro' ether ring,
Till earth exulting own the eternal King,
Till ruling planets, from their orbits hurl'd,
Announce the dissolution of the world.[16]

The concluding lines of this poem significantly set forth the millennial doctrine which exists also in the works of Dwight, Barlow, and most other poets of the time. Although this work must certainly be considered as important evidence of the vogue of classical models in American literature, it must not be assumed that the designation of classical prototypes is peculiarly an American phenomenon or that the practice makes American literature any more classical than others in Western Europe. Goethe, who deplored the popularity of poetic imitation in Germany, remarked in his *Autobiography* concerning the common practice: "We now possessed, if not Homers, yet Virgils and Miltons; if not a Pindar, yet a Horace; of Theocrituses there was no lack."[17] Looking back from the perspective of the nineteenth century, Goethe realized that the period of neoclassical imitation had passed and that

[16] *Massachusetts Magazine* 1 (1789): 117-18.
[17] Trans. John Oxenford, 2 vols. (Chicago, 1974), 1: 293.

different standards and objectives were necessary for the literature of his age.

The same judgment may, of course, be rendered post facto against the American critics who awaited the appearance of new Virgils or new Ovids. They failed to realize that the time for neoclassical imitation had passed in America also. Not only were Latin and Greek models about to lose their vogue, but the traditional genres were giving way to new ones such as the novel, the romance, the short story, and the personal lyric. Apart from the prose of Franklin and Paine, the first works of American literature to obtain international recognition grew out of the new wave of what is now known as Romanticism. The first of the poets of this school, William Cullen Bryant, took full advantage of the classical tradition—witness, for example, the title of his best-known lyric "Thanatopsis"—but he reacted against the artificial or superficial elements of neoclassical rhetoric. He remarked in 1827, "I am aware that in modern poetry nothing is generally so nauseous and revolting as the introduction of the Pagan deities. Nothing turns us away from the perusal of a copy of verses so soon as any talk about Venus and Cupid, about Bacchus and his bowl, and about Sol and his chariot."[18]

Two of the labels that have been used for the period under discussion—the quarter of a century from the Revolution to the end of the eighteenth century—are paradoxically conflicting, but still relatively accurate. It was a new Age of Augustus in the rhetoric and structure of its literature, based as it was upon arbitrary rules requiring adherence to a single standard of propriety and order. It was the Federal period in ideology, however, allowing for a mixture of intellectual codes in the sense that "in the shallow structures of the mind several cultural codes can

[18] R. B. Silber, "William Cullen Bryant's Lectures on Mythology" (Ph.D. diss., State University of Iowa, 1962), p. 123.

operate successfully at the same time."[19] Intellectually, the Federal period was as pluralistic as the political system of the newly organized United States of America.

The history of the debate in eighteenth-century America over the educational value of Latin and Greek has been exhaustively treated by Meyer Reinhold in two articles in the *Proceedings of the American Philosophical Society*: Vol. 112 (1968): 221-34 and Vol. 119 (1975): 108-32. In the later article, Professor Reinhold declares that it is "methodologically wrong" to view the dispute over classical languages in the schools "as a renewal of the debate between the Ancients and the Moderns in the earlier Battle of the Books in Europe, or as a contrast between conservatives and liberals" [p. 116]. My own methodology in the preceding survey has consisted entirely in quoting American authors and suggesting parallels to notions expressed in the European debate. I am inclined to believe, however, that one could legitimately argue that the fundamental issues of the controversy were very much alive in eighteenth-century America and that the debate was continued there rather than merely renewed. The ancient side was favorably presented by John Wesley in his *Survey of the Wisdom of God in the Creation*, which contains long extracts from a work originally printed in French by John Dutens, *An Inquiry into the Origin of the Discoveries attributed to the Moderns: Wherein It is Demonstrated, That our most celebrated Philosophers have, for most part, taken what they advance from the Works of the Ancients*. The Dutens extracts were added to the second edition of Wesley's work (Bristol, 1777) and repeated in subsequent editions. It is impossible to tell how extensively this work circulated in America during the eight-

---

[19] James McLachlan, "Classical Names, American Identities: Some Notes on College Students and the Classical Tradition in the 1770's," in *Classical Traditions in Early America*, ed. James W. Eadie (Ann Arbor, 1976), p. 93.

eenth century, but it appears to be one of those books which people read in their homes, but was not bought for libraries. It is not listed in Evans, *American Bibliography*. The Library of Congress holds the "3d American ed., rev. and enl.; with notes, by B. Mayo. New York, Pub. by N. Bangs and T. Mason, for the Methodist Episcopal Church, 1823." I do not know when the first American edition appeared. The British Museum contains only three editions, the first (Bristol 1763) [which does not have the Dutens extracts], the second (Bristol, 1777) and an un-numbered "new edition . . . adapted to the present state of science by R. Mudie. 3 vol. London, 1836."

As far as political principles are concerned, I am not aware of any serious attempt to join the debates over either classical languages in the curriculum or the preeminence of ancient or modern learning to party or social divisions. Freneau and Barlow conveyed democratic ideals whereas Dwight, Humphreys, and Robert Treat Paine revealed aristocratic sentiments. By and large, however, the democratic writers (those loyal to the administration of Thomas Jefferson in the first decade of the nineteenth century) continued to predict eventual American supremacy in the realm of literature; whereas the opponents of Jefferson (the Federalists) lamented what they considered to be the lack of distinction in American letters.

The opposition to classical languages in the academic curriculum has been partly attributed to the influx of Scottish educators such as William Smith of Pennsylvania and John Witherspoon of Princeton. Perhaps because the speech of their country had been traditionally ridiculed by the English, they placed a premium upon the strength and purity of the English language and maintained that this purity was threatened by the emphasis on Latin and Greek. Even before Smith's appearance in Philadelphia, however, Franklin had proposed that in the institution that eventually became the University of Pennsylvania "all should not be compell'd to learn *Latin*, *Greek*, or the modern foreign languages."[20] He later called Latin and Greek "the quackery of literature."[21] Benjamin Rush, although ambivalent about Scottish educators, expressed grave doubts concerning the value of classical instruction in his *Observations upon the Study of the Latin and Greek Languages* (1789).

Many in the Federal period agreed with Franklin that the classical languages were nothing but elegant and useless ornaments. Thomas Paine not only shared this opinion, but maintained in addition that organized religions had imposed the study of dead languages in order to preserve the system of Christian dogma and to prevent its falsehood from being exposed through scientific discoveries. "It became necessary to their purpose," he charged in *The Age of Reason*, "to cut learning down to a size less dangerous . . . , and this they effected by restricting the idea of learning to the dead study of dead language."[22] This reasoning was duplicated by one of Paine's Latin American disciples, Camilo Henríquez of Chile, in an essay "On the Influence of Enlightenment Writings on the Fate of Humanity" (1812), an essay which is equally as relevant to the final chapter of this book as to the present one. Continuing to teach sciences in Latin, Henríquez affirmed, is the major obstacle which can be offered not only to the diffusion of the Enlightenment, but also to its perfection. "The method of scholasticism, the system of studies of the schools, the obstacles which the popularization of useful books has encountered, have had an enormous influence in the backwardness of letters."[23]

---

[20] *Papers of Benjamin Franklin*, ed. Leonard W. Labaree et al. (New Haven, 1961), 3: 415.

[21] "Papers of Benjamin Rush," *Pennsylvania Magazine of History and Biography* 29 (1905): 15-30.

[22] *Complete Writings*, ed. Foner, 1: 483.

[23] Quoted in A. O. Aldridge, "Thomas Paine and the Classics," *Eighteenth-Century Studies* 1 (1968): 370-80.

SEVEN

THE APEX OF AMERICAN LITERARY NATIONALISM

DURING THE PERIOD of the American Revolution, many writers considered that the level of intellectual achievement in America was high, and they were not reticent about declaring their opinion to the world. John Dickinson in the seventh of his Farmer's *Letters* described the inhabitants of the American colonies as in general "more intelligent than any other people whatever." Paine in the last of his *Crisis* papers maintained that the American Revolution had "contributed more to enlighten the world, and diffuse a spirit of freedom and liberality among mankind, than any human event (if this may be called one) that ever preceded it." And a decade later in his *Rights of Man*, Paine quoted Edmund Burke to the effect "that the people of America are more enlightened than those of Europe, or of any other country in Europe."[1] The euphoria of the Revolution lasted in America until the end of the eighteenth century when it gave way to doubts and fears about the efficacy of the experiment then being carried on in democratic government. This emotional transition coincided roughly with the gradual replacing of the Enlightenment with Romanticism, but no connection other than that of chronology has yet been demonstrated between these shifts in public opinion and literary trends.

[1] *Complete Writings*, ed. Philip S. Foner, 2 vols. (New York, 1945), 1: 366.

European observers remained tolerant of American pride and complacency until early in the nineteenth century. At this time a statement emanating from the Congress of the United States declaring the American nation to be the most enlightened in the world turned the American people into objects of ridicule. In December 1796, the House of Representatives resolved itself into a Committee of the Whole to consider the text of a reply to a state of the union address recently delivered by President George Washington. In this tentative reply to the chief executive appeared an astounding phrase describing the United States literally as "a whole nation, the freest and most enlightened in the world." In the resulting debate over the entire text, one of the more moderate members moved to strike out the boastful phrase. "Although, said he, I wish to believe that we are the freest people, and the most enlightened people in the world, it is enough that we think ourselves so; it is not becoming in us to make the declaration to the world; and if we are not so, it is still worse for us to suppose ourselves what we are not."[2]

The phrase claiming the United States to be the most enlightened nation in the world was never incorporated into an official Congressional document, but it did appear in the printed annals of Congress. Not surprisingly, this pretension to a superior degree of enlightenment provoked varying degrees of critical response from European observers. A contemporary French traveler in America, the Duke de la Rochefoucauld Liancourt, with gentle irony referred to the congressional debate as evidence of the "good opinion" which the people of the United States have of themselves. He cited caustically the labor and long discussion necessary to persuade the House to sacrifice "this superlative, with which the modesty of the

[2] *Debates and Proceedings in the Congress of the United States* (Washington, D.C., 1849), 6: 1614.

majority of the United States had not been embarrassed" and added seriously that "almost all the books printed in America, and the individual conversations of the Americans" furnish proof of their inordinate nationalistic pride.[3]

It might be noted in connection with "inordinate nationalistic pride," however, that one of La Rochefoucauld's countrymen, the novelist Balzac, a few years later described their own nation to be "la plus intelligente du monde."[4] What might be condoned as natural pride or even mildly criticized as excessive vanity in a French author, however, would have been harshly condemned in the early years of the nineteenth century as presumption and insufferable arrogance in a citizen of the newly formed United States. It is quite possible, indeed even probable, that the congressional debate over "the most enlightened people in the world" led the British critic Sydney Smith to phrase in the *Edinburgh Review* of 1820 his now-famous rhetorical question, "In the four quarters of the globe, who reads an American book? or goes to an American play? or looks at an American picture or statue?" Reason for believing that Smith had read the report of the debate in the House of Representatives is found in a sentence in his review in which he specifically reprobated the epithets by which American "orators and newspaper scribblers endeavour to persuade their supporters that they are the greatest, the most refined, the most enlightened, and the most moral people upon earth."

After Smith's attack, the phrase "most enlightened people of the world" continued to attract attention. In the middle of the nineteenth century, an even more vicious denunciation of American arrogance was published by a conservative German count, Adelbert Heinrich Baudissin,

---

[3] *Travels through the United States of North America*, 2 vols. (London, 1799), 2: 657.

[4] *La Duchesse de Langeais*, Edition Livre du Poche, Gallimard (Paris, 1958), p. 143.

under the pseudonym of Peter Tütt. His book, entitled *Zustände in Amerika* (1862), is now quite rare, but it had in its own time at least three editions. Baudissin revived the phrase concerning American enlightenment in a colorful passage depicting the state house of Tennessee as an example of the anomalous combination of filth and luxury to be found everywhere in the United States. Although the ceiling of the legislative chamber was adorned with murals and the floor with thick carpets, the legislators sat with their feet on their desks and spat tobacco juice into the air. The German critic wondered how it could be "possible that *the most enlightened people of the world* should leave the weal and woe of the whole nation in the hands of raw and dishonorable men." We are not concerned with this observer's conservative political opinions, but with the persistence of the phrase "the most enlightened people of the world," which Baudissin quoted in English and which he had, therefore, presumably found to be in widespread use. Incidentally, tobacco chewing and spitting without the amenity of a spittoon were among the aspects of American life that the German poet Heinrich Heine, a contemporary of Baudissin, adduced as making him wary of American civilization.[5]

Few European observers at the beginning of the nineteenth century expressed much hope for the imminent development of letters in America. An English gentleman, for example, who had formerly lived in the United States published in the London *Monthly Magazine* for 1802 a survey of what he termed the "disgraceful" and the "wretched state of American literature."[6] He refused to accept as relevant or valid the excuse which many Americans offered "in defence of a literary dearth, that *their's*

---

[5] Benno von Wiese, "Goethe und Heine als Europäer," in *Teilnahme und Spiegelung*, ed. B. Allemann and E. Koppen, (Berlin, 1975), p. 313.

[6] 14 (January, 1803): 624-27.

is a young country, and consequently that science must be in its cradle." This English observer tartly affirmed that "The Americans were the same people as the British, coëval with them; sprung from the same stock; children of one family, inhabiting distant parts, yet speaking the same language, enjoying the very same advantages of preceding authors whereon to form their tastes. Why then should Americans be behind-hand in science with the Britons?" At this period in English journalism the word *science* was loosely used to represent intellectual activity of almost any kind. According to this critic, English books were being constantly sent to the colonies, but little or nothing came back to London in return. It was irrelevant that the Americans paid for their books as a commercial transaction; in his opinion nothing but a cultural exchange could place the two nations on equal terms. "Between nations, genius cannot be bartered but for itself; it is a restless, ever-stirring quality of the human mind, which can only be satisfied with itself, which increases only to be increased; enlightens only to be enlightened the more." This austere English critic would not accept even the works of Franklin as an example of a "literary production to which America hath given birth, stamped with original genius."

These British strictures can be considered as in large measure a reply to an overdrawn appeal for American nationalism that Noah Webster, the pioneer American lexicographer, had issued in his *Dissertations on the English Language* (1789). Webster had proposed therein establishing an independent national language for North America on the grounds that "customs, habits, and *language* as well as government should be national." In his opinion, "to copy foreign manners implicitly is to reverse the order of things, and begin our political existence with the corruption and vices which have marked the declining glories of other republics." It is not strange, therefore, that the writer for the *Monthly Magazine* should have attacked Webster's proposed model for American writing as a "collection of Stuff, having the same affinity to science, which an *Olla podrida*, or hotch-potch, hath to cookery."

A famous French traveler in America during the same period, Brissot de Warville, also believed that the Americans should devise their own language. They should detest the English, he felt, and should carry their hatred so far as to efface all traces of their linguistic origins. In support of this notion, Brissot expressed a principle that would now be considered anathema by French linguists anxious to preserve their heritage from Franglais. According to Brissot, "one is the enemy of the human race and of universal peace by attaching oneself, as do certain writers, to preserving what they call the genius of each language." Brissot advised the Americans to adopt ways of expression peculiar to the French tongue. There would be, he argued, a double advantage in his method of universal naturalization. In his words, "The Americans would draw closer to other peoples and further away from the English; they would manufacture a language that would be appropriate to them; and they would have an American language."[7]

The defensiveness of Webster and many other Americans in regard to their cultural achievements grew out of resentment at a philosophical doctrine originating with Buffon and promulgated by many Europeans throughout the eighteenth century, the doctrine that European biological species of all kinds degenerated when introduced into the Western Hemisphere. Buffon had originally maintained that only plants and animals in the New World were inferior, but in 1768, a French abbé, Cornelius de Pauw, a protégé of Frederick the Great and associate of

---

[7] *Nouveau voyage dans les États-Unis . . . par J. P. Brissot*, 3 vols. (Paris, 1791), 1: 99-100.

Voltaire, published a shocking book, *Recherches philosophiques sur les Américains*, extending the notion of degeneration to the human race.[8] The book had a *succès de scandal*, and for a while almost everyone in Europe, including the abbé Raynal who adopted its doctrine in his own history of the New World, accepted the notion. In 1776, de Pauw applied the concept of inferiority to American letters in an article "Amérique," which appeared in the Pancoucke *Supplément* to the *Encyclopédie*. Here de Pauw remarked that "one does not notice that the professors of the university of Cambridge in New England have formed any young Americans to the point of being able to launch them in the literary world."

Franklin and Jefferson, among major writers, attempted to refute Buffon and de Pauw by pragmatic evidence, and a host of belligerent and satirical squibs against their theory appeared in American newspapers. Thomas Paine in the introductory essay to the *Pennsylvania Magazine*, which he edited before the publication of *Common Sense*, unequivocally affirmed, "degeneracy is here almost a useless word."[9] Foreign vices, he declared, "either expire on their arrival, or linger away in an incurable consumption." Among the category of noxious foreign products, Paine included European wit, which he decried as "one of the worst articles we can import." The *New Haven Gazette* published in 1787 an essay entitled "American Antiquities" devoted to a spurious epic poem, which presumably antedated Homer and predicted the nature of the modern world. The entire essay satirized the doctrine of biological degeneration and its principal exponents Buffon, De Pauw, and Raynal [13 September]. A more sober "Essay on Amer-

---

[8] Full documentation on the history of the theory of biological degeneration may be found in Antonello Gerbi, *The Dispute of the New World*, trans. Jeremy Moyle (Pittsburgh, 1973). This is one of the most important books related to the intellectual background of American literature.

[9] *Complete Writings*, ed. Foner, 2: 1110.

ican Genius," which appeared in the same volume of this newspaper [1 February], both attacked the doctrine of biological degeneration, and celebrated American writers and painters, including Trumbull, Barlow, West, and Copley. A similar essay, praising the literary achievement of Franklin, Edwards, Trumbull, and the memorials of Congress, concluded that "of no other nation can so honourable things be mentioned, at so early a period of their existence" [27 April 1786]. These essays were by no means unusual in their exaggerated view of national esthetic achievement, and contemporary poetry was every bit as extreme. A recent survey has revealed that "during the Revolution and the Period of Confederation [1775-1788], three out of every ten poems which were printed in magazines contained some type of patriotic exploitation; in the 1790 decade the proportion increased."[10]

Long before the doctrine of biological degeneration developed in Europe, the contrary notion of a special pure and salutary environment to be found in America had emerged in the British colonies. This notion has contributed to a type of isolationism or separatism that has existed in North American culture ever since Puritan times. Sometimes known as "exceptionalism" or "historical uniqueness," it has appeared under various guises, including millennialism and Manifest Destiny. One of the most common colonial forms of exceptionalism consisted, as we have already seen, in a variant of the European theme of the westward movement of the arts and sciences from the place of their birth in ancient Greece and Rome. Later writers expatiated on the delights and advantages of America without introducing the *translatio* theme to explain them.

[10] Unpublished dissertation by C. W. Coles quoted by Gordon E. Bigelow, *Rhetoric and American Poetry of the Early National Period*, University of Florida Monographs, Humanities, no. 4 (Gainesville, Fla., 1960), p. 52n.

David Humphreys, who shared with Barlow the distinction of being among the first American poets to attain any degree of international notice, wrote an entire poem on the theme of the salutary environment of his country to which he gave the unequivocal title, "On the Happiness of America" (1780).[11] The following lines are typical:

> All former empires rose, the work of guilt,
> On conquest, blood or usurpation built:
> But we, taught wisdom by their woes and crimes,
> Fraught with their lore, and born to better times;
> Our constitutions form'd on freedom's base,
> Which all the blessings of all lands embrace;
> Embrace humanity's extended cause,
> A world our empire, for a world our laws.

The emergence of a native literature is associated with the author and his fellow poets.

> Thou spirit of the West, assert our fame,
> In other bards awake the dormant flame.

Humphreys also produced a companion piece with the explicit title, "A Poem on the Future Glory of the United States of America" (1800?). Its prose "Advertisement," deliberately seeking to vindicate the theme of aggressive prophecy, makes use of the theological doctrine of the millennium, that divine order has appointed America for the ideal society. In Humphrey's words, "America, after having been concealed for so many ages from the rest of

[11] One of Humphrey's Revolutionary poems, "Address to the Armies of the United States of America," was translated by the Marquis de Chastellux, published in Paris, and favorably received in the *Journal de Paris*, 7 May 1786. Since Humphreys served in Madrid as minister plenipotentiary to Spain, it is not surprising that the list of subscribers to his *Miscellaneous Works* (New York, 1804) should include the king and queen of Spain as well as diplomats at Madrid from Denmark, Sweden, Norway, Portugal, Great Britain, Prussia, and France.

the world, was probably discovered, in the maturity of time, to become the theatre for displaying the illustrious designs of Providence, in its dispensations to the human race." Humphreys argues also that the function of the poet is precisely that of looking into the future. "The poet and the prophet have been considered so intimately blended together, that a common name (at least in one language) was expressive of both."

Four years before the Declaration of Independence, Philip Freneau composed for commencement exercises at Princeton University a superpatriotic poem entitled "The Rising Glory of America," in which he established a tradition of pride by anticipation. After consigning to poetic oblivion Memphis, Athens, Rome, and Britain, he affirmed that

> A theme more new, tho' not less noble, claims
> Our ev'ry thought on this auspicious day;
> The rising glory of this western world.

Then celebrating Philadelphia as the "seat of arts, of science, and of fame," the happy city, "where the muses stray," Freneau indicated that fair science "transplanted from the eastern climes, dost bloom / In these fair regions" while "Greece and Rome no more / Detain the muses on Cithaeron's brow."

In a later poem entitled "Literary Importation" (1786, 1788), intended primarily to oppose the bringing over of an English bishop, Freneau suggested that the religious purity of America would lead to intellectual superiority over England.

> Can we never be thought to have learning or grace
> Unless it be brought from that horrible place
> Where tyranny reigns with her impudent face;
>> And popes and pretenders
>> And sly faith-defenders

> Have ever been hostile to reason and wit,
> Enslaving a world that shall conquer them yet.

In other "Stanzas on the Emigration to America" (1785), Freneau predicted the supremacy of his nation in every possible human activity.

> Far brighter scenes, a future age,
> The muse predicts, these States shall hail,
> Whose genius shall the world engage,
> Whose deeds shall over death prevail,
> And happier systems bring to view
> Than all the eastern sages knew.

In a prologue to a French play presented in Philadelphia in 1782, Freneau developed a double contrast, cultural and political.

> Even here where Freedom lately sat distrest,
> See a new Athens rising in the west!

Another prologue, by Robert Treat Paine for the opening of the Federal Street Theatre in Boston in 1794, joined to traditional esthetic excellencies the architecture of the building.

> An Athens, Rome, Augusta, blush to see,
> Their virtue, beauty, grace, all shine—combined in thee.

Crèvecoeur, in his famous *Letters from an American Farmer* (1782) in which he described Americans as "a new race of men," also portrayed his countrymen as perfecting the civilization that had been inadequately developed in Europe. "Americans," he said, "are the western pilgrims, who are carrying along with them that great mass of arts, sciences, vigour, and industry which began long since in the east; they will finish the great circle."[12]

---

[12] Edited by Warren B. Blake (London, 1913), Letter III.

The *translatio* theme, which was obviously exactly the opposite of the notion of biological degeneration, was given a revolutionary twist by Thomas Paine, who defiantly charged in his manifesto of political independence *Common Sense* that "Freedom hath been hunted round the globe" until at last it found a refuge in America. When Paine himself returned to America in 1802 following a disappointing experience with the French Revolution, he told the citizens of the United States that it is "through the New World" that "the Old must be regenerated."[13]

Paine also proclaimed the topographical theme—that the vast and sublime landscape of America together with its salubrious climate will inspire noble and sublime thoughts in its natives and lead to great deeds and artistic triumphs. Although this environmental theme is usually associated with Walt Whitman, who later developed it out of all proportion with the help of his self-recognized bombast, it actually originated in the early years of the republic. According to Paine, the scene that America "presents to the eye of a spectator, has something in it which generates and encourages great ideas. Nature appears to him in magnitude. The mighty objects he beholds, act upon his mind by enlarging it, and he partakes of the greatness he contemplates" [*Rights of Man*, Part Second, Introduction]. The idea was by no means original to Paine. Six years previously the *Columbian Magazine* had associated the esthetic appeal of American sylvan scenes with the production of literature. "The face of nature, throughout the United States, exhibits the *sublime* and *beautiful*. . . . Our mountains, vallies, plains, and rivers, are formed upon a great scale; the extent of the country itself is great; and the whole is rendered magnificiently beautiful." If patriotic deeds are also taken into consideration, "we must

---

[13] *Complete Writings*, ed. Foner, 2: 912.

allow that nothing can allow more noble themes for our native bards" [October 1786].

In fairness to American authors, one might point out that Goethe makes a similar reference to the influence of the landscape upon mental processes. He remarks in his *Autobiography* that "the undetermined, widely expanding feelings of youth and of uncultivated nations are alone adapted to the sublime, which, if it is to be excited in us through external objects, formless or moulded into incomprehensible forms, must surround us with a greatness to which we are not equal."[14] This is close to, if not identical with, a statement by Thomas Paine, shortly before the publication of *Rights of Man*: "Great scenes inspire great Ideas. The natural Mightiness of America expands the Mind and it partakes of the greatness it contemplates."[15]

The first American author to challenge the topographical argument was the Gothic novelist Charles Brockden Brown. A British traveler who greatly admired Rousseau once asked the Philadelphia author "whether a view of nature would not be more propitious to composition; or whether he should not write with more facility were his window to command the prospect of the Lake of *Geneva*. Sir, said he, good pens, thick paper, and ink well diluted, would facilitate my composition more than the prospect of the broadest expanse of water, or mountains rising above the clouds."[16]

Somewhat later the poet Longfellow expressed the same pragmatic attitude in a novel *Kavanaugh* (1849). By means of one of his characters, the village schoolmaster, Longfellow rejected the call for a "national literature commensurate with our mountains and rivers."

[14] *Autobiography*, Part II, Book VI.
[15] A. O. Aldridge, *Man of Reason, The Life of Thomas Paine* (New York, 1959), p. 109.
[16] John Davis, *Travels of Four Years and a Half in the United States of America* (London, 1803), pp. 149-50.

Great has a very different meaning when applied to a river, and when applied to a literature. . . . A man will not necessarily be a great poet because he lives near a great mountain. Nor being a poet, will he necessarily write better poems than another, because he lives nearer Niagara. . . . Switzerland has produced no extraordinary poet; nor, as far as I know, have the Andes, or the Himalaya mountains, or the Mountains of the Moon in Africa.

[Chapter XX]

One of the paradoxes in American writing at the turn of the century is that glowing predictions of literary glory coexisted with recognition that the social and economic conditions requisite for extensive literary production were almost entirely lacking. A poem by Warren Dutton, *The Present State of Literature*, delivered at the commencement exercises of Yale College in 1800, lamented in allegorical terms the neglect of the muses in "fair freedom's last retreat." Dutton condemned French writers associated with the French Revolution and praised some English writers, but the only American he even mentioned was Royal Tyler because of his having preceded Gifford in satirizing the Della Cruscans.

In the same year, the president of Yale, Timothy Dwight, attempted to explain the dearth of American talent in a discourse on the eighteenth century. "Great literary and scientific attainments," he affirmed, "cannot be made without great leisure, as well as great talents and application. Such leisure is rarely found here. No ample literary foundations are furnished here for the support of ingenious and speculative men, in the pursuits of learning and science."[17]

When British reviewers failed to hail the sporadic productions from western pens as belonging to the category

---

[17] *A Discourse on Some Events of the Last Century* (New Haven, 1801), p. 16.

of genius, a natural reaction of American writers was to accuse British publishers and reviewers of prejudice. One of the earliest examples of this attitude is a poem by John Trumbull castigating British critics for neglecting American works, allegedly for political motives. His poem, "Lines addressed to Messrs. Dwight and Barlow, on the projected publication of their Poems in London," which was written in December 1775, affirms the existence of bias among British reviewers even though the anticipated publication of the verse of his friends had not taken place.

> And see, where yon proud Isle her shores extends
> The cloud of Critics on your Muse descends!
> From every side, with deadly force, shall steer
> The fierce Review, the censuring Gazeteer.

Not all British journals, however, should be considered hostile or condescending toward polite letters in the United States. An early, perhaps the first, significant Old World recognition of American literature as an independent entity consists of a "Half-Yearly Retrospect of American Literature," a regular feature appearing every six months in the London *Monthly Magazine* beginning in 1809. These regular surveys, parallel to others on domestic English, French, German, and Spanish literatures, sought to attain objectivity and fairness, and in large measure succeeded in doing so.[18]

Even some native Americans expressed adverse opinions about the quality of the literature being produced at the turn of the century, but these were for the most part politically inspired, directed by Federalists against the Democratic-Republican Administration of Jefferson. The

---

[18] A prior publication *Bibliotheca Americana* (London, 1789) is primarily a catalog of books about both North and South America. Its introductory discourse "On the Present State of Literature in those Countries," which will be discussed in Chapter Nine, has an intriguing title, but does not live up to its promise.

Federalists' philosophy was conservative and elitist; the Democratic-Republican, populist and eclectic. The Federalists found one more weapon against the Democrats by citing alleged deficiencies in the cultural milieu. The *Monthly Anthology* affirmed, therefore, in 1805 that "in literature we are yet in our infancy; and to compare our authors, whether in prose or poetry, to those of the old world, can proceed only from the grossest ignorance, or the most insufferable vanity." The *Port Folio*, edited by Joseph Dennie, devoted in 1807 parts of three issues to an "Examination of the causes that have retarded the progress of literature in the United States."[19] Although completely rejecting the doctrine of biological degeneration as a fantasy of discredited French philosophy, the author nevertheless presented the theme of *translatio* in a skeptical light (a rare, almost unique example of such a treatment). Unsympathetic to Puritanism and the egalitarian political notions associated with it, he caustically referred to the early settlers of America "who under we know not what pretext of civil and religious liberty, wandered to the Wilderness of the West." The poor showing of American literature he ascribed to commercialism and avarice, the lack of a national university, the indifference of the federal government, the lack of patronage, and the neglect of classical learning. A hardened Federalist, Fisher Ames, ironically asked in 1809 whether Joel Barlow could be matched with Homer or Hesiod, or Thomas Paine with Plato, but he was not much more flattering to England, which, he affirmed, had not produced a first-rate poet for a long time. In his opinion, if America were to lag behind merely to the same degree as her parent country, "it will not be thought a proof of the deficiency of our genius."[20]

The most extensive analysis of the obstacles to the growth

---

[19] 3 (1807): 385-89; 4 (1807): 342-46, 356-59.
[20] "American Literature," in *Works* (Boston, 1854), pp. 430-38.

of American letters together with a survey of the contemporary status of American culture came in 1803 in a
two-volume treatise entitled *Brief Retrospect of the Eighteenth Century*, by Samuel Miller, a Presbyterian clergyman from New York. His method of classifying the various literary genres as well as his categories of the major
literatures of Europe probably derived from the twice-yearly
"retrospects" in the London *Monthly Magazine*, previously mentioned. The forthcoming publication of Miller's
own *Brief Retrospect* had been announced therein in flattering terms.[21] Much more moderate than some of his
countrymen concerning the past and future glories of
America, Miller provided the standard explanations to account for the relatively slow rise of literary eminence, but
he made a unique contribution by comparing the status
of America with, in his own words, that of other "nations
lately become literary." After admitting that "the conspicuous poets" of the United States were not numerous,
and then naming only a half dozen examples, Miller concluded that "we are by no means to ascribe this circumstance either to the paucity or the barrenness of American
genius." A far more likely cause he considered to be the
lack of "respite from the toils of professional and active
life" among those who have any taste for letters.

According to Miller, the previous century had been notable for "the rise of several nations from obscurity in the
republic of letters, to considerable literary and scientific
eminence." Passing over several nations "of inferior character," he considered "the most important of those which
. . . have become literary" to be Russia, Germany, and the
United States. At the beginning of the century, he maintained, the whole Russian empire had been "sunk in ignorance and barbarism," and almost nothing was done to
alleviate this condition until Peter the Great came to power.

[21] 11 (July 1801): 614.

Although noting that some progress had been made in printing, the fine arts, the study of languages, and the dissemination of newspapers and literary journals, Miller had little confidence that the fundamental illiteracy of the Russian nation would be unchanged even after another century.

Turning to Germany, Miller admitted that long before the eighteenth century much in the way of science and literature had existed there, but all works of importance were written in the Latin tongue. In Miller's opinion, "the cultivation of the German language; . . . and especially the commencement of a just taste in German literature, may all with truth be ascribed to the eighteenth century." Although citing only Mosheim, Gottsched, and Schlegel among the names that are now considered great, Miller concluded that Germany had produced during the second half of the century "historians, poets and dramatists, whose writings evince that judgment, acuteness, imagination, elegant taste, and every qualification for fine writing." Without mentioning Goethe's *Werther*, which was both admired and condemned in the United States, Miller concluded his survey of Germany with the pronouncement that with the possible exception of France there was no country on earth in which literary enterprise was "made the medium for conveying so much moral and theological poison as in Germany." He may have had in mind the sentimental and sensational plays of Kotzebue without wishing to provide them with additional notoriety by citing them. One would never realize from reading Miller that Kotzebue was the most popular author on the American stage in the last two years of the eighteenth century.[22] The stage provides another interesting example of German-American relations. The setting of a play by Friedrich

[22] Henry A. Pochman, *German Culture in America* (Madison, Wis., 1957), pp. 349-51.

M. Klinger that gave the name to a period of German literary history, *Sturm und Drang* (1776) is America. The action, however, unlike that in the novel *Mis MacRae* by Hilliard d'Auberteuil has no connection with political events on the continent.

Miller prepared his readers for the paucity of materials concerning American literature by affirming that its annals were "short and simple." Even though adding that "the history of poverty is usually neither very various, nor very interesting," he argued that the small amount of literature that did exist in America was better than could have been expected considering the circumstances under which it was produced. During the seventeenth century, he explained, literature was retarded by the general poverty of the colonists, their struggles with a hostile environment, and the rigorous censorship of the press. During the eighteenth century, progress was still being hampered by "defective plans and means of instruction in our Seminaries of learning," the absence of leisure, the lack of encouragement to learning, such as books and libraries, and the dependence upon Great Britain. Americans themselves, he felt, did not sufficiently appreciate their own writers and were "too apt to join with ignorant or fastidious foreigners, in undervaluing and decrying our domestic literature." But Miller closed on an optimistic note: when the time shall arrive when native authors will have equal leisure and equal encouragement with their European counterparts, "it may be confidently predicted, that letters will flourish as much in America as in any part of the world."

Even though it may appear from a twentieth-century perspective that Miller was presumptuous in comparing the United States with Russia and Germany as nations lately become literary, he was by no means overgenerous in assessing the merits of American authors. He was just as aware as the most rigorous British critics of the obsta-

cles to be overcome in the emergence of a national literature. He represents, moreover, indubitable proof that
not all Americans were, in the words of Sydney Smith,
anxious to persuade the world that they were "the greatest, the most refined, the most enlightened, and the most
moral people upon earth." Miller should be credited in
addition with preceding Channing by thirty years in exposing the need for a comparatist perspective on American
literature and in providing one. Henry Pochman, in praising Miller's coverage of German letters, remarks that his
"broad survey was all the more effective because German
achievements were set against the background of all other
European as well as American accomplishments, thus
providing the reader with a perspective which made comparisons inevitable."[23] This comment has equal validity
in reference to the other European literatures in Miller's
survey.

In the next decade, an article in *Niles' Weekly Register*
(28 September 1816) on the "Progress of the United States
in Literature" seemed to be a deliberate continuation of
Miller's retrospective view. After repeating Miller's application of Thomas Gray's phrase "short and simple annals" to the "depressed literature of our country," the
author in a tone of mingled humiliation and hope attributed the neglect of literature in America to the previous
subjugation of the people under colonial rule, the low
regard for classical learning in public journals, the mercenary nature of the national character, and the influence
of religion over the cultivation of intellect.

This common sense attitude would seem to lead to the
conclusion that the arrogance and exaggeration of post-
Revolutionary years soon gave way to a period of reas-
sessment during which more sober and realistic opinions
prevailed. Unfortunately such a conclusion is not sup-

[23] Ibid., p. 523.

ported by historical fact. In 1818 a minor poet, Solyman Brown, revitalized the theme of an autonomous national literature in tones as strident and aggressive as any that had been heard at the turn of the century. There followed a steady stream of books and essays vociferously defending the merits of American writing. Because of chronological limits, we shall not go beyond Solyman Brown. In the prose preface to a versified *Essay on American Poetry*, he affirmed that "The proudest freedom to which a nation can aspire, not excepting even political independence, is found in complete emancipation from literary thraldom. Few nations, however, have arrived at this commanding eminence. Greece once possessed it, and she was the glory and wonder of the world." According to Brown, Rome also achieved this enviable position before the coming of the Dark Ages. France was the first in the modern world to recover intellectual eminence and then England attained ascendancy, but used it to smother the rising genius of both Scotland and Ireland. England was now attempting to maintain superiority over America. Brown charged that English writers first portrayed their American brethren as cannibals and savages and when this falsehood was exposed treated them "as a race of intellectual pigmies; bunglers in Art and pedants in Science." Brown specifically accused the British ministry of exporting books to the United States to prevent the growth of an indigenous publishing industry, of filling their books with slanders on American achievements in order to discourage emigration, and of exciting among Americans "a prejudice against the literary work of their compatriots." It had become "the determined resolution of men of letters, in the parent country, not to give the smallest credit to American productions, how meritorious soever." As a result of all these policies, America was left with "native genius without patrons, and the shelves of the bookseller bending beneath a weight of imported volumes." Like Barlow, Brown con-

sidered North and South America as a geographical unit
and presumably an esthetic one as well, but he mentioned
no Hispanic poets. In the verse section of his work, he
did not name either Bryant or Ladd, who had already begun to publish. His favorites were Robert Treat Paine,
Dwight, and Barlow, and he addressed the last as "Music's
heir—Apollo's child."

William Cullen Bryant noticed Brown's work in the
North American Review (July 1818), but in keeping with
the custom of the times had very little to say about the
book itself, but presented an independent critical and historical essay of ten pages on American poetry. Without
attempting to disparage the poets of his nation, he concluded that "on the whole there seems to be more good
taste among those who read, than those who write poetry
in our country." Admitting that it is natural that national
pride should wish to foster the infant literature, Bryant
observed that it is "detrimental to bestow on mediocrity
the praise due to excellence. . . . We make but a con-
temptible figure in the eyes of the world, and set ourselves
up as objects of pity to our posterity, when we affect to
rank the poets of our own country with those mighty
masters of song who have flourished in Greece, Italy and
Britain."

Solyman Brown's declaration was published toward the
end of the period marking the emergence of the literature
of the United States—the period when Philip Freneau,
Washington Irving, and William Cullen Bryant were making respectable contributions, but a decade before the appearance of Poe and James Fenimore Cooper. It is somewhat of a paradox that the writers of the Revolutionary
period had predicted a resurgence of literature in the classical vein, new Livies, Platos, Ovids, and Virgils; whereas
the most significant authors of the nineteenth century
chose Romantic themes and developed new forms such
as the novel. Brown himself, however, could be cited as

a practitioner of the neoclassical version of the Virgilian georgic. In addition to his *Essay on American Poetry*, he published in 1840 *Dentologia: a poem on the diseases of the teeth, and their proper remedies.*

A great contrast exists between Brown's dedication to "complete emancipation from literary thraldom" and William Ellery Channing's advocacy of a more extensive knowledge of "the different modes of viewing and discussing great subjects in different nations." The latter's cosmopolitanism is worthy of comparison to a famous declaration by Goethe in conversation with his friend and secretary Eckermann in 1827. "I like to look at other nations," Goethe said, "and I advise everyone to do the same. National literature has little meaning today; the time has come for the epoch of world literature to begin, and everyone must now do his share to hasten its realization."[24] Even though few voices but Channing's could be found in the United States to echo Goethe's opinion, most critics by the time that American literature had come of age in the 1830s had ceased to make exaggerated claims for the genuine talent that existed and to blame the rest of the world for conditions that had allegedly prevented Americans from producing works of great merit. By that time, there was no longer any need for either diffident apology or chauvinistic puffing.

[24] *Gespräche mit Eckermann.* Quoted by François Jost, *Introduction to Comparative Literature* (New York, 1974), p. 16.

PART III

THE TWO AMERICAS: NORTH AND SOUTH

MANY PARALLELS exist between the literature of Latin America and that of English America before 1830. Both areas went through periods of conquest and exploration, colonial domination, struggle for political independence, and national recogition. Although these stages in development are completely parallel, they were widely separated chronologically on the two continents. Conquest and exploration in South America took place in the sixteenth century, but not until a hundred years later in North America. The relationship is noticed in one of the best New England poems of the seventeenth century, but otherwise almost completely ignored.

> The Spanish project working well, tooke sudden such
>> impression
>> In minds of many *Europe* held, who fell to like
>> progression.
> It's strange to see the Spanish fleete so many should
>> provoke,
>> In *English* searching for like prize, they are vanisht
>> into smoake.
>> [Edward Johnson, "Good News from New-England"]

In Spanish America, literature began to flourish almost concurrently with settlement, and it reached a high level of development before the establishment of the first printing press in New England. Highly sophisticated examples of the epic, the satire, and the lyric were produced in Spanish America during the first century of European occupation, but very little of comparable quality can be claimed for the first century of the English colonies, during which nearly all writing was religious or utilitarian. Before 1700, the muses harmonized south of the border, while they remained almost mute in northern climes. In the eighteenth century, however, the situation was reversed. The active struggle for independence began in the English colonies toward the middle of the century and was successfully concluded before its end, decades before the emergence of an independence movement in the Spanish colonies. The Spanish-Americans led in the development of imaginative literature during the era of colonization, but fell behind in literature concerned with independence and political organization.

The two American hemispheres could serve as a useful test case of the theory of literary zones, which has recently been proposed by critics in Eastern Europe. According to this theory, "common characteristics, analogues and parallel features of literatures" belonging to a particular geographical zone may be ascribed to "their common or similar history."[1] To ascertain whether the Western Hemisphere represents a unified literary zone during the period under discussion, that is, in the period before 1830, one should find out the extent of similarities and differences between the northern and southern continents and then to decide whether the similarities derive from a common historical and geographical tradition or from broad literary movements originating in Europe. A major difficulty consists in defining the scope of the zone or zones. Should one conceive of Latin American literature and Anglo-American literature as two separate, more or less homogeneous zones or should an attempt be made to combine the two and consider them together as constituting a single comprehensive zone? Problems arise even with the notion of Latin American or Anglo-American literature. The major countries of the south draw inspiration directly from the various literatures of Europe and North America (not only from the Portuguese and the Spanish), and this connection with Europe and Anglo-America has historically been stronger than any communication with each other. The same principle applies to North America. The literatures of Canada and the United States draw more upon English literature than they do upon each other, and that of French Canada has closer ties with Paris than with New York or Toronto. The concept of literary zones is merely a theory whereas that of independent national literatures represents historical reality, no matter what ties may exist between these independent literatures. Bringing the literatures of the two continents together merely as the products of a geographical-historical zone results in a purely arbitrary classification comparable to other arbitrary units such as separate colonies or *virreinatos*, in-

---

[1] I am quoting the language of György M. Vajda in his summary of a colloquium concerning the comparative history of literature. "Conclusions," *Neohelicon* 1 (1973): 329. Objections to the theory are presented on pages 149-52 of the same issue of *Neohelicon*.

dependent nations, individual states in the United States, and groups of states (e.g., Southern literature of the United States). While cultural and historical differences may justify such classifications as Canadian literature, the literature of the United States, Mexican or Argentinian literature, the comparatist seeks to transcend these differences. A zone comprising both continents is a more comprehensive unit than that of a state or province, but from the broadest international perspective it has no more logic to recommend it than the smaller divisions. A workable compromise might be to think in terms of universal literature, or of a world system comprising subsystems, as the Mexican poet Octavio Paz has suggested. The two literatures using the Spanish language, Spanish literature and Hispanoamerican literature, would represent subsystems. Similarly individual literatures using the English language, including those of England, the United States, Canada, Australia, and more than a dozen other countries, would also represent subsystems. As far as the literatures of the two American continents are concerned, it is possible to see parallels, analogies, and influences without conceiving of them in terms of a single zone.

One of the irrefutable arguments against treating Anglo-America and Ibero-America as a cohesive unit in the particular period with which we are concerned is that until the nineteenth century the two areas were for the most part unaware of each other's literary production.[2] This situation changed radically, however, after the English colonies became the United States of America. Political leaders in Latin America, in seeking independence from

[2] Interesting material on this point is found in Hans Galinsky, " 'Colonial Baroque': A Concept Illustrating Dependence, Germinal Independence and New World Interdependence of Early American Literature," in *Proceedings of the 7th Congress of the International Comparative Literature Association*, ed. Milan V. Dimic and Eva Kushner (Stuttgart, 1979), 1: 48-49.

Spain, profited from the example of their neighbor to the north and drew upon its political literature. Most important in Latin America were the writings of Thomas Paine. Spanish America did not by any means depend exclusively upon the independence literature of the United States, but drew as well, and perhaps more extensively, upon the advanced political theory of Europe, particularly that of England and France. The social and political writings of Locke, Rousseau, and Montesquieu are part of a broad literary and historical movement known as the Enlightenment, and they circulated in both North and South America.

A distinction should be made between the overlapping movements of classicism and the Enlightenment. The former emphasizes esthetic concepts and the latter, social and political ones, but both rest upon presuppositions of rationalism. Eighteenth-century classicism should be known as neoclassicism, since it consists primarily of the revival and imitation of the ancient writers of Greece and Rome. In a broad sense, the esthetic values of classicism exalt stability over change, norms over individual eccentricities, and the absolute over the relative. The Enlightenment comprises concepts such as deism, religious toleration, human rights, and economic and social reform. Neoclassicism exalts and illustrates reason and order in artistic expression: Enlightenment philosophy seeks to establish principles of reason and order in religion, government, and social relations. Many European figures such as Pope, Swift, Voltaire, and Diderot combine the ideals of neoclassicism and the Enlightenment in their literary work, but many others—in both Europe and America—emphasized one or the other approach, sometimes adhering firmly to one and rejecting the other. Timothy Dwight, for example, followed neoclassical models in poetic style, while vigorously attacking Enlightenment notions of rational religion. Paine, on the other hand, fervently expressed Enlightenment ideals in all areas, but did so in a prose style strongly tinged with elements of Romanticism. His much less successful attempts at poetry, however, do not deviate in their absolute adherence to neoclassical standards. As literary periods, neoclassicism and Romanticism are mutually exclusive, but in both North and South America many writers simultaneously revealed techniques and attitudes reflecting both of these antithetical movements.

The first of the next two chapters will demonstrate the direct influence of Paine's political prose upon various figures in Latin America, and the second will reveal parallel portrayals of various Enlightenment themes and concepts in the literatures of the two continents.

EIGHT

THOMAS PAINE AND
LATIN AMERICAN
INDEPENDENCE

T HE WRITINGS of Thomas Paine provide an outstanding example of literature used for social and political ends. His major works all concern political and
social reform, but are not uniform in their purposes and
direction. For this reason they met varying fortunes in the
several cultures that they penetrated. Paine's two propaganda tracts for the American Revolution, *Common Sense*
and *The American Crisis*, attained a phenomenal circulation in North America, where they were first published;
achieved moderate success in France and Germany; but
were practically ignored in England. In Latin America they
were translated only in part, but used as symbols by leaders of the independence movement. Paine's two-volume
treatise, *Rights of Man*, an attempt to apply the ideals of
the French Revolution to the British Isles, was hotly debated in Great Britain and widely read in the United States,
but was known only to small groups of political thinkers
in France and Germany and virtually not at all in the
Spanish world. His manifesto of deism, *The Age of Reason*, attained an extraordinary circulation in Great Britain
and the United States, acquired a certain prestige in Germany, but made very little impression in any other country.

In England and America Paine was a historical figure—
a personality almost as well known as Franklin and Washington. The rest of the world, however had virtually no

knowledge of his biography and personality. Even in France, where Paine served briefly in the Convention, he did not shine as a public figure. A striking difference may be observed in the reception of his works in North America, where he was a personality, and in South America, where he was merely a name. In both areas he served as a symbol, but in one his behavior was at issue, in the other his political doctrine.

In the Anglo-Saxon world, Paine's opponents attempted to discredit his doctrines by accusing him of drunkenness. Ever since James Cheetham's notorious *Life of Thomas Paine* (1809), the first muckraking biography in American literature, Paine's detractors have pictured him as a disgusting inebriate. The famous phrase of Theodore Roosevelt, "filthy, little atheist," has stuck to him like a burr. Roosevelt used this inaccurate and prejudicial phrase in a biography of Gouverneur Morris, one of Paine's most vindictive ideological enemies. Even Washington Irving in both his *Salmagundi* and his *History of New York* used this simile "red as Thomas Paine's nose."

The contrast with South America is striking. Where nothing was known about Paine as an individual, his name served only as symbol of toleration and individual rights.

As early as 1783, Paine met one of the liberators of South America, Franciso de Miranda, in New York.[1] Ten years later in Paris, where Paine was serving in the Convention and Miranda held the rank of general in the army, the latter was put on trial for treason. Paine, called as a character witness, testified that the success of the French Revolution was intimately linked with the favored object of the general's heart, the deliverance of South America and the opening of its commerce to the rest of the world.[2] Somewhat later Paine grew suspicious that Miranda was

---

[1] A. O. Aldridge, *Man of Reason, The Life of Thomas Paine* (New York, 1959), p. 111

[2] Ibid., pp. 198-99.

acting as a British agent, but he remained on friendly terms and subsequently tried to obtain Miranda's release from a French prison.[3] There is no reason to believe that Miranda ever exerted any effort to make Paine's writings known in his native Venezuela, even though this was the first place in Spanish America where they were extensively circulated.

A twentieth-century historian, Enrique de Gandía, who has devoted considerable attention to Paine's ideology, has made the paradoxical statement that "the influence of Thomas Paine in the events that led to Hispano-American independence was absolutely nil. It did not exist at any moment or at any time."[4] Time and events are the key concepts in his remarkable statement, which rests upon a distinction between ideology and political action. Gandía gives Paine full credit for providing Hispanic patriots with a clear and logical ideology to justify their efforts to overthrow Spanish rule. He nevertheless argues that by the time Paine's work became known in Spanish America, the independence movement was already in full swing. This historian gives 1810 as the date of the penetration of Paine's thought into the Spanish colonies, the year in which a partial translation of his work was ready for the printer. Before this date, according to Gandía, the number of Hispanics who had even heard of Paine was

[3] Ibid., p. 247. Miranda, while visiting the British Parliament in 1791, noted that copies of the second part of Paine's *Rights of Man*, at that time proscribed by the British government, were being sold along with sandwiches in the House of Commons *Archivo del General Miranda* (Caracas, 1930), 4: 309. In the next year, Miranda received a letter from Major A. Jardine with an intriguing passage concerning American men of letters: "We Europeans ought to invite more of these wise Americans among us. You see Franklin, Paine, Barlow, have scattered more truths of importance among us than all Europe could do for themselves." *Archivo* (Caracas, 1930) 6: 218.

[4] *Historia de las ideas políticas en la Argentina,* 6 vols. (Buenos Aires, 1960), 1: 407.

negligible. Gandía admits elsewhere, however, that "ideas run from man to man without the need of being printed,"[5] and it is obvious that Paine's first Spanish translator made his original contact without the aid of a Spanish text. Gandía also maintains that Paine's basic ideas already existed in liberal Hispano-American culture; indeed, that apart from the native Indians "all the inhabitants of Spanish America thought either like Thomas Paine or like his most extreme critics."[6] Liberal political ideology allegedly derived from St. Thomas Aquinas, Francisco de Vitoria, Francisco Suárez, Juan de Mariana, and especially Jean Jacques Rousseau.[7] For illustration, Gandía cites a Hispanic republican, Antonio Picornell, whose thought presumably reveals notable similarities and coincidences with Paine's. In Gandía's opinion, the resemblances derive, not from direct contact, but from "a common ideological substratum: both are established upon Locke, on Rousseau, and, without being aware of it, on St. Thomas." This is probably the only time Thomas Paine has ever been associated with Thomas Aquinas.

The notion of an ideological substratum uniting Paine and liberal Latin American thinkers can be accepted only to the extent that both ultimately depend upon Christian theology. Paine derives, however, from a Protestant tradition and the Latin Americans from a Catholic one. The particular contribution of St. Thomas to political tradition consists in the argument that if the people have the right to elect a king they have a right to dethrone him also.[8] This argument exists in Locke as well, but it is by no means certain that it came to him from St. Thomas. The concept, moreover, is not to be found in Paine's *Common Sense*. Without doubt, Locke, Rousseau, and Paine contributed to an ideological substratum, but this does not

[5] Ibid., 1: 247.
[6] Ibid., 1: 407.

[7] Ibid., 1: 408.
[8] Ibid., 5: 508.

mean that the partisans of one of these thinkers would necessarily be receptive to the arguments of the others or that Paine necessarily depended upon Locke. To this day, scholarship has been unable to discover passages in *Common Sense* that can be conclusively proved to be inspired directly by either Locke or Rousseau. Many of the concepts in Paine that appealed to the Spanish-American liberals, moreover, have nothing in common with either Locke or Rousseau, and still less with St. Thomas or Suárez. Even though a substratum of political thought parallel to Paine's may have existed in the Hispanic tradition, none of Paine's translators or commentators referred to such a substratum nor did they seek to associate his writings with those of any predecessors.

Gandía has two excellent chapters interpreting Paine as "the man who with the exposition of clear and profound ideas that spoke of liberty contributed more than any other ideologue of his time to the triumph of the North American Revolution and of the French Revolution and to the awakening of an infinite number of minds in the civil war for the liberty of the great empire of Hispano-America."[9] Gandía admired Paine greatly despite his paradoxical attempt to minimize Paine's influence. Whether Paine contributed to the birth of the independence movement or served merely to reinspire or invigorate it is relatively unimportant to his fame. What counts for literary history is that he was translated, quoted, and widely respected as a political thinker.

As previously noted, Gandía gives 1810 as the date for the introduction of Paine's ideas into the Hispanic world. He isolates this date because it was in this year that parts of *Common Sense* were first translated into Spanish, but he does not take into account the possibility of the pen-

[9] Ibid., 1: 243-44.

etration of French versions. In my opinion, there is absolutely no reason to believe that the French translations of *Common Sense* which I have mentioned in the fifth chapter traveled physically across the Atlantic, but Paine's ideas may have been transmitted by means of a widely read book of major interest to Spain and her colonies, Raynal's *Histoire philosophique et politique*, the work that picked up Franklin's Polly Baker. Raynal did not actually translate Paine in his *Histoire*, but gave a thorough paraphrase of his main ideas. Raynal's treatise was translated into Spanish, moreover, before the end of the eighteenth century.[10] One cannot, therefore, unequivocally rule out Paine's influence before 1810.

There exists, moreover, in the work of a writer known as "the Peruvian Rousseau," convincing evidence that Paine was known in Hispano-America before the publication of the first Spanish translation. This writer, Manuel de Vidaurre, had rounded the Horn on a voyage to Spain early in 1810. On 13 May of that year he wrote the dedication to a work setting forth a political program for his native land entitled *Plan del Perú*. In a prologue, he says that he had composed this remarkable work of over 100 tightly packed pages in eleven days. Vidaurre recommends Paine as one of the basic political writers that should be read in the schools of Peru. In his words, "the first books to be read should be the histories of Spain and the Americas; afterwards *Common Sense* by Thomas Paine, the constitution of the Spanish monarchy, and universal morality." Vidaurre's *Plan del Perú* was not printed until 1823 (in Philadelphia) at which time he added extensive notes, including a number of favorable references to Paine's religious ideas. In various other documents, Vidaurre cites

---

[10] *Historia política de los establecimientos ultramarinos de las naciones europeas*, 5 vols. (Madrid), 1784-1790).

and quotes Paine almost as frequently as he does his other idol, Rousseau.

The most important translations of Paine's works intended for Latin America were originally published in Philadelphia, primarily because of the rigid censorship in the Spanish colonies, and other Spanish translations were published in London. Second editions of two of these translations, however, were printed in the Hispanic world, one in Mexico and the other in Peru. The first translation of any of Paine's work into Spanish was published in Philadelphia under the title *La independencia de la Costa Firme justificada por Thomas Paine treinta años ha*. Although it bears the date 1811 on the title page, the dedication is dated December 1810. In the following year a companion volume appeared, *Historia concisa de los Estados Unidos desde el descubrimiento de la América hasta el año de 1807*, the two works complementing each other and forming "a complete body of doctrine in the service of one idea: the enlightenment of Hispanoamérica."[11] Both volumes were edited by Manuel García de Sena, a native of Venezuela temporarily residing in Philadelphia. The *Historia concisa* consists of a rather rough translation of a utilitarian historical text by a minor writer, John M'Culloch, and *La independencia de la Costa Firme* consists of translations of carefully selected passages from the works of Paine and other North American political authors.

Except for parts of *Common Sense*, the contents of the *Independencia* are dry and prosaic, in large part documentary in nature, and in our day they would seem rather forbidding reading. The prosaic cast of the book makes its vogue in South America seem all the more remarkable. A summary of the contents will indicate why one might not have expected an avid audience for the work. The

[11] Pedro Grases and Albert Harkness, *Manuel García de Sena y la independencia de Hispanoamérica* (Caracas, 1953), p. 31.

selections from Paine consist of the first two parts of *Common Sense;* the *Dissertation on First Principles of Government;* and the *Dissertations on Government; the Affairs of the Bank and Paper Money.* The sections from *Common Sense* include Paine's famous distinction between government and society and his demonstration of the superiority of republican over monarchical government. The *Dissertation on First Principles* further attacks the hereditary principle, repudiates the concept of a property qualification for voting, and defends the principle of majority rule. The work on the bank and paper money explains the concept of public good, distinguishes the lawmaking function of a state from that of merely carrying on public business, and vindicates a state bank and paper currency.

The other documents in the collection comprise the Declaration of Independence, the Articles of Confederation, the Constitution of the United States, and the state constitutions of Massachusetts, Connecticut, New Jersey, Pennsylvania, and Virginia. Although the extracts from *Common Sense* make up only a small part of García de Sena's book, they received the major attention in the press of Latin America. This is not surprising since *Common Sense* is one of the world's greatest works of forensic literature, whereas the constitutions of the various American states seldom stir the hearts of their readers. But at this period of Latin American history, even the state constitutions were likely to have had some popular appeal: government by constitution was still a novelty since prior to this time the only parallel documents in political science had been charters and royal grants. The edition of García de Sena's translation was a relatively large one for the time and place, for records exist showing that six boxes were consigned to Caracas, each box containing 125 copies of the work.[12] A contemporary observer remarked

[12] Ibid., p. 54.

that it circulated from hand to hand in Caracas and became fashionable reading.[13]

García de Sena, in dedicating the *Independencia* to his brother Ramón, took pains to point out that it contained not a single word contrary to their Roman Catholic religion. This caution was necessary, he felt, since the Spanish government had not only sought to conceal the truth that Paine expounded, but had sacrilegiously attempted to make its people believe that monarchical rule had the same divine sanction as their religion, "to turn into an almost divine precept that which was in reality an act of despotism."

García de Sena's anticipation of the charge of irreligion together with his need to defend himself against it underscores a fundamental contrast between the climate of opinion in the Anglo-Saxon world and that in the Spanish. In England at the time of Paine, nobody any longer seriously believed that God had appointed any particular set of temporal rulers, and the arguments for monarchy and hereditary aristocracy which Paine was attacking had nothing to do with theories of divine right.

In the Spanish world, however, the monarchy and the Church were so closely affiliated that the belief was imposed and apparently widely accepted in all sections of society that the monarchy had been constituted by God. The first step for propagandists in Latin America, therefore, was to attack and defeat that concept. Paine, as we all know, made extensive use of Scripture in *Common Sense*, but he did not even bother to notice the concept of divine right; it was monarchy as a mere secular institution that he condemned. It was customary in the North American colonies to appraise any doctrine or mode of behavior by scriptural standards, and Paine merely fell in with this custom. He probably did not have any more belief in divine inspiration at this time than when he

---

[13] *Ibid.*, p. 52.

wrote *The Age of Reason*. Despite the efforts of Paine's translator to remove from his work any suspicion of the taint of irreligion, it was nevertheless condemned by the Inquisition in Mexico in 1815 and placed on the list of forbidden books.[14]

Soon after the publication of *La independencia* in Philadelphia, the section from *Common Sense* on hereditary succession was extracted in two issues of *La Gazeta de Caracas* [14 and 17 January 1812], supplemented by three long footnotes attributed in the text to the editor. The editor was an important revolutionary leader, Francisco Isnardy, but Juan Germán Roscio, another Venezuelan patriot, is thought by some to be the author of the notes. One of them is even more radical than Paine's text in disassociating monarchy from Christianity and suggesting that Scripture had been deliberately misinterpreted by monarchical rulers to mislead their people.

In reference to Paine's affirmation that "all anti-monarchical parts of Scripture have been very smoothly glossed over in monarchical governments, but they undoubtedly merit the attention of countries which have their governments yet to form," the note implies that government should be established with no reference whatsoever to the Christian Scriptures, a position with which Paine would have undoubtedly agreed at the time he wrote *Common Sense*. "If we answer truthfully," ran the note, "perhaps we shall be suspected of heresy in the opinion of those who make use of this scarecrow in order to avoid the reform of certain abuses incompatible with the republican form of government."

Paine had referred to the Book of Samuel, but since his remarks were published in Venezuela on 14 January, shortly after Twelfth Night or the Feast of the Three Kings, the editor made a topical comment on the relationship be-

---

[14] Ibid., p. 55.

tween religion and government by citing the three Wise
Men of Scripture. "We shall not fail to reveal," he affirmed,

> that those wise foreigners, sanctified in the adoration
> of the newborn God, were imperceptibly converted by
> vile glossary-makers into crowned Kings. Despots, con-
> cerned to make their slaves believe that their authority
> is all divine and that heaven cares profoundly for their
> person, were able to impose upon their subjects by hav-
> ing them accept the fiction that the Three Wise Men
> who came from the orient to Jerusalem were sovereigns,
> seeking the place where the King of the Jews had been
> born. Using the same artifice, they had managed to make
> people believe that comets were destined to announce
> the death of monarchs. In the Gospel of St. Mark, where
> this story is narrated, three philosophers and astrologers
> are found denying the royal character which tyranny
> combined with religious fanaticism has attributed to
> them.

In connection with Paine's reference to the eight civil
wars and nineteen rebellions which the concept of hereditary monarchy had brought on in England, his commentator affirmed that the record in Spain and France had
been equally bloody. "Catalonia and Aragon will never
forget the troubled epoch of the introduction of the Bourbon dynasty: and France will always regard with horror
the memory of the League, the Barricades, and St. Bartholomew, during which were reciprocally assassinated
fathers, brothers, kinsmen, and friends for the rights of a
king and a family which afterwards cost France itself all
the evils of its last revolution and the foreign despotism
to which it was submitted." The Caracas newspaper was
thus much bolder than Paine's translator, García de Sena,
in condemning the Spanish monarchy per se, not merely
as an instrument of colonial exploitation and despotism.

Enrique de Gandía has noticed that Roscio, who may have been Paine's newspaper annotator, uses in one of his own political tracts the argument from *Common Sense* that many verses from the Old Testament demonstrate that the origin of monarchy is not divine.[15] Roscio's work is entitled *El patriotismo de Nirgua y abuso de los reyes* (1811). Gandía does not assert direct influence in this "echo of Thomas Paine," but rather a coincidence of style. In a later work published in Philadelphia in 1817, *El triunfo de la libertad*, Roscio refutes a wider range of arguments in favor of monarchy based on Scripture. An even more significant echo of Paine, moreover, appears in a manifesto of 1811 drawn up by Roscio based on the American Declaration of Independence, *Manifesto que hace al mundo la confederación de Venezuela . . . de las razones en que ha fundado su absoluta independencia de la España*. In reference to "the moral abuse of the maternity of Spain in regard to America," Roscio affirms that "it is widely recognized that in the order of nature it is the father's duty to free his son, so that when leaving his minority he is able to make use of his forces and his reason in order to provide for his subsistence; and that it is the duty of the son to do it [assert his freedom] when the cruelty or dissipation of the father or guardian compromises his destiny or jeopardizes his patrimony."[16] In *Common Sense*, Paine had developed the same metaphor of parental relationship: "But Britain is the parent country say some. Then the more shame upon her conduct. Even brutes do not devour their young, nor savages make war upon their families."[17] In *Crisis* no. VII, Paine returned to the metaphor: "The title she assumed of parent country, led to, and pointed out, the propriety, wisdom and advantage of

---

[15] *Historia*, 5: 506.

[16] *Obras*, ed. Pedro Grases, 3 vols. (Caracas, 1953), 2: 65.

[17] *Complete Writings of Thomas Paine*, ed. Philip S. Foner, 2 vols. (New York, 1945), 1: 19.

a separation; for as in private life, children grow into men, and by setting up for themselves, extend and secure the interest of the whole family, so in the settlement of colonies large enough to admit of maturity, the same policy should be pursued."[18]

On the day after the Declaration of Independence of the American Confederation of Venezuela, 5 July 1811, Antonio Nicolás Briceño read before the Assembly García de Sena's translation of the American Constitution.[19] One of the fathers of Venezuelan independence, Francisco Javier Yanes, had sought to have independence formally declared on 4 July so that it would coincide with that of the United States. Later, in his respected political treatise, *Manual político del venezolano*, he listed Paine among those who had perfected representative government in the New World and gave him credit for saying that representative government is the invention of the modern world and that its foundation rests upon the equality of rights.[20] Even more important than this explicit recognition of Paine's historical significance is a paragraph from the preface that duplicates the opening lines of *Common Sense*, completely without acknowledgment.

> . . . De lo dicho se conoce que la sociedad y el gobierno so diferencian esencialmente en su origen y objeto. La sociedad nació de las necesidades de los hombres; y de los vicios de éstos el gobierno. La sociedad se dirige siempre al bien; y el gobierno debe tirar a reprimir el mal. . . . La sociedad, en fin, es esencialmente buena; el gobierno puede ser, y efectivamente es, malo en muchas partes del globo.

Comparison with Paine's text reveals that Yanes is translating rather than paraphrasing.

[18] Ibid., 1: 154.
[19] Grases and Harkness, *García de Sena*, p. 56.
[20] Ed. Ramón Escovar Salóm (Caracas, 1959), pp. 61, 52.

> Some writers have so confounded society with govern-
> ment, as to leave little or no distinction between them;
> whereas they are not only different, but have different
> origins. Society is produced by our wants, and govern-
> ment by our wickedness; the former promotes our hap-
> piness *positively* by uniting our affections, the latter
> negatively by restraining our vices. . . . Society in every
> state is a blessing, but government even in its best state
> is but a necessary evil.

Indeed Yanes follows Paine more closely than do some
Latin American texts actually described as translations.

In 1811, the same year as García de Sena's *Independencia*, there appeared in London a more extensive translation of *Common Sense* under the title *Reflecciones políticas, escritas baxo el título de "Instinto común,"* published at the expense of the translator, who is described
on the title page as a Peruvian Indian, Anselmo Nateiu.
The latter was a pseudonym based on an anagram for
Manuel José de Arrunátegui.

In his preface Nateiu states that he is translating merely
the sections "applicable to the actual circumstances of
South America." He warns that although Paine's principles are important and incontestable, great prudence must
be exercised in presenting them to the people all at once.
"A violent metamorphosis in their political situation,"
he affirms, could dislodge the people "from the true circle
of liberty and cause them to degenerate into a frenzy de-
grading them into anarchy or despotism." He nevertheless
considers it desirable for the Spanish-Americans to imitate their Anglo-American brothers in forming a patriotic
union and making themselves equally deserving of the
liberty that the latter are enjoying. In one of his footnotes
he follows the *Gazeta de Caracas* in drawing attention
to the passage concerning the large number of civil wars
and rebellions in the history of England. The Spanish peo-

ple have suffered through internal strife, he says, for the famous war of the Spanish succession had no other cause but the personal disputes of the houses of Austria and Bourbon.[21] In another note he displays a remarkable feeling of identity with the North Americans, suggesting not only that the two peoples are alike in their political situations, but that they share a common character. In reference to Paine's praise of American courage and resolution, his translator proudly affirms that recent events in Buenos Aires "are the most authentic testimony of that which the American character is capable of."[22]

A Mexican patriot, Servando Teresa de Mier, made a similar attempt to associate Spanish-American and Anglo-American bravery in reference to Paine. The following significant paragraph appears in his *Historia de la revolución de Nueva España*, written in 1813.

> Enough blood has been shed already to demonstrate that they [the Spanish-Americans] are not cowardly orangutans but very worthy of appearing at the side of the Anglo-Americans. It is impossible that *Common Sense* should not already have said to them as well as to others: "A greater interest has never concerned the nations. It is not the matter of a single town or province, but that of an entire immense continent, or of half of the globe. It is not the interest of a day, but of centuries."

> [Demasiada sangre han derramado ya para evidenciar que no son cobardes uranutanes, sino mui dignos de figurar al lado de los Anglo-americanos. Es imposible ya que su *Sentido común* no les esté diciendo como á los otros: "Jamás un interés más grande ha ocupado a las naciones. No se trata del de una villa ó provincia,

---

[21] *Reflecciones políticas*, p. 18. A second edition was published in Lima, Peru, in 1821.

[22] Ibid., p. 31.

es el de todo un continente inmenso, ó de la mitad del globo. No es el interés de un día, sino el de siglos."][23]

Mier's translation is exceedingly loose. Paine's exact words are:

> The sun never shined on a cause of greater worth. 'Tis not the affair of a city, a country, a province, or a kingdom, but of a continent—of at least one eighth part of the habitable globe. 'Tis not the concern of a day, a year, or an age; posterity are virtually involved in the contest, and will be more or less affected, even to the end of time, by the proceedings now.

Mier uses fewer words than Paine, but expands his concepts. Paine has been accused of exaggeration in speaking of one eighth of the globe; Mier inflates the area to one half. He covers fifteen pages of Paine's text in two of his own, not only shortening and paraphrasing, but adding comments and embellishments that are not in Paine at all. When Paine refers to England or Great Britain, Mier substitutes Spain, as in the following passage: "La autoridad de la España sobre América tarde o temprano debe tener un fin. . . . España está demasiado lejos para gobernarnos." ["The authority of Spain over America must sooner or later come to an end. . . . Spain is too far away to govern us."] No better proof could be offered of the relevance of Paine's words to the situation of the Spanish colonies.

Despite the great liberties that Mier took with Paine's text, he took pride in his rendition as a fair translation. In a manuscript not published during his lifetime, he credits Paine for analyzing political principles in the light of the common sense which provided the title of his work. He then adds, "I translated his speech in Book IV of my *History of the Revolution*, accommodating it to our sit-

---

[23] Facsimile ed., 2 vols. (Mexico, 1922), 2: 272. Accentuation is that of the original.

uation, and as despotism has concealed it, I shall reproduce this piece of eloquence."[24] The manuscript does not
include Mier's translation, but it may be found in another
work of Mier published in Philadelphia in 1821, his *Memoria politíco-instructiva*, republished in Mexico in the
next year.

A separate translation of Paine's *Dissertation on the
First Principles of Government* was published anonymously in London in 1819. The translator, who was Gen.
José María Vergara according to a handwritten note in the
copy at the British Museum, believed that this was the
most useful of Paine's works. He devotes most of his prologue, however, to defending Paine for not treating Montesquieu's theories of the influence of climate on human
character and social institutions. Vergara replies that
Montesquieu's theories have not been generally accepted
and as proof quotes an extensive refutation of them by
Voltaire. He vehemently rejects the idea that since most
of Latin America lies within the torrid zone, its inhabitants are sluggish and unfit for democratic government.
Republicanism, he maintains, is the only form of government originating in the nature of man, and climate does
not make man lose his rights or change his nature. Paine's
principles, therefore, are valid for all people, including the
Latin Americans, regardless of the climate or latitude where
they live. In his notes, Vergara seems far less liberal than
Paine. Although accepting all of Paine's criticisms of hereditary monarchy, he argues that defects of absolutism
would be avoided in a constitutional limited monarchy
with an elected House of Representatives. He also believes
that the rights of man would not be violated in a republic
with hereditary succession.[25]

---

[24] "Nos prometieron constituciones," in *Escritos inéditos de Fray Servando Teresa de Mier*, ed. J. M. Miquel i Vergas and Hugo Díaz-Thomé
(Mexico, 1944), p. 359.

[25] *Disertación sobre los primeros principios del gobierno por Tomas
Pain [sic]* (London, 1819), pp. 25, 38.

One of the most active political and intellectual figures in the history of Latin American independence, Vicente Rocafuerte, edited sections of *Common Sense* and the entire *Dissertation on the First Principles of Government* in a compilation entitled *Ideas necesarias a todo pueblo americano independiente, que quiera ser libre* (1821) [*Ideas necessary for all the independent people of America who wish to be free*]. A second edition was published in Puebla, Mexico, two years later. Born in Ecuador, Rocafuerte, after studies in France and a political apprenticeship in Spain, came to Philadelphia, where he published *Ideas necesarias* and led a propaganda campaign against the imperialistic aims of Iturbide of Mexico. He later became president of Ecuador (from 1835 to 1839) and fathered a new constitution. The material from Paine in *Ideas necesarias* is essentially a reworking of García de Sena's previous translation with only minor textual changes. In his preface, which is original, Rocafuerte eulogized Paine for doing more than anyone else to tear the reins of government from despotic hands. "The intrepid American," he wrote, destroyed the trappings of monarchy in order that it would never return to establish itself in this precious part of the globe. Rocafuerte also reprinted his adapted translation of *Common Sense* in his defense and interpretation of the United States Constitution entitled *Ensayo político: el sistema colombiano, popular, electivo, y representativo, es el que más conviene á la América independiente* (1823), published not in Philadelphia, but in New York.

Apparently it required almost five years for García de Sena's translation to make its influence felt in the southern part of the continent, for it was not until 6 April 1816 that it was advertised, along with the *Historia concisa*, in *La Gazeta de Buenos Aires*, as being "extremely worthy of the attention of the people during the present crisis." Five days later it was advertised as well in another periodical of Buenos Aires, *El Censor*, with the comment that

"nothing in the present times would better serve to nourish the minds of the young with those ideas which could
strengthen and instruct" them in the cause that was then
being defended. On 16 April 1816, both of García de Sena's
books were advertised in the third newspaper of the city,
La Prensa Argentina, as well as on 15 October 1816, this
time Paine's title being abbreviated to *El sentido de Tomas
Payne*.[26]

During the preceding six years, sentiments of revolution and republicanism had created a climate of opinion
receptive to Paine's forthright mode of expression. According to Bartolomé Mitré, "There was not only the abstract *Contrat social* of Rousseau, the vade mecum of the
revolutionaries; also popular among the youth were the
clear, practical and radical principles of the book of Thomas
Paine on *The Rights of Man*."[27] As we examine the evidence that Paine was well known in Buenos Aires, however, we shall observe that *Common Sense* rather than
Rights of Man represented the source of his fame.

Paine's *Rights of Man* was not translated into Spanish
until 1821, when it was made available under the title *El
derecho del hombre* by an Italian-American language
teacher, Santiago Felipi Puglia, and published in Philadelphia by Matthew Carey. Despite a second edition which
appeared in the following year, no evidence has yet been
uncovered of its being circulated or exerting any influence. Puglia's translation includes both Parts I and II, but
omits all polemics against Burke, all historical descriptions of the French Revolution, all complimentary references to the United States, and all of the famous passage
in which Paine declares "my country is the world." Puglia

[26] In an anonymous *Compendio de la historia de los Estados Unidos*
(Philadelphia, 1825), the title of *Common Sense* was translated as *Luz
de la razón*.

[27] *Historia de Belgrano y de la independencia argentina*, 4 vols., 5th
ed. (Buenos Aires, 1902), 3: 13.

had earlier defended Paine's ideas in a highly original treatise entitled *Desengaño del hombre* (Philadelphia, 1794), and an extract from the manuscript had been published in the form of a prospectus in English in the previous year. Hamilton and Jefferson were among the subscribers to the Spanish edition of 500 copies. In addition to defending Paine's political ideas, the work attacked the abuses of institutionalized Christianity on moral grounds, a rather important development since the work preceded *The Age of Reason*. No evidence of the circulation of *Desengaño del hombre* has yet been discovered other than its being decreed as blasphemous by the Inquisition of Mexico in the year of its publication, a distinction soon to be shared by García de Sena's translation.[28]

The Argentinian periodical that gave greatest space to Paine was *El Censor*, edited at that time by Antonio José Valdés, a Cuban and former deputy to the Cortes. In keeping with its title, *El Censor* exercised a kind of magisterial censorship over the government, and its editors enjoyed a feeling of privileged immunity. The issue of 4 January 1816 devoted its entire eight pages to a single article introduced by the following epigraph in English, "It is not in number, but in unity, that our great strength lies.— T. Paine." The article itself, however, has no reference to *Common Sense*, from which the quotation is taken.

On 20 June 1816 appeared without title but with an anonymous epigraph in French an article on the need for a realistic appraisal of the political situation in Buenos Aires. This article contains a historical anecdote of the North American Revolution attributed to Paine. During a session of Congress, according to this anecdote, a letter from the commander-in-chief to the executive council

---

[28] All of the material on Puglia is based upon A. O. Aldridge, "A Spanish Precursor of the Age of Reason," in *Papers on French-Spanish, Luso-Brazilian, Spanish-American Literary Relations*, ed. Marie A. Wellington (Elmhurst, Ill., 1969), pp. 1-4.

threw the assembly into consternation by its desperate tone. No one in the assembly uttered a word for some time, until a member known for his readiness to submission said: "If the report in this letter presents the true state of things and we are really in the situation which it represents, it seems to me useless to dispute the affair any longer." Another more courageous spirit dissipated the melancholy atmosphere, however, exclaiming, "It is useless to despair; if events do not go as we should like, we must try to improve them." Thus it was, according to this article, that the members of Congress "preserved their votes, their lives, and their fortunes, and the nation was saved." Neither this narrative nor any other resembling it, however, is to be found in the work of Paine.

On 9 July 1816, the Congress of the United Provinces of Argentina, meeting in the city of Tucumán, issued a Declaration of Independence. *El Censor* on 25 July printed the text of this declaration [pp. 1-3] as well as a political article [pp. 3-12] introduced by the following epigraph in English:

> Notwithstanding our wisdom, there is a visible feebleness in some of our proceedings, which gives encouragement to dissentions. The continental belt is too loosely buckled; and if something is not done in time, it will be too late to do any thing, and we shall fall into a state in which neither RECONCILIATION nor INDEPENDENCE will be practicable.—*T. Paine.*

This is an accurate quotation from *Common Sense*.

On 22 August, Valdés printed a very important quotation in Spanish translation from Paine's *Rights of Man*. This is the first reference I have found to *Rights of Man* anywhere in the Spanish world, and few others followed in the period of the liberation of Spanish America. It preceded by five years Puglia's partial translation in Philadelphia. The quotation does not mention Paine by name, but is preceded by the headline "Rasgo Extractado de los Derechos del Hombre." It corresponds to the following passages in Paine's English text:

> The independence of America, considered merely as a separation from England, would have been a matter but of little importance, had it not been accompanied by a revolution in the principles and practise of governments. She made a stand, not for herself only, but for the world, and looked beyond the advantages herself could receive. . . .
>
> From the rapid progress which America makes in every species of improvement, it is rational to conclude, that if the governments of Asia, Africa, and Europe, had begun on a principle similar to that of America, or had not been very early corrupted therefrom, that those countries must, by this time, have been in a far superior condition to what they are. Age after age has passed away, for no other purpose than to behold their wretchedness. Could we suppose a spectator who knew nothing of the world, and who was put into it merely to make his observations, he would take a great part of the old world to be new, just struggling with the difficulties and hardships of an infant settlement. He could not suppose that the hordes of miserable poor, with which old countries abound, could be any other than those who had not yet had time to provide for themselves.[29]

This passage is extremely important in the history of ideas because it incorporates a unique argument in favor of the Moderns in the controversy over ancient versus modern learning which was not only still going on in the eighteenth century, but which had been carried by Paine

[29] *Complete Writings*, ed. Foner, 1: 354-55.

and others from Europe to the New World. Following is the Spanish text, which is not quite a literal translation:

> La independencia del Norte de América, considerada solamente como una separación de Inglaterra, sería materia de poca importancia, si no fuese accompañada por una revolución de los principios y práctica de los gobiernos. Ella hizo una parada, no tan sólo notable a la misma América, sino á todo el mundo, y la América logró ventajas muy excedentes á las que se propuso.— Por sus rápidos progresos en todo género se puede concluir racionalmente, que si los gobiernos de Asia, Africa y Europa hubiesen empezado por los mismos principios que esta parte del nuevo mundo, habrían executado adelantos asombrosos, y aquellas naciones se hallarían en estado muy diverso que el que experimentan en el día. No habrían visto sucederse las edades unas á otras sólo para presenciar sus miserias.—Si supusiésemos un espectador, absolutamente ignorante de nuestro globo, en un punto en que le pudiese observar con ojos filosóficos, deduciría ciertamente que la mayor parte del mundo antiguo era nuevo: y la América libre una nación antigua y experimentada. Era imposible que así no lo supusiese al ver los estados de Asia, los del Africa, y gran parte de los de Europa forcejeando con las miserias, ignorancia y dificultades de pueblos nacientes.

After this quotation, Valdés made a pertinent personal comment, applying the experience of the continent of the north to that of the south.

> Efectivamente la América del Norte ha dado un paso tan asombroso á la civilización, al comercio y población, que el año de 1807 en que yo la visité, los ministros extrangeros residentes en ella se admiraban de su sistema y progreso singular. Todo esto ha ido en más rápido aumento desde aquel tiempo: la guerra con los ingleses

los ha hecho más avisados, y la ruina del imperio francés ha dado un empuje soberbio á su felicidad. Una vecindad tan estimulante coadyuva ventajosamente á la insurrección de Nueva España.

[Indeed North America has given such an astonishing thrust to civilization, to commerce and population, that in 1807, the year in which I visited it, the foreign ministers residing there marvelled at its system and unusual progress. All this has gone on with even more rapid speed since that time; the war with the English (in 1812) has made them more informed, and the ruin of the French Empire has given a superb thrust to their felicity. A neighbor so stimulating aids advantageously in the insurrection of New Spain (Mexico).]

The passages that Valdés extracted from *Rights of Man* are among the most pertinent to Latin America, but there is another passage in this work even more directly concerned with the Southern Hemisphere, which all commentators of the time completely overlooked. In the last section of his work, Paine proposed a kind of North Atlantic Alliance, consisting of a confederation of the fleets of England, France, and Holland together with the dismantling of all the navies in Europe.[30] These confederated powers, he suggested, "together with that of the United States of America, can propose, with effect, to Spain, the independence of South America, and the opening those countries, of immense extent and wealth, to the general commerce of the world, as North America now is." It may be that the patriots of South America would not have been enthusiastic about this method of acquiring their independence, but they would probably have approved of Paine's subsequent remarks concerning trade. "The opening of South America," he affirmed, "would produce an immense field for commerce, and a ready money market for

[30] Ibid., 1: 448.

manufactures, which the Eastern world does not. The East is already a country of manufactures, the importation of which is not only an injury to the manufactures of England, but a drain upon its specie." This remark concerning the economic destiny of Latin America seems to have gone entirely unnoticed to this day. Indeed a scholarly historian of Venezuelan independence affirms "ninguna obra de Paine se refiera específicamente a la Independencia de Hispanoamérica."[31]

Valdés in the month after his reference to *Rights of Man* published in *El Censor* an essay attacking the complete freedom of press in Buenos Aires, using Thomas Paine as a justification for his point of view [26 September 1816]. This is probably the only time in any country when the name of Thomas Paine has been used to oppose the free expression of opinion. The article in *El Censor* belongs to an extended polemical discussion between Valdés and the editor of a rival periodical, Vicente Pazos Silva, a Peruvian of mixed Indian blood, who had come to Buenos Aires early in the Revolution. After taking orders in the Roman Catholic Church, he visited London and returned to Buenos Aires, no longer wearing clerical garb, and bringing with him a wife and a printing press on which he printed a new republican periodical, *La Crónica Argentina*. Silva added to his Spanish names an Indian name Kanki, by which he is now most frequently known.

Kanki in *La Crónica Argentina* began the periodical debate with a magisterial article opposing the scheme of two leaders of the nation to establish an empire in Argentina based on the ancient one of the Incas. Kanki opposed this romantic idea because of its all too apparent monarchical complexion.

Valdés replied in *El Censor* to this criticism of the pro-

---

[31] Pedro Grases, *La conspiración de Gual y España y el ideario de la independencia* (Caracas, 1949), p. 61.

posed empire with a defense of constitutional monarchy as found in England. And since Kanki had handled him rather roughly along with the power-minded politicians behind the scheme, Valdés argued for restraints upon the freedom of press. In order to enlist historical authority on his side, he cited the proscription of the works of Paine by the British government. Somewhat inconsistently, however, he supplied his article with an epigraph in English attributed to Paine: "It is darkness attempting to illuminate light." The essence of Valdés's argument is that Argentina was not yet ready for the complete freedom of the press, a condition that suits only well-established and highly cultured societies. If a free press were to be introduced into a backward country like Turkey, he reasoned, it would lead to disturbances, bloodshed, and ruin. And in a developing country like Argentina, the press would be taken over by impetuous spirits, preaching division and revolution.

> Thomas Paine produced marvelous effects in the United States because he knew the genius of the people, their propensities, and their geographical conditions. Thomas Paine would have written among us in another vein, however, or he would have made a mistake involving us in a thousand evil happenings, as indeed he had contributed to bring them about during the French Revolution. Among us a few superficial geniuses drink his alluring and dangerous doctrine, and without being capable of digesting it, make opportune application and belch pestilences with their proud and insubstantial philosophy. Thus we see all around us in print and in manuscript the principles of Payne, more appropriate to be read than to be adopted in practice.

Dramatically Valdés expressed the hope that his fellow citizens would not weep with tears of blood as a consequence of the enthusiastic extravagancies of Thomas Paine.

In this diatribe against Paine, Kanki was not directly

accused of being the disciple of the author of *Rights of Man*, but since Valdés attempted to discredit his rival by disparaging Paine, Kanki was certainly being condemned by association. He therefore repudiated this method of argument and at the same time rose to the defense of Paine. *"El Censor,"* he wrote, "deceives himself or wishes to deceive the public by indicating Paine as our favorite author."

> Let us grant it, however, for the sake of argument: If the principles of Paine are impracticable how is it that they have been successful in North America? And in what way are our propensities and geographical conditions any different from those of North America? The main consideration is that which has already been accomplished—that is, to have dethroned the king and reassumed our own government. And in what page does Thomas Payne [*sic*] teach that the citizens of a Republic should cut each other's throats, as has taken place in France. This was the effect of other causes and not of his principles. No matter what they were, they are not the basis of the reasoning which we used to discredit in a convincing manner, and not by the use of proscription, the projected Inca monarchy.

Kanki observed that Valdés was in effect opposing not only the freedom of press but also the freedom to read. This would be the logical outcome of the argument that Paine should be prohibited in Argentina since he had been prohibited in England. Drawing on recollections of his sojourn in London, Kanki explained the paradox of the British government prosecuting Paine's works under a system of a free press. The British people, Kanki affirmed, are allowed to condemn the institution of kings and monarchs or to revile ministers as assassins, as they do every day, but they must not speak against their actual king or reigning house. And this is the reason why the reprinting of Paine's works was prohibited. Kanki went on to describe a recent incident involving a London printer who had been condemned to stand in the pillory for the offense of publishing Paine. The enlightened English public, however, instead of abusing or insulting the printer, as was expected, paid tribute to him with flowers and music, thereby turning the event into a triumph over the sentence of the judges. Kanki was indeed very generous toward the British nation in his description of how it maintained a free press, but unfortunately his explanation is not very accurate. *Rights of Man* was actually prosecuted as a seditious publication, not because it condemned George III as an individual, and the story of the printer's triumph in the pillory is, as far as I have been able to determine, purely imaginary.

Valdés in the following number of *El Censor* completely passed over the question of freedom of the press and concentrated his continuing criticism of Paine on the subject of monarchy. Paine's strongest argument, he believed, is that the present generation has no right to establish a monarchy since it would thereby be enslaving all future generations to the monarch and his successor. To Valdés, this reasoning was superficial and sophistical. By failing to make provision for the stability of future generations, he countered, the present one would be enslaving itself to these later generations, since it would be obliged to live in continuous disorder merely to keep from limiting future generations. The latter, he argued, would be much more grateful to have as their heritage, instead of a turbulent and ruinous republic, a constitutional monarchy in which the ruler protects order as prescribed by the constitution and guarantees to each citizen the free and certain possession of his rights. Paine, according to Valdés, had used his natural genius to expose the defects of monarchy, but in so doing had confounded the constitutional type of monarchy with the absolute. His magnification of democracy had nevertheless acquired for him an infinity of unsophisticated proselytes.

As an example of Paine's subtlety, Valdés cited his interpretation of the Book of Samuel, in which he had depicted the Hebrew people as constituting a republic and bringing down the anger of God upon them by asking for a monarch. In refutation, Valdés argued that the Hebrews had never had a republican form of government, but had been a patriarchy until the time of Moses, and subsequently they had been ruled by judges and tyrants, the latter designed by God as a punishment for the crimes of the Chosen People. The rule of the judges, Valdés maintained, represented a theocracy mixed with aristocracy. When the Hebrews called for a king, they were, therefore, rejecting their God in favor of a despot, not a constitutional king. This interpretation, Valdés considered, was corroborated by the words of God to Samuel: "they have not rejected thee, but they have rejected me" [I Samuel 8:7]. Finally, Valdés observed, as many others have done, an apparent inconsistency in Paine's attitude toward the Scriptures, that in *Common Sense* he regarded the Old and New Testaments as an authority to persuade his readers; whereas in *The Age of Reason* he labeled them apocryphal. This is the first time that Paine's work on religion is known to have been mentioned in Latin America.

Kanki in replying (30 November) made no effort to carry on the debate over Scripture, but returned to the concept of a free press. The very prohibition of Paine's works in England, Kanki affirmed, "is the best recommendation they contain, for the English are too enlightened and too liberal to fear incendiary writers merely because they are heated." Paine had not been proscribed because he spoke in general terms against the ruling house, but because "disseminating principles opposed to the constitution of the state with the aid of his vivid imagination, he had forced the common sense of his readers to an irresistible conviction, and this is what they have reason to fear and have feared."

Since Valdés had leveled the charge of inconsistency against Paine, Kanki turned it against Valdés. He cited the previous numbers of *El Censor* in which Paine had been warmly praised, specifically the issue in which the García de Sena translation had been recommended for its ability "to nourish the minds of the young with those ideas which could strengthen and instruct them in the cause that we defend" (11 April) and the issue containing the Argentinian declaration of independence (25 July), in which an epigraph from Paine had introduced the lead article. Kanki reminded his opponent that he had "publicly praised Thomas Paine, proposed him as a model for the enlightenment of youth, and pointed to him as a teacher to form their minds."

After this controversy, Paine disappeared from Argentinian periodicals until 23 December 1825, when an intriguing item appeared in the *Mensajero Argentino* reporting the circulation of a Portuguese translation of *Common Sense*.[32] The report does not indicate where the translation was published or what title it bore, but since it is based upon a letter from Liverpool, presumably the translation itself also originated in England. According to the Liverpool letter, five thousand translated copies of *Common Sense* were introduced clandestinely into Brazil. The size of this edition is enormous compared to the press run of 750 copies of García de Sena's *Independencia* and 500 of Puglia's *Desengaño*. What is more surprising, however, is that no other trace of this Portuguese edition has ever been uncovered; there is not a single copy known to exist today. According to the *Mensajero Argentino*, the successful introduction of Paine's work into Brazil should

---

[32] Merle E. Simmons, *U.S. Political Ideas in Spanish America before 1830: A Bibliographical Study* (Bloomington, Ind., 1977), p. 55.

be considered as "very favorable to inflame the fire, which aggravated by the attempted crimes of despotism, appears from time to time in all parts of the empire" ["muy propio a encender el fuego, que a pesar de los conatos del despotismo, aparece de cuando en cuando en todos los lugares del imperio"].

The direct influence of Paine in the southern part of the hemisphere was by no means limited to discussions in the periodical press of Buenos Aires. Evidence indicates that a number of important political personalities drew inspiration from Paine's works as presented in the García de Sena translation. At the opening of the Biblioteca Pública in Montevideo in January 1816, the inaugural discourse given by an ecclesiastic listed Paine's works among "the classic texts that speak of our rights." That this speaker attributed great significance to Paine's ideas is revealed by the complete list of his classic texts: these comprised "the wisest constitutions, including among others the Britannic, with its commentator Blackstone; that of North America with the acts of its Congress up to the present, the state constitutions, and principles of government by Paine; that of the Peninsula, with the journals of the Cortes; that of the Italian Republic by Napoleon and his famous Code of the French People."[33]

José Artigas, the chief of the Uruguayan Orientals, wrote to the Cabildo of Montevideo on 17 March 1816, describing the two translations of García de Sena as "the two volumes which you promised me concerning the discovery of North America, its revolution, the various contrasts, and its progress up to the year 1807." Artigas added that he would rejoice if each one of the eastern states could have this very interesting history. Two months later he wrote to the Cabildo of Corrientes, transmitting "the

[33] Hugo D. Barbagelata, *Artigas y la revolución americana* (Paris, 1930), pp. 118-19.

compendium of the history of North America, anxious
that its light be sufficient to clarify the ideas of the Magistrates and everything contribute to bring about our progress."[34]

One of the greatest of the liberators, José de San Martín,
the George Washington of Argentina and Chile, also knew
the work of Paine and proposed to circulate it through his
own efforts. On 15 December 1816, he wrote to the local
leaders of Buenos Aires, "We are in need of a number of
copies of the work of Thomas Paine, *Historia de la revolución de Estados Unidos e Independencia de la Costa
firme* in order to distribute them in Chile. I hope your
excellencies will bring this to the attention of the supreme
government."[35]

In the following year, when a diplomat from the United
States, Henry Marie Brackenridge, visited Artigas near
Montevideo, he reported the leader of the Orientals to be
"under the guidance of an apostate priest, of the name
Monterosa," who professed "to be in the literal sense, a
follower of the political doctrines of Paine."[36] In Montevideo itself, Brackenridge engaged in conversation with a
merchant's clerk, who "thought Rousseau's Social Contract a visionary theory, but Paine's Common Sense and
Rights of Man, sober and rational productions."[37]

The various Latin American translators of Paine or pop-
ularizers of his work considered up to this point were not
literary figures, as opposed to statesmen or politicians
(with the exception of Puglia, who perhaps should be best
labeled as a pioneer in adult education or bilingual edu-

[34] These extracts are printed by Pedro Grases and Albert Harkness in
their introduction to *Manuel García de Sena y la independencia de
América.*

[35] Ricardo Levene, "El constitucionalismo de Mariano Moreno," *Historia* 3 (1958): 53-71.

[36] *Voyage to South America*, 2 vols. (London, 1820), 1: 209.

[37] Ibid., 1: 235.

cation). In Chile, however, Paine's works did attract the attention of a professional man of letters, Camilo Henríquez, the pioneer dramatist of his country and, like Paine, a journalist and zealous partisan of Enlightenment thought. Although a Roman Catholic clergyman, at one stage in his career called "el fraile de la Buena Muerte," Henríquez held religious ideas bordering on the deism of Paine. He was scarcely more orthodox than the French abbés Raynal or Morellet, notorious in the eighteenth century for their independent thinking. One of his contemporary clerical opponents even accused him of holding that philosophy had been neglected for a period of eighteen centuries, but the dawn of its triumph was impending and beginning to raise its luminous countenance, which meant, according to Henríquez's attacker, that impiety and error would prevail over the religion of Jesus Christ. Not only did Henríquez embrace with Paine the ideals of tolerance, free inquiry, and universal education associated with the Enlightenment, but he was the first to call for an independent Chile.

Before discussing in detail the impact that Paine made upon Henríquez and as a consequence upon the people of Chile, it is necessary to make a few preliminary observations upon the various types and degrees of literary influence. Ordinarily one considers the translator of the works of another writer as a disciple or a follower of the original writer if the translation has been performed as a labor of love and is not mercenary hackwork. A writer may also be considered a disciple if he directly acknowledges an indebtedness or does so indirectly by frequently quoting or imitating his author. A writer may draw upon a preceding author, however, without his becoming in either of these senses a disciple: the influence may either be only moderate in itself or combined with the influences of so many other authors that its single force is greatly outweighed by the others. Although major writers are sometimes so greatly dominated by a single author that they may properly be classified as his disciples, they are more likely to come under the spell of so many and so diverse predecessors that no real discipleship exists to any single one of them. In literary history, this kind of moderate influence upon a major author is sometimes more significant than an extensive influence upon a minor one.

As we have seen, Paine had some translators in Latin America, who may justly be called his disciples, but Henríquez hardly belongs to their number. He never translated more than a few lines of Paine's works, and he derived his liberal political philosophy from a multitude of sources besides Paine. Yet because of his eminent position as a man of letters and his key role in the history of Chilean independence, his achievement in circulating the ideas of Paine below the equator is certainly as notable as that of Paine's Spanish-American translators. As a journalist, Henríquez was gifted with the same powers as Paine to prevail upon his fellow citizens through a lucid, penetrating, and persuasive style to adopt enlightened principles of government. Paine's Hispanic translators, on the other hand, were not literary men at all, and their translations have absolutely no pretense to stylistic excellence.

We shall see that although Paine's influence upon Henríquez's intellectual development was extensive, the latter referred to Paine only once in *La Aurora de Chile* (1812), the first periodical and first publication of any kind to be produced in Chile, and twice in the succeeding *El Monitor Araucano* (1813), the second periodical published in Chile. In the *Aurora*, Henríquez included a brief translation of one paragraph from Paine's *Common Sense*. In the *Monitor* he based one feature article upon an English sentence from Paine's *American Crisis* and concluded his article with a translation of merely ninety-three words from the same source. In a later number he made a further complimentary reference to the *Crisis*. The most remarkable link between the patriot of North America and the patriot of Chile is poetical. In a third periodical, Henríquez translated one of Paine's complete poems under the strange illusion that it was the national anthem of the United States.

Henríquez probably gained his first knowledge of Paine from three citizens of the United States who went to Chile expressly to operate the printing press that produced *La Aurora*, the first and only printing press then in the country. It had been imported as a commercial venture by a naturalized North American of Swedish descent, Hoevel, who wrote his given names in the Spanish style, Mateo Arnaldo. The press had been accompanied on its voyage from the United States by the three printers, Samuel Burr Johnston, William H. Burbidge, and Simon D. Garrison. The government bought the press from Hoevel, hired the three Americans as printers, and engaged Henríquez as editor to publish an official periodical "para unificar la opinión pública a los principios del Gobierno." Probably Hoevel or one of the three printers had a copy of Paine among his possessions, which he showed to Henríquez.[38]

He learned English thanks in great measure to Hoevel. This genial man of the world received a number of periodicals from the United States from which he made translations for Henríquez, and later he gave English lessons to the dedicated editor. If we are to believe Henríquez's statement in *La Aurora* (9 April 1812), two months after the founding of the journal, he learned this difficult language in record-breaking time: The editor, he wrote, animated by a fervent desire to please the public and to earn the confidence of his country, took upon himself the study of the English language, and in the space of less than a

---

[38] Biographical material concerning Henríquez is documented by A. O. Aldridge, "Camilo Henríquez and the Fame of Thomas Paine and Benjamin Franklin in Chile," *Inter-American Review of Bibliography* 17 (1967): 51-67.

month qualified himself to translate English newspapers without help. Only the people who know this language, Henríquez added, would be able to appreciate the greatness of this work or the extent of the fatigue involved. According to Henríquez's biographer, this is not vainglory, but merely a means of giving readers confidence in the editor's veracity. It also seems to indicate that methods of modern language teaching have not actually made much progress since the early nineteenth century.

The American diplomat, Brackenridge, who met Henríquez in Beunos Aires five years later, had the following comment on his literary and linguistic attainments:

> . . . Henríques, [sic] is a Chilean of considerable literary acquirements, of a philanthropic turn of mind, and an enthusiastic admirer of our institutions, which he has endeavoured to explain to his fellow citizens. He understands the English language extremely well, and translates from our newspapers such articles as are likely to be useful.[39]

Brackenridge's further testimony concerning the journalism of this period is invaluable in giving us some idea of circulation figures. Information of this kind is extremely difficult to obtain, and for most early periodicals in both North and South America is virtually nonexistent. Brackenridge tells us that the journals of Buenos Aires in 1817 circulated to the rate of about two thousand weekly. Also in reference to the translation of García de Sena, he remarked: "I believe these have been read by nearly all who can read, and have produced a most extravagant admiration of the United States, at the same time accompanied with something like despair."

Less than two months after Henríquez made his statement in *La Aurora* concerning his mastery of English, he

[39] *Voyage to South America*, 2: 138.

introduced Paine's *Common Sense* to the Chilean public
in a lead article (4 June 1812) bearing the title "Exemplo
Memorable." Here he sketched the plight of Boston in the
early days of the Revolution, while it was suffering the
hardships of the blockade and other British efforts to bring
it to submission. The great need of the English colonies
at this time, Henríquez explained, was that of forming a
constitution—to prove that the conflict was not brought
on by private individuals seeking to gratify personal ambition, but that it was a struggle between the Parliament
of England and the Congress of America, that is, a war
between two nations. At this point Henríquez turned to
his printed authority:

Ayudó á determinarlos á tomar esta resolucion una
obra que se publicó en aquellos dias intitulada el *Sentido Comun*: decia entre otras cosas,—"Sea nuestro
primer paso una constitucion que nos una. Este es el
momento de formarla. Mas tarde se expondria á un por-
venir incierto, y á los caprichos del acaso. Será mas
dificil mientras mas nos aumentemos y seamos mas
ricos. ¿Como conciliar entonces tantos intereses, y tan-
tas provincias? Los hombres se unen por grandes des-
gracias, y grandes temores: entonces nacen esas amis-
tades fuertes y profundas, que asocian entre si las almas
y los intereses. Entonces el genio de los estados se forma
por el espiritu errante del pueblo, y las fuerzas espar-
cidas forman un cuerpo único y formidable. Pocas naciones se aprovecharon del momento oportuno para for-
marse un gobierno. Este momento no vuelve por muchos
siglos, y el descuido es castigado por la anarquia ó la
esclavitud. Aprovechemonos de este instante único. Podemos organizar la constitucion mas bella que ha co-
nocido el mundo. Habeis leido en los libros santos la
historia de la especie humana abismada en la inundación general del globo. Una sola familia escapó, y fué

encargada por el Ser Supremo de renovar la tierra. Esta familia somos nosotros. El despotismo lo ha inundado todo, y nosotros podemos renovar otra véz el mundo. Vamos en este momento á decidir de la suerte de una raza de hombres mas numerosa tal véz que todos los pueblos de la Europa reunidos. Esperaremos ser presa de un conquistador, y que se destruya la esperanza del universo? Sobre nosotros estan fixos los ojos de todas las generaciones futuras, y nos piden la libertad. Nosotros vamos á fixar su destino. Si defraudamos sus esperanzas, si les hacemos trahision, ellas algun dia arrastrarán sus cadenas sobre nuestros sepulcros, y nos cargarán de inprecaciones."

[*Common Sense*, a work published in those days, helped them to make up their minds to undertake the revolution. Among other things, it said: "Let our first step be a constitution which will unite us. This is the moment to form it. At a later time the project would be exposed to an uncertain future and to the caprices of chance. The task will be more difficult after our population grows and we become richer. How would it be possible then to reconcile so many interests and so many provinces? Men unite themselves through great tragedies and great fears. It is then that those great and profound friendships are born which bring people and their interests together. The genius of the state is formed by the wandering spirit of the people, and the extended forces form one whole and formidable body. Few nations have taken advantage of the opportune moment to form a government for themselves. This moment may not return for many centuries, and failure to act is punished by anarchy or slavery. Let us take advantage of our unique moment. We are able to create the most perfect constitution that the world has ever known. You have all read in the Holy Books the history of the human species engulfed by the general inundation of the globe, allowing only one family to escape. It was sent by the Supreme Being to restore the earth. We are this family, despotism has flooded everything, and we are able to renovate the world. Let us in this moment decide the future of a race of men more numerous perhaps than that of all the peoples of Europe together. Are we waiting to be victims of a conqueror? Is the hope of a Union to be destroyed? Upon us are fixed the eyes of all future generations, asking us for freedom. It is up to us to decide their destiny. If we disappoint their hopes, if we commit treason against them, they will some day drag their chains over our tombs and curse us."]

Immediately after these words, Henríquez added his own equally stirring appeal: "Comencemos declarando nuestra independencia" ["Let us start to declare our independence"].

One would look in vain for this long passage in *Common Sense*, for, despite Henríquez's statement, it is not there. Indeed only part of the passage has any resemblance to Paine's original. Henríquez's first three sentences in the Spanish text may be based upon the following from *Common Sense*: "Should an independency be brought about by the first of those means [the voice of Congress], we have every opportunity and every encouragement before us, to form the noblest, purest constitution on the face of the earth." Henríquez's ninth sentence resembles the following in *Common Sense*: "Should we neglect the present favorable and inviting period, and an Independance be hereafter effected by any other means, we must charge the consequence to ourselves." Henríquez's twelfth to fifteenth sentences were probably suggested by the following in *Common Sense*: "A situation similar to the present, hath not happened since the days of Noah until now. The birthday of a new world is at hand, and a race of men, perhaps as numerous as all Europe contains, are to receive their portion of freedom from the event of a few months."[40] The rest of the alleged transcription of Paine's thought is not even a paraphrase, but an elaboration of sentiments previously sketched.

A similar mystery exists in regard to Henríquez's use of *The American Crisis*. Henríquez began the sixty-third number of his *Monitor Araucano* with the following epigraph:

> There [sic] are the times that try men's souls. Paine. American crisis n. 2.
>
> [September 2, 1813]

Apart from the substitution of "There" for "These," which is probably a typographical error, the great puzzle in this epigraph is why the quotation should be attributed to *Crisis* no. 2, when it is universally recognized by all who have read Paine as the opening sentence of *Crisis* no. 1. The mystery may be cleared up by reference to the publishing history of Paine's works. The first London printer of the *Crisis*, Daniel Isaac Eaton, was not certain of exactly which writings of Paine were originally issued under this title, and in his edition published in 1796 he included as no. 1 an essay from an earlier "Crisis" series published in London by another author. In a later issue of his edition, also in 1796, Eaton included a note acknowledging that no. 1 of his collection was not by Paine.

This bibliographical circumstance shows that the *Crisis* did not make its way into Henríquez's hands directly from Philadelphia, but that he used a copy published in England. This suggests that his copy of *Common Sense* may also have come from England and that other Latin Amer-

---

[40] All three sentences from *Common Sense* are to be found on the same page in *Complete Writings*, ed. Foner, 1: 45.

icans may likewise have read London imprints as well as Philadelphia ones or the García de Sena translation.

In a sense, Henríquez's entire essay is an elaboration of Paine, for he begins with the opening sentences of *Crisis* no. 1 and concludes with its final sentences. Paine is used as a means of introducing the theme of revolutionary struggle:

> El célebre Paine en las vicisitudes de la fortuna de la revolución de Norte América decía: *estos son los tiempos que prueban las almas*. En verdad en las revoluciones todo se descubre a nuestra vista: los talentos, las virtudes, la incapacidad, los visios, los caracteres nobles y sublimes, y los seres pequeños y ridículos que suspiran por la opresión y la infamia de la servidumbre.

Henríquez's last paragraph, as we have already indicated, consists of his translation of the conclusion of the first *Crisis*:

> Tal es nuestra situación, y todos la conocen. Por la perseverancia y fortaleza tenemos el prospecto de un éxito dichoso; por la cobardía la perspectiva de los males más terribles; la devastación del país; la despoblación de las ciudades; la deshonra de las familias; las habitaciones sin seguridad; una esclavitud sin esperanza; una posteridad infame; la patria cubierta de cadalsos; miseria, desesperación: ¡Oh! Contemplad esta pintura, y penetraos de ella: si hay alguna tan insensible que no se horrorice, o que no lo crea, sufra estos males, y no haya quien lo lamente.

This translation is relatively close to its original, except for the softening beyond all recognition of one of Paine's forthright and original thrusts—the dire prediction that, unless the Americans were victorious in battle, they would have their "homes turned into barracks and bawdy-houses for Hessians, and a future race to provide for, whose fathers we shall doubt of." Henríquez's "una posteridad infame" hardly conveys the same idea. Probably the traditional Spanish reticence toward treating sexual matters in print rather than failure to understand Paine's English explains the discrepancy.

One month later in an article on the need for joint action of all the American peoples against the European powers, Henríquez again paraphrased Paine in calling for the organization of constitutional government in all the American countries:

> Estos cuerpos soberanos y legislativos son los únicos que pueden autorizar a los Plenipotenciarios y para ello es indispensable que conste a todo el mundo que están en libertad y constituidos legítimamente. Da mucha fuerza a lo expuesto el siguiente artículo de la preciosa obra de Tomás Paine, titulada *The American Crisis*. El Continente corre riesgo de ser arruinado si pronto no se organiza y constituye en independencia.
>
> [October 2, 1813]

The importance of this article is not in a particular quotation or translation, but in the implication that Paine's ideas had stimulated Henríquez's own thinking.

Almost concurrently with the appearance of *El Monitor*, a young native of Guatemala, Antonio José de Irisarri, was editing in Santiago a weekly political organ, *El Semanario Republicano*, which ran from 7 August 1813 until 19 February 1814. Henríquez succeeded the younger man as editor on 23 October 1813.

Following the example of Henríquez, Irisarri drew upon Paine's *Common Sense* to inculcate liberal political principles. As a matter of fact, he was more democratic than Henríquez; Irisarri wanted a republican form of government, whereas Henríquez preferred a limited monarchy. In 1817 Henríquez even translated Robert Bisset's *Sketch of Democracy*, an attack upon popular government in favor of monarchy, in which Paine is compared to Wat Tyler and Jack Straw.

In his article "Sobre el origen y la naturaleza de las monarquías," a determined attack, Irisarri cites one of the fundamental principles of *Common Sense*: "El Gobierno, dice Paine, es un mal necesario para los Pueblos." In the same article, Irisarri adopts Paine's scriptural argument to refute the doctrine of divine right: "Dicen algunos que las Monarquías son instituídas por Dios, y para esto se valen de una aplicacíon violenta de los textos de la sagrada escritura. El autor del Sentido Común, rebate poderosa-mente este error con una convicción, que me ha, parecido digna de imitarse." After a close paraphrase of Paine's reasoning, Irisarri follows him in quoting a long passage from 1 Kings, and then comments:

> En vista de estas palabras de Samuel, dice Paine, es preciso convenir en una de dos cosas, o en que Dios es enemigo de los Reyes, o en que es falsa la escritura. Si creer lo último es una impiedad, debemos aceptar lo primero como uno de los misterios de nuestra santa religión. ¿Cómo, pues, los Católicos hemos sido tan ignorantes que creyésemos a los Reyes establecidos por la voluntad de Dios?

Henríquez certainly had a valuable ally in his campaign to promote both political and theological liberalism.

When Henríquez succeeded Irisarri as editor of *El Se-manario*, the only Paine material he then published was his translation of Paine's poem already mentioned, in a sense the most important of all his writings inspired by Paine.

Not even Paine's warmest admirers consider his poetry much better than mediocre: it is labored, conventional, and amateurish. Here again the parallel with Henríquez stands firm. The text of the poem that Henríquez chose for translation, "Hail Great Republic of the World," exists in two widely different versions, one that now appears in collected editions of Paine's works and another, presumably earlier, that was printed in *Tom Paine's Jests* (Philadelphia, 1796) and not reprinted.[41] The second version is the basis of Henríquez's translation, but he presumably used an anonymous copy. Otherwise, he would probably have given the author's name and he would also have been spared from describing the work as the national anthem of the United States. He included it in *El Semanario Republicano*, "Extraordinario—Miércoles 10 de Noviembre de 1813."

Following is the text from *Tom Paine's Jests* together with the text as translated by Henríquez:

HAIL GREAT REPUBLIC OF THE WORLD

Hail great Republic of the world,
    Which rear'd her empire in the West,
Where fam'd Columbus' flag unfurl'd,
    Gave tortured Europe scenes of rest;
      Be thou forever great and free,
      The land of Love and Liberty!

Beneath thy spreading, mantling vine,
    Beside each flowery grove and spring,
And where thy lofty mountains shine,
    May all thy sons and fair ones sing,
      Be thou forever, etc.

From thee may rudest nations learn,
    To prize the cause thy sons began;
From thee may future, may future tyrants know,
    That sacred are the Rights of Man.
      Be thou forever, etc.

From thee may hated discord fly,
    With all her dark, her gloomy train;
And o'er thy fertile, thy fertile wide domain,

---

[41] A. O. Aldridge, "The Poetry of Thomas Paine," *Pennsylvania Magazine of History and Biography* 79 (1955): 94-95.

May everlasting friendship reign.
  Be thou forever, etc.

Of thee may lisping infancy,
  The pleasing wond'rous story tell;
And patriot sages in venerable mood,
  Instruct the world to govern well.
    Be thou forever, etc.

Ye guardian Angels watch around,
  From harms protect the new born State;
And all ye friendly, ye friendly nations join,
  And thus salute the Child of Fate.
    Be thou forever, etc.

VERSIÓN LIBRE DEL CÁNTICO NACIONAL DE ESTADOS UNIDOS "HAIL GREAT REPUBLIC OF THE WORLD"

AL PUEBLO DE BUENOS AIRES

¡Salve, gloria del mundo, República naciente
Vuela a ser el imperio más grande de occidente,
¡Oh Patria de hombres libres, suelo de libertad!

Que tus hijos entonen de vides a la sombra,
O entre risueñas fuentes sobre florida alfombra:
¡Oh Patria de hombres libres . . . !

Que a estimar la gran causa aprendan los
    humanos,
Y a hacer que sus derechos veneren los tiranos.
¡Oh Patria . . . !

Que canten tus jijuelos con balbucientes labios,
Y enseñando a los pueblos en la vejez tus sabios.
¡Oh Patria . . . !

Tus ángeles custodios te cubran con sus alas;
Y unidas las naciones en fe y amistad pura,
Te saluden con lágrimas, lágrimas de ternura.
¡Oh Patria . . . !

It will be noticed that Henríquez omitted Paine's fourth stanza, possibly because it did not appear in the copy from which he worked. As far as I know, this is the only poem by Paine ever translated into any language. And, as we have seen, Henríquez himself probably did not know that Paine was the original author. Yet it cannot be denied that Paine made a significant impression upon Henríquez.

If, as Enrique de Gandía maintains, Paine did not influence the events leading up to the Latin American independence movement, he certainly made a significant contribution to the development and final success of that movement. Before 1825, there were three separate translations of *Common Sense*, two of a *Dissertation on the First Principles of Government*, and one of *Rights of Man*. Paine's doctrines were discussed in seven different newspapers in Venezuela, Argentina, and Chile; sections of *Common Sense* were paraphrased in the *Manual politico* of Francisco Yanes and in the *Memoria* of Servando Teresa de Mier; Paine's reasoning was echoed in the *Manifesto* concerning Venezuelan independence by Germán Roscio; and his *Crisis* no. 1 was paraphrased by Camilo Henríquez. As Paine had argued in Philadelphia that the struggle against England was the affair of a whole continent, not of individual cities or colonies; so his disciples in Spanish-America used his words to preach the doctrine of unity in the Hispanic world. His concepts were not confined to merely one or two parts of the Spanish colonies, but were promulgated by at least a dozen translators or commentators in the major population centers from Mexico to Chile.

NINE

THE ENLIGHTENMENT IN THE AMERICAS

O NLY WITHIN recent years has the term Enlightenment been generally applied to the literature of
either North or South America. The traditional
term has been that of "colonial" in both areas for most
of the eighteenth century and that of "revolutionary" for
North America after 1776 and for South America after
1810. At the present time historians of Latin American
literature speak freely of *las luces* or *la ilustración*; whereas
critics of North American literature still seem hesitant
to utilize the term Enlightenment, confining themselves
to the more traditional expressions "rationalism" or "Age
of Reason." This is paradoxical since the Anglo-Saxon
tradition in general was rich in the philosophical thought
associated with the Enlightenment; whereas the Hispanic
world, suffering during this period under the influence of
a despotic monarchy and a stifling religious Inquisition,
could make little claim to an atmosphere of free inquiry
or political reform.

The degree to which either culture can be said to have
participated in the Enlightenment depends primarily on
the way this movement of ideas is defined. If it is considered primarily from the epistemological and scientific
perspectives, that is, considering reason as the basis of all
knowledge, recognizing experimental science as the road
to progress in human development, and favoring secular-
ization of social relations, the Hispanic world may indeed

be said to have participated in the movement. But if it is considered in addition—as it is in France, Germany, and England—as open opposition to every form of superstition and fanaticism; as toleration of a wide diversity in religious opinions and practices; and as reform of political, economic, and social abuses of the state, the Spanish mainland was hardly touched at all by this powerful current of ideas, and Spanish America was little affected until the period of independence early in the nineteenth century.

The pioneers in drawing attention to the Enlightenment as a unified movement in the Americas have been historians rather than literary critics. For more than thirty years intellectual historians have been associating the Enlightenment with Latin America,[1] but the term "American Enlightenment" in reference to North America had no currency, if indeed it was used at all, until the publication in 1965 of an anthology with that title edited by Adrienne Koch. This significant collection of documents is based entirely on the writings of five major "philosopher-statesmen," namely, Benjamin Franklin, John Adams, Thomas Jefferson, James Monroe, and Alexander Hamilton, and the emphasis is understandably not on literature. The only one of these five who knew Spanish was Thomas Jefferson. For this and other reasons he enjoyed considerable renown in Latin America, comparable to that which Franklin gained in France.

In the Bicentennial year another historian, Henry F. May, published an excellent work entitled *The Enlightenment in America*, but its focus is on politics and religion, specifically the balance between deism and Christianity, and it considers literary matters only incidentally. The brief definition of Enlightenment which the author

---

[1] See, for example, Arthur P. Whitaker, ed., *Latin America and the Enlightenment* (Ithaca, N.Y., 1942, rev. ed., 1961).

provides, moreover, is unfortunately inadequate. This intellectual attitude, which dominated much of the eighteenth century, according to May, consisted merely in the belief in two propositions, "first, that the present age is more enlightened than the past; and second, that we understand nature and man best through the use of our natural faculties."[2] This definition is at once too comprehensive and too limited. Not all Enlightenment thinkers believed in the doctrine of progress, and the exceptions included many of the defenders of the ancients whom we have previously treated as well as the advocates of primitivism. The second proposition would cover almost everyone in the entire century except religious enthusiasts. It would certainly comprise stalwart anti-Enlightenment figures such as Jonathan Edwards and Edmund Burke. In addition to sense perception, both reason and instinct were regarded as natural faculties, and except for divine revelation no other sources of knowledge were considered possible. It has also been convincingly argued that social action among the major Enlightenment thinkers counted for much more than reasoning, ideas, or acquiring knowledge. It is a mistake to overlook the great emphasis on scientific research and social reform, which were almost the lifeblood of the Enlightenment.

The best definition of the Enlightenment spirit that I have ever encountered comes from a contemporary French disciple of Voltaire, abbé André Morellet, who played a major role in French-American literary relations. This emancipated ecclesiastic was a close friend and correspondent of Benjamin Franklin; he translated Jefferson's *Notes on Virginia*, and he served as intermediary between Thomas Paine and the Archbishop of Toulouse in an exchange of letters involving Edmund Burke, which Paine described in his *Rights of Man*. Referring to the intellec-

---

[2] (New York, 1976), p. xiv.

tual activity of the *philosophes* involved with the *Ency-clopédie*, Morellet wrote: "All of these men had an identical philosophy; it is this desire to know, this mental activity which refuses to leave an effect without seeking its cause, a phenomenon without an explanation, an assertion without proof, an objection without a reply, an error without combatting it, an evil without seeking the remedy, a possible good without trying to attain it; it is this general movement of minds which characterized the eighteenth century and which will be its glory forever."[3]

One of the major types of evidence used to prove the existence of an Enlightenment spirit in Spain and Latin America consists of lists of books by enlightened authors of other countries available in libraries or private collections during that chronological period. The assumption is that if the works of such luminaries as Voltaire, Montesquieu, and Rousseau were on the shelves of libraries in any part of the world, they must have contributed to the dissemination or indigenous development of Enlightenment ideology in that area. Daniel J. Boorstin, however, has denied that library holdings in themselves prove strong evidence of intellectual influence.[4] Books in a library may not be read or they may be read to be refuted. According to Boorstin's skeptical view, even though the works of Voltaire and Montesquieu circulated in the Americas, they may not have contributed to fostering a spirit of toleration or other ideals of the *philosophes*. Most scholars, however, continue to regard library holdings as realistic evidence of the spread of ideas, particularly since the recent vogue

[3] This definition was originally published by Morellet in his "Eloge de Marmontel." I have previously used it in a collection of essays by various scholars concerning North America, South America, and the Iberian Peninsula under the title of *The Ibero-American Enlightenment* (Urbana, Ill., 1971), p. 5.

[4] "The Myth of an American Enlightenment," in *America and the Image of Europe* (New York, 1960), pp. 65-78.

of quantitative methodology in historical studies. Certainly, from the literary perspective, bibliography is an indispensable part of research—all aspects of bibliography, including that which takes account of actual copies as well as titles. It is relevant to add, moreover, that even though library holdings do not offer absolute proof that works were being read with approval in a particular milieu, the lack of evidence of physical presence and circulation does not prove, on the other hand, that books were not being read. Sometimes the most popular and widely circulated books at a specific time leave almost no trace in libraries. An example is John Wesley's *Survey of the Wisdom of God*, which was discussed in the sixth chapter.

Ideas were successfully disseminated, moreover, by means of monthly journals published in England and on the continent, the prototype of which was the *Journal des Sçavans*, which began publication in 1665. Others from the seventeenth century included *Acta Eruditorum, Nouvelles de la République des Lettres, Bibliothèque Universelle et Historique*, and the first in English, *Universal Historical Bibliothèque*. Norman Fiering has provided an absorbing account of these journals and traced the circulation of several later ones in America, including *History of the Works of the Learned* (established 1699), *Memoirs of Literature* (established 1710), and *The Present State of the Republick of Letters* (established 1728). According to Fiering, the first book written by an American to be noticed by a learned journal on the continent was by a Harvard professor, Charles Morton. His *Enquiry into the Physical and Literal Sense of that Scripture Jerem. VIII, 7. "The Stork in the Heaven knoweth her appointed Times"* was announced in the January 1687 issue of the *Bibliothèque Universelle*. Concerning the scientific problem of the migration of birds, Morton argued that they migrated back and forth from the moon. The first essay by an Amer-

ican in a learned journal was Samuel Johnson's "Intro-
duction to the Study of Philosophy," which, according to
Fiering, appeared in the May 1731 *Present State of the
Republick of Letters.*

In a further article, Fiering maintains that "the very
first American enlightenment was French, if the advent
of Cartesianism may be thought of as at least a pre-en-
lightenment." This qualification extends the definition of
Enlightenment so broadly, however, that it would also
include most of Hispanic America as well as the New
England colonies. We must remember that Voltaire and
others insisted that the system of Descartes in contrast
to that of Newton was almost as obsolete as that of the
Church fathers. The early contribution of French thought
to the American colonies consisted in the dissemination
of notions of free inquiry by means of learned journals,
but the concept of Enlightenment as knowledge in action
in the sense in which we have defined it earlier in this
chapter came originally to America through the writings
of the English deists.[5]

Henry F. May and David Lundberg in a quantitative
survey of major European writers in American libraries
and bookstores in North America from 1700 to 1813 have
compiled impressive evidence of the availability of the
works of the dominant Enlightenment figures.[6] Another

---

[5] "The Transatlantic Republic of Letters: A Note on the Circulation
of Learned Periodicals to Early Eighteenth-Century America," *William
and Mary Quarterly*, 3rd ser., 33 (1976): 642-60; "The First American
Enlightenment: Tillotson, Leverett, and Philosophical Anglicanism,"
New England Quarterly 54 (1981): 307-44. I have quoted from p. 322.
This second article won the Walter Muir Whitehall Prize in Colonial
History in 1981.

[6] "The Enlightened Reader in America," *American Quarterly* 28 (1976):
262-301. An exhaustive account of books in North American libraries
about Latin America is provided by Harry Bernstein, "Las primeras relaciones intelectuales entre New England y el mundo hispánico (1700-
1815)," *Revista Hispánica Moderna* 5 (1938): 1-17. See also Harry Bern-

scholar, on the basis of personal sampling in libraries in the Philadelphia area, moreover, has concluded that May and Lundberg have considerably undercounted the actual numbers.[7] One of the most significant findings of May and Lundberg is that the various printings of some works actually exceeded the number of individual copies recorded. During this period, for example, there were forty-seven different issues or editions of Pope's *Essay on Man*, but the compilers were able to locate only thirty-three single copies.

In the British colonies of North America, neoclassical trends in style virtually coincided with Enlightenment subject matter. Neoclassicism could be discerned early in the eighteenth century; signs of the Enlightenment were apparent soon after; and the movement reached its apex in the period between 1765 and 1815, "an age of revolutions and constitutions," as John Adams remarked. Adrienne Koch has even suggested "the continuing hold" of Enlightenment ideals not only throughout the half century before the Civil War but even beyond.[8]

In peninsular Spain, neoclassicism did not flourish until the middle of the eighteenth century, far later than in England or France; and in the Spanish colonies the lag was even greater. Scant evidence of its existence can be found in Latin America before the last two decades of the eighteenth century, and the period of its highest development was the first half of the nineteenth century. In-

---

stein, *Making of an Inter-American Mind* (Gainesville, Fla., 1961); A. Owen Aldridge, "An Early Cuban Exponent of Inter-American Cultural Relations: Domingo del Monte," *Hispania* 54 (1971): 348-53; José de Onís, *The United States as Seen by Spanish American Writers, 1776-1890* (New York, 1952); Estuardo Nuñez, *Autores ingleses y norteamericanos en el Perú* (Lima, 1956).

[7] Arthur H. Scouten, "The Paradox of Deism in Colonial America," *Lex et Scientia* 14 (1978): 222-25.

[8] "Aftermath of the American Enlightenment," *Studies in Voltaire and the Eighteenth Century* 56 (1967): 762.

deed, neoclassicism and Romanticism arrived in Hispanic America almost simultaneously. Historians of the comparative development of literature should be aware of this phenomenon, not only of the existence of neoclassicism and Romanticism side by side in the same chronological period but also of the merging of characteristics of the two movements in particular literary artifacts. Examples are so numerous as to be superfluous, but the poetry of José de Olmedo could be considered a *locus classicus*. Even in North America the same blending of neoclassicism and Romanticism may be seen in many of the poems of Philip Freneau.

In studying the Enlightenment, one must be on guard against the process that Daniel Boorstin has described as homogenizing; that is, of assuming the presence of a complex of ideas or climate of opinion in a particular culture merely because these intellectual currents existed somewhere else in the same chronological span. A type of distortion just as serious as homogenizing, however, is that of provincializing; that is, of attributing a special or unique character to the people or way of life of a certain region while ignoring international currents.

The first step in studying the Enlightenment in North and South America is to seek evidence as to whether this complex of ideas and ideals actually existed. If the evidence is affirmative, one may next try to determine whether it was primarily a native growth in each area or whether it was part of the spirit of the times. In the scope of a single chapter, I cannot hope to provide definitive conclusions, but I shall attempt to introduce some relevant parallels and relations. I shall not deal with political prose, however, which has generally been considered as the chief claim of the Americas to the Enlightenment, but shall concentrate instead on belletristic works. Nor shall I treat a significant document on Enlightenment ideas in the tradition of the picaresque novel, *El Periquillo Sarniento*

(1816), by Fernández de Lizardi. It was preceded in North America by Hugh Henry Brackenridge's *Modern Chivalry* (1792-1797), which also uses the picaresque genre with emphasis on humor. In this work, however, it is ideals of the Enlightenment that are frequently satirized.

One of the most important Latin American poets of the period of independence is José Joaquín de Olmedo of Ecuador. His best poem is generally recognized to be "La Victoria de Junín: Canto a Bolívar" ["The Victory of Junín: Song to Bolívar"], a tribute to the revolutionary general Bolívar for a decisive military victory, published in 1825 and written with the advice and consultation of the general himself. Olmedo also published a translation of the first three epistles of Alexander Pope's *Essay on Man*. From an international perspective this translation represents prima facie evidence of the Enlightenment spirit. From an indigenous point of view, however, Olmedo's tribute to Bolívar is equally a document of the Enlightenment. This poem not only celebrates two famous battles in the struggle for independence, but also reincarnates, in the spirit of the traditional epic, the ghost of the Inca emperor Manco-Capac who prophesies the future glorious destiny of America. In passing, Olmedo celebrates Las Casas, the protector of the Indians, as a national hero, and eulogizes the people of the United States as "primogénito dichoso de libertad." The dedication of the author to political liberty and social equality is obvious, but the poem also contains cosmological overtones typical of the Enlightenment. In the introductory lines, for example, Olmedo describes the enormous extent of the Andes mountains and suggests in a note that their size is intended to help compensate for the difference in land mass between the Northern and Southern Hemispheres.

Since Pope's *Essay on Man* is one of the most significant deistic documents in world literature, the connection of Olmedo's translation with the metaphysics of the Enlightenment can be assumed without commentary. Olmedo himself, however, points out an ethical relationship which otherwise would have gone unperceived. In the notes of the first epistle published in 1823, Olmedo affirmed that he conceived of his translation of Pope as a means of giving the people of his country a sound moral system to compensate for their lack of a comprehensive code of laws, the Spanish statutes having been rendered obsolete by the independence of the former American colonies.[9]

A remarkable parallel to this political intrepretation of the *Essay on Man* exists in a North American poem, almost a century earlier, which provides hitherto unsuspected political applications of precepts in Pope's *An Essay on Criticism*. A satirical poem published in the *Pennsylvania Gazette* in 1733 entitled "Against Party-Malice and Levity, usual at and near the time of Electing Assembly-Men" [no. 252, 28 September 1733] is interlarded with quotations from the English neoclassicist. In the following example, the first four lines are by the Pennsylvania author, the last two by Pope:

> For little Faults great Merit should not fall;
> First find th' applauded Man with none at all.
> In brave old Patriots, when small Faults are seen,
> Think of the Weight they've borne and check your
>   Spleeen!
> "Of Old, those met Rewards who cou'd excel,"
> "And such were prais'd as but endeavour'd well."

Olmedo also translated a "Fragmento del Anti-Lucrecio," which is published in his *Poesías completas* directly after his translation of *An Essay on Man*. There is a good reason for this placement. The section from the famous

---

[9] *Ensayo sobre el hombre. De M. Pope. Versión del inglés* (Lima, 1823), p. 9. This note is not reprinted in *Poesías completas*, ed. A. E. Pólet (Quito, 1945).

Latin poem of Cardinal de Polignac [Book IX] is filled with concepts of natural religion comparable to those in Pope.

Olmedo's "Canto a Bolívar" provides an excellent illustration of the high regard in which many Latin American authors held the Indian races native to their land. By and large South American authors identified with the Indians and considered the natives as part of their own race and tradition, although some Argentinian authors represent an exception to this characteristic. Esteban Echeverría in a narrative poem, *La Cautiva*, portrays Indians as debauched, and Sarmiento in prose considers the race as inferior. Yet, as we have seen in the preceding chapter, a political group in Argentina in the second decade of the nineteenth century had actually proposed the creation of an empire based on the past glories of the Incas. North American authors, on the other hand, at best patronized the Indian in the manner of the European Noble Savage tradition, considering him as physically powerful, but intellectually primitive and naive. Perhaps the most significant early portrayal of the Indian in favorable terms was that of William Penn in a letter to the Free Society of Traders in August 1683, in which he maintains that Europeans, despite their superior knowledge, have not been able to surpass the Indians in a wholesome way of life. This letter was immediately printed in London and has been reprinted many times. It was incorporated into a travel book by Richard Brome, which was translated into French as *L'Amérique angloise* (Amsterdam, 1688) and may have been partly responsible for the glowing portrayals of the American Indian in the works of Diderot and Montesquieu. The most sympathetic North American portrayal appeared in the verse of Philip Freneau, who preceded Chateaubriand in delineating the Indians as a noble race predestined to extinction through the predatory advance of the white man. Even Freneau, however, kept the red man on an inferior intellectual and spiritual level.[10] Many North Americans, moreover, even poets, were bitterly hostile toward the Indians and openly paraded their animosity in literary works. A forthright example is a poem published in 1764 entitled "A New and mild Method totally to extirpate the Indians out of No. America." The method advocated was to encourage drunkenness.[11]

Joseph Dennie, who disliked Indians about as heartily as he detested Jeffersonian Democrats, published an essay in the *Port Folio* entitled "An Indian Plagiary," which supported two of his favorite themes, that close imitation of European models contributed to the wretched condition of the literature of the United States and that the Indian should not be portrayed as a noble sage, but as a "natural brute beast."[12] The essayist reprints from a Ver-

---

[10] See, for example, Freneau's "The Indian Burying Ground" and William Cullen Bryant's "An Indian at the Burying-Place of His Fathers." In a sprightly narrative with the misleading title, *God's Protecting Providence Man's Surest Help and Defence* (Philadelphia, 1699), Jonathan Dickinson provided a realistic portrayal of encounters with Indians. Dickinson, who was shipwrecked off the coast of Florida, described his trip by land and canoe northward to Philadelphia during the course of which he was humanely received by the Spanish governor of St. Augustine, a rare example of early contact between the two cultures. His book, which despite the pietistic title consists of a day-by-day account of his experiences, belongs to the related literary genres of shipwreck and Indian captivity and is one of the first American best sellers. In addition to the first printing, there were fourteen others between 1700 and 1826 together with a Dutch translation published in Leyden, a German translation published in Germantown, Pennsylvania (1756), and a further German translation published in Frankfort (1774). The Dutch translation contains an appended sixty-line poem of commentary. See *Jonathan Dickinson's Journal*, ed. E. W. Andrews and C. M. Andrews (New Haven, 1945).

[11] J. A. Leo Lemay, *A Calendar of American Poetry in the Colonial Newspapers and Magazines and in the Major English Magazines through 1765* (Worcester, Mass., 1972), p. 271.

[12] 5 December 1807. The essay is presented as a contributed piece, but it could be by Dennie himself.

mont journal an anecdote which had "run its merry round through most of the newspapers as a proof of Indian genius." An Indian, discovering that some venison which he had hung up in his hut to dry had been stolen, set out in search of "a *little old white man* with a *short gun* and accompanied by a *small dog* with a *bobtail*." When asked how he knew all these details, the Indian replied that the thief was little because he had made a pile of stones to stand on when stealing the venison, he was old because of his short steps, and he was white because his tracks showed a turning out of his toes, which Indian tracks never do. His gun, moreover, was little because of the mark it made on the bark of a tree on which it was leaning, and the dog was small and bobtailed because of its tracks and the mark it made in the dust when sitting down while his master engaged in thievery. The essayist considered this journalistic composition to be as "rude as the rocks of Scandinavia" even though he proceeded to expose it as a plagiary from a passage in Voltaire's *Zadig*, which by contrast he held to be "full of the glory of Invention, and the brightness of Genius; . . . embellished by Taste, and consummated by Art, . . . the style of Refinement and Civility." The essayist thereupon reproduced the third chapter of *Zadig* in the original and in translation even though Smollett's translation of the entire work had already been reprinted in two issues (one separately under the title *The Princess of Babylon* and once in Voltaire's *Miscellanies*) in Philadelphia in 1778. In the relevant chapter, Zadig recognizes by deductions similar to those of the Vermont Indian that the king's horse was five feet high with small hoofs and a tail three and a half feet in length, that the studs on his bit were twenty-three carat gold, and the silver of his shoes was almost pure. What the American essayist did not know is that the story was no more original with Voltaire than it was with the Vermont scribe who adapted it. Voltaire's source is a story in the *Bibliothèque orientale* of Barthélemy d'Herbelot (1697) about three Arab brothers who deduce the major physical features of a lost camel. The anecdote in its Arabian, French, and Vermont versions obviously provides a splendid example of Early American letters in contact with universal literature. A parallel to the charge of plagiarism in the *Port Folio* exists, moreover, in a French periodical *L'Année littéraire*, edited by one of Voltaire's most persistent enemies, Elie Fréron. In 1767, Fréron accused Voltaire of plagiarizing another episode of *Zadig* (Chapter XVIII) from the English poet Parnell.[13]

A theme more closely linked to Enlightenment thought than the relative intelligence of the natives of America is that of the dissemination of knowledge. It is indicated in an ode "Sobre la invención y libertad de la imprenta" published by an Argentinian Juan Cruz Varela in 1822. It is strongly indebted to a very similar ode "A la libertad

---

[13] *L'Année littéraire* (Amsterdam, 1767), Vol. 1, Letter 3. The *Port Folio* also introduced to America an original translation of another of Voltaire's *contes*, "The World as it Goes, or the Vision of Babouc." It was not identified as Voltaire's, however, but merely as "from the French" [20, 27 April and 4 May 1805]. This was apparently the second translation in the English-speaking world, the only previous one consisting of a pamphlet, *Babouc, or the World as it Goes* (London, 1754, and Dublin, 1754). None of the foregoing material appears in the excellent study by M. M. Barr, *Voltaire in America, 1744-1800* (Baltimore, 1941). Barr indicates, however [p. 45], that the second chapter of *Zadig* was translated in the *New York Weekly Museum*, 20 August 1796, under the title "The Nose." Voltaire's contribution to the Enlightenment in America has never been thoroughly treated as such although the basic materials are available in Barr's study. His poem "Temple du gout" was actually noted as early as 9 August 1733 in Franklin's *Pennsylvania Gazette*. Voltaire's *Treatise on Toleration* especially was widely known and respected. As could be expected, he was regarded by the anti-Enlightenment forces as the epitome of evil. The outstanding example of this attitude is the ironic dedication to Voltaire of Timothy Dwight's poem *The Triumph of Infidelity* (Hartford, 1788) in which Voltaire is portrayed as teaching "that the chief end of man was to slander his God, and abuse him forever."

de imprenta," by an exponent of liberal ideas in Spain, Manuel José Quintana. Praise of the printing press for making possible the efficient diffusion of ideas was widespread in most western European literatures of the eighteenth century. As we have already seen, it was expressed in 1728 by James Sterling and in 1795 by Robert Treat Paine.

Even more important, one of the pioneer printing craftsmen of America, Isaiah Thomas, published in 1810 an encyclopedic *History of Printing in America* in two volumes, which was printed on his son's press at Worcester, Massachusetts. The work also contains a "Concise View of the Discovery and Progress of the [Printing] Art in Other Parts of the World." For his discussion of Spanish America, Thomas was forced to rely exclusively on secondary sources, including two famous histories of the Conquest, one by the Scotsman William Robertson and the other by the Mexican Francisco Javier Clavigero. Thomas also provided a rather extensive bibliography, drawn entirely from Robertson, of books printed in Mexico and Lima on the history of America, together with a comparison of book production in both western continents, a perspective remarkably free from chauvinism or religious intolerance. Within seven years of its publication Thomas's book was known in Chile, where it was cited by the leading journalist of Santiago, Camilo Henríquez, as the source of a statement concerning the large number of periodicals being published in North America.[14]

The only neoclassical poem of the English colonies to obtain any kind of renown in England was a topographical piece based on Virgil's *Georgics* entitled "A Journey from Patapsco to Annapolis, April 4, 1730." It was reprinted in Britain at least five times. Implying the deistic belief that the beauty and order of the universe reveal the existence

[14] *El Censor*, no. 88 (22 May 1817).

of a benevolent deity, the author, Richard Lewis, describes a typical farmer, the fruit trees of his orchard and those of the forest, together with thoughts on life and immortality in a day's journey through the country. Many parallels are to be found in a Spanish georgic written almost one hundred years later, "To the Agriculture of the Torrid Zone" ["A la agricultura de la zona tórrida"] (1826), by Andrés Bello. It features such commonplaces on the Enlightenment as social peace and order, the dignity of labor, and the benevolence of the Creator, but dwells upon the organizing of nature through agriculture rather than on the landscape in general. Except for their relative brevity, these two poems resemble James Thomson's *The Seasons* and Saint-Lambert's *Les Saisons* as closely as the English and the French georgics resemble each other. A poem in the Virgilian tradition preceding Bello's was *Rusticatio Mexicana*, by Rafael Landívar, published in Latin in 1781. This description of rural life in Mexico is clearly neoclassical, but its being composed in Latin partially disqualifies it as an Enlightenment document since progressive thought of the movement exalted the vernacular over the ancient languages. Landívar's inclusion of a good deal of natural science, however, certainly represents an Enlightenment tendency.[15] The only complete translations of the poem into Spanish belong to the twentieth century, although the Cuban poet José María Heredia in 1836 translated a lengthy section concerning cockfighting.[16]

Bello, in another poem of the same decade as his panegyric to agriculture, "Alocución a la poesía," called upon the genius of poetry to leave Europe and to take up her abode among the burgeoning nations of America. Since

[15] Graciela P. Nemes, "Rafael Landívar and Poetic Echoes of the Enlightenment," in *The Ibero-American Enlightenment*, ed. Aldridge, pp. 299-301.

[16] Heredia, "Pelea de gallos," in *Poesías líricas*, ed. Elías Zerolo (Paris, n.d.), pp. 91-94.

we have already given several examples of *translatio studii* in North American literature, we shall provide only one more at this time, an anonymous poem of 1729 attributed to Richard Lewis.

E'er Time has Measured out an hundred Years
Westward from *Britain*, shall an *Athens* rise,
Which soon shall bear away the learned Prize;
Hence Europe's Sons assistance shall implore,
And learn from her, as she from them before.[17]

Both in Europe and America, the theme of westward movement was applied to liberty as well as to learning and the arts. One example is "El regreso" (1830), by Esteban Echeverría.

La libertad de Europa fugitiva,
Un asilo buscando,
Ha passado el Oceano,
Su dignisimo trono levantando
Do se agitan los pechos a su nombre,
Y do con dignidad respira el hombre;
En el hermoso suelo americano.

[The fugitive liberty of Europe,
Seeking an asylum,
Has traversed the ocean,
Raising its sublime theme
On the fair American soil,
Where hearts exalt its name
And where men breathe with dignity.]

A more interesting example is "En el aniversario del 4 de julio de 1776" (1825) by José María Heredia, which associates liberty with both North and South America. The poet addresses "sacred liberty," which, enlightened by

---

[17] J. A. Leo Lemay, *Men of Letters in Colonial Maryland* (Knoxville, Tenn., 1972), p. 132.

Athens and Rome, has left the tyranny of Europe and braved the horrors of the ocean waves to find a refuge in America.

After the American Revolution the theme of the westward movement of the arts merged into a more strident nationalistic affirmation of the superiority of the western world in physical nature and in human virtue. Patriotic fervor expressed itself through pride in geographic location, military exploits, and national identity however, rather than common awareness of an intellectual heritage.[18] In Latin America as well the wars of independence inspired scores of patriotic odes and verse discourses comparing the New and the Old Worlds to the disadvantage of the latter, but the cultural heritage of Spain and Portugal was nearly always recognized, even though sometimes rejected.

So far we have seen several parallel themes that have united the Enlightenment in North and South America, but very little in the way of direct influence of one area upon the other. Before the beginning of the nineteenth century, practically none existed. The first and major impact of the United States upon the land to the south was political. The writings of Paine, Jefferson, Hamilton, and Monroe were quoted, reprinted, and discussed during the struggle for independence from Spain and the succeeding period of quest for sound government. Washington, moreover, became a symbol in Latin American poetry of military hero, patriot, and father of his country much as he was in the literature of the United States and many European countries. Heredia, for example, in 1824 addressed a poem "A Washington escrita en Monte Vernón," and wrote an essay in prose entitled "Washington," in which he both expressed reverence for the "sublime character"

---

[18] An excellent study of this phenomenon is Merle Curti, *The Roots of American Loyalty* (New York, 1946).

of the North American hero and affirmed, contrary to many contemporary and later historians that "the war of 1776 was strictly a war of principles."[19] Heredia also translated the first act of Voltaire's drama against the use of religion as a political weapon, *Mahomet*. Heredia's translation, under the title "El fanatismo," is in verse and closely follows the original text.[20] The Cuban author also conceived the project of an *Ensayo filosófico sobre la historia universal*, on the scale of Voltaire, from earliest times to the present, but the idea was never executed.[21]

At this period the North American public was still for the most part totally unaware of the intellectual life in Hispanic America. Jared Sparks, influential New England scholar and editor, wrote in September 1825, "The difference of language, and the infrequence of communication, have sent out as many errors as truths. Hardly an editor in this country knows the Spanish language, and there is not to this day taken in Boston a single regular file of a newspaper from the whole South American continent, or Mexico."[22]

---

[19] *Poesías líricas*, ed. Zerolo, p. lxix.

[20] It was completed in 1821. Pedro J. Guiteras, "José María Heredia," *La Revista de Cuba* 9 (1881): 25.

[21] Ibid., p. 24.

[22] E. F. Helman, "Early Interest in Spanish in New England (1815-1835)," *Hispania* 29 (1946): 344-45. One of the few echoes of peninsular Spanish letters in an English colony consists of an essay by Dr. Alexander Hamilton in the *Maryland Gazette*, 29 June 1748, signed Quevedo and loosely following the structure of the *Sueños* of the luminary of the Golden Age as paraphrased in English by Sir Roger L'Estrange. Lemay, *Men of Letters*, p. 233. A reference to Portugal occurs in a remarkable short story by Charles Brockden Brown in which he treats a mythical biography of the absolutist ruler Pombal, who is usually considered an exponent of enlightened despotism. Brown's work is remarkable, however, not because of its reference to Pombal or even an ingenious parallelism between Pombal and Cicero, but because of the literary genre to which it belongs. Entitled "Walstein's School of History," it purports to be an essay on a German historian, but the historian and his books

280

ENLIGHTENMENT IN THE AMERICAS

Two reasons may be advanced to account for North American ignorance or indifference. One is the generally recognized principle that intellectual relationships usually follow political and economic ones, and the language of the dominant race or nation invariably takes precedence over the less developed one. Another is the Anglo-

are purely imaginary. To be sure, there is nothing unusual about inventing nonexistent professors and writers. Swift and Voltaire did it brilliantly before Brown. What is remarkable about Brown is that his invented works are not instruments of satire, but fictional materials devoted to a serious portrayal of life and art. His work, which I have called a short story, has amazing resemblances to the style and method of Jorge Luis Borges, and it deserves to be treated as a valuable precursor of the fiction of the Argentinian master, particularly "El acercamiento a Almotásim" ["The Approach to Al-mu'tasim"]. "Walstein's School of History" appeared originally in the *Monthly Magazine and American Review* (August-September 1799), and has been reprinted in *The Rhapsodist and Other Collected Writings by Charles Brockden Brown*, ed. Harry R. Warfel (New York, 1943), pp. 145-56.

Borges himself deserves special mention as perhaps the only major creative writer outside of the United States possessing an extensive knowledge of early North American literature. In his autobiography he ranked Jonathan Edwards as author of one of the world's masterpieces, a view rarely expressed elsewhere. Borges wrote, moreover, an *Introducción a la literatura norteamericana* (Buenos Aires, 1967), a book of less than 100 pages which contains, nevertheless, some interesting insights and novel perspectives. It has been translated under the somewhat inaccurate title *An Introduction to American Literature* [ed. L. Clark Keating and Robert O. Evans (Lexington, Ky., 1971)]. In his first chapter entitled "Origins," Borges treats John Winthrop, William Bradford, Cotton Mather, Jonathan Edwards, and a single poet, Philip Freneau. He recognizes "The Indian Burying Ground" as the best-known of Freneau's poems and "The hunter and the deer, a shade" as its most famous line, reminding him of a hexameter in the eleventh book of the *Odyssey*. Borges shows particular interest in the narrative poem "The Indian Student," about a gifted native who abandons Harvard College for his natural haunts, which Borges calls "at once a poem and a short story." He treats Franklin in his second chapter along with Cooper, Irving, Prescott, and Parkman. Like Balzac, he draws attention to Franklin's enjoyment of mystifications (a major characteristic of Borges as well) and compares him in this regard to Poe.

Saxon distrust of the Spanish character prevailing in the eighteenth and early nineteenth century, which was based on Protestant suspicion of the Catholic religion, particularly the notorious Spanish Inquisition, together with horror of the alleged mistreatment of the Indians during the period of the Conquest, the equally notorious Black Legend.

The well-known author of *Letters from an American Farmer* (1782), the French-American St. Jean de Crèvecoeur, also wrote a "Sketch of the Contrast between the Spanish and the English Colonies," which even today is almost unknown.[23] In the spirit of Voltaire and the *philosophes*, Crèvecoeur tore into the religious ostentation and "multiplicity of priests" in Lima. The Spanish in America, he charged, had kept their country so closely shut against foreigners that it was virtually impossible to know anything about it. Crèvecoeur, nevertheless, contrasted the ostentation, superficial observances, and ceremonies of religion in South America with the simplicity, sincerity, and social benevolence of that in North America; the oppressive government of the one with the toleration of the other.

The conclusion of Crèvecoeur's essay even more starkly reveals the depth of his distrust of the Spanish colonies and his admiration of the United States.

An incomprehensible Gov't [in South America] permits but few branches of Industry to flourish—How can the Earth be tilled? How can manufactories araise [*sic*]? how can trade improve? how can population increase? how can a people become opulent & strong where so many

[23] Ed. H. L. Bourdin and S. T. Williams, *University of California Chronicle* 28 (1926): 152-63. The editors indicate that a free translation appears in Crèvecoeur's *Lettres d'un cultivateur américain*, 2 vols. (Paris, 1784), but I have found that the only resemblances are remote and superficial. See, for example, 2: 361.

canker worms gnaw the great vital Root of the National tree, suck & exhaust the Sap which was Intended to Vivify its numerous Branches. . . .

. . . .

Happy provinces *these* [in North America] on the contrary now become the azilum [*sic*] of all the unfortunate from the old world, which can boast of the happiest Gov't, the Mildest Laws, the Simplest Relligion. How happy for Mankind that the Era of their different Foundations was that of Knowledge & science by which they were taught to divert themselves of those antient civil errors to which many had fell victims. Happy Regeneration for Mankind! Human Nature everywhere Insulted & oppressed, here can breathe the Purest air & boast of that which I believe no society ever cou'd before, of the full enjoyment of every Natural & necessary Right, consistent with a State of Society. I sincerely wish that the Spanish Colonies may one day become partakers of some of those great blessings by being placed so contiguous to these Provinces, that from the large & copious Source of Freedom which they contain some happy Sparks of it may be disseminated to all the world.

Crèvecoeur's very unflattering view of South America can be contrasted not only with the favorable view of North America in his sketch, but also with his even more rhapsodic picture of the Northern Hemisphere in his widely read "What Is an American?"[24]

A similar denigratory portrayal of eighteenth-century

---

[24] *Letters from an American Farmer* (London, 1782). In the first quarter of the nineteenth century, a debate took place in Chile concerning the character of a North American—one author accused the citizens of the United States of materialism and greed; another attributed to them virtually all the same qualities claimed by Crèvecoeur. A. O. Aldridge, "The Character of a North American as Drawn in Chile, 1818," in *Hispania* 49 (1966), 489-94.

Latin America appeared in *Bibliotheca Americana; or, a Chronological Catalogue of the most Curious and Interesting Papers, &c. upon the Subject of North and South America*, which was published in London in 1789.[25] Its "Introductory Discourse on the Present State of Literature in those Countries" charges that South America is in a state of bondage and consequently produces "nothing conducive to the good or happiness of mankind." Personified as the elder sister, South America is portrayed as "decorated with gold; but that gold, fabricated into chains, and as is too commonly the fate of wealth, serving only to exclude, what is conducive to happiness, and to confine what is essential to misery." The twin forces which oppose all "scientific," that is, intellectual progress, are the Inquisition and censorship of the press. Despite this disparaging portrayal of South American letters, *Bibliotheca Americana* includes a seven-page catalog of European and Creole authors who have written on Christianity and moral subjects in the indigenous languages of New Spain, transcribed completely from "that curious, entertaining, and valuable Work, entitled The History of Mexico," by Francisco Javier Clavigero, which had already acquired an international reputation.

Although the literature of North America is said to be in much better condition than that of the Latin countries, the author of the "Discourse" is unable to provide a much more impressive catalog. In his words: "At the head of their philosophers and politicians, stands the venerable Franklin. In the first class, the ingenious Lorimer must not be forgotten.—In mathematics, the self-taught Rittenhouse.—In divinity, Weatherspoone.—In history, criticisms, and policy, the modern Tacitus (Payne).—In poetry, Barlow, Smith, and Ray.—In painting, West" [pp.

---

[25] Several names have been proposed as the compiler of the work, including Lehman Thomas Rede.

10-11]. We are presented here with two major authors, Franklin and Paine, and two minor ones, Barlow and Witherspoon, but the only poets named, Smith and Ray, are so obscure that it is doubtful that anyone in London had ever read their works.[26] And the philosopher Lorimer seems to be as legendary as the continent of Atlantis. The remainder of the discourse is primarily concerned with the printing, distribution, and sale of books in North America. We are told that the "demand for foreign literature is inconsiderable, . . . very little for French books, and still less for Italian, Spanish and Portuguese." German works sell relatively well in districts inhabited by the Germans, but these are principally school and devotional texts. "When a Dutchman is not at prayers, he is either at work or asleep." Finally, the French have tried to introduce their language and literature, but "without success."

The first Latin American work to influence a major North American author was a lyric "En una tempestad" ["In a Tempest"] by Heredia published in New York in 1825. During this period of Cuban history, many advocates of independence or at least reform of the Spanish administration were living, like Heredia, in voluntary or forced exile in the United States. "En una tempestad" is a typically neoclassic statement of the relationship of a particular aspect of nature to the cosmic order, a theme that belongs to the Enlightenment as well as to neoclassicism. The poem served as the basis of a free rendering in English by William Cullen Bryant under the title "The Hurricane" written in 1827 and published five years later.[27] Bryant also published in 1832 an original poem on the same theme, "After a Tempest." Thirty-five years before

[26] Presumably these are Charlotte Smith, *Elegiac Sonnets* 1787; and William Ray, *Poem on Visiting the Academy of Philadelphia*, 1753; *Ode on the New Year*, 1753.

[27] *Poems by William Cullen Bryant, An American*, ed. Washington Irving (London, 1832).

Heredia's poem, moreover, Philip Freneau had published another verse description of a storm with the identical title, "The Hurricane." With no reference to the Creator, or to the ordered universe, but with a statement of personal fear and loneliness, Freneau's eighteenth-century poem paradoxically has more of the Romantic spirit than either Heredia's or Bryant's in the nineteenth century.

Bryant also had a hand in an English translation of the poem regarded by some critics as Heredia's best, an ode, "Niágara," which records his feelings on visiting the famous waterfall. The translation by Thatcher Taylor Payne was revised and corrected by Bryant and published in January 1827 in the *United States Review and Literary Gazette*, of which Bryant was one of the editors.[28] Probably the earliest verses on Niagara Falls in any language were those contained in a descriptive poem "Night," published in 1728 by a Pennsylvanian James Ralph, a friend of Benjamin Franklin, whose name was appropriated by Voltaire as the purported author of *Candide*.[29]

Bryant was not only a major poet, but also a literary critic of extraordinary range and acuteness. In addition to his extensive criticism of European and North American literature, he also published the first essay to be written in any language on a Latin American historical novel, *Jicoténcal*. This work on the conquest of Mexico by Cortez has the distinction of being the first historical novel ever written in the Spanish language. It was published

[28] Héctor H. Orjuela, "Revaloración de una vieja polémica literaria: William Cullen Bryant y la oda 'Niágara' de José María Heredia," *Thesaurus. Boletín del Instituto Caro y Cuervo* 19 (1964): 248-73.

[29] James Ralph, *Night: A Poem. In Four Books* (London, 1728). Pope parodied the poem in his *Dunciad* probably because Ralph in his preface quoted a passage from Pope's *Homer* but suggested that it contained various infelicities which could have been avoided had he used blank verse instead of rhyme. Charles M. Dow's *Anthology and Bibliography of Niagara Falls* (Albany, 1921) lacks these details and includes practically no eighteenth-century poetry.

anonymously in Philadelphia in 1826, and to this day its author can still not be definitely ascribed, although there are good reasons for believing that it was Félix Varela (a Cuban, not the Argentinian Varela, author of the poem on printing).[30] Bryant published his analysis of the novel in February 1827 in the *United States Review and Literary Gazette* [1, 336-46]. Although not enthusiastic about *Jicoténcal* as a work of fiction, Bryant praised its "just and enlightened notions on political government and other important subjects." He also contrasted the progressive spirit of Latin America with the backwardness of Spain. "It might almost seem," he wrote, "as if a nobler race of men had grown up in those countries."

> In the midst of their political storms, they have taken care to found institutions for the purpose of forming the minds of those, who are soon, under better auspices, to take the place of the men who threw off the Spanish yoke. In the mean time, more enlightened notions of government are diffusing and perfecting themselves, and a tolerant spirit is fast displacing the old bigotry.

It is a coincidence worthy of notice that the first novel written in English with a Mexican setting was *Francis Berrian, or, The Mexican Patriot* by Timothy Flint, published in the same year as *Jicoténcal*. Another novel concerning Mexico, *Calavar, or, the Knight of the Conquest* (1834) by Robert Montgomery Bird, was translated into German and published in St. Louis in 1848. It was followed in the next year (1835) by another romance concerning the Conquest, *The Infidel; or The Fall of Mexico*.

The illustrations of Enlightenment themes and tendencies presented so far show for the most part that English America was at least a half century in advance of Spanish America. This is not the result of arbitrary selection of

---

[30] Luis Leal, "*Jicoténcal*, Primera novela histórica en castellano" *Revista Iberoamericana* 25 (1960): 9-31.

texts. It would be impossible to find illustrations proving the reverse situation. Priority in developing Enlightenment themes in North America, however, does not necessarily mean artistic superiority. As a matter of fact, the quality of Spanish-American literature in the first forty years of the nineteenth century was much better than that in English America before the Revolution.

During the eighteenth century, moreover, no work of formal history written in the English part of North America attained the European reputation of the work of the Mexican historian, Francisco Javier Clavigero, *Historia antigua de México*, to which we have already alluded. Since the author was a Jesuit and like many of his order lived in Italy after the disbanding of the Jesuits, the first edition of 1780 was published in Italian. The first Spanish edition was a posthumous translation in 1826.[31] Two editions in English appeared in North America before the Spanish edition, one in Philadelphia in 1806, the other in Richmond in 1817.[32] Clavigero made several animadversions on William Robertson's *History of America* to which Robertson responded in later editions.[33] More important, Clavigero was the first author in either North or South America to undertake a formal refutation of the notorious thesis of Buffon and de Pauw which held that biological species degenerated when transplanted to the western world.[34]

Another historical work from Latin America promptly

[31] 4 vols. Colección de Escritores Mexicanos (Mexico, 1945), 1: 13.

[32] Bernstein, *Making of an Inter-American Mind*, p. 34; neither of these editions is mentioned in the Mexico, 1945, edition.

[33] (London, 1817), 8: 382, 9: 320.

[34] Antonello Gerbi, *The Dispute of the New World: The History of a Polemic 1750-1900*, trans. Jeremy Moyle (Pittsburgh, 1973), pp. 196-211. Clavigero also enjoyed extensive relations and exchange of compliments with Gian Rinaldo Carli, author of *Delle lettere americane* (1780), [Gerbi, p. 239]. Jefferson's *Notes on Virginia* is in part a rebuttal of Buffon. In Argentina, Felix de Azara published a parallel *Memorial concerning the rural conditions of the Rio de la Plata in 1801*.

taken up in the United States was a treatise on Chile published originally in Italian by Juan Ignacio Molina, which was translated from French and Spanish versions in 1808 by Richard Alsop as *The Geographical, Natural and Civil History of Chile*. The appendix, bearing a separate title page, consisted of a "Sketch of the Araucana with Copious Translations from that Poem." The sketch was taken from William Hayley's notes to an essay on the epic and the translations, all of the third and fourth cantos, were taken from another English author, the Reverend H. Boyd, who had also translated Dante. The prose summary to a harangue delivered by an ancient warrior is prefaced by the remark that it was preferred by Voltaire to the speech of Nestor on a similar occasion in the *Iliad*.

One would assume that *La Araucana*, published originally in the sixteenth century (1569 and 1578), well before the birth of Anne Bradstreet, would, because of its subject matter, have been of interest to colonial British America, especially to authors dealing with the subjugation of the Indians there. No evidence of any awareness whatsoever of this work in the British area of North America, however, can be found until the Revolution, when as we have seen Joel Barlow adopted some of its themes and structural features for his epic in English, *The Vision of Columbus*. In 1805, when Barlow returned to the United States from a long sojourn in Europe, Voltaire's chapter on Ercilla was extracted from his essay on epic poetry and published in the *Port Folio*.[35] A contributor who had never seen a copy of *La Araucana* and who believed that it was difficult for the "jaundiced eye of the philosopher of Ferney, to discover any beauties, in another author," nevertheless translated Voltaire's remarks because the poem was "little known" and because he believed Ercilla to be "the only epic poet, that Spain can boast." Thanks to Voltaire and the *Port Folio*, therefore, the attention of

[35] 12 January 1805.

many North Americans was drawn to the existence of a major epic concerning the foundations of the civilization of South America which antedated by two centuries the efforts of Dwight and Barlow in the genre.[36]

The objection might perhaps be raised that apart from the connection with Voltaire, the topic of epic poetry has little or nothing to do with the Enlightenment. To the contrary, the portrayal of South American Indians in Barlow's *Vision of Columbus* is intimately involved with concepts of rational government and rational religion. Between the second and third books of his epic, Barlow inserted a prose "Dissertation on the Genius and Institutions of Manco Capac," the legendary leader and lawgiver of the pre-Columbian Indians in Peru. In his portrayal, Barlow treats Manco Capac as superior to parallel figures in Jewish, Mahometan, and, by suggestion, Christian societies. His system of government, according to Barlow, was "the most simple and energetic conceivable, and capable of reducing the greatest number of men under one jurisdiction." In treating the religion of Manco Capac as pure deism, Barlow completely ignores the Christian tradition.

Perhaps no single criterion can be given, which will determine more accurately the state of society in any age or nation, than their general ideas concerning the nature and attributes of the Deity. In the most enlightened periods of antiquity, only a very few of their wisest

[36] Another resident of Connecticut, Richard Alsop, to whom the translation of Molina's history has been attributed, tried his hand in the epic style with an international theme in *The Conquest of Scandinavia*. Only an excerpt from this work has ever been published, the introduction to the fourth book, in Elihu Hubbard Smith, ed., *American Poems* (Litchfield, Conn., 1793). Alsop, the first literary millionaire in America, also translated from the Greek, Latin, Italian, and Spanish. Another of his historically significant translations is one of the earliest in America from Dante. Joseph G. Fucilla, "An Early American Translation of the Count Ugolino Episode," *Modern Language Quarterly* 11 (1950): 480-85.

Philosophers, a Socrates, a Tully, or a Confucius, ever formed a just idea on the subject, or described the Deity as a God of purity, justice and benevolence. Can anything then be more astonishing than to view a savage native of the southern wilds of America, rising in an age, void of every trace of learning or refinement, and acquiring by the mere efforts of reason, a sublime and rational idea of the Parent of the universe!

We have seen that both North and South Americans made a conscious effort to separate the Old World from the New, to create a New World personality or climate of opinion based on political independence. We may wonder whether there also existed a consciousness of an Enlightenment spirit—an awareness of an intellectual movement transcending political relationships. In France, for example, the writers associated with the *Encyclopédie* were known as the *philosophes* and they considered themselves as part of a common effort to reform their society in nearly every aspect.

In Hispanic America one likewise encounters a specific awareness of the Enlightenment as a philosophical movement vitally affecting the political and social institutions of the times. One example is a poem of Heredia celebrating (1826) the opening of the Institute of Mexico ["En la apertura del Instituto mejicano" (1826)].

> Es la alma libertad madre fecunda
> De las artes y ciencias; ella rompe
> La atroz cadena que al ingenio humano
> Los déspotas cargaron, y á la sombra
> De su manto benéfico y su oliva
> Crece la ilustración.

The application to contemporary life is made even more specific by Varela in his poem of 1822 on the invention of printing.

> Por esta noble libertad se llama
> el siglo en que vivimos
> el siglo de las luces.

> [For this noble liberty is called
> The century in which we live
> The century of enlightenment.]

These references to a period of enlightenement are completely different in character and spirit from the assertions of Paine, Dickinson, and the House of Representatives that the United States as a political entity was the most enlightened in the world. Thomas Paine's title *The Age of Reason* is hardly relevant to our subject since his book has no special reference to America, and it was both written and published in Europe. A tentative approach to recognition of the years immediately following the American Revolution as a period of enlightenment, however, may be found in a circular letter of June 1783 from George Washington to the governors of the thirteen states. According to Washington, "The foundation of our Empire was not laid in the gloomy age of ignorance and superstition, but at an Epoch when the rights of mankind were better understood and more clearly defined, than at any former period; the researches of the human mind after social happiness, have been carried to a great extent, the treasures of knowledge, acquired by the labours of Philosophers, Sages and Legislators, through a long succession of years, are laid open for our use, and their collected wisdom may be happily applied in the establishment of our forms of government."[37]

A similar tentative statement in more traditional literature may be found in Enos Hitchcock's *Memoirs of the Bloomsgrove Family*, a treatise on education in the form of an epistolary novel, based on Rousseau, which was

[37] Adrienne Koch, ed., *The American Enlightenment* (New York, 1965), p. 24.

published in Boston in 1790. According to this enterprising author, "The present may with propriety be styled the age of philosophy; and America, the empire of reason. The agitations which usually follow such convulsions are rapidly subsiding, and she is fast rising into superior consequence. America now promises fair to be the asylum of genius and liberty, the seat of arts and learning, and the universal emporium of wealth and commerce."[38] In kindred vein, Samuel Miller, in his *Brief Retrospect*, sketched the achievement of French and English authors usually associated with the Enlightenment and came to the moderate conclusion "that the century of which we have just taken leave has produced an unusual number of revolutions, and at least some improvements."[39] Although Miller devoted a long chapter to Oriental literatures, including Hebrew, Persian, Hindu, and Chinese, he had absolutely nothing to say about Spanish literature or Spanish culture. His only references to Spanish America were geographical, apart from an admission that printing existed in Mexico not long after the middle of the sixteenth century.[40] In Miller's mind and in his literary achievement, incredible narrowness and provinciality coexisted with a spirit of free inquiry.

There may be some connection between the near-contemporary references to the Enlightenment as a movement in Latin American letters and the frequent usage of the term in twentieth-century scholarship in the same area. We have already indicated that the Spanish equivalent for "Enlightenment" has been used in Latin American intellectual history much earlier than in that of the United States. Since the cultural traditions of Hispanic America go back to the early sixteenth century, literature there has commonly been viewed in parallel terms with

[38] 2: 10-11.
[39] 2 vols. (New York, 1803), 1: 7.
[40] Ibid., 2: 332.

that of the Peninsula, comprising Renaissance, Golden Age, the baroque [since the use of this term], neoclassicism, and the Enlightenment. The early literature of North America, on the other hand, has conventionally been divided into strictly national segments, Colonial, Revolutionary, and Federal, and even in the nineteenth century Romanticism is ordinarily not used as a period designation. Once more the paradox may be noted that scholars have talked extensively about the Enlightenment in Latin America, but that the movement existed to a much greater degree in English America.

Also to be noted is that writers in the former Spanish colonies of South America bitterly denounced Spain for its failure to reflect the ideals and principles of the Enlightenment which were widespread in France and England. From the perspective of the New World, Spain was an intellectually backward nation, and in its colonies it deliberately opposed the dissemination of learning and toleration as part of a conscious policy of oppression. A Colombian critic, Camilo Torres, for example, accused the Spanish government of completely prohibiting the study of natural rights. The barbarous cruelty of Spanish despotism, he charged, made that nation "the enemy of God and men."[41] Even the most determined opponents of British rule in the American colonies such as Thomas Paine, however, respected the intellectual achievements of England and never suggested that the British government sought to keep the colonies in a condition of philosophical ignorance. To the contrary, the colonists separated British culture from British rule, remaining loyal to the first and declaring independence of the second. To be sure, there

[41] *Memorial de agravios* (1809; reprinted, Bogota, Colombia, 1960), p. 388. I am unable to develop this concept further in this book, but I have dealt with it at length in a previous article, "Las ideas en la América del sur sobre la ilustración española," *Revista Iberoamericana* 24 (1968): 282-97.

were some priests and royalists in South America who defended the Spanish monarchy against "los afrancesados y los liberales" just as there were a number of ministers and Federalists in the United States who denounced the French Revolution. But the French Revolution was by no means identical with the Enlightenment.

The Enlightenment was primarily a period of philosophies and ideas and one cannot say that it existed in any particular area merely because a group of authors claimed that it did so. In both North and South America, the major manifestations of the Enlightenment were in the political realm, but political aspirations and achievements were also reflected in literary works. Direct literary relations between North and South America seem to have been extremely limited during this period, but many resemblances in theme and subject matter may be discovered, resemblances that may reasonably be attributed to the combination of ideas and attitudes known as the Enlightenment.

TEN

CONCLUSION

S INCE the foregoing chapters do not pretend to give a
comprehensive or synoptic view of early American
literature, but present instead a number of selective
illustrations of relations with other literatures, a great
deal in the way of broad conclusions can hardly be expected. It is clear, however, that the major literary movements of Europe between the beginning of the sixteenth
century and the end of the eighteenth, that is, Renaissance, baroque, neoclassicism, Enlightenment, and Romanticism, had repercussions of one kind or another in
Anglo-America. Anne Bradstreet was strongly affected by
one particular continental author, and Edward Taylor,
without attaching himself to any single British or continental predecessor, developed a close and pervasive affinity to the baroque style. These two representatives of New
England Puritanism have been treated in the foregoing
pages, not because their resemblances to writers in other
cultures stand out in particular, but rather because Bradstreet is indelibly registered in literary history because of
her early chronological position and Taylor is highly regarded by many contemporary critics for his poetic
achievement. Even Jonathan Edwards, one of the least
cosmopolitan of authors, could (and should) be treated
from the comparatist perspective. Without venturing in
quest of philosophical parallels into the nebulous territory
of Spinoza, one could uncover analogies with various European necessitarians, particularly atheists such as Fred-

erick the Great, as well as with introspective metaphysicians such as Pascal.

The most innovative literary work produced in Anglo-America before the nineteenth century is also the most universally famous—Franklin's autobiography, which has been accorded merely cursory mention in this book. Today this work is as well known in some remote parts of the world as it is throughout the United States. In Taiwan and Japan, for example, it is part of the curriculum of many secondary schools. Franklin's "Speech of Polly Baker" gained almost immediate attention in France, but it does not seem to have made any impression whatsoever upon the Hispanic world. To this day, no Spanish translation exists. In the Anglo-Saxon world the speech has been treated as either a factual account or as an amusing hoax, but in France its ideological overtones have been seriously heeded.

Many of the intellectual themes associated with the Enlightenment and eighteenth-century Europe have been vigorously discussed in America. These include the Golden Age, the quarrel of ancients and moderns, biological degeneration in the New World, *translatio studii*, deism, and natural rights. Other major units in the history of ideas not treated at length in this book but equally important in early American literature are the state of nature, primitivism, and determinism. The major contribution of American letters to the rest of the world was in the area of political thought. In the words of the English observer quoted in the eighth chapter, "Franklin, Paine, Barlow, have scattered more truths of importance among us than all Europe could do for themselves."

Although many parallels exist in the historical development of Anglo-American literature in the North and Ibero-American in the South, few direct contacts between the two existed until the very end of the eighteenth century. But both literatures maintained close connections with the mainstreams of Europe, not only with the national tradition from which they developed, English, Spanish, or Portuguese. The literature of the British colonies of North America and of the first decades of the United States with which we have been primarily concerned is not a product of men and women writing in isolation. It is not as individual as it is sometimes portrayed (whether exceptional, exclusive, original, on one hand, or confined, insular, provincial, on the other), and for good or for bad it has more in common than appears on the surface with the writing of other nations. It is, in other words, a small, but respectable, part of universal literature.

BIBLIOGRAPHY

Bibliographies, Collected Works, and Editions

Amacher, Richard E. *Franklin's Wit and Folly. The Bagatelles*. New Brunswick, N.J., 1953.

Balzac, Honoré de. *Oeuvres complètes*. Edited by Jean-A. Ducourneau. 26 vols. Paris, 1965-1976.

Bibliotheca Americana: or a Chronological Catalogue of the Most Curious and Interesting Papers, &c. upon the Subject of North and South America. [Edited by Lehman Thomas Rede?]. London, 1789.

Borges, Jorge Luis. *An Introduction to American Literature*. Edited by L. Clark Keating and Robert O. Evans. Lexington, Ky. 1971.

Bowe, Forrest, and Mary Daniels, eds. *French Literature in Early American Translation. A Bibliographical Survey of Books and Pamphlets Printed in the United States from 1668 through 1820*. New York, 1977.

Bradstreet, Anne. *Works*. Edited by Jeannine Hensley. Cambridge, Mass., 1967.

Brown, Charles Brockden. *The Rhapsodist and Other Collected Writings*. Edited by Harry R. Warfel. New York, 1943.

Bryant, William Cullen. *Poems*. Edited by Washington Irving. London, 1832.

Butcher, Philip, ed. *The Minority Presence in American Literature*. 2 vols. Washington, D.C., 1977.

Camoëns, Luiz de. *Os Lusiadas*. Edited by Theophilo Braga. Lisbon, 1898.

Clavijero, Francisco Javier. *Historia antigua de México*. 4 vols. Colección de Escritores Mexicanos. Mexico, 1945.

Condorcet, M.J.A.N.C. de. *Oeuvres*. Edited by A. O'Connor and F. Arago. 12 vols. Paris, 1847-1849.

Crashaw, Richard. *Poems*. Edited by L. C. Martin. Oxford, 1927.

Crèvecoeur, Michel Guillaume St. Jean de. *Letters from an American Farmer*. Edited by Warren B. Blake. London, 1913.
———. "Sketch of a Contrast between the Spanish and the English Colonies." Edited by H. L. Bourdin and S. T. Williams. *University of California Chronicle* 28 (1926): 152-63.

Cruz, Sor Juana Inés de la. *Obras escogidas*. Edited by Juan Carlos Merlo. Barcelona, 1968.

Debates and Proceedings in the Congress of the United States. Printed and Published by Gales and Seaton. 42 vols. Washington, D.C., 1834-1856.

Dickinson, John. *Letters from a Farmer in Pennsylvania*. Edited by R.T.H. Halsey. New York, 1903.

Dickinson, Jonathan. *Journal*. Edited by E. W. Andrews and C. M. Andrews. New Haven, 1945.

Diderot, Denis. *Oeuvres complètes*. Edition Club français du livre. 15 vols. Paris, 1969-1973.

Dow, Charles M. *Anthology and Bibliography of Niagara Falls*. Albany, 1921.

Du Bartas, Guillaume de Salluste. *Bartas His Devine Weekes and Workes (1605)*. Translated by Joshua Sylvester. Facsimile ed. Gainesville, Fla., 1965.
———. *Works*. Edited by Urban Tigner Holmes Jr. et al. 3 vols. Chapel Hill, N.C., 1935-1940.

Ercilla y Zúñiga, Alonso de. *La Araucana*. Edited by José Toribio Medina. 5 vols. Santiago de Chile, 1910-1918.

Franklin, Benjamin. *Papers*. Edited by Leonard W. Labaree et al. New Haven, 1959-

Freneau, Philip. *Poems*. Edited by Harry Hayden Clark. New York, 1929.
———. *Prose*. Edited by Philip M. Marsh. New Brunswick, N.J., 1955.

Goethe, Johann Wolfgang. *Autobiography*. Translated by John Oxenford. 2 vols. Chicago, 1974.

Grimm, Melchior. *Correspondance littéraire*. Edited by Maurice Tourneux. 16 vols. Paris, 1877-1882.

Henríquez, Camilo. *Escritos políticos*. Edited by Raúl Silva Castro. Santiago de Chile, 1960.

Heredia, José María. *Poesías líricas*. Edited by Elías Zerolo. Paris, n.d.

Madison, James et al. *The Federalist.* Edited by Max Beloff. New York, 1948.

Mier, Servando Teresa de. *Escritos inéditos.* Edited by J. M. Miquel i Vergas and Hugo Díaz-Thomé. Mexico, 1944.

Miranda, Francisco de. *Archivo.* 24 vols. Caracas, 1929-1950.

Monaghan, Frank. *French Travellers in the United States, 1765-1932: A Bibliography.* New York, 1933.

Olmedo, José Joaquín de. *Poesías completas.* Edited by A. E. Pólet. Quito, 1945.

Paine, Robert Treat. *Works in Verse and Prose.* Boston, 1812.

Paine, Thomas. *Complete Writings.* Edited by Philip S. Foner. 2 vols. New York, 1945.

Rush, Benjamin. *Letters.* Edited by L. H. Butterfield. 2 vols. Princeton, 1951.

―――. "Papers." *Pennsylvania Magazine of History and Biography* 29 (1905):15-30.

Smith, Elihu Hubbard, ed., *American Poems.* Litchfield, Conn., 1793.

Smith, Sydney. *Works.* Boston, 1874.

Taylor, Edward. *Poems.* Edited by Donald E. Stanford. New Haven, 1960.

Trumbull, John. *Poetical Works.* Hartford, 1820.

Varela, Juan de la Cruz. *Poesías.* Edited by Vicente D. Sierra. Buenos Aires. 1916.

Voltaire, François-Marie Arouet de. *Complete Works.* Edited by Theodore Besterman et al. Geneva, Banbury, and Toronto. 1968-

―――. *Oeuvres complètes.* Edited by Louis Moland. 52 vols. Paris, 1877-1885.

Yanes, Francisco Javier. *Manual político del venezolano.* Edited by Ramón Escovar Salóm. Caracas, 1959.

BACKGROUND, GENERAL WORKS, AND SPECIFIC STUDIES

Aldridge, A. Owen. *Benjamin Franklin et ses contemporaines français.* Paris, 1963. [An expanded version of *Franklin and His French Contemporaries.*]

―――. *Benjamin Franklin Philosopher and Man.* New York, 1965.

BIBLIOGRAPHY

Aldridge, A. Owen. "The Character of a North American as Drawn in Chile, 1818." *Hispania* 49 (1966):489-94.

———. "An Early Cuban Exponent of Inter-American Cultural Relations: Domingo del Monte." *Hispania* 54 (1971):348-53.

———. *Franklin and His French Contemporaries*. New York, 1957.

———. "Las ideas en la América del sur sobre la ilustración española." *Revista Iberoamericana* 24 (1968):282-97.

———. "The Influence of Thomas Paine in the United States, England, France, Germany and South America." In *Proceedings of the Second Congress of the International Comparative Literature Association*, edited by W. P. Friederich, 2:369-83. Chapel Hill, N.C., 1959.

———. "Jacques Barbeu-Dubourg, a French Disciple of Benjamin Franklin." *Proceedings of the American Philosophical Society* 95 (1951):331-92.

———. *Man of Reason, The Life of Thomas Paine*. New York, 1959.

———. "The Poetry of Thomas Paine." *Pennsylvania Magazine of History and Biography* 79 (1955):81-99.

———. "A Religious Hoax by Benjamin Franklin." *American Literature* 36 (1964):204-9.

———. "Thomas Paine and the Classics." *Eighteenth Century Studies* 1 (1968):370-80.

———. "Thomas Paine and the idéologues." *Studies in Voltaire and the Eighteenth Century* 152 (1976):109-17.

———, ed. *The Ibero-American Enlightenment*. Urbana, Ill., 1971.

Arner, Robert D. "The Connecticut Wits." In *American Literature, 1764-1789*, edited by Everett Emerson. Madison, Wis., 1977.

———. "The Structure of Anne Bradstreet's *Tenth Muse*." In *Discoveries & Considerations*, edited by Calvin Israel. Albany, 1976.

Arnold, Hans. "Die Aufnahme von Thomas Paines Schriften in Deutschland." *Publications of the Modern Language Association* 74 (1959):365-86.

Arrunategui, Manuel José de [Anselmo Nateiu]. *Reflecciones políticas, escritas baxo el titulo de "Instinto común."* London, 1811.

Azara, Félix de. *Memorias sobre el estado rural del Rio de Plata en 1801.* Madrid, 1847.

Baker, Ray Palmer. *A History of English-Canadian Literature to the Confederation: Its Relation to the Literature of Great Britain and the United States.* Cambridge, Mass., 1920.

Barbagelata, Hugo D. *Artigas y la revolución americana.* Paris, 1930.

Barlow, Joel. *The Columbiad.* Baltimore, 1807.

―――. *Vision of Columbus.* Hartford, 1787.

Barr, Mary Margaret. *Voltaire in America, 1744-1800.* Baltimore, 1941.

Baudissin, Adelbert Heinrich [Peter Tütt]. *Zustande in Amerika.* Altona, 1862.

Beck, Thor J. *Northern Antiquities in French Learning and Literature (1755-1855).* 2 vols. New York, 1934-1935.

Bernstein, Harry. *Making of an Inter-American Mind.* Gainesville, Fla., 1961.

―――. "Las primeras relaciones intelectuales entre New England y el mundo hispánico (1700-1815)." *Revista Hispánica Moderna* 5 (1938):1-17.

Bigelow, Gordon E. *Rhetoric and American Poetry of the Early National Period.* University of Florida Monographs, Humanities, No. 4. Gainesville, Fla., 1960.

Boccaccio, Giovanni. *The Decameron . . . Translated into English Anno 1620 with an Introduction by Edward Hutton.* London, 1909.

Boerner, Peter. "The Images of America in Eighteenth-Century Europe." *Studies in Voltaire and the Eighteenth Century* 99 (1976):323-32.

Boorstin, Daniel J. "The Myth of an American Enlightenment." In *America and the Image of Europe.* New York, 1960.

Brackenridge, Henry Marie. *Voyage to South America.* 2 vols. London, 1820.

Brissot de Warville, Jacques Pierre. *Nouveau voyage dans les États-Unis.* 3 vols. Paris, 1791.

Brome, Richard. *L'Amérique angloise.* Amsterdam, 1688.

Brown, Ruth Wentworth. "Classical Echoes in the Poetry of Philip Freneau." *Classical Journal* 45 (1949):29-34.

Brown, Solyman. *Essay on American Poetry.* New Haven, 1818.

BIBLIOGRAPHY

Brumm, Ursula. *American Thought and Religious Typology.* New Brunswick, N.J., 1970.

Burrus, E. J. "The First Literary Production of the New World." *Classical Journal* 43 (1947):31-33. [Three Latin dialogues published in Mexico City, 1554.]

Cazden, Robert E. "The Provision of German Books in America during the Eighteenth Century." *Libri* 23 (1973):81-108.

Channing, William Ellery. "On National Literature." *Christian Examiner* 36 (1830):269-95.

Charpentier, François. *De l'excellence de la langue françoise.* Paris, 1683.

Cheetham, James. *Life of Thomas Paine.* New York, 1809.

Chinard, Gilbert. *L'Amérique et le rêve exotique dans la littérature française au XVIIᵉ et au XVIIIᵉ siècle.* Paris, 1933.

————. *Volney et l'Amérique d'après des documents inédits et sa correspondance.* Baltimore, 1923.

Compendio de la historia de los Estados Unidos. Philadelphia, 1825.

Condorcet, M.J.A.N.C. de, marquis de, ed. *Bibliothèque de l'homme publique* 9 (1791).

Curti, Merle. *The Roots of American Loyalty.* New York, 1946.

Dabezies, André. "The First American Faust (1720)." *Comparative Literature Studies* 8 (1971):303-9.

Davies, Thomas M. and Arthur Forslater. "Edward Taylor's 'A Fig for Thee Oh! Death.' " In *Discoveries & Considerations,* edited by Calvin Israel. Albany, 1976.

Davis, John. *Travels of Four Years and a Half in the United States of America.* London, 1803.

Del Monte, Domingo. "Bosquejo intelectual de las Estados Unidos." In *Escritos,* edited by José A. Fernández de Castro. Havana, 1929.

De Onis, José. *The United States as Seen by Spanish American Writers, 1776-1890.* New York, 1952.

Desmarets de Saint-Sorlin. *Discours pour prouver que les sujets chrétiens sont seuls propres à la poésie heroïque.* Paris, 1673.

Dutens, Jean. *An Inquiry into the Origin of the Discoveries attributed to the Moderns.* London, 1769.

Dutton, Warren. *The Present State of Literature.* New Haven, 1800.

Dwight, Timothy. *A Discourse on Some Events of the Last Century.* New Haven, 1801.

―――. *Dissertation on the History, Eloquence, and Poetry of the Bible.* New Haven, 1772.

―――. *The Triumph of Infidelity.* Hartford, 1788.

Echeverría, Durand. *Mirage in the West. A History of the French Image of American Society to 1815.* Princeton, 1957.

Emerson, Everett. "The Cultural Context of the American Revolution." In *American Literature, 1764-1789,* edited by Everett Emerson. Madison, Wis., 1977.

Englekirk, J. E. "Franklin en el mundo hispano." *Revista Iberoamericana* 21 (1956):319-71.

Fess, Gilbert M. *The American Revolution in Creative French Literature (1775-1937).* Columbia, Mo., 1941.

Fiering, Norman. "The First American Enlightenment: Tillotson, Leverett, and Philosophical Anglicanism." *New England Quarterly* 54 (1981):307-44.

―――. "The Transatlantic Republic of Letters: A Note on the Circulation of Learned Periodicals to Early Eighteenth-Century America." *William and Mary Quarterly,* 3rd ser., 33 (1976):642-60.

Flanagan, John T. "An Early Novel of the American Revolution." [*Mis Mac Rae* by Hilliard d'Auberteuil]. *New York History* 32 (1951):316-22.

Fridlender, G. M. " 'Voskresenie' L'va Tolstogo i 'Reč' Polli Beker' B. Franklina," in E. A. Smirnova, ed., *Sravnitel'noe izučenie literatur [The Comparative Study of Literatures]* Leningrad, 1976.

Fucilla, Joseph G. "An Early American Translation of the Count Ugolino Episode." *Modern Language Quarterly* 11 (1950): 480-85.

Galinsky, Hans. "Anne Bradstreet, Du Bartas and Shakespeare in Zusammenhang kolonialer Verpflanzung und Umformung europäischer Literatur." In *Festschrift für Walther Fischer,* 1:43-51. Heidelberg, 1959.

―――. " 'Colonial Baroque': A Concept Illustrating Dependence, Germinal Independence and New World Interdependence of Early American Literatures." In *Proceedings of the 7th Congress of the International Comparative Literature*

Association, edited by Milan V. Dimíc and Eva Kushner, 1: 43-51. Stuttgart, 1979.

————. "Exploring the 'Exploration Report' and Its Image of the Overseas World: Spanish, French, and English Variants of a Common Form Type in Early American Literature." *Early American Literature* 12 (1978):5-24.

————. "Frühkoloniales Amerika in dreifacher europäischen Sicht: Pedro de Castañeda, Samuel de Champlain, Thomas Hariot." In *Beiträge zur vergleichenden Literaturgeschichte: Festschrift für Kurt Wais,* edited by Johannes Häsle and Wolfgang Eitel. Tubingen, 1972.

————. "Kolonialer Literaturbarock in Virginia: eine Interpretation von *Bacons Epitaph* auf der Grundlage eines Forschungsberichtes." In *Amerika und Europa. Sprachliche und Sprachkünstlerische Wechselbeziehungen in amerikanistischer Sicht.* Berlin, 1968.

Gandía, Enrique de. *Historia de las ideas políticas en la Argentina.* 6 vols. Buenos Aires, 1960.

Gerbi, Antonello. *The Dispute of the New World: The History of a Polemic 1750-1900.* Translated by Jeremy Moyle. Pittsburgh, 1973.

Góngora, Luis de. *Obras en verso del Homero español, 1627.* Facsimile edition. Madrid, 1963.

Grant, Loomis C. "An Unnoted German Reference to Increase Mather." *New England Quarterly* 14 (1941):374-75 [in W. E. Tentzel's *Unterredungen,* September 1694, on converting Indians. See L. Országh below].

Grases, Pedro. *La conspiración de Gual y España y el ideario de la independencia.* Caracas, 1949.

————, and Albert Harkness. *Manuel García de Sena y la independencia de Hispanoamérica.* Caracas, 1953.

Grégoire, Henri. *De la littérature des Nègres.* Paris, 1808.

————. *Critical Observations on the Poem of Mr. Joel Barlow.* Washington, D.C., 1809.

Grueningen, John Paul von, ed. *The Swiss in the United States.* Madison, Wis., 1940.

Guiteras, Pedro J. "José María Heredia." *La Revista de Cuba* 9 (1881):20-30.

Gummere, Richard M. "The Heritage of the Classics in Colonial North America: An Essay on the Greco-Roman Tradition." *Proceedings of the American Philosophical Society* 99 (1955): 68-78.

———. *Seven Wise Men of Colonial America*. Cambridge, Mass., 1967.

Hall, Max. *Benjamin Franklin and Polly Baker*. Chapel Hill, N.C., 1960.

Haus, Rudolph. "Some American Contributions to World Literature." *Yearbook of Comparative and General Literature* 26 (1977):17-23.

Hedges, William L. "Toward a Theory of American Literature, 1765-1800." *Early American Literature* 4 (1969):5-14.

Helman, Edith F. "Early Interest in Spanish in New England (1815-1835)." *Hispania* 29 (1946):339-351.

Hennings, August. *Olavides*. Copenhagen, 1799.

———. *Philosophische Versuche*. 2 vols. Copenhagen, 1779.

Hilliard d'Auberteuil, Michel René. *Mis MacRae Roman historique*. Philadelphia [Paris?], 1784.

Hitchcock, Enos. *Memoirs of the Bloomsgrove Family*. 2 vols. Boston, 1790.

Humphreys, David. *Miscellaneous Works*. New York, 1804.

Ilie, Paul. "Franklin and Villarroel: Social Consciousness in Two Autobiographies." *Eighteenth-Century Studies* 7 (1974):321-42.

Isari, Mukhtar Ali. "Edward Taylor and Ovid's *Art of Love*: The Text of a Newly-Discovered Manuscript." *Early American Literature* 10 (1975):67-74.

Jacobson, David L. *John Dickinson and the Revolution in Pennsylvania 1764-1776*. University of California Publications in History. Berkeley and Los Angeles, 1965.

Jaffe, Adrian H. "French Literature in American Periodicals of the Eighteenth Century." *Revue de littérature comparée* 38 (1964):51-60.

Jantz, Harold. "American Baroque." In *Discoveries & Considerations*, edited by Calvin Israel. Albany, 1976.

Johnson, James William. "The Meaning of 'Augustan.' " *Journal of the History of Ideas* 19 (1958):507-22.

BIBLIOGRAPHY

Jones, Howard Mumford. *America and French Culture, 1750-1848*. Chapel Hill, N.C., 1927.
——. *Revolution & Romanticism*, Cambridge, Mass., 1974.
Jost, François. "German and French Themes in Early American Drama." *Journal of General Education* 28 (1976):190-222.
——. *Introduction to Comparative Literature*. New York, 1974.
Kaestle, Carl F. "The Public Reaction to John Dickinson's Farmer's Letters." *Proceedings of the American Antiquarian Society* 78 (1968):322-59.
Kane, Elisha Kent. *Gongorism and the Golden Age*. Chapel Hill, N.C., 1928.
Keller, Karl. *The Example of Edward Taylor*. Amherst, Mass., 1975.
Koch, Adrienne. "Aftermath of the American Enlightenment." *Studies in Voltaire and the Eighteenth Century* 56 (1967): 735-63.
——, ed. *The American Enlightenment*. New York, 1965.
La Motte, Antoine H. de. *Discours sur Homère*. Paris, 1714.
La Rochefoucauld Liancourt, François A. F. duc de. *Travels through the United States of North America*. 2 vols. London, 1799.
Leal, Luis. "*Jicoténcal*, Primera novela histórica en castellano." *Revista Iberoamericana* 25 (1960):9-31.
Lebano, Edoardo A. "Vittorio Alfieri and the United States of America." *Comparative Literature Studies* 8 (1971):310-16.
Le Breton, Maurice. *The French in Boston in the Eighteenth Century*. Bordeaux, 1929.
Lemay, J. A. Leo. *A Calendar of American Poetry in the Colonial Newspapers and Magazines and in the Major English Magazines through 1765*. Worcester, Mass., 1972.
——. "Franklin and the Autobiography. An Essay on Recent Scholarship." *Eighteenth Century Studies* 1 (1968):185-211.
——. *Men of Letters in Colonial Maryland*. Knoxville, Tenn., 1972.
——. "The Text, Rhetorical Strategies, and Themes of 'The Speech of Miss Polly Baker.' " In *The Oldest Revolutionary. Essays on Benjamin Franklin*. Philadelphia, 1976.
Levene, Ricardo. "El constitucionalismo de Mariano Moreno." *Historia* 3 (1958):53-71.

Lind, Sidney E. "Edward Taylor: A Reevaluation." *New England Quarterly* 21 (1948):519-30.

Longfellow, Samuel Wadsworth. *Kavanagh*. Boston, 1849.

Lopez, Claude-Anne. *Mon Cher Papa*. New Haven, 1966.

Marino, Adrian. "Benjamin Franklin in Rumanian Literature." *Comparative Literature Studies* 13 (1976):132-42.

Marraro, Howard R. "Views on America and the American Revolution in Contemporary Italian Reviews." *Forum Italicum* 5 (1971):67-81.

May, Henry F. *The Enlightenment in America*. New York, 1976.

———. "The Problem of the American Enlightenment." *New Literary History* 1 (1969):201-14.

———; and Lundberg, David. "The Enlightened Reader in America." *American Quarterly* 28 (1976):262-301.

McKee, Kenneth N. "The Popularity of the 'American' on the French Stage during the Revolution." *Proceedings of the American Philosophical Society* 83 (1940):479-91.

McLachlan, James. "Classical Names, American Identities: Some Notes on College Students and the Classical Tradition in the 1770's." in *Classical Traditions in Early America*, edited by John W. Eadie, pp. 81-98. Ann Arbor, 1976.

McMahon, Helen. "Anne Bradstreet, Jean Bertault, and Dr. Crooke." *Early American Literature* 3 (1968):118-23.

Medlin, Dorothy. "Thomas Jefferson, André Morellet, and the French Version of *Notes on the State of Virginia*." *William and Mary Quarterly* 35 (1978):85-99.

Mier, Servando Teresa de. *Historia de la revolución de Nueva España*. Facsimile ed. 2 vols. Mexico, 1922.

———. *Memoria político-instructiva*. Philadelphia, 1821.

Miller, Samuel. *Brief Retrospect of the Eighteenth Century*. 2 vols. New York, 1803.

Mirollo, James. *The Poet of the Marvelous, Giambattista Marino*. New York, 1963.

Mitré, Bartolomé. *Historia de Belgrano y de la independencia argentina*. 4 vols. 5th ed. Buenos Aires, 1902.

Molina, Ignacio. *The Geographical, Natural and Civil History of Chile*. Translated by Richard Alsop. Middletown, Conn., 1808.

Morellet, André. *Eloge de Marmontel*. Paris, 1805.

Morse, Jedediah. *American Universal Geography.* Worcester, Mass., 1796.

Murphy, Francis. "Edward Taylor's Attitude toward Publication: A Question concerning Authority." *American Literature* 34 (1962):393-94.

Nelson, Lowry. *Baroque Lyric Poetry.* New Haven, 1963.

Nemes, Graciela P. "Rafael Landívar and Poetic Echoes of the Enlightenment." In *The Ibero-American Enlightenment,* edited by A. O. Aldridge. Urbana, Ill., 1971.

Newcomb, Robert. "Benjamin Franklin and Montaigne." *Modern Language Notes* 72 (1957):489-91.

Nuñez, Estuardo. *Autores ingleses y norteamericanos en el Perú.* Lima, 1956.

———. *El nuevo Olavide.* Lima, 1970.

Olmedo, José Joaquín de, trans. *Ensayo sobre el hombre. De M. Pope. Versión del inglés.* Lima, 1823.

Orjuela, Héctor H. "Revaloración de una vieja polémica literaria: William Cullen Bryant y la oda 'Niágara' de José María Heredia." *Thesaurus. Boletín del Instituto Caro y Cuervo* 19 (1964):248-73.

Országh, Ladislas. "A Seventeenth-Century Hungarian Translation of a Work by Increase Mather." *American Literature* 34 (1962):94-96. [A Latin letter in 1688 on converting Indians. See L. C. Grant above.]

Pablón y Suárez de Urbina, Jesús. *Franklin y Europa 1776-1785.* [Included primarily for the title.] Madrid, 1957.

Pace, Antonio. *Benjamin Franklin and Italy.* Philadelphia, 1958.

———. "The Fortunes of Luigi Castiglioni, Traveler in Colonial America, with an Extract from a Recently Discovered Manuscript of *Viaggio nell'America Settentrionale* (1785-1787)." *Italian Americana* 1 (1974):247-64.

Pauw, Cornelius de, abbé. *Recherches philosophiques sur les Américains.* 2 vols. Berlin, 1768-1769.

Penn, William. *Some Account of the Province of Pennsylvania.* London, 1681.

Picón-Salas, Mariano. *De la conquista a la independencia.* México, 1944.

Pochman, Henry A. *German Culture in America.* Madison, Wis., 1957.

Pocock, J.G.A. *The Ancient Constitution and the Feudal Law.* New York, 1967.

Poggioli, Renato. *The Oaten Flute.* Cambridge, Mass., 1975.

Puglia, Santiago Felipi. *El derecho del hombre* [translation of Paine's *Rights of Man*]. Philadelphia, 1821.

———. *Desengaño del hombre.* Philadelphia, 1794.

Quillen, Elisabeth M. "Relations américaines d'André Chénier." *Revue de littérature comparée* 47 (1973):556-75.

Raymond, Agnes G. "Figaro, fils naturel de Polly Baker? ou la Réhabilitation de Marceline." *Comparative Literature Studies* 12 (1975):34-43.

Raynal, Guillaume Thomas François. *Histoire philosophique et politique des deux Indes.* 6 vols. Amsterdam, 1770.

———. *Historia política de los establecimientos ultramarinos de las naciones europeas.* 5 vols. Madrid, 1784-1790.

Reinhold, Meyer. "Opponents of Classical Learning in America during the Revolutionary Period." *Proceedings of the American Philosophical Society* 112 (1968):221-34.

———. "The Quest for 'Useful Knowledge' in Eighteenth Century America." *Proceedings of the American Philosophical Society* 119 (1975):108-32.

Reish, Joseph G. "Mme de Genlis and the Early American Stage." *Proceedings of the Pacific Northwest Conference on Foreign Languages* 28 (1977):22-25.

Rice, Howard C. "Cotton Mather Speaks to France: American Propaganda in the Age of Louis XIV." *New England Quarterly* 16 (1943):198-233.

Robertson, William. *History of America.* 4 vols. 13th ed. London, 1817.

Rocafuerte, Vicente. *Ensayo político: el sistema colombiano, popular, electivo, es el que más conviene a la América independiente.* New York, 1823.

———. *Ideas necesarias a todo pueblo americano independiente, que quiera ser libre.* Philadelphia, 1821.

Roscio, Juan Germán. *El triunfo de la libertad.* Philadelphia, 1817.

Rousset, Jean. *La Littérature de l'âge baroque en France. Circé et le paon.* Paris, 1954.

Rush, Benjamin. "An enquiry into the Utility of a knowledge of the Latin and Greek languages as a branch of liberal studies." *American Museum* 5 (1789):525-35. Reprinted as "Observations upon the Study of the Latin and Greek languages." In *Essays, Literary, Moral, and Philosophical*, pp. 21-56. Philadelphia, 1798.

Scheick, William J. *The Will and the Word*. Athens, Ga., 1974.

Scouten, Arthur H. "The Paradox of Deism in Colonial America." *Lex et Scientia* 14 (1978):215-28.

Seeber, Edward D. "The French Theatre in Charleston in the Eighteenth Century." *South Carolina Historical and Genealogical Magazine* 42 (1941):1-7.

Sharma, Mohan Lai. "Of Spinning, Weaving and Mystical Poetry: The Fine Yarn of Taylor, Indian Yogis, and Persian Sufis." *Mahfil* 6 (1970):51-61.

Silber, R. B. "William Cullen Bryant's Lectures on Mythology." Ph.D. dissertation, State University of Iowa, 1962.

Simmons, Merle E. *U.S. Political Ideas in Spanish America before 1830: A Bibliographical Study*. Bloomington, Ind., 1977.

Smith, John. *Generall Historie of Virginia, New England and the Summer Isles*. London, 1624.

Spell, J. R. "An Illustrious Spaniard in Philadelphia: Valentín de Faronda." *Hispanic Review* 4 (1936):136-40.

Spurlin, Paul M. *Montesquieu in America, 1760-1801*. Baton Rouge, La., 1940.

———. *Rousseau in America, 1760-1809*. University, Ala., 1969.

Stanford, Ann. *Anne Bradstreet: The Worldly Puritan*. New York, 1974.

Stillé, Charles J. *The Life and Times of John Dickinson*. Philadelphia, 1891.

Sullerot, Evelyne. *Histoire de la presse féminine en France, des origines à 1848*. Paris, 1966.

Thomas, Isaiah. *History of Printing in America*. 2 vols. Worcester, Mass., 1810.

Tichi, Cecelia. "Charles Brockden Brown, Translator." *American Literature* 44 (1972):1-12.

Tilton, Elizabeth M. "Vashington: A Revolutionary Tragedy." *French Review* 49 (1976):975-84.

Tourtellot, Arthur Bernon. *Benjamin Franklin The Shaping of Genius.* Garden City, N.Y., 1977.

Trumbull, John [painter]. *Autobiography.* New York, 1841.

Tyler, Moses Coit. *A History of American Literature during the Colonial Period, 1607-1765.* 2 vols. New York, 1898.

———. *The Literary History of the American Revolution, 1763-1783.* New York, 1897.

Vajda, György M. "Conclusion [regarding a comparatist history of literature]." *Neohelicon* 1 (1973):326-35.

Van Doren, Carl. *Benjamin Franklin.* New York, 1938.

Vergara, José María. *Disertación sobre las primeros principios del gobíerno por Tomas Pain* [sic]. London, 1819.

Victory, Beatrice M. *Franklin and Germany.* Philadelphia, 1915.

Vidaurre, Manuel de. *Plan del Perú.* Philadelphia, 1823.

Wade, Ira O. *The Clandestine Organization and Diffusion of Philosophic Ideas in France from 1700 to 1750.* Princeton, 1938.

Wadepuhl, Walter. *Goethe's Interest in the New World.* Jena, 1934.

Waggoner, H. H. *American Poets: From the Puritans to the Present.* Boston, 1968.

Waldo, Lewis P. *The French Drama in America in the Eighteenth Century.* Baltimore, 1942.

Walsh, Henry Hill. "On the Putative Influence of Benjamin Franklin on Tolstoi." *Canadian-American Slavic Studies* 13 (1979):306-9.

Walz, John A. "Increase Mather and Dr. Faust." *Germanic Review* 15 (1940):20-31.

Warfel, Harry R. *Noah Webster, Schoolmaster to America.* New York, 1936.

Warnke, Frank J. *European Metaphysical Poetry.* New Haven, 1974.

Warren, Austin. *Rage for Order. Essays in Criticism.* Chicago, 1948.

Watanabe, Toshio. "Benjamin Franklin and the Younger Generation of Japan." *American Studies International* 18 (1980): 34-49.

Watts, George B. "Thomas Jefferson, the *Encyclopédie,* and the *Encyclopédie méthodique.*" *French Review* 38 (1965):318-25.

BIBLIOGRAPHY

Webster, Noah. *Dissertations on the English Language*. Boston, 1789.

Wellek, René. *Concepts of Criticism*. New Haven, 1963.

Wesley, John. *Survey of the Wisdom of God in the Creation*. 2nd ed. Bristol, 1777.

Whitaker, Arthur P., ed. *Latin America and the Enlightenment*. Ithaca, N.Y., 1942.

White, Elizabeth Wade. *Anne Bradstreet, "The Tenth Muse."* New York, 1971.

Wiese, Benno von. "Goethe und Heine als Europäer." In *Teilnahme und Spiegelung*, edited by B. Allemann and E. Koppen, pp. 295-315. Berlin, 1975.

Wilhite, John. "The Inter-American Enlightenment." *Revista Interamericana de Bibliografía* 30 (1980):254-61.

Wolf, Edwin L. "The Classical Languages in Colonial Philadelphia." In *Classical Traditions in Early America*, edited by John W. Eadie. Ann Arbor, 1976.

Woods, M. J. *The Poet and the Natural World in the Age of Góngóra*. Oxford, 1978.

Zunder, Theodore Albert. *The Early Days of Joel Barlow*. New Haven, 1934.

INDEX

Library of Congress Cataloging in Publication Data

Aldridge, Alfred Owen, 1915-
  Early American literature.

  Bibliography: p.
  Includes index.
  1. American literature—Colonial period, ca. 1600-1775
—History and criticism.   2. American literature—
Revolutionary period, 1775-1783—History and criticism.
3. American literature—1783-1850—History and criticism.
4. Literature, Comparative.   I. Title.
PS185.A38   1982   810'.9'001   82-47580
ISBN 0-691-06517-9

A. Owen Aldridge is Professor of Comparative Literature at the
University of Illinois. Currently president of the American Comparative Literature Association, he is founder and editor of *Comparative Literature Studies* and the author of many books, including biographies of Franklin, Paine, and Voltaire.

DOING BUSINESS

IN

MEXICO

DOING BUSINESS

IN

MEXICO

Chistopher Engholm
Scott Grimes

PRENTICE HALL
Paramus, New Jersey 07652

Library of Congress Cataloging-in-Publication Data

Engholm, Christopher.
  Doing business in Mexico / by Christopher Engholm and Scott
Grimes.
      p.   cm. — (The Prentice Hall emerging world market series)
    Includes index.
    ISBN 0–13–260738–7 (cloth)
    1. Mexico—Commerce—United States.   2. United States—Commerce—
Mexico.   3. Investments, American—Mexico.   4. Mexico—Economic
conditions—1994-   I. Grimes, Scott (David Scott)   II. Title.
III. Series: Prentice Hall's emerging world market series.
HF3238.U5E54   1997
658.8'48'0972—dc21   97–9597
                                                                      CIP

Acquisitions Editor: *Tom Power*
Production Editor: *Tom Curtin*
Formatting/Interior Design: *Dee Coroneos*

ISBN 0-13-260738-7

ATTENTION: CORPORATIONS AND SCHOOLS

Prentice Hall books are available at quantity discounts with bulk purchase for
educational, business, or sales promotional use. For information, please write to:
Prentice Hall Career & Personal Development Special Sales, 240 Frisch Court,
Paramus, NJ 07652. Please supply: title of book, ISBN, quantity, how the book
will be used, date needed.

PRENTICE HALL
Career & Personal Development
Paramus, NJ 07652
A Simon & Schuster Company

On the World Wide Web at http://www.phdirect.com

Prentice Hall International (UK) Limited, *London*
Prentice Hall of Australia Pty. Limited, *Sydney*
Prentice Hall Canada, Inc., *Toronto*
Prentice Hall Hispanoamericana, S.A., *Mexico*
Prentice Hall of India Private Limited, *New Delhi*
Prentice Hall of Japan, Inc., *Tokyo*
Simon & Schuster Asia Pte. Ltd., *Singapore*
Editora Prentice Hall do Brasil, Ltda., *Rio de Janeiro*

ACKNOWLEDGMENTS

ᛃ

Like so many books created in this age of cyber-communications, this one is the result of many people in diverse locations sharing their opinions and experiences in digital form. As the "authors" of the book, we have many people to whom we are indebted for stuffing our e-mail boxes with millions of bits of wit, anecdote, and expertise, and for doing so—it always seemed—at a moment's notice, and whenever we asked. We thank you.

And there are some truly special people who worked on parts of the book as its "correspondents" in Mexico: journalist Stan Gotlieb, known as *The Gringo of Oaxaca* among fans of his online column, who hunted down and interviewed adventurous foreigners running businesses in southern Mexico; researcher and marketing wonk Dave Fletcher of The Engholm Group, who conducted interviews of Americans doing business in Cabo San Lucas; and journalist Yolanda Torres, a valuable helping hand to us and researcher in Mexico City.

We would also like to thank the individuals and organizations who made the time to subject themselves to our interrogations. They are, in random order: environmental writer Ron Mader, international trade consultant Rolando Garcia, David R. Hostler of Aerolyte, Dick DeVoss of Amway Corporation, Gabriel Covarrubias of the World Trade Center, folk art importer Carolyn Majors, Valente Souza of Booz, Allen in Mexico City, Mike Hart of Collateral Mortgage, Ltd., Dr. Antonio Souza Saldivar of Banco Nacional de Mexico, folk art importer Ginger Blossom, psychologist and author Dr. Marc Erhlich, eco-tour guide and author Rick Fisher, restaurateur Mary Bragg in Cabo, coffee shop owners Mignon and Kenny Kent in Cabo,

author and publisher Don Merwin, mezcal distiller Jake Lustig in Oaxaca, adventure tour operator Roger Remacle in Canada, mortgage broker and author Stephen Conway, importer Susana Trilling in Oaxaca, protocol expert Mari-Betts Johnson, marketing consultant and actress Barbara Chronowski, the Institute of the Americas, the American Chamber of Commerce in Mexico City, the Department of Commerce in Mexico City, the Library at the Graduate School of International Relations and Pacific Studies (IR/PS) at U.C. San Diego, and SECOFI in Mexico City.

We would also like to thank our agent, Julie Castiglia, and our editor at Simon & Schuster/Prentice Hall, Tom Power.

CONTENTS

PART I
COMING TO MEXICO

PART II
SELLING TO MEXICO

PART III
BUYING FROM MEXICO

PART IV
MANUFACTURING AND INVESTING

PART V
LIVING AND WORKING IN MEXICO

PREFACE

V

THE PRENTICE HALL
EMERGING WORLD MARKET SERIES

Everybody knows about the importance to the U.S. economy of exports, which from 1985 through the early 1990s were the number one source of new job creation in America and the largest engine of economic growth. As part of the Clinton Administration's National Export Strategy, the U.S. Department of Commerce has classified key countries as "Big Emerging Markets" or BEMs. These markets represent the core exporting opportunities through the balance of the 1990s and into the 21st century. While the major industrialized nations will continue to be the largest markets for U.S. goods and services, the emerging economies of the world hold the greatest opportunities for gains in U.S. exports. That is, our traditional markets in Canada, Japan, and the European Community will remain important for U.S. exporters; however, they are mature markets that will remain flat in terms of growth. Growth in exports toward the century's end will be seen in countries such as China, Vietnam, Mexico, Brazil, Indonesia, South Korea, Argentina, South Africa, Poland, and Turkey. This is the "A" list of Big Emerging Markets, chosen by the Commerce Department from over 130 of the world's developing economies.

Incidentally, nearly three-quarters of world trade growth is to come from developing countries over the next twenty years. The countries of the "A" list above—all of which feature large populations, high growth, and untapped markets—will account for one-half of that growth. BEMs already purchase about one-

quarter of America's exports, well over $100 billion worth each year. American companies are a perfect match to supply the needed production equipment, business services, engineering expertise, computer hardware and software, health products, and—once wages climb—consumer goods to the world's emerging nations. Our effort is warranted because by 2010, the top 10 BEMs will import more than the European Union and Japan combined. Already they account for over 40 percent of world imports, not including the United States.

Another commonality shared by BEMs: each country's emergence will act as a locomotive pulling along neighboring economies in its tracks. For instance, the emergence of China has fueled growth in Hong Kong, Taiwan, and the Russian Far East. India's participation in the world economy will affect Sri Lanka, Pakistan, and perhaps Myanmar, which was formally Burma. Poland, the first Central European country to achieve positive economic growth since the fall of the Berlin Wall, will pull along neighboring Hungary and Belarus, and will provide a consumer market to benefit the adjacent Czech and Slovak Republics.

The key to success is to set up a corporate presence in these regional economic drivers and expand in each region as the country emerges. The purpose of the Prentice Hall Emerging World Market Series is to both encourage companies to make an early commitment to this endeavor, and assist them in adroitly navigating their way.

Will succeeding in the BEMs be tough for U.S. companies?

Yes. There is nothing fast or easy about dealing with countries that share positive as well as negative commercial characteristics. These are countries in transition, both economically and politically. They are undergoing structural reforms of their commercial and legal systems which are tectonic in scope. Naturally, the risks to foreign companies pioneering in these countries are significant. Yet the wait-and-see approach pursued by many U.S. corporations may be even more risky, given the tangible advantages which early entrants eventually wield in emerging economies like Mexico's. For example, major infrastructure projects are planned and decided upon

early in a BEM's development, and established foreign vendors and contractors gain a significant edge over latecomers to the game. Similarly, widespread brand name awareness can be achieved overnight before the competition drives up advertising costs. The few capable indigenous business partners who run the best-endowed enterprises tend to go fast as Japanese and European companies race to tie up agreements along with their American competitors. In fact, many analysts argue that the future battles of U.S.-Japan-Europe industrial competition will be decided in the Big Emerging Markets.

Which brings us to the ultimate objective of the publisher of this series and its authors—to contribute to the process by which corporate America designs and implements its strategies to meet the tough challenges ahead in markets that will matter the most to our economic future. We seek to prepare you to enter these volatile markets with your eyes open, aware of the mistakes your corporate brethren have made in them already, and to approach them with the right information and enough savvy to keep the cost of the effort under control while enhancing your chances for long-term success.

ABOUT THE AUTHORS

∀

CHRISTOPHER ENGHOLM is an international business consultant and a frequent speaker on the topic of emerging markets, business culture, and protocol. He has designed and conducted seminars for firms such as Hughes Aircraft, Chevron, and NYNEX. Among his books about international business culture and practice are: *DOING BUSINESS IN THE NEW VIETNAM,* and *INTERNATIONAL EXCELLENCE: SEVEN BREAKTHROUGH STRATEGIES FOR PERSONAL AND PROFESSIONAL SUCCESS.* He is founder of The Engholm Group in Fallbrook, California, providing custom business information and Internet training services. He is the publisher of *INTERNATIONAL EXCELLENCE Online* at:

http://www.tmisnet.com/~engholm/group.htm,

as well as co-author of the *PRENTICE HALL DIRECTORY OF ONLINE BUSINESS INFORMATION.*

SCOTT GRIMES is an international market research consultant who specializes in emerging economies and online business ventures. His clients include law firms, think tanks, international development banks, and Fortune 500 companies. He also serves as a research analyst at The Dialogue, the regional public policy program at the University of California, San Diego. He is the co-author of the *PRENTICE HALL DIRECTORY OF ONLINE BUSINESS INFORMATION.*

INTRODUCTION

V

MEXICO—A PLACE TO LIVE, WORK, AND SUCCEED

Coming through the airport at Mexico City, one is amazed by the most obvious manifestations of change here in the years since the ratification of NAFTA. The canopy of orange gauze your jet descends through to get to the world's most populous city remains unchanged—if not slightly worse in hard statistical terms—but inside the airport the recent transformation of this society is palpable. A 17-year-old Mexican boy sits in a cafe wearing Okley sunglasses and reading *Men's Health,* one of the most visible magazines here. Most everyone wearing a business suit also carries a cellular phone. And the clothes worn by women are chic, the gold adornments more conspicuous and the cosmetics shading their faces more subtle. There are payphones everywhere and, miraculously, they all work, though you have to purchase a Ladatel phone card in dominations of 25 or 50 pesos in order to use them. Another sign of changing times: on the back of the Ladatel phone card appears an advertisement for Banamex, including the company's website address.

There seems a whole new orderliness about the place, epitomized by the fact that the just-arrived must now queue up to pre-hire a taxi and pay a regulated fare to a selected destination, instead of being subjected to certain extortion by a taxicab driver. And in the airport restaurant promotional girls sashay in red suits and sashes emblazoned with the logo of the cable company, DirecTV.

We sit down to a meal and a dose of MTV, which is MC'd by a Gen-X Latino-looking guy named "Claudio," from Miami. The Hollywood high-tech imagery and techno-erotic lyrics are subtitled in Spanish: "Ah, ah, . . . amor." (In fact, we found that during our stay in Mexico conducting research for this book, it was all but impossible to elude the sounds of Madonna, Michael Jackson, and The Artist Formerly Known as Prince.) We ended our meal, having endured a 10-minute TV interview with a bleached-blonde female Mexican rock idol named Marta Sanchez, during which she repeatedly compared her band to Guns & Roses. A sophisticated-looking businessman sitting at the next table responded to our question concerning whether there was any resentment felt in Mexico about the apparent Americanization of the country's media and, indeed, the look and feel of its urban culture.

"There is no resentment," the man replied in crisp English. "There is a shift in Mexico now—a change. People are into making money."

As you come into the city in a taxicab, the air stings your eyes as you peer up at Pearl Jam posters, the familiar neon of McDonald's arches, and a huge billboard advertising Playboy condoms. Entering the once-quaint Zona Rosa, one encounters a cacaphony of tony boutiques with names like Gucci, Rolex, and Armani; a grim-faced guard nuzzling a semi-automatic rifle stands aside the entryway of each shop. Upscale women window shop wearing fitted tee-shirts that advertise foreign perfumes. These are the images of the "new" Mexico.

DOING BUSINESS IN THE "NEW" MEXICO

Turbulent and unpredictable, Mexico's market economy—recently opened by the NAFTA—is by far the most popular destination for U.S. investment among the so-called Big Emerging Markets. Mexico is our third-largest trading partner, yet American business persons are doing much more than just trading with their neighbor to the South. They are partnering in jointly managed ventures both large and small, exchanging

technology, and working together in cross-border teams...often in cyberspace. In fact, more U.S. subsidiaries are located in Mexico than in any other country besides Brazil; an astonishing 400,000 jobs in America now depend on our commercial relationship with Mexico.

Today, the "new" Mexico has recovered from the economic downturn of 1994-1995 and is again emerging as a source of global business opportunities. The Mexican economy is growing at a brisk 7.4% clip and imports of consumer goods have jumped by 50 percent. More importantly, Mexico continues to draw investment from around the world. As a result of the NAFTA, many of the world's leading manufacturing companies have shifted their production to Mexico, including such common household names as Sony, Panasonic and Samsung. The growth of manufacturing at *maquiladora* plants near the border has created new sources of business for American firms wishing to invest in or market to these multinational companies.

A PLACE FOR THE SMALL COMPANY AS WELL AS LARGE

The Presidency of Ernesto Zedillo has continued a reform process that is fundamentally transforming Mexican society. As a result of privatization and decentralization, exciting new opportunities are arising for American companies in a number of fields. Joint venture projects in energy, shipping, telecommunications, financial services and health care are generating hundreds of millions of dollars in revenues for U.S. firms, and future privatization will ensure new opportunities for enterprising American companies. Most importantly, these opportunities are not limited to the Fortune 500. Small and medium-sized U.S. companies have enjoyed significant success in establishing supplier relationships with Mexican companies and larger U.S. firms doing business in Mexico. The real-life profiles contained in this book are proof that even the sole individual with a dream and a passion for achieving it can find prosperity in the Mexico that has emerged from economic crisis.

HOW THIS BOOK CAME TO BE
 Ⅴ

This book was inspired by the Americans and Canadians we have met and interviewed in Mexico who are truly "making it" South of the border, business people who embody a sense of adventure and adaptability in actualizing their unique visions of working in Mexico. Often their visions were born of travel in the country or working with Mexican people in the United States. Their motive was not always merely to make money, per se, but to forge a deeper link to the country; to create a different lifestyle for themselves . . . to escape the rat race and crime of El Norte.

Consider the archeologist-turned-importer of indigenous art objects; the well-known American architect whose non-profit foundation erects hospitals in Tijuana; the canyon eco-adventurer who can't ignore the starving Tarahumara Indians and finds a way to combine his company's eco-tours with aid projects to save Indian villages; the Hispanic-American insurance agent working in San Diego who "discovers" a whole new clientele South of the border, and now works both sides as if the border has vanished completely.

No doubt about it, many Americans have pursued their dreams in Mexico as an exit route from the corporate realities of the Norte. There's Suzanne Lopez, who in the 1960s was a city kid working at a coffee house in the Soho district in Manhattan. Now she owns and manages a jungle resort in Puerto Angel on the southern Pacific coast of Mexico, where meals are organically grown and yoga classes are convened on the roof top of the hotel. And there are many others. In fact, according to the U.S. State Department, about 500,000 Americans live in Mexico, which is an increase of

about 20 percent since 1990. These are people who have come to the country to work or to retire where the quality of life can be high relative to the cost of living. Bivouacked in quaint colonias in and around Guadalajara, Guanahuato, Cabo San Lucas, and San Miguel de Allende, Americans are finding real estate bargains and a tranquil lifestyle South of the border.

What do you need to know to make it in Mexico?

What do you need to know to pursue your dreams in the land of the sun? There are three things, really. The first is *country background,* including an acquaintance with the political and economic scene and the changes, as well as the business opportunities, brought about by NAFTA. It would include as well an understanding of the 1994 peso crisis and Mexico's partial recovery from it, and how this affects your business plan. You also need some insight into how the different regions of the country relate to the center and stand alone as unique places in which to engage in business.

Second, you need to know *how to deal with Mexico's business bureaucracy.* Where are the doors to getting your business licensed? How do you find reliable information about the market, and about the rules of commercial endeavor?

And third, you will need to prepare yourself *to cross into Mexican business culture* with an appreciation for the local customs and commercial protocol. Business in Mexico is more social, personal, and relationship-based. How will you present yourself and your proposal, and to whom?

Hence, three areas of expertise emerge:

➤ knowledge of the country
➤ understanding the rules, and
➤ cultural sensitivity

WHAT'S INSIDE THIS BOOK
FOR YOU
V

Doing Business in Mexico is designed for small and medium-sized companies seeking to grow their businesses by tapping into marketing opportunities south of the border. It also provides a helpful update for Fortune 1000 business executives who are "rediscovering" Mexico in the wake of a rebounding economy and the implementation of the NAFTA. Through this book, we hope you will gain a better understanding of Mexico, its future course, and where the country should fit into your business plan.

We've tried to make the book a complete guide to selling to, buying from, and partnering with Mexican businesses. Its question-and-answer format is a "one-stop consultant" for anyone interested in starting a business south of the border, living and working there, or even retiring there. We've included how-to sections covering five essential areas of business know-how:

COUNTRY BACKGROUND

SELLING TO MEXICO

BUYING FROM MEXICO

MANUFACTURING AND INVESTING

LIVING AND WORKING IN THE COUNTRY

Many essential business contacts and addresses are included, as well as a full complement of Internet destinations related to Mexico.

We hope you enjoy the book, and your business days in Mexico.

Christopher Engholm   **Scott Grimes**
Fallbrook, California   *Encinitas, California*

DOING BUSINESS

IN

MEXICO

PART I
∀

COMING
TO MEXICO

---

*"The advent of a 'modern Mexico'—business-oriented,
outward-looking, and sympathetic to most things
American—borders the contours of a 'different Mexico,'
one that, despite the convergence of ideas among
the elites of both nations, remained profoundly different
than the United States, and capable of generating
the very surprises that have cropped up in the
past couple of years."*

Jorge G. Castañeda
*Mexican journalist and
social thinker*

Chapter 1
∨

MAKING IT IN MEXICO:
IS YOUR FUTURE SOUTH
OF THE BORDER?

When you think about setting up a business in Mexico, a number of initial apprehensions might come to mind. For example, "how much is this going to cost?"; and, "are other foreigners like me making money in the country?" You may also wonder whether the obstacles—like Mexico's well-known government corruption—are insurmountable. More specifically, the businessperson might ask whether small and medium-sized businesses can make a go of it in Mexico alongside the Fortune 500 companies. This chapter will help you gauge whether Mexico is a place for you. It looks at Mexico as a place for small and medium-sized companies to do business, whether it's starting a small restaurant after you retire, serving as a supplier to a maquiladora, or importing high-quality Mexican goods for sale in the United States. Here we look at the experience of others in Mexico and try to lay out a road map for your own business success.

Is it possible to make money south of the border, especially as a small or medium-sized foreign business? And do the successes outnumber the failures?

If the interviews of business owners included in this book are any indication, you can be assured that it is indeed possible for a small American company to prosper in Mexico. Larger Fortune 500 companies have maintained a presence in Mexico

for 50-100 years; most maintain a corporate presence in Mexico, and are managed, for the most part, by Mexican nationals as opposed to expat Americans. In terms of personnel, these companies are fully integrated into the country's business community. For smaller companies, the challenge is to initiate a business with fewer prior connections to the local business players, less capital, and less manpower. Although one quickly recognizes while in Mexico that small and medium-sized American companies are simply not set up in Mexico in great numbers, we were personally cheered by the ease with which we did locate American entrepreneurs who had engineered methods for surmounting the difficulties of entering the Mexican market, and had made it pay. These pioneers have set up an amazing array of ventures that testify to a deeply felt determination and will to succeed in an emerging market. You will learn more about these folks later in the book.

A great deal of future money will be made by American companies who pursue the opportunities in servicing the exporting maquiladora manufacturing plants along the border, where medium-sized American companies can be very effective. Also, the larger retail marketing companies from the United States have already been—and will continue to be—highly successful, including the likes of Office Depot, Mail Boxes, Etc., and Price Club, which has formed a venture with Gigante, one of Mexico's largest retail chains. And certainly our successes outnumber our failures in the context of multinational investments in the maquiladoras. This is where most foreign investment and foreigners are located. The maquiladoras and their suppliers benefit from their proximity to the American market; the border communities where most are located are quasi-dollar economies, and are thus partially insulated from the risks of a peso devaluation. The most successful business ventures in Mexico are those maquiladoras that are producing consumer goods for the U.S. market. Small and medium-sized firms have experienced success by creating supplier relationships with these companies, particularly with firms whose products are strongly affected by the local content requirements in the NAFTA.

Will doing business in Mexico really take more time and patience, as everyone always says?

Undoubtedly. However the rewards are likely to be worth the investment. Business planning for Mexico must reflect the time, the "person hours," required to develop substantive business relationships. Just as important, businesses need to budget significant "economic time" for Mexico and design strategies for long-term success. Fluctuations in the value of the Mexican currency mean that income projections denominated in dollars will not always be dependable in the out years of a business plan.

Furthermore, a small American company will likely lack the limitless resources of a multinational corporation and thus, must pay special attention to being well-positioned in the Mexican market. As a small business in Mexico, for example, you will be vulnerable to changes in the Mexican economy, particularly in the value of the Mexican currency. You need to be in a position to alter your business strategy in response to fluctuations both in the Mexican economy and in the Mexican government budget. Ideally, your business should be in a position to supply inputs or consumer goods to Mexico, or to purchase goods for import into the United States, depending on the economic conditions and the exchange rate of the peso. For example, a wine marketing firm might export California wines to Mexico, but should also be ready to import Mexican wines or wine grapes if need be.

What is the cost of doing business in Mexico compared to other emerging countries?

The real costs of doing business in Mexico reflect a number of important factors about the country. Included in these are the significant currency risk undertaken by Mexican investments, institutionalized and under-the-table corruption, and the variable productivity of Mexican workers. On the other hand, Mexican investments realize significant cost savings in comparison to other export platforms due to its proximity to

the U.S. market, the relatively low cost of Mexican labor, and the availability of educated local employees.

Can a foreigner do business in Mexico without having to compromise his or her business ethics or values; that is, can clean business be conducted in a society renowned for bribery and corruption?

Many Mexicans would argue that a tradition of bribery has arisen from public officials neither qualified nor sufficiently educated to serve. For many, bribes have become endemic. "They know you will lose money if they have the plant closed down," says a Mexican investor in a fertilizer plant which the government has closed down three times. "And so they extort you to keep it open."

A civil servant culture does not yet exist in Mexico. What exists, says Valente Souza, Consultant in Energy and Environment with Booz, Allen & Hamilton in Mexico City, recently, "is personal, team, cronyism. They live and breathe via loyalties to teams, and there is no concern for the public good."

There exists a near total lack of organized schooling for public officials. Training courses for bureaucrats are being conducted, but all too slowly. Civil servants like to call themselves "the authorities." But, as one frustrated Mexican business person screamed at such an authority on the phone recently, "Come on, you're a public servant, and we pay your salary!" In the final analysis, we side with the advice proffered by most of our interviewees—that to pay bribes only invites more requests for them, and to keep one's nose clean, and one's deal above board, is the most prudent long-term approach.

Are violations of human rights part of Mexican society today? And is it a safe place for foreign business people and residents?

Human rights violations are not a standard part of Mexican life in most states. They are particularly rare in Mexico City

and the border states. Groups such as Human Rights Watch and Amnesty International have pointed to the systematic exploitation of indigenous peoples in the southern Mexican states, notably Chiapas and Oaxaca and can provide more detailed information.

A related question is the quality of living conditions for workers who live in the border cities and work for maquiladora factories. Critics such as Ross Perot are correct when they point out that workers in the barrios of these cities often dwell in conditions that are appalling by First World terms. However, many of these workers have emigrated from very poor states in Central and Southern Mexico, and many are sending a portion of their wages back to their home villages. These populations represent a mass internal immigration that has overwhelmed the limited capacities of state and local governments on the border. Moreover, the barrios of Brownsville and El Paso are in many cases no better than those of Matamoros and Cuidad Juarez, so Americans should be careful of lobbing too many criticisms at Mexico before they have inspected their own back yards.

There is no question that crime has increased substantially in Mexico over the last few years, particularly in Mexico City where crime in 1996 increased 10 percent from the previous year. Part of this is attributable to the economic crisis of 1994-1995; in addition, the rise of narcotics trafficking and organized crime has contributed to the growing number of violent crimes nationally. Despite the government's anti-corruption campaign in the civilian police force, crime remains a critical issue for many middle-class Mexicans. There are close links between the military and the police, and some critics have questioned the growing militarization of the police force.

Ironically, the Mexican crime wave has created new opportunities for foreign businesses such as car alarms and home security systems. Still the incidence of crime in Mexico City and other major urban areas is concentrated in residential, primarily lower middle-class and poor neighborhoods, but

does not really affect the commercial sector. As a result, foreign businesspersons should feel reasonably safe.

What are the personal qualities necessary to live, work, and succeed as a foreigner in Mexico?

Of the people we met and spoke to about doing business in Mexico, virtually all of them had Mexico in their blood. That is, they had fallen in love with the country and its people long before setting up a business there. In short, we discovered that the foremost requirement for success is an appreciation, if not adoration, for the Mexican way of life. All the stereotypes one hears about Mexicans are based on reality; they just don't take into account the exceptions. One will need to be prepared, as an example, to accept the country's "work to live, don't live to work" philosophy. One needs to understand that the mañana syndrome is not a cliché, it's a distinct outlook on life and work and the relationship between the two. Also, one needs to understand and accept the importance of religion and family in a person's life. Moreover, to live and succeed in the country, the language barrier must be broken. A commitment needs to be made to penetrate the culture as a new citizen rather than an expat on a brief stint. (We'll talk much more about Mexican business culture in a later chapter.)

GETTING TO KNOW
THE MEXICAN PEOPLE

A big part of succeeding in business anywhere is simply not to set yourself up for failure. There is one proven recipe for doing just that in Mexico: go into a business venture there believing that with NAFTA, with our proximity, with Mexico's move toward an open market democracy, our two countries and our two people are more the same than fundamentally different. To go into Mexico with the mindset that our two countries have embraced based on notions of free trade and democratic ideals, and that our NAFTA-confirmed relationship has inspired such commonality that our long-time differences in culture, economic status, and historical experience have been rendered inconsequential and benign, is to invite disaster. Mexico is different from the United States in crucial ways, and will remain so regardless of what documents their leaders ratify at ceremonies. This chapter reviews the history and cultural mindset of Mexico, and examines the ways in which it differs fundamentally from the United States. It also looks at the current demographic characteristics of the Mexican population, which should drive any company's business plan for Mexico.

How has Mexico's geographic location and topography
influenced its industrial and agricultural sectors?

Mexico is the 13th largest country in the world, with a total area of approximately 760,000 square miles. The country

varies from arid deserts in the far north to tropical rain forest in the south. Much of Mexico is mountainous, primarily due to two parallel mountain ranges that run from the northwest to the southeast. The plain between these two mountain ranges in central Mexico comprises the Altiplano Central, or the central Mexican plateau which is the site of Mexico's largest cities and its heaviest concentration of industry.

Nearly half of Mexico is arid, with 23 percent of the country experiencing a temperate climate and 28% sub-tropical or tropical. Only 13 percent of Mexico's land is considered arable, and most of this is under cultivation. A large percentage of the country is composed of forests, perhaps 24 percent, offering a dangerously unexploited resource.

What demographic trends in Mexico are important to business planning?

Mexico has a young, transient, and rapidly-urbanizing population. As a consumer market, Mexico holds genuine promise as a leading purchaser of consumer goods from the United States. However, consumption in Mexico is tied to the central government's control of key economic instruments, particularly the value of the currency. Depending on the state of the peso and the rate of inflation, Mexican households can experience rapid swings in their annual disposable income.

Following are key demographic facts regarding Mexico that should be incorporated in a company's marketing plan:

➤ **Race**: The Mexican government has not collected official data on race and ethnicity for over 60 years. Unofficial estimates by demographers claim that about 55% of Mexicans are mestizos. Approximately 29% are Native Americans, 15% are Caucasians, and 1% fall into other categories.

➤ **Language**: The most recent census data suggest that approximately 90% of Mexicans speak Spanish as their primary language. Other major languages are Nahuatl, used in east-central Mexico; Maya, used primarily in the Yucatan; Zapotec and Mixtec, which are spoken in Oaxaca state; and Otomi, spoken near Mexico City and in parts of

Puebla and Veracruz. The 1990 census estimated that over 6.3 million Mexicans could speak a dialect of one of these languages.

➤ **Religion:** Approximately 90% of all Mexicans are Roman Catholics. Protestants account for roughly six percent of the population and five percent identify themselves as non-religious. Foreigners should be aware that Roman Catholicism varies widely throughout Mexico and many indigenous peoples who identify themselves as Roman Catholics actually practice a blend of Catholic and native beliefs.

➤ **Population:** The population of Mexico is estimated to be nearing 100 million people. Projections indicate the country's population will grow to 109,480,000 by the year 2000 and 118,445,000 by 2010. The Mexican census bureau, INEGI, estimates the natural rate of population growth to be 1.9%. The Mexican government has succeeded in slowing the rate of natural increase through a vigorous family planning program; however, the birthrate in the country is still high.

➤ **Age:** In comparison to many industrialized countries, Mexico's population is extremely young. Eighty percent of the population is under 40 and over half of all Mexicans are under 20 years of age. Due to the rapid growth of the population and the relative youth of its citizens, experts argue that Mexico must produce 800,000 to one million jobs each year to keep a substantial portion of its population working.

➤ **Urbanization:** Mexico has experienced an extraordinary internal migration of its peoples from rural to urban areas in the last fifty years. An estimated 71% of the population now resides in cities and towns. The strongest example of this phenomenon is Mexico City, whose metropolitan area now includes a population of 22 million people. A similar phenomenon has occurred on the U.S.-Mexico border, as migrants from the interior have traveled north to seek work in the maquiladoras. Their migration has swelled the

populations of the border towns such as Tijuana and Cuidad Juarez past one million.

What are the key events in Mexico's history that shape Mexican character?

History is very important to Mexicans; it is what Professor Jorge Castaneda calls the "essence of the present." Writing in *The Atlantic Monthly,* Castaneda notes that the "Mexican Memory serves a role in Mexican society that is akin to the place of the American dream in the United States."[1]

Key events in Mexican history that should be understood by foreign businesspersons include:

PRE-COLUMBIAN CIVILIZATIONS

Pre-Columbian civilizations in Mexico included the Maya in the Yucatan Peninsula and civilizations of the central highlands. They created the first advanced forms of social organization in Mexico, including a strong class hierarchy and a byzantine bureaucracy, two characteristics that are still apparent in contemporary Mexican society. These civilizations represent an important source of pride and inspiration for many of Mexico's indigenous peoples, and are useful for leaders attempting to spark rebellions in the southern states.

THE AZTEC AND THE SPANISH CONQUEST

The Aztec built an extensive and complex society in the fifteenth and sixteenth centuries A.D. Their capital was at Tenochtitlan, on the site of present-day Mexico City. A Spanish expedition led by Hernan Cortes between 1519 and 1521 overcame the Aztecs, a triumph through the use of superior military weaponry and mercenaries drawn from other indigenous tribes.

---

[1] Jorge G. Castenada, Professor of International Affairs, National Autonomous University of Mexico, "Ferocious Differences," *The Atlantic Monthly,* July, 1995.

Another factor: the Aztecs were conflicted in their opposition to Cortes, because he posed as the "white" god Quetzalcoatl. According to traditional legends, Quetzalcoatl was an exiled god whose return had been expected "from the East."

SPANISH RULE

Key aspects of the Spanish era include the rise of the Catholic Church and the conversion of the majority of Mexico's indigenous peoples, and the growth of self-sufficient economic units that were governed as feudal fiefs by Spanish overlords. Mexico became the colony of "New Spain," although there was always tension between local Spanish rulers and the mother country. The Spanish began their period of rule by trying to break the country into feudal *encomiendas,* land grants that included Indian villages with their associated populations and production. These grants started the colonial tradition of chopping Mexico into regional fiefdoms that were largely self-sufficient.

This process was exacerbated after the collapse of the native population due to disease and overwork. By 1700 perhaps a million Native Americans still lived in the colony of New Spain, in comparison to an estimated population of 11 million plus in the early 1500s. The colony's extensive cattle and sheep operations destroyed the indigenous people's farmland, and the Spanish monopoly on irrigation water limited their ability to grow food. Ironically, the collapse of the economy actually increased the remaining population's dependence on Spanish rule, and much of the population retreated onto rural estates called *haciendas.* These estates were even more autonomous from the central government, and they consolidated a tradition of regional centers of power that continues to the present day.

INDEPENDENCE, THE AGE OF SANTA ANNA, AND THE MEXICAN REVOLUTION

Mexico's history is slightly confusing to outsiders because Mexican Independence and the Mexican Revolution are two dis-

tinct events. Mexico achieved independence from Spain in 1821, after an almost two-decade struggle between Mexican nationalists and the remnants of the Spanish colony. After independence Mexico was ruled off and on over a 22-year period by General Antonio López de Santa Anna, a tumultuous period that was highlighted by the loss of almost half of Mexico's national territory to the U.S. after the Mexican-American war. Note that this occasion is referred to in Mexico as the First Northern Intervention (1846-1848) and is the source of significant lingering bitterness.

In 1910-1911 Mexican revolutionaries combined forces in a concerted attack against the Dictator Porfirio Diaz. Diaz was exiled whereby the revolutionaries promptly began to fight amongst themselves. This period is referred to as the Mexican Revolution, and is a source of great pride to many Mexicans.

MODERN MEXICO AND THE RISE OF THE PRI

In the first decades after the 1910 revolution, the country was mobilized to modernize. Solidarity with the country's central political establishment was high. During the 1920s and 1930s, the country industrialized and people were overwhelmingly loyal to Mexico's leadership, which was headed by the Partido Revolucionario Institucional (PRI). As the PRI developed the country the time came for democratic pluralism to develop through reform of the system. Students protested in Tlatelolco Square in 1968 and were gunned down by government police in the country's own version of Tiananmen. During this decade, the country's president, Echeverria, brought the finances of Mexico's central bank under the personal control of the president, changing the relationship of the PRI and the Mexican people. Suddenly, the PRI and industry were in bed together. Concessions got doled out to friends and family. PRI officialdom became complacent, becoming a class of apparatchiks, a nomenclatura. An official culture was born made up of people who survived in the shadows of their benefactors, rising with them, falling with them, "loyal to their boss until he dies."

A public loss of faith in the ruling party occurred after the taking of control of the central banking system by the president. The massacre of students moved the country out of its naive adolescence and toward mature questioning of authority. Unfortunately, the protesters were subsequently co-opted by the system, compromised by it, eventually to buy into it and become the "technocrats" of the Salinas era.

Salinas is considered by elites to be Mexico's greatest modern president. He may be despised by the person-on-the-street, but hindsight tells us that he was singularly responsible for starting a battle within the PRI aimed at changing its very structure. He signed NAFTA. He privatized industry. Meanwhile, the aging Echeverria, who is said to have worked in tandem with Grupo Hank, moved quickly to sabotage Salinas' effort to reform the party. A whole class of privileged nomenclatura was at stake. His faction of the PRI took advantage of Salinas' last year in office, in which all presidents are weak, to strike. In fact, on New Year's Day, 1994, the Zapatista rebellion was launched in Chiapas. (Some commentators claim that the ERP militant group is backed by Echeverria's gang as well, and is just another attempt to destabilize Zedillo's regime.) Thus began an internecine war with the PRI.

For now, President Ernesto Zedillo may be too weak to carry out substantive reforms which, ironically, are aimed to reduce the power of the presidency.

What are the most important aspects of Mexican culture and how will these affect business relations with foreigners?

The two key aspects of Mexican culture that will affect foreigners' business relations with Mexico are time and history.

Mexican concepts of *time* are fundamentally different from American. In practice, this translates into Mexicans frequently being late to appointments or failing to show up at all. Patient acceptance is a far better tact in this situation than anger, frustration or reprisals. Tardiness is discussed in more detail below; however, a few quick words here on failure to keep appointments are in order.

The bluntness or directness that is often prized in America is alien to Mexican culture. In order to avoid giving offense, Mexicans will often refuse to say "no" to an invitation. To the Mexican mind, it is better to accept an invitation and fail to attend than to directly refuse the offer. And no explanation for any absence will be forthcoming.

Time concepts in Mexico create a national propensity for tardiness. Not only will individuals be late to meetings and appointments, but entire events will start later and end far later than was officially announced. A Mexican party will rarely start on time, but will definitely extend well into the night. Americans' sense of Mexicans' tardiness is further exaggerated by the different daily routines followed in the two countries. Traditionally Mexicans take five meals in the course of the day: *desayuno,* a light early-morning meal, often of coffee and pastries, *almuerzo,* an early lunch, *comida,* the late substantial lunch that is the main meal of the day, *merienda,* a light early evening meal, similar to a tea, and *cena,* the late supper. Most professional Mexicans will have been up the previous night until after midnight, and a substantial segment of their work day occurs after 4:00 P.M.

At a more fundamental level, Mexicans understand time in a manner different from North Americans. As political scientist Jorge G. Castaneda has commented: "The difference is not merely a question of punctuality, formality, or responsibility but rather one of the conception of time, its role in life, and its social function."

Again in *The Atlantic Monthly,* Castaneda argues that time simply is not the driving force in Mexicans' lives:

> Because so many Mexicans work, live, and even love informally, time is not of the essence. Letting and watching time go by, being late (an hour, a day, a week), are not grievous offenses. They simply indicate a lower rung on the ladder of priorities. It is more important to see a friend or the family than to keep an appointment or make it to work . . .

There may even be a climatic explanation for the Mexican conception of time as Castaneda notes:

Everything is slow in Mexico, but not because Mexicans cannot do things quickly. Everything is slow because the passage of time is not very noticeable. Time is flat: too frequently nothing changes with time, and the sense of its going by— the reason for putting a premium on it—is absent. Much of Mexico lacks seasons except when it rains and when it doesn't, and in the countryside the dry season is basically devoted to waiting for rain; for this and more complex reasons as well, time in Mexico is not what it is in the United States.

The importance of *history* to Mexico has already been noted. History is a unifying force in Mexico; it helps to bind a country that is deeply divided by ethnicity, region and class. Mexican historians have noted that history in Mexico is slower, a continuum of evolutionary change occasionally interrupted by short bursts of violent intense activity.

The role of history in Mexican culture is so profound that the "official" version of Mexican history has become a major source of debate in the country. For most Mexicans, it is more important that there be a national consensus regarding the country's history than that the history be accurate. For foreigners, the best stance is to stay out of the often heated debates that erupt over Mexico's past.

In general, the relevance of Mexican history for U.S. businesspersons is the need for heightened sensitivity. The most old guard, traditional, enfranchised members of the establishment may still think of themselves as revolutionaries. In a sense, all Mexicans are revolutionaries and may have a natural sympathy for historical revolutionary figures such as Pancho Villa or contemporary revolutionaries such as the Zapista army in Chiapas.

HOW MEXICAN COMMERCE WORKS:
WHAT'S CHANGED WITH NAFTA

The Mexican economy has undergone fundamental changes in the last decade as a result of the NAFTA and two successive presidential administrations that have emphasized economic reform and marketization. This chapter reviews the Mexican commercial environment in light of the major changes underway in Mexican society. Here we look at strategic trends affecting Mexico, including the effects of an emerging free trade regime and the consequences of the 1994-1995 economic crisis. The chapter examines the pace of privatization of industry in Mexico and identifies key industrial sectors slated for further privatization before the end of the millennium. In addition, we examine major commercial regions in the country and note their distinguishing characteristics. Finally, we look at Mexico's regulatory environment, and review the government agencies responsible for overseeing foreign trade and investment.

How has the Mexican economy changed since the 1980s?

The Mexican economy has been fundamentally changed since the 1980s by four interrelated factors: privatization, marketization, controlled inflation and the NAFTA.

PRIVATIZATION

As part of its efforts to resolve Mexico's long-term debt crisis, the administration of President Carlos Salinas initiated an ambitious privatization drive of government assets in the early 1990s. Salinas began by privatizing eighteen of Mexico's largest commercial banks, which had been nationalized in 1982 by President José López Portillo. As preparations for ratifying the North American Free Trade Agreement commenced, Salinas also privatized Telmex, Mexico's traditional telephone monopoly, and a variety of other state enterprises. Between 1990 and 1993 the Salinas administration privatized more than three hundred companies and, in the process, attracted billions of dollars of foreign capital to Mexico.

The process of privatization also served the interests of the elite business clans in Mexico, which profited from sweetheart deals offered by the Mexican government to encourage the purchase of government assets. Many companies were sold to private interests without a commensurate elimination of regulations that allowed the company to monopolize its markets. Other companies were offered significant government subsidies as part of the transition to competition in an open market. Many of these deals were offered to members of the Council of Mexican Businessmen *(Consejo Mexicano de Hombres de Negocios),* a private group of industrialists with close ties to the PRI.

MARKETIZATION

Mexico's middle class has benefited substantially from an increased availability of new consumer goods, many from the United States. New sales and distribution channels provide a path for consumer goods to reach the shelves of expanded grocery store chains, discount stores, and foreign franchises. The marketization of Mexico's economy is also being driven by new advertising channels, including cable systems and satellite net-

works that bring U.S. programming and commercials from the United States.

INFLATION

Inflation has been controlled from the mid-1980s through the present period. It dropped from a rate of 160% in the mid-1980s to single digits in the early 1990s. Although it rose substantially during the Mexican economic crisis of 1994-1995, it has declined in recent months. Projected annual inflation rates for 1997 range between 15% and 18%, down from a 27% annual rate for 1996.

NAFTA

NAFTA has served to substantially increase the volume of trade between the United States and Mexico since its ratification in 1994. In the first year after NATFA's implementation U.S. exports to Mexico rose 20%. Even after the devaluation of the peso, the NAFTA helped to cushion the Mexican recession and maintain a reasonably favorable balance of trade with the U.S. In 1995 the United States exported $46.3 billion worth of U.S. goods to Mexico, a drop from 1994 but still nearly $5 billion more than the pre-NAFTA level. In addition, the United States has captured a significant share of the Mexican market from other foreign countries. In 1995 the U.S. share of Mexico's import market climbed to 75%, up from less than 70% prior to the implementation of the NAFTA.

NAFTA also removed impediments to investment, including lengthy government screening of potential foreign investors and requirements regarding the use of Mexican inputs and the percentage of goods manufactured in Mexico that must be exported.

What about the peso and the recent economic crisis? What effect did this have on the Mexican people?

December 19, 1994 is a day the Mexican people remember and refer to, just as Americans recall Black Friday in October,

1987. On that day, the prosperous times which Mexicans had worked for and enjoyed during the Salinas regime collapsed. The Mexican government announced that the peso was to be devalued from 3 to a dollar to 4.5 to a dollar. The shock was immediate as people's real wages were slashed and their dollar-denominated debt—much of it in the form of high-interest credit card debt—rocketed out of sight. Then, just into the New Year, the peso was devalued again, and again, until it came to rest at a paralyzing 7 to the dollar, representing a crushing 120 percent decrease in personal and corporate wealth.

Since the crisis, Mexico has adjusted to the loss of personal income and the peso has appreciated to some degree against the dollar. The Mexican government has repaid the bailout loan granted by the Clinton Administration, although it has accomplished this primarily by issuing the same dollar-denominated short-term debt that helped to spark the crisis in the first place. However, the painful transition—not unlike that underway in Eastern Europe and the former Soviet Union—is still underway in the country. You can feel it when people refer angrily to "December 19th" and see it on the faces of people who are forced to don clown faces or hawk Salinas masks in the fume-filled air of Mexico City's streets to make ends meet. The important thing is that you, as a business person from outside, appreciate the situation which Mexicans have been through, and carry with you an understanding that times are harder there than you have experienced in the States. Foreign business representatives need to have an appreciation for the lingering dismay, hardship, and sense of resentment against the Mexican government and indeed, against the leaders of the United States.

What types of enterprises are there in Mexico? Is Mexico's economy completely privatized or are some industries still controlled by the state?

The Mexican economy is reasonably diversified, with a strong emphasis on natural resources, particularly oil, natural gas and mining. For example, Mexico is the world's leading pro-

ducer of silver. Many natural resources are located in the tropical southern portion of the country and have not yet been developed.

There is a large concentration of enterprises in agriculture. In manufacturing, food, beverage and tobacco processing is the largest sector in terms of gross output, followed by metal products, machinery and equipment (including autos). Chemicals, petroleum-related products and plastics are third, followed by textile and apparels. These four sectors account for over three-quarters of all Mexican manufacturing.

The Mexican economy has been significantly privatized since the late 1980s, particularly in telecommunications, media, finance and business services. However, the feeling among elites in Mexico is that the government is partially to blame for the country's industrial and economic woes. Its industrial policies, they say, tend to discourage companies from using their profits to upgrade technology and train the workforce for long-term benefits.

Many enterprises are still run as state monopolies or quasi-private oligopolies that enjoy significant state patronage. The most notable of these enterprises is Pemex, the government-run oil monopoly. President Ernesto Zedillo has had to pull back from his plans to privatize portions of Pemex because of pressures from old guard leaders in the PRI. However, Zedillo has indicated there may be compensatory privatization in other sectors, such as in transportation and telecommunications. The President has indicated an interest in changing the Mexican Constitution in order to allow the privatization of railroads and satellite communication systems.

What are the key commercial regions of the country?

Broadly speaking, Mexico's geographic and economic landscape can be divided into four parts. Each of these regions has developed a unique business subculture that should be understood by Americans seeking to do business in Mexico.

For over 150 years the central region surrounding Mexico City and encompassing the state of Mexico and the city of

Guadalajara has been the business, financial and government center of the Republic of Mexico. From traditional indigenous societies to the present, Mexico City has been the capital and focal point of economic and political life in Mexico. Today it is arguably the largest metropolitan region in the world, and is home to 25% of the Mexican population.

The Northern region, including the major city of Monterrey, is characterized by rugged mountains and the dry Sonoran desert. These conditions are often noted as explaining the fierce and aggressive qualities of the *nortenos.* Midday meals start an hour earlier in Monterrey than in Mexico City, a fact worth noting given the importance of this meal in establishing and maintaining business relationships.

The border region, known as *la frontera,* stretches along the U.S.-Mexican border from Tijuana in the west to Matamoros in the east. These border cities, often paired with sister cities in the U.S., have created a unique business and social culture that is an invigorating mix of Mexican and American. There is a strong sense of dynamism and innovation in the region, which is characterized by large levels of investment from the U.S. and Asia in maquiladora plants and other joint venture projects. The workforce is young, transient and poor, although work is plentiful and unemployment nearly nonexistent.

The south and southeastern portion of Mexico is hot, humid, tropical lowlands populated by a variety of poor, predominantly rural indigenous peoples largely employed in subsistence agriculture.

How is commercial activity regulated in Mexico?

Mexico is governed by a civil legal code that regulates commercial enterprise. State and federal agencies enforce a variety of statutes and regulations that affect foreign businesses. Economic reformers in Mexico have tried to streamline regulations, and continue to revise laws dealing with foreign commerce. The creation and operation of corporations in Mexico is governed by the Mexican General Law of Commercial

Companies. Foreign corporations must register before conducting business in Mexico with the National Registry of Foreign Investment.

Foreign businesses should be particularly aware of new Mexican laws that cover intellectual property and the environment. The intellectual property regulations are discussed in more detail later in this book. The environmental laws are serious new regulations designed to protect Mexican natural resources as the country tries to eliminate its reputation as a pollution haven for multinational corporations.

Obviously, the major laws governing foreign trade with Mexico are codified in the North American Free Trade Agreement (NAFTA). Specific aspects of the treaty will be discussed in more detail in other sections of this book. For further information on NAFTA, contact the Office of the NAFTA in Washington D.C., a special organization set up within the Department of Commerce to help American firms and individuals understand the treaty and its related economic opportunities. You can reach this office at (202) 482-0300.

How is trade with foreign countries regulated?

The major law now governing trade between Mexico and foreign countries is the North American Free Trade Agreement (NAFTA). The NAFTA was signed by the United States, Canada and Mexico in 1993 and took effect January 1, 1994. It was designed to allow greater market access for the participating countries, increased opportunities for bilateral trade and increased competitiveness vis-à-vis other countries outside of the trading bloc.

NAFTA KEY FEATURES INCLUDE:

➤ The elimination of tariffs and non-tariff barriers to trade between the three Parties.

➤ The creation of strong "North-American-made" rules of origin or "local contents requirements" to restrict non-NAFTA countries from gaining duty-free access to the free trade area.

➤ The opening of the services market in Mexico to U.S. and Canadian firms.

➤ The strengthening of patented, trademarked and copyrighted goods made in North America.

➤ The establishment of a panel for dispute resolution regarding trade issues between the NAFTA countries.

A secondary result of the NAFTA is its role in encouraging investment in Mexico by countries outside of the trade bloc. In the past, foreign companies, particularly those from Asia, have chosen to invest in Mexico through its maquiladora program to take advantage of the country's inexpensive labor and proximity to the U.S. market. Today a new rush of investment capital is entering Mexico from Asia and Europe to take advantage of the preferential trade regime erected by the NAFTA.

In addition, NAFTA provisions call for a reduction in input licensing and quotas that will further increase trade between the parties.

Mexico is also a signatory of GATT and is governed by its international trade conventions.

The two major cabinet-level agencies that regulate trade with Mexico are the *Secretaria de Comercio y Fomento Industrial* (SECOFI) and the *Secretaria de Hacienda y Crédito Público* (Hacienda). Specific departments within these agencies are responsible for various aspects of international business, and will be discussed in later sections of this book.

Chapter 4

V

THE POLITICS OF
MEXICAN BUSINESS

The crossover between the commercial realm and politics in the United States in routine business dealings is infrequent. While we may rail at local bureaucracies and zoning ordinances or look to the federal government for protection and subsidy, politics can be removed from American business life. In Mexico, business and politics intersect more often and more deeply. If you want to succeed in the commercial realm, you will need to move and shake to some degree in the political realm, at least at the local level. This political involvement can take the form of support for community projects and charity work, backing a candidate for office, or dealing with the leadership of a labor union. All of these activities work to enhance your clout within the surrounding bureaucracy and among the elite who make decisions. This chapter will bring you up to date with Mexico's current political scene, with how the government is organized, and what may lie ahead for Mexican politics. We briefly review some of the more titillating aspects of contemporary national politics, but focus on underlying changes in the Mexican political economy that will fundamentally affect the business climate in the 21st century.

How is Mexico's government organized to make commercial decisions?

Mexico is a highly centralized country where most significant powers rest with the federal government, particularly the

executive branch. While local and state officials are often helpful when trying to attract foreign investment, key decisions regarding permits, investment, financing, and trade are made by agencies of the federal government. The Mexican federal government is organized along lines not dissimilar to the United States. Significant power rests in the Mexican Presidency, at *Los Piños,* the Mexican White House. The central government bureaucracy is organized into a series of secretariats or ministries, similar to the cabinet level departments in the U.S. government. Key secretariats for foreign business include the *Secretaría de Hacienda y Crédito Público* (Hacienda) and *Secretaría de Comercio y Fomento Industrial* (SECOFI). These entities will have specific agencies, often called Directorates, that issue permits, register foreign companies and approve investments.

Underneath the federal government Mexico is divided into state governments that enjoy varying degrees of autonomy from Mexico City. Most states do not have independent sources of tax revenue and therefore depend on Mexico City for the funding of their annual budgets. There is significant tension between the federal government and several of the more independent states, particularly those in the northern portion of the country. Many of these state governments are controlled by the PAN, the major opposition party to the ruling PRI party.

How widespread is government corruption and commercial bribery, and what laws exist to discourage them?

In recent years the Mexican government has taken significant steps in cracking down on bribery and corruption at all levels. This is not to say bribery no longer occurs, but it is much more subtle and is less likely to involve visitors from the United States. The tradition of bribery, or the *mordida* (the "bite"), predates the Mexican Republic, and one may still be asked for a "contribution" from time to time.

Small-scale bribery often involves minor officials who regularly deal with foreign businesspersons and tourists. A likely

scenario for bribery is a businessperson who needs to extend a tourist card or visa. Paying the *mordida* is straightforward but discreet. Hand over a few dollars (American) and you hope that will be the end of it. The official may shake his head, in which case you'll need to add another dollar or two.

In larger cases of a bribe being required for a permit or other certificate issued to foreign businesses, our recommendation is to not pay the requested amount. Issues of bribery in business dealings are described in greater detail later in this book.

How is Mexico's leadership changing, and what will be the effect on the business atmosphere?

Traditionally the PRI (the *Partido Revolucionario Institucional*) has been the dominant ruling party of Mexico. It was established after the 1917 Mexican revolution, and has held the Mexican Presidency ever since. The PRI controls the Mexican legislature and the majority of state governorships. In the eyes of many, it is less a legitimate political party, even in the sense of a single-party, and more an electoral tool for dominating Mexican politics. The PRI has never been guided by a dominant ideology, although it frequently employs revolutionary or socialistic rhetoric as part of its communications strategy. In reality, the PRI is run by the Mexican President in cooperation with a set of leading clans, or *camarillas,* who have representatives in top positions in the government. This group represents a political family that has effectively ruled Mexico through most of the twentieth century. Even the tension between the old party leaders, "the dinosaurs," and the new generation of technocrats is more a generation split than a split between factions. The real source of tension derives from clan leaders whose business interests may be working at cross-purposes. These tensions have been exacerbated in recent years by the spate of privatizations that have left many of the clans continuing to fight over a smaller pie of government largesse.

In *Bordering on Chaos,* Andres Oppenheimer describes the Mexican political system as being organized into a three-part hierarchy:[2]

> *The Ruling Class.* Composed of camarillas, or clans. The Mexican President and the core of his administration will be drawn from this group.

> Influential Interests. This group of perhaps several hundred men are not necessarily formal PRI members, but are drawn from influential circles in finance, industry and the military. They have access to the Presidency, but are not part of the inner circle.

> The Bureaucracy. The PRI bureaucracy, including party leaders and government officials, exist primarily to get the PRI presidential candidate into office every six years. After this is accomplished, the bureaucracy is expected to serve as a docile tool of the presidency.

The PRI's ability to remain the dominant force in Mexican politics may depend largely on the continued effective use of its traditional political apparatus. Many Mexicans blame the PRI for the recent economic crisis and are further incensed by revelations of official corruption. On Nov. 10, 1996, the PRI lost more than one-fourth of the city government posts up for election in three Mexican states. Compare this to 1993 when the PRI controlled the electorate in these states and won up to 98% of the vote. Today political scientists estimate that the years of patronage have left the PRI with a loyal base of 38% of the electorate. Using the base to build from, many project the party will succeed in keeping its majority in next year's nationwide congressional elections.

The direction of the PRI has become more clouded in the wake of recent party reforms. At its last convention it decided that it will no longer choose candidates as its nominees

---

[2] Andres Oppenheimer, *Bordering on Chaos* (New York: Little, Brown & Company, 1996)

for governorships or the presidency of Mexico unless they have held previous elective office. The party decision may indicate a gradual erosion of the influence of U.S.-educated technocrats, led by President Ernesto Zedillo and his immediate predecessors, Carlos Salinas and Miguel de la Madrid.

Although President Zedillo's term runs until 2000, many analysts are now questioning his ability to command the loyalty of the party. This is partially due to the fact that he has managed to convince the country that he will not hand-pick a PRI candidate to succeed him. As a result, he has abandoned many of the dictator-like powers that Mexican presidents have traditionally had over the PRI party machine, the Congress, and the government bureaucracy.

In a sense, Zedillo has become Mexico's first lame duck President of the modern era.

The result seems bound to be a politically less stable, less predictable Mexico, with a more fractious PRI and a more assertive Congress, even if the PRI survives challenges by newly energized opposition parties in the midterm elections.

Although few would turn the clock back to Mexico's statist past, the split in the PRI between old-line pols and technocratic reformers could give the opposition parties—the center-right National Action Party (PAN) and the center-left Party of the Democratic Revolution (PRD)—an unprecedented chance to end the PRI's control of Congress in next year's elections.

Another factor influencing the direction of Mexican politics is the country's decision to extend citizenship (and the franchise) to Mexican natives residing in the United States. The Mexican Congress has enacted a revision to the country's Constitution that would allow millions of Mexican immigrants to seek U.S. citizenship without fear of losing rights in Mexico, including the right to own property. The move would allow over 5 million Mexican natives resident in the United States to acquire or retain Mexican citizenship.[3]

---

[3] *Los Angeles Times,* December 9, 1996, Section I.

The government plans to increase spending on infrastructure and social programs by over 25% in next year's budget. Some economists worry that these spending proposals may alter the country's trade balance by artificially increasing consumer demand, while positioning Mexico for higher 1997 interest rates due to a larger-than-projected budget deficit.[4] The increased social and infrastructure spending is thought to be aimed at enhancing support for Mexico's ruling party, the Institutional Revolutionary Party, or PRI, in advance of the 1997 congressional elections.

What is the Mexican attitude toward foreign business, and vice versa in the post-NAFTA era?

Mexico's attitude toward foreign business is still highly encouraging, particularly toward firms who are investing in real assets throughout the country. The government also continues to encourage the importation of foreign capital by issuing short-term bonds denominated in dollars. Competition for foreign investment is more intense at the border, where consortiums of private commercial real estate developers and local government officials aggressively wine and dine potential investors who are weighing alternative site locations. Often the competition is between other border locations and alternative emerging market production sites, such as Southern China and Vietnam.

Mexican society seems quite unconcerned about the incursion of culture and values from the States. To its credit, the society exhibits an ability to meld its own images, fashions, and sounds with those of America to create a true hybrid, indeed one pervasive enough to assimilate the contributions of America and elsewhere without losing its national identity. This is made possible by the fact that Mexican society is extraordinarily open and very young.

Are local government officials friendly to foreign business?

Yes, but their capacity is limited. Few local governments have the budget flexibility to be able to offer investment incentives

---

[4] Dow Jones News Service, 11/11/96.

to potential foreign investors. Because there are no state or local income taxes, there are few available tax incentives. Those that do exist typically consist of subsidies or waivers that concern nominal local property taxes.

Local officials may be more aggressive in terms of offering infrastructure resources to potential foreign investors. This is particularly relevant at the U.S.-Mexico border, where limited water supplies make water for manufacturing a scarce and valuable commodity. Many local officials in border communities have pledged significant rights of first use for water resources to major multinational companies investing in their communities. Often these pledges are made without sufficient planning for the long-term sustainability of the regional water system.

THE OPPORTUNITIES AND THE RISKS:
VENTURING SOUTH WITH YOUR EYES OPEN

Perhaps the wisest approach in an emerging market is to pin-point opportunities embodying the richest reward, while also constantly monitoring what you can lose in the attempt. With the U.S. government engaged in what one business expert called "cheerleading" for the future of Mexico and U.S. interests in the country, it can be difficult to keep sage advice in mind and not become opiated by the pronounced opportunities. Here, we provide you with a sober stocktaking of where potential rewards lie in Mexico, by concentrating on key industrial sectors and subsectors that hold promising opportunities for foreign companies. We focus primarily on those sectors where plans of reform and marketization are most advanced, or where Mexico's competitive advantages are strongest in comparison to other emerging markets. In addition, this chapter discusses the key strengths and weaknesses of Mexico's business environment and offers some thoughts on strategic planning for the country. We also review leading sources of online information for executives and entrepreneurs who want to use the Internet to learn more about specific aspects of Mexico's commercial environment.

Where are the current and future opportunities to be found by foreign business people in Mexico? What's hot and what's not?

The Mexican economy is undergoing rapid changes due to the effects of the NAFTA, foreign investment, and the decen-

tralization and privatization plans of the Mexican government. To capitalize on emerging opportunities in Mexico, businesses need to be aware of day-to-day changes in the Mexican economy, investment laws and foreign trade regimes.

The following summarizes key sectors of the Mexican economy that contain promising opportunities for foreign businesses.

OIL AND GAS

Mexico is one of the world's major producers of oil and natural gas.

Its reserves are located in the southeastern region of the country and in territorial waters off the coast in the Gulf of Mexico. Approximately 20 percent of these reserves are in natural gas. Oil production is critical for export revenues and as a significant percentage of total government revenues. Currently Mexican businesses are seeking consultants and engineers to assist them in the development and construction of new petroleum facilities. In addition, there is strong demand for equipment related to petroleum extraction.

PETROCHEMICALS

Mexico is a leading producer of petrochemicals and Mexican firms are interested in joint venture opportunities with foreign companies that can bring investment capital and upgrade their manufacturing processes. Currently the Mexican government has brought to a halt its planned privatization of the petrochemical sector; previously it had announced a plan to privatize the vast majority of its petrochemical companies, including critical secondary petrochemical plants. These plants produce ethylene, ammonia, propylene and other secondary chemicals. Moreover, under new regulations foreigners will be permitted up to 49 percent

ownership of secondary petrochemical processing plants. While there was some effort to legislate new regulations that would allow up to 100 percent foreign ownership of new petrochemical facilities, this initiative has been put on "hold" by the current government.

DIRECT-TO-HOME (DTH)
SATELLITE SERVICES

The Mexican market for direct-to-home satellite television is exploding. This service, similar to DirectTV in the United States, competes with Mexican cable television. Under Mexican telecommunications law, U.S. firms may enter this market in partnership with Mexican companies if the Mexican firm has majority capital in the joint venture. The major players in direct-to-home include Televisa, which has a joint venture with NewsCorp and Telecommunications International, and TV Azteca, which is in partnership with Hughes Electronics (the owner of DirectTV).

PAGING

The paging market in Mexico has been traditionally limited by the lack of commercial frequencies. The Secretariat of Communications and Tranport (SCT) auctioned over 70 frequencies in 1996, most of which have gone to private companies. Several of the frequencies span the entire nation, and the balance are devoted to specific regions. Companies that have won the concessions must start to provide paging services to 25 percent of their region within a year, and expand to 50 percent within two years. The American Chamber of Commerce in Mexico estimates the size of the paging market in Mexico at 270,000 users. Leading companies in the market include Servicios Modernos, TV Azteca's Biper, Avantel, and Telmex's Buscatel. Additional frequencies are expected to be concessioned in 1997, including multiple microwave frequencies (MMDS).

PENSION PLANS

In December of 1995 the Mexican government passed a law that authorizes the privatization of the Mexican pension system. Under the law, Mexico's pensions, which have been previously controlled by the Mexican Social Security Institute (IMSS) will be placed in private pension funds, or Afores, which will be managed by private companies. Currently the Afores are scheduled to be created on July 1, 1997. The plan to privatize the system is designed to increase the productivity of the country's savings and to improve individual workers' preparation for their retirement. New regulations allowing foreign participation in securities firms should open opportunities for investment bankers from abroad to participate in the management of these pension funds.

WAREHOUSES

Mexico's vast warehouse system is currently on the block for privatization. The country's National Deposit Warehouses (ANSDA) are scheduled to be auctioned in June of 1997. ANSDA is composed of three state companies that currently control 3.9 million meters of storage space, with a total storage capacity of 4.3 million tons. These warehouses are particularly important in the storage and distribution of the nation's agricultural output. It is hoped that the privatization of these storage systems will enhance the productivity of distribution systems for a variety of Mexican goods.

TELECOMMUNICATIONS

By the end of 1997 the Mexican telecommunications sector should be fully open to foreign competition. Even with the status of the Mexican economy, the local and long-distance telephone market is expected to grow to close to $9 billion from the present $6 billion by 1999. As a result, a number of major

multinational telecommunications corporations have entered the Mexican market, primarily by forming strategic partnerships with Mexican firms. AT&T and GTE have joined forces in a cooperative relationship with the Mexican industrial conglomerate Alfa, Telefonica de Espana and Bancomer, the second largest bank in Mexico. Another major player is Avantel, a joint venture between MCI and Mexico's largest bank, Banamex. The focus of their efforts will be Telefonos de Mexico, or TelMex, the former telephone monopoly. Analysts expect the new rivals to capture between 20 to 50 percent of the market from TelMex.

As Mexico's about-to-be-opened telecommunications industry braces itself to meet an onslaught of foreign competition, a public relations war has been declared by Telmex. Parodying the prototypical ugly American, an actor in a new Telmex television ad announces: "Hi, I'm Burton Helms. I came to Mexico for the pleasure of doing your business." The play on the Helms-Burton Act, trade legislation which the U.S. enacted to punish companies doing business with Cuba and which most Mexicans decry, is followed by the claim—voiced in heavily gringo-accented Spanish—that the phone service this American offers is called long distance "because we're going to run it from Chicago!"

RAILROADS

To date, the plan for the privatization of Mexico's railroad system has been halting at best. The Mexican government has authorized the privatization of twenty-eight railroads throughout the country; however, so far only one of the railroads has been placed at auction, and it was withdrawn after the Secretary of Communications and Transport (SCT) failed to receive a satisfactory bid. The Chihuahua-Pacific Concession received only one bid, and its value came in at 55 percent below the government's estimated worth of the concession.

Nevertheless, long-term prospects for a privatized railroad system are promising. Many potential bidders have indicated that the Chihuahua-Pacific line was not their first choice, and

that there are much higher levels of interest in other railroads still to be auctioned. The 50-year concessions being offered by the SCT represent important long-term business opportunities. The Mexican National Railroad System, or *Ferrocarriles Nacionales de Mexico (FNM)*, has reported that over 85 companies have expressed interest in privatization opportunities, and other firms are lining up as potential suppliers to the private railroads.

Mexican railroads only serve an estimated 6 million passengers per year. However, the railroad system has an underutilized capacity for cargo transport, which will become increasingly important as domestic consumption rises and as the spatial location of Mexican manufacturing becomes more diversified.

TOURISM AND ECOTOURISM

Given excellent climate, natural resources and archeological sites, Mexico has successfully developed an enterprise tourist industry. The country welcomes in excess of 7 million visitors annually, excluding regular visitors to the border zone. Tourism is Mexico's second largest source of foreign exchange earnings.

Mexico has targeted its rich ecological resources as a potential source of tourism dollars. The country's tourism agencies are aggressively marketing the country's attractions as part of a global boom in "ecotourism"—tourism designed to promote and sustain ecological and biological diversity. In ecotourism, emphasis is placed on sites and activities that preserve rather than exploit natural resources. For example, key areas in Mexico include the peninsula of Baja California, particularly Baja California Sur, and the southern tropical states of Oaxaca, Chiapas and Quintana Roo. In many of the southern states, destinations such as rainforests, cloud forests and sensitive coral reefs are combined with encounters involving the region's indigenous peoples. In Baja, many such tours are organized around whale-watching during the migration of the gray whales.

Business opportunities in this area for Americans revolve around organizing and marketing tours to key market segments in the United States. There is a strong need to make ecotourism more manageable for U.S. travelers, and to combine relatively cheap Mexican transportation options with high value-added ecotourist destinations.

MINING

Mexico's largest mineral production is in iron and salt. The country's largest iron mines are found in the state of Durango, while salt is made in large evaporation ponds on the eastern shore of Baja California. Mexico is also the world's leading producer of silver, accounting for approximately 15 percent of global production, and also has significant lead and zinc resources, copper, sulphur, fluorite, coal, and manganese.

Mining exploration in Mexico is frequently financed by foreign investors. Local partners are typically involved after ore is discovered. In addition, there are significant opportunities for suppliers of equipment and business services targeted at mining and related extractive industries.

FISHING AND AQUACULTURE

Fishing is an underdeveloped resource in Mexico, despite its proximity to major fisheries in the Gulf of Mexico, the Sea of Cortez and the Eastern Pacific. Aquaculture is an infant industry in Mexico, but one with vast promise. The natural bays and lagoons of the Baja peninsula, as well as desert sinks near the shoreline, offer abundant opportunities for aquaculture development. Operations cultivating shrimp, seaweed, and abalone are already thriving in Baja California. As transportation links to North America improve there should be expanded opportunities for fresh-frozen and aquaculture-reared seafood to be distributed in America's expanding fresh fish markets.

DRUGS

While hardly a recommended opportunity for foreign businesspersons, any analysis of major economic sectors in Mexico must take into account the role of drug trafficking and other related illegal activities. Narcotics and arms smuggling form the core of a huge economic sector that increasingly dominates the political economy of Mexico. Policy analysts debate the actual value of Mexican drug trafficking, but a conservative estimate of $100 billion suggests profits to Mexican drug lords of $25 billion per year. This figure is twice the total revenues of the entire Mexican oil sector. Part of the resentment many average Mexicans feel towards ex-Presidente Salinas can be traced to their perception that Salinas allowed the country to become controlled by narcotics cartels. Many Mexicans feel they are becoming more like Colombia, residents of a narco-democracy.

What are the strengths and what are the weaknesses in Mexico's commercial environment?

The following are major strengths that characterize Mexico's current business climate.

➤ **Regionalization and Globalization.** NAFTA has reduced trade barriers and opened the Mexican economy to a wide range of high-quality goods and services from the United States. Mexico is attracting multinational investments from throughout the world in real assets—plants, buildings, equipment, workforce training—both as a platform for export manufacturing and to serve the domestic market. Mexico is also positioning itself as a logical gateway to Latin America and should be set to take advantage of opportunities that arise from admitting Latin American countries such as Chile into a hemispheric free-trade zone.

➤ **Relative Transparency of Regulations.** While Mexico may seem confusing and bureaucratic by U.S. standards it is actually among the most transparent of the big emerging markets. The extreme centralization of authority in Mexico can actually make it easier for foreign businesses to con-

duct business, particularly in comparison to the multi-layered bureaucracies of many Asian countries.

➤ **Political Stability.** Despite the potential for significant political change in Mexico, there is no serious threat of revolution or truly destabilizing political turmoil in the country for the foreseeable future. Many commentators have noted that Mexico's revolutionary rhetoric is actually a mask for a political culture that is highly resistant to change.

➤ **Demographics.** The demographic portrait of Mexico strongly favors U.S. business interests seeking to market products in the country. Mexico's young, consumption-oriented class is embracing a hybrid culture that is part Mexican, part Tejano and part North American. This trend will only be enhanced by the rise of cable television and direct satellite systems that expose more young people to American and Hispanic-American products.

The key risks associated with Mexico revolve around the Mexican government and its manipulation of the economy for political purposes. If the government repeats the pattern of 1994-1995 and overvalues the currency by assuming high levels of short-term foreign debt, a subsequent adjustment can have a real impact on Mexican consumption patterns and the value of goods and services controlled by foreign companies in pesos. Businesspersons dealing with Mexico need to develop flexible business plans that allow them to anticipate and react to changes in the value of the Mexican currency.

Should a firm get involved now, and grow with Mexico, or wait until the country surmounts the impediments to its modernization?

Like all of the emerging markets, Mexico's modernization is a long-term prospect. Forty percent of the population lives at the "community level," the strata of the municipality or below. This huge sector lives in servitude to the status quo, bargaining and sacrificing via their unions which support the PRI. In exchange, the local affiliate of the PRI builds a drain through their village. This is the give-and-take system

that they have known for so long that they know nothing else. In short, these people are not prepared to function as participants in a modern pluralistic state.

Despite its proximity to the United States and its membership in NAFTA, there is no reason to assume the pace of modernization in Mexico will be any quicker than that in Hungary, China or Turkey. The country is undergoing deep and painful transformation. The 1994 peso devaluation was a real horror for millions of Mexicans, many of whom lost their jobs. Nevertheless, significant opportunities exist for foreign businesses in Mexico today, and should not be overlooked because of the associated risks. Fundamentally, right now one can manufacture and export high-quality goods in Mexico for distribution in the United States to a consumption-hungry public. If nothing else, the relative strength of the U.S. economy and the comparative advantages of Mexican manufacturing suggest that, like Sony, Hewlett-Packard and GM, you should be in Mexico today.

In addition, a significant consumer class resident in Mexico is worth the attention of U.S. exporters, particularly companies offering high-quality consumer goods. While it is true that Mexican consumers do not have the purchasing power of their U.S. or Canadian counterparts, there is a growing demand for middle—and high-end consumer goods among the middle class. Almost a third of the Mexican adult population has a credit card and increasing numbers of consumers are developing loyalties to foreign-owned retail businesses and identifiable foreign brand names.

What will be the expected, and unexpected, costs of conducting business in Mexico, including business travel?

Expect delays. In transportation. In clearing customs. In manufacturing. In quality improvements. Delays are going to happen. Beat them by developing personal relationships with your employees and business partners. The investment of your time will pay off over the long-term.

For business travelers, a few minor considerations can reduce headaches once you are in Mexico. Surprisingly, there are

limited international air service connections directly to Mexico. Often travelers will have to fly to the U.S. first if they are coming from a third country. Expect traffic to be busy and congested in most major urban areas. Taxis are your best option for local transportation, but be prepared for delays in the cab. Consider walking if the trip is reasonably short. Note that both Mexico City and Guadalajara have large, well-designed and safe public underground rail, or Metro, systems.

Telephone service in Mexico is sporadic at best. There is a significant shortage of lines; plan on six months to get a new line installed. You may have difficulty in making a connection, or your connection may be severed mid-conversation. Public phones are often broken; plan on using your hotel phone for local calls. Mexico's international phone tolls are extremely expensive. Consider purchasing a pre-paid calling card from one of the major U.S. long-distance companies before you leave, or, better yet, take advantage of new call-back options that will return your call using a low-cost connection from the United States.

What are the most common reasons for foreign business failure in the country?

Clearly, the most obvious explanation for many foreign business failures in Mexico is that the company failed to sufficiently insulate itself from fluctuations in the Mexican economy. However, there are more fundamental cultural reasons why some business ventures succeed and others fall apart.

One high-profile case study of business venture failure in Mexico is the example of Corning Inc. In the summer of 1994 Corning announced it was closing down a two-year, $130 million joint venture between the ceramic cookware manufacturer and Vitro, a major Mexican glass manufacturer. Interestingly, the core explanation for the collapse of the venture was cultural differences.

Corning found that their Mexican partners often delayed making major sales and marketing decisions because senior executives needed to be consulted and were unavailable. Corning favored a much more aggressive sales strategy,

which was disconcerting to the Vitro management. Both sides insisted on retaining their traditional work schedules, so Americans would work eight-hour days while Mexicans would break for long lunches and return late in the afternoon for an evening meeting which they expected would last until nine at night.

Interviews with both parties after the break-up of the venture revealed important perceptions that contributed to the partnership's internal "culture war."

➣ The Mexican managers saw the Americans as too direct, too impatient and disinclined to admit fault. The American managers saw the Mexicans as too polite and too slow.

➣ The Americans wanted rational, linear decisions while the Mexicans wanted to consider other issues such as relationships, traditions, and personal loyalties, and often reached their decisions by consensus, in a "gentlemanly" way.

➣ The Americans had no problem with criticizing or laying blame on a person while the Mexicans preferred to focus on the positive aspects of the partnership.

➣ The Mexicans at Vitro valued strong interpersonal relationships, human dignity, and enjoying life as you live it. Therefore, their behavior was characterized by consideration of people's "face" and personal loyalties; polite, respectful speech; and the tendency to take long breaks during the workday. The Americans at Corning valued aggressively attacking problems, egalitarian conduct, and accomplishing tasks. Their propensity for openly criticizing individuals, their difficulty with titles, and their desire to work straight through the day to complete their goals, reflected this.

What are the surest methods of tracking Mexico in order to monitor risk and stay tuned to opportunities? What business resources exist both on and off-line?

Two good periodicals for following changes in the Mexican commercial environment are *Business Mexico,* which is pub-

lished monthly by the American Chamber of Commerce in Mexico, and the Economist Intelligence Unit's *Mexico Country Risk Monitor,* which is published quarterly by Economist magazine.

New sources of updated information online provide an excellent way for foreign businesspersons to remain current on Mexico's business climate.

The *Mexico Trade and Business Forum* on CompuServe is a lively, interactive crossroads for a variety of local and international players in Mexican business. *The Forum* contains investment guides, trading offers and live chat rooms for networking with other businesspersons.

We also recommend the following sites on the World Wide Web for high-quality Mexican business information.

SimPex
http://mexico.businessline.gob.mx

This extensive online database is maintained by BancoMex, the Mexican Bank for Foreign Trade. SimPex offers information on foreign trade with Mexico, including import/export regulations and financing options. There is also a directory of over 4,000 Mexican firms seeking foreign trading or investment partners.

Mexico World
http://www.mexicoworld.com

An excellent source of daily business and financial news from Mexico. Mexico World hosts several Mexican news organizations, including news updates, daily financial papers and business forecasts. Most of the publications are in Spanish.

The NAFTA Home Page
http://iepnt1.itaiep.doc.gov/nafta/nafta2.htm

This is the home page of the Office of the NAFTA at the U.S. Department of Commerce. The page provides a basic overview of commercial conditions in Mexico and the role of the NAFTA in governing U.S.-Mexico trade. There is also

a menu of more detailed documents regarding specific provisions of the NAFTA that can be ordered from their FlashFax fax retrieval service.

U.S. Commercial Service in Mexico
http://www.uscommerce.org.mx

This website is maintained by the office of the U.S. Foreign Commercial Service at the American Embassy in Mexico City. It provides direct contact to country officers who work in Mexico promoting U.S. business interests and trade between the two countries.

Mexico Business Home Page
http://www.nafta.net/mexbiz/index.html

An on-line version of a popular monthly business magazine published in English. The site provides sample articles from the print magazine and discussion boards that address current issues in Mexican business.

Mexico—A Big Emerging Market
http://www.stat-usa.gov/bems/bemsmex/bemsmex.html

A summary page of information regarding business in Mexico published by the U.S. Department of Commerce. The Commerce Department has classified Mexico as one of the world's "Big Emerging Markets." As such, it receives significant attention from the Department's market research analysts. Many of their reports and publications are offered on this site.

PROFILES

INTERVIEW WITH ROGER REMACLE
Owner of Land Trek Expeditions, Ltd. in Canada

Roger Remacle has been involved in the transportation industry since 1980. After years of traveling in Mexico for pleasure, he sold his trucking company in 1990 with the intent to start something new. He had looked into setting up a business in Mexico prior to NAFTA, but found that commercial transportation businesses run by foreign companies were prohibited. With NAFTA, however, business involving the transportation of tourists and requirements regarding the nationality of drivers were eased, and thus Mr. Remacle formed a tour company to conduct innovative tours for adventurous travelers utilizing an old-fashioned mode of travel.

The name of his company's bus: *The Spirit of Jules Verne.* Your guide will be Roger Remacle and his friend of 25 years, John Hagemans, originally from Holland, who combined their multiple years of experience driving and traveling in Mexico. They offer 11 seats on this modernized version of the Merry Pranksters bus to intrepid souls beguiled by the notion of spending 40 days traversing the width and length of Mexico at a slower pace.

The tour begins in Victoria/Vancouver and travels down Interstate 5 through California and then into Mexico. As Roger tells it: "We look like a circus. We pull into a nice RV park and people gather around and they bring cameras. At one point we thought they would start throwing peanuts."

What kind of bus is it?

It's a 38-foot Bluebird with a school bus design, which has been stripped and rebuilt to feature high-back recliners that face each other. It's not luxurious but it's reliable, and has high clearance. It's outfitted with a mobile kitchen and heater as well as tools—a strong-built machine that was originally built in 1980.

What route do you follow on your grand tour through Mexico?

The Mexican part of the tour begins in Mexicali and proceeds through Hermosillo, Tepic, Guadalajara, and the mountains of Michoacán to see the monarch butterflies—just an incredible site where we drive up to a 6,000 foot elevation and then we board trucks that take us up the mountain to 10,000 feet where you literally walk into a wall of millions of butterflies. Then it's on to Mexico City, Puebla, Cholula, Vera-cruz, Villahermosa, Palenque, Merida, Uxmal, Chichén Itzá, and Cancun. On the return leg, the tour passes through colonial Mexico, including stops in Teotihuacan, Guanajuato, Zacatecas, and Chihuahua.

What do you charge for the tour?

From Canada, the cost is $2,190 plus about $18 per day, which goes into a kitty fund for breakfast, supper, water, and campsite rentals. So, all told, the fee from Canada is about $3,000; that's Canadian dollars, and includes 7 nights staying in hotels. John and I do the driving, the cooking, and all janitorial tasks.

How did you get the Mexican government to approve your venture?

To get the bus over the border we have to "import" it into Mexico. The import license allows us to come into the country for six months, as long as we agree not to sell the bus while we are there. Upon leaving Mexico, we produce the papers that show that the same bus is leaving Mexico which we brought in. I am also required to obtain a temporary immigration visa in order to work in Mexico during the tour. But overall, the red tape is minimal and the Mexican government has been very helpful and easy to deal with. What helps is the tour is entirely self-sufficient; we pay for our hotels, RV park fees, tolls, without relying on the Mexican government in any way.

We take advantage of the fact Mexico has constructed over 4,000 miles of autopistas, which are four-lane toll roads that crisscross the country and connect cities like Nogales, Mexico City and Villahermosa, and on which there are no speed limits. We pay a total of $325 in road tolls for the entire trip, and I think that's extremely reasonable.

Has the tour encountered any problems on the road in Mexico, in terms of crime or safety?

We've received nothing but help from the Mexican people, including those who give directions just for the asking. Someone will hop onto the bus to help us find our way when we've gotten lost, and then refuse to accept taxi fare to get home again. One time the bus lost its muffler and a Mexican policeman hopped on and spent the next half hour helping us locate another one, again refusing a fee for the help. Another time, we had a problem with the bus' fuel tank. Mexican police allowed us to park the bus in Mexico City's central Zócalo overnight. In the morning, the police brought in their own mechanic who had the clogged filter in the bus repaired in fifteen minutes and we were off.

Perhaps the most harrowing evening was in Culiacán, Sinaloa. The rule of driving in Mexico is not to do it at night, and of course that's what we were doing, as we looked for this campground on a deserted road in the middle of nowhere. Finally we came upon the sign for it, but two men came out of a house near the gate, and one carried a gun. They told us to back up and come in through a rear service road. This looked grim until the bus arrived at a series of camp huts and a bathroom, and a small store. It turned out the guys with the guns were hired private police, which are common in Mexico. The next morning we found that we were parked in the middle of a huge resort with a view of a beautiful lake. There were bars and restaurants. In the middle of the night the campground had been opened for us with no prior reservation.

Have you used the Internet to market your tour company?

I've used the Internet to market the tours, with mixed feedback. It's been trial and error dealing with newsgroups and the Web. I've gotten flamed a few times for advertising on the newsgroups. I offer an FAQ to travelers going to Mexico with information about shopping, camping, road condition, and tolls. And some business has come through the Internet connections.

What future tours are planned?

We're adding a new journey through Baja, including La Paz, with a ferry ride to Mazatlán, and another stop in Puerto Vallarta.

Set back along one of the main streets in the bustling Mexican tourist town of Cabo San Lucas is Pancho's Restaurant. The front half of the place is roofless and sunny with four tables out in the tropical sun. The first thing you notice is the colorful tablecloths, then the walls covered with original photos of Pancho Villa, for whom the place was named. Behind the bar stand hundreds of bottles of tequila, mezcal, and pulque—all potent elixirs of the maguay plant. Pancho's owner, John Bragg, has traveled all over Mexico studying this "Crema De Cacti" and will share his favorites to the querying guest.

Mary Bragg, John's wife, is the force behind the restaurant. The couple, says Mary, "failed at retirement" in slow-paced Cabo, starting up and later selling a successful coffee house, to then start up Pancho's and turn it into one of the most profitable restaurants in town. And we haven't mentioned Mary's wedding shop or her active charity work.

In short, the Braggs have a lot to teach us about pursuing dreams South of the border, and making it pay in Margaritaville.

After four years down here are you still excited about doing business in Cabo San Lucas?

Our primary reason for coming here and staying is the lifestyle. We came here to retire and we failed at retirement. In reality, doing business here is a piece of cake for us. The first year was a bear, but now we understand the best way to work within the system. We don't do anything that is under-the-table or could be brought to someone's attention as wrong. Because eventually that sort of thing is going to come back and bite you in the butt.

You have made the choice not to engage in any funny business?

Like the *mordida*. We've never paid it. If you start paying it you'll never get away from it, and that's certainly been proven true by other people in town here who can't get anything done now without paying somebody off. We just chose not to do it.

Going back to the beginning of your activities here, was setting up your business in the first place difficult?

Yes, it was. At the time when we started, a foreigner could not own 100 percent stock in a Mexican corporation. We had a Mexican partner. It was the only way we could do business at that time. To form a corporation was not difficult but it had to be done correctly. We had to have a good attorney, and we were fortunate to find an excellent attorney in Tijuana who had been educated in the United States as well as Mexico, who speaks English as well as I do, and has a good business background. We took his advice and he advised us very well.

Is it easier now to set up a business here?

Absolutely. Incorporation is very reasonable today, but you do have to have some financing behind you when you open a corporation here. Not a tremendous amount but they want to know the valuation of your business. The thing I find that most people do not do when they come to Mexico to do business, is they don't spend enough time really coming to understand the market—looking at what's going on. Cabo San Lucas is really different from most other places in Mexico. It's a tourist economy here. It's pure tourism. If you're going to do business in other parts of Mexico that are outside tourist areas, you're marketing to an entirely different clientele. You've really got to understand who it is you're marketing to. We had to make

a decision about four years ago about who our customer was. We had to decide if our customer was the Mexican who lived in Cabo San Lucas, or the tourist who was coming in. We decided on the tourist, and we went after that market. Because you're marketing in a completely different way. We do a lot of marketing in the States, before the customer gets here. For example, we do a lot of marketing electronically because we're dealing with a consumer who finds out about our kind of business here in that way.

How do you market using the Internet?

Very simple. Of the 200 dinners we serve here a night, probably 40 to 50 percent of those people are involved with the Internet. And when they tell us that Pancho's is such a great restaurant and it's been their best experience in Cabo, I ask them to put a little note on the Internet. That's how I found out about the Net. People started coming in with little print-outs that said, "Go to Pancho's, it's the best place in Cabo." That was like, "wow."

We also work with marketing people in the United States who are bringing people here like Sun Tours in San Jose; when they come, it's dinner-on-us because these are the people who influence people coming here.

Marketing here is so different. You have people for one week if you're lucky; the average stay here is five days. So in that five days you have to be able to attract them. And the hotels aren't going to help you because they want to fill up their restaurant. And we cannot count on the OPC—the people who are out on the street corner handing out flyers because they only hand out flyers for the restaurants who have their OPCs in them to sell time shares, and we don't allow that in our restaurant. We don't want our customers bothered. They ask us all the time and will pay $10,000 per month in rent to come into the restaurant, and that's hard to turn down. But we believe in the longevity of our busi-

ness and we don't want our customers being bothered. So you have to find other methods that are going to work.

If a person wanted to open a restaurant in Mexico, what tips would you offer?

I would recommend that that person come to Mexico and work in a restaurant here for awhile. If I had done that I would have saved myself a lot of time and a lot of effort. I would have seen how certain things are done and I would have had to make those mistakes. Secondly, I'd sit down and talk to a lot of restaurant owners to find out what kind of business line to get into, and whether my idea is realistic. I'd talk to the local restaurant association— and there is one in Cabo. Every business in Mexico has to be affiliated with what we would call a chamber of commerce. Our chamber is called CANIRAC. And there's one for the shop owners, and one for the dive shop owner. Everyone has to be a member of one of the chambers; it's required by law. Meet with the chamber and ask questions: what kind of products are available locally? availability of employees? what kind of training is there? I remember when we were trying to determine where to locate our restaurant, I went around and talked to all kinds of people about where they go and where they don't. I went to the airlines and asked how many people were being unloaded everyday in Cabo San Lucas. I went to hotel owners and asked what their occupancy rates were year-round. I didn't care anything about the population of Cabo San Lucas because that didn't matter to us.

If you don't speak Spanish is it wise, and is it possible, to hire a bilingual manager?

The number one barrier will be the language. And someone who doesn't have the respect to learn the language of the country where the business is has an arrogant attitude.

54

People do that and then they wonder why they can't get anything done. Hey, wait a minute! This is their country. They don't have to learn English; we have to learn Spanish.

We have what we call our *administradora*—she's our administrator in our company. She cannot sign checks or legal documents, but she can do purchases for us, communicate—anything of that nature. She is bilingual and Mexican. She has a great business background and was an executive secretary for a large manufacturing company in Mexico. You've got to have somebody who really understands business. Not just somebody who is bilingual. That person has to understand profit and loss.

Are these people easy to find?

Not here at all, but on mainland Mexico they are.

Businesses in Cabo rely tremendously on their accountant. We don't have to utilize our accountant (as a bilingual cultural translator) because we have Norma and I speak Spanish. But it's extremely difficult on my husband, who doesn't speak Spanish and has to use Norma to get anything done.

The language barrier also affects your employees. We don't have a lot of employee turnover here. Why? Because they're happy. They know that I care about them, and they care about us. Turnover is huge in Cabo because workers feel they're not being paid enough or they're not satisfied with the work. Same as anywhere else. We pay more here than most places pay, but not a lot more.

You need to be able to communicate both verbally and in writing. Mexico is a country where you need to get everything in writing. Everything. You don't leave anything to interpretation.

Is doing business in Cabo all that different than doing business in the States?

It's not much different doing business here than anywhere else in the world. But there are fewer rules to follow here. This is what makes doing business in Mexico a joy. I don't have to worry that I'm going to get sued if somebody tips over in a chair and cracks his head. Because Mexican law says that if the person is stupid enough to lean back in the chair like that and break his head, that's a lack of personal responsibility; and that person can't sue you. If I give someone poison to eat, that's another matter. Then he can take everything I own and probably put me in jail for the rest of my life, if there is intent to harm.

So that makes doing business here a joy. We have no fear of lawsuits here. And that is a major difference between doing business here and probably most other places in the world, certainly the United States.

On the other hand, if you need money down here, you better make sure you've got enough behind you because you're not going to be able to go to your bank and get it. You can't afford the cost of a bank loan. So you have to have your own personal financing to get started and carry your cash flow. That's something that makes business different here: you have to be very willing to accept that this is a cash economy. Employees are paid daily or weekly, certainly no longer than that. They don't have 30-day net. They don't understand "net." Cash only.

What would be minimum investment to start up a restaurant in Cabo?

It depends on the size of the restaurant and how many hours you'll be open. But I'd say a minimum of $250,000. And that doesn't include buying the property outright, which we did. We own the Pancho's property 100 percent.

How do taxes compare to what you would pay in the States?

The Hacienda—the equivalent of the I.R.S. here—can fine the hell out of you, so you have to be very careful. People complain about the high amount of taxation in Mexico, and it's very high. Extremely high. However, we've actually figured what we paid out in taxes in the United States and compared it to what we pay out here. And we actually pay less here than we did in the States. Our net here is about 70 percent after taxes, and that's very good. So we take home about the same as we did in the States, about $300,000, but look how much further it goes in Mexico!

Is the future rosy for expats like you in Cabo San Lucas?

It's rosy if you've done you homework. If you have spent enough time really researching what you're going to do, and you're sure you have the wherewithal financially, emotionally, and psychologically to do it . . . because it sounds easy talking to me but it's not. Everyday there's something.

This interview was conducted in Cabo San Lucas by Dave Fletcher of the Engholm Group.

INTERVIEW WITH STAN GOTLIEB
Expat Writer and Publisher of Letters from Mexico

We found Stan, as most people do, on the Internet at a site called *Letters from Mexico*. Not long after he started posting his "columns" about life in Oaxaca and things Mexican, his site was awarded Point's *Top 5% of the Web* medal. His topics range from local politics to the Zapatistas, from expat culture shock to drug interdiction. The articles are now available in book form as well. Stan's story is both a "lone eagle" story about how to use cyberspace to eke out a living in an exotic clime, as well as a tale of the trials and rewards of relocating to deep Mexico.

> *Tell us: How did you rip up your roots in the States and transplant yourself to Mexico to become the Internet's man-on-the-scene in Oaxaca?*

I am a traveler. Some people are drunks and some play Bingo. I like to pack a suitcase and boogie. I get restless when I have been too long in the same place, the same job, the same social scene. That's why I travel: for stimulation. So far, I have lived in over 15 cities in four countries on three continents.

On the other hand, I like my comforts, the more so the older I get. I am not a loner, so I look for places with the possibility of community. And, having been born and raised in Minnesota, I like warm places.

With all this, I had no intention of going anywhere for some time when, in 1993, an aunt died and left me a few thousand dollars (I didn't know she was rich, and I wasn't sure she liked me). At the time I was working in a legal aid office dealing with domestic issues, and the combination of overwork and icky cases was burning me out. So, in the fall of 1993, I gave notice, and in January of 1994 I packed my bags, rented out my house, and headed south. I chose Mexico because I had visited many locations over

the previous 20 years, and Oaxaca, because since first coming here in 1973 it had remained in my mind. Mexico, I told my friends, is the ideal place: very close to here, but very far away.

When I got to Puerto Escondido, my first stop in Mexico, I wrote a letter to Ed Felien, a friend in Minneapolis who owns a small monthly neighborhood newspaper. I continued to write to him over the next few weeks, through my move to Oaxaca city and my enrollment in Spanish classes. Imagine my surprise and my consternation when one day, about four months after arriving, I received a check for $75, with a note saying that he had published three of my letters at $25 each, and keep 'em coming. Why consternation, you might ask? I would answer: because at that point I had become a Paid Author, a heavy responsibility for someone who had thought of himself only as a layabout who wrote letters.

Soon, another letter arrived, from my oldest and best friend. He was, and is, a master computer programmer (his company, The Dream Machine, has been providing PC programming since the earliest days of the Commodore Pet) and political philosopher of the first order. He told me he was going to found a "home page" on the Internet, through Dream Machine Network Services, and invited me to publish my articles. I replied "where's the money?," and he answered "aside from Eddie, who's paying you now? This is a chance to get read by a large audience that is doubling every month. Where else will you get such an opportunity?" I went for it.

As I discovered, writing was only half the Internet battle. It has also been necessary to shamelessly promote myself on the Internet. That means getting other content providers to exchange Web addresses with me, making sure that all the "search" utilities contain cross-references

to my stuff, and spending time in "chat" forums: keeping my name before the public. In fact, I have gotten so good at this that I now perform this service (free) for other providers in the Dreamagic stable.

How many columns have you written now, and is your website as popular as ever? Is it true you've got an anthology published in book form?

I will have written over 60 articles, a "letters to the editor" column with commentary, a list of answers to "frequently asked questions" about life in Oaxaca and Mexico, and many special articles for other webmasters and the print media. Due to some very clever packaging and merchandising by the Dream Machine, I am enjoying ever-increasing popularity. I am particularly satisfied by my "stick around" factor (on the average, everyone who accesses my pages reads 3.5 articles) and my reader responses (5 to 6%, or many times that of print journalists, who consider 1% to be good). Of course, that is one advantage of publishing electronically: people read you because they are *looking* for what you provide, as opposed to print media, where they buy the newspaper or magazine for the headline, and read you because they paid for it and you are there. On the other hand, that is also the challenge: if they don't like what they read at first, they will change channels in a hurry.

As well as in *International Excellence Online,* I have been featured in the rec/travel side of Straw.com (a crafts and travel-oriented website), and reproduced in numerous places.

In the fall of 1995, I was contacted by Peter Weiss, a "fan" from upstate Illinois, who was coming to Mexico for vacation and asked (via e-mail, of course; I only write letters to a few Luddites who are too dear to dump in spite of their anachronistic behavior, and corporate and government entities whom I need for my continued existence) if I would find him and his wife a place to live. I did, we

60

became very good friends during their three months here in early 1996, and we ended up publishing a book together. He has advanced computer and laser printer equipment. He downloaded my columns, scanned and reworked (my wife) Diana's photos to grayscale (color being too expensive); now he prints out however many copies I need and ships them to me. He sells in the U.S., and I sell in Mexico. His e-mail address is bandwent@inter-access.com (book). U.S. price is about $17.95, tax and delivery included (160 pp, 44 illustrations). We expect to have a new edition, with some old columns dropped and some newer ones added, some time in the summer of 1997.

I also write and distribute an "insider newsletter" which I distribute directly to subscribers via e-mail. The cost is $25 for 20 issues a year.

You seem to be enjoying the information-age fantasy of making your living by observing a foreign culture and reporting your findings to all of us back home via the Internet; what's the reality?

I use the Internet as a medium because it is so cheap compared to sending written materials, and because it is so friendly to new faces compared to the established print media which are ossified and hard to break in to. I enjoy my role immensely, and I often think of it as just that: a sort of persona that time and circumstances invented for me. It tickles me that a whole lot of people find what I have to say worth reading, even if it is mostly free—with five million or more information providers on the Internet, also giving it away, I take pride in that.

The *reality,* day to day, is not a hell of a lot different than it was "back there": work, sleep, eat, socialize, make love (and occasional war) with Diana, scratch for the rent, and go to the beach whenever the time and money permit.

Also, I have to admit, it's fun being a medium-sized frog in a very small pond. I like the notoriety, such as it is, and it makes me feel good when I can give others information (power) that they didn't have before, like how to get to x and where to find y and have you seen z. Because aside from writing, which is fun, I am really a "matchmaker" by nature: a living walking connection between here and there, so-and-so and such-and-such.

Of course, I miss my old friends, most of whom could not for various internal and external reasons share in my expatriate wanderings. It takes a long time for new friends to become old friends—although I have observed that the process is speeded up in small town atmospheres such as we have in the expatriate community of Oaxaca.

Was it a difficult transition for you to relocate to Oaxaca, in terms of cultural differences, language, climate, access to media, making friends, American cooking, etc.?

Nothing about Oaxaca was difficult for me. I love the "vamos a ver" (let's go and see how it works out) attitude, and I haven't worn a watch in thirty years. I accept the fact that I will always be an outsider to the local folks: people from the next State are so viewed, so why not me? I have my "family" here among the extranjero (foreigner) community, and like all families, I like some better than others and some not at all. The climate (5,100 feet) suits me.

As to cultural access, this is one of the blessings of life here, and absolutely necessary to me. We have the only English language lending library between San Miguel Allende, north of Mexico City, and Antigua Guatemala. It is the social, cultural and intellectual center for us. But that is not all: we have wonderful musical performances going on all the time, from Norteño mariachi music to baroque chamber orchestras, to fine jazz, to marimba music in the

town square; movies shown in the museums and at several movie theaters (90% in English with Spanish subtitles); contemporary artists of major talent; and over, under and around it all the traditional indigenous arts and crafts that make this place special.

As to the culinary arts, we can get almost anything here that we got there, and it is usually riper, fresher and more healthy. And the few things that we miss (horseradish for me, balsamic vinegar for Diana, for instance) we and our friends bring with us on our trips from the States.

What about access to health care as a foreigner living in Mexico? Are you a member of the Mexican National Health system, and what has been your experience with Mexican doctors and hospitals?

I am a member of the National Health. Unfortunately, I have very little direct experience to relate. The one time I went to the clinic to which I am assigned, I was interviewed as opposed to examined. The doctor took testimony from me as to my symptoms, and prescribed medication for me. The whole process would have taken three minutes if I were more fluent in Spanish.

The issue of health care is very prominent among the expatriates whom I know, and I have gathered a great deal of testimony from them without being able to reach any conclusions. Some have private health insurance, which runs about three times as much and carries deductibles (still cheap by U.S. standards). Some self-insure and use private practitioners. Each group has its tales of woe and of glory.

Based on little personal experience, anecdotal unscientific information from my readers and my neighbors, and the voices in my head, I would offer the following advice: Be redundant, if you can afford it. Take the National Health against the eventuality of emergencies, major elective surg-

eries and catastrophic illness, and in order to take advantage of free medicine if you have a chronic treatable condition (such as high blood pressure). For worrisome conditions requiring serious diagnosis, go to a medical specialist in private practice who has been recommended by at least one non-hysterical friend. Or, try both private and public medicos every time you feel the need for attention. If you do this for a year, you can do your own evaluation.

What does it take in an American person to relocate to Mexico; what kind of personality traits, interests, temperament? And what kind of person shouldn't even think about moving to Mexico?

Carl Franz says "wherever you go, there you are." He's not the first person to say that, but he made it the central empowering notion of a valued travel guide, and that is why I give him the quote. To me, the notion that you can "transplant" yourself is an erroneous simile. It's like saying you can grow a cranberry bush in the Sahara. The successful process is more like grafting, where you join your developed personality to roots that are already viable.

This means that if you value punctuality above everything else, you would find life here very frustrating, but if you know how to be punctual but don't value it more than reading a good book you could probably adjust. The cultural values regarding punctuality compose one of the roots of plants that grow in this soil. Others are patience, tolerance, a sense of humor and a non-judgmental attitude, to name a few.

The Mexicans reciprocate in kind: they accept us as they find us. Sure, we scandalize them sometimes, but most often they just shrug their shoulders and assume that our craziness is just the way "we" behave.

Your journalistic endeavors in Mexico have been made possible by the Internet. How widespread is the use of E-mail and the Web in the Oaxaca area, and what does an Internet connection cost there?

There are four major providers in Oaxaca, only one of which is a national network with local access. Costs vary slightly according to plan, running between six and ten pesos per hour (75 cents to $1.25 usd). Compuserve and AOL are in Mexico City, Monterrey and other northern megacities, but haven't ventured this far south yet. Everyone is awaiting the much publicized "opening up" of phone lines for competition, and rumors of AT&T and MCI coming in with super-cheap connections are probably exaggerated both in installation date and savings. Even so, we know that our patience will someday be rewarded and we all await the millennium.

Stan Gotlieb can be reached at

stang@pemail.net

SELLING
TO MEXICO

"Many foreigners (and Mexicans too) have overestimated how much the Mexican people have to spend. This affects foreigners coming here to sell things to the Mexicans. A Mexican will spend everything they have and more for a good fiesta, but be unable to buy a new coat or pair of shoes."

Susana Trilling
*Owner, Seasons of My Heart Cooking
School, Oaxaca*

Chapter 6

∀

WHAT MEXICO
WANTS TO BUY

The time has arrived for us to take a closer, perhaps painstaking, look at Mexico's appetite for imported goods and services. The goal of this exercise is to discover whether what we have to sell will find a market down South. We don't have space here to provide detailed market data for all industrial sectors in Mexico, but we can review the leading categories of Mexican imports and discuss key opportunities in specific industrial and commercial subsectors. Most of the data is derived from the U.S. Department of Commerce and INEGI, the Mexican statistics bureau. It is worth noting that the composition of Mexico's imports has remained essentially consistent through the boom years of the early 1990s, the crisis of 1994-1995, and into the current period. The devaluation of the peso limited the power of Mexicans to purchase foreign goods, but not their appetites or tastes. Also, because so many products imported into Mexico are purchased by the Mexican government or state-owned firms, the types of goods required tends to stay reasonably constant. In this chapter we also briefly discuss the tastes and preferences of the Mexican consumer and make recommendations for where you can go to conduct your own market research for Mexico.

What is the composition of Mexico's international trade?

Despite Mexico's economic difficulties, the effects of the NAFTA have served to enhance the competitiveness and

accessibility of U.S. exports. Due to delays in reporting statistics from Mexico, 1995 is the most recent year for which complete data on international trade are available. In 1995, despite the financial crisis, $46.3 billion in U.S. goods were exported to Mexico, 8.9% lower than in 1994 but $4.7 billion higher than before NAFTA in 1993. U.S. goods have also gained significant ground in Mexico vis-à-vis its foreign competitors. The U.S. share of Mexico's import market rose to nearly 75% in 1995, from less than 70% in 1993.

What does Mexico buy from the United States?

Most of Mexico's imports from the United States are destined for use in the country's manufacturing industries. Even when imports for use in the maquiladoras are excluded from official statistics, the major categories of imports still appear as manufacturing imports, even raw materials such as foodstuffs destined for processing. Another significant category of imports is consumer goods, which include processed foods and beverages destined for retail distribution.

Over the past five years, these categories have remained reasonably consistent. The biggest import categories represent inputs temporarily imported for use in maquiladora manufacturing. Top imports include automobile subassemblies and parts, electrical apparatus and parts, radio and television apparatus, telephone apparatus, meat, iron and steel, and aircraft parts.

Excluding maquiladora inputs, the major categories of imports from the U.S. have included machinery, staple foodstuffs (corn, beans, soybeans, and sorghum), radio and television equipment, sugar, powdered and condensed milk, computers and computer parts, paper and paper products, apparel and pharmaceuticals.

Major institutions in Mexico including Pemex purchase large quantities of specialized goods from foreign suppliers. Note that a common requirement is that the supplier maintains an office and/or service presence in the country. After-sales service is, in fact, often more important than price in the buying decision. The hit-and-run approach will not address the needs of the large-scale Mexican purchaser.

What are the selling opportunities in Mexico?

In Mexico, the strongest selling opportunities lie with those U.S. products and services that are linked to Mexico's export sector and the Mexican government's industrial modernization program. The Mexican government continues to stress value-added exporting and the upgrading of production technology as the new engines of the country's economy. In addition, the rising disposable income of Mexico's middle and upper classes is creating important possibilities for disposable goods and consumer services. Included in this sector are opportunities for franchising U.S. business models to Mexican entrepreneurs.

According to the International Trade Administration of the U.S. Department of Commerce, the following product and service categories offer the strongest potential markets for U.S. exporters looking to Mexico.

BEST PROSPECTS FOR U.S. EXPORTERS TO MEXICO

Sector	Est. Market Size (U.S. $ Millions)	Est. Imports from U.S. (U.S. $ Millions)
Automotive Parts and Services	8608.0	3806.0
Franchising Services	6423.1	2433.0
Pollution Control	2290.1	1402.5
Chemical Production Machinery	1146.0	836.0
Telecommunications Equipment	4696.4	828.3
Building Products	1535.6	626.7
Management Consulting Services	1393.3	533.4
Apparel	5670.0	446.0
Aircraft and Parts	544.7	320.1
Electronic Components	610.5	271.5
Water Resources and Equipment	447.5	231.4
Architecture/Construction/Engineering	1177.9	217.5
Air Conditioning and Refrigeration Equipment	797.0	191.7
Medical Equipment, Instruments and Disposables	856.0	180.0

In addition, private sector analysts have also noted key opportunities in Mexico for selling prefabricated housing systems, medical instrument manufacturing equipment, advanced apparel manufacturing equipment and agricultural equipment.

Do Mexican consumers have an appetite for, and the disposable income to purchase, imported goods?

While wealth has been traditionally concentrated among Mexico's elites, many foreign marketing executives are often surprised at the real purchasing power of upper-middle class Mexican households. The top 10 percent of Mexican consumers earn an income that is roughly proportional to the average salary in the United States. This percentage earns approximately 40 percent of the Mexican national income. Since the next 20 percent of the population earns 30 percent, 70 percent of the income of the country is concentrated in the top 30 percent of the population. This is bad news for economic development officials but important for marketers. Mexico's population is nearly 100 million, and even the top 30 percent represents a significant market for disposable consumer goods.

Given the success of new foreign products in Mexico, it is clear the country has an appetite for foreign products. However, Mexicans are very loyal to their own brand products. Also, there is not a clear positive overall image associated with American brands. Mexicans will develop brand loyalty to specific products that are high-quality and complemented by positive advertising. In certain key sectors this process has already occurred. In areas such as fast food and beverages, American brands are clearly preferred.

What regions of Mexico represent important consumer markets?

Mexico City, Monterrey, Guadalajara, and the border corridor, as well as major resort developments on the Yucatan and the Pacific Coast. Perhaps the strongest retail opportu-

nities lie in the rapidly growing cities along the U.S.-Mexico border. Many large American retail chains have achieved success in the border corridor, where they have been protected from the devalued peso by the fact so many shoppers cross over the border from the States to shop with dollars.

What are the best ways to research demand for your product in Mexico?

Use a combination of public and private resources to investigate product demand in Mexico. The U.S. Foreign and Commercial Service in Mexico conducts market research projects regularly in a wide variety of industries. The findings of these projects are summarized in Market Profile reports that are published electronically via the National Trade Data Bank (NTDB). The NTDB is described in greater detail in Section III of this book. In addition, several market studies are available directly via the World Wide Web on the Commercial Service's website. The website address is:

http://uscommerce.org.mx.

An alternative approach is to hire a market research company to conduct a generalized market profile using its existing data or a specialized market study based on secondary information and original survey research. A pioneer in this field is Rincón & Associates, a market research firm based in Dallas, which has been analyzing the purchasing patterns of U.S. Hispanics for over a decade. The company has conducted specialized market research for firms such as American Airlines, American Express, JC Penney and Coca-Cola. In 1995 Rincón completed the largest and most detailed study ever conducted in Mexico by a U.S. market research firm. The study, entitled "Mexico: A Market Profile," analyzed product flows and demographics using government statistics and census data. In addition, the company conducted one-on-one interviews with 1,200 randomly selected residents living in Mexico's three largest markets: Mexico City, Guadalajara and Monterrey.

THE KEY FINDINGS OF THE STUDY

> While Mexican fertility levels are decreasing, Mexican families still have significantly more members per household—average of five members—than the average U.S. household, or the average U.S. Hispanic household.

> Mexicans on average are younger than Americans. The average age in Mexico is near 20, while the average U.S. citizen is in the thirties.

> Mexicans are big consumers of non-alcoholic beverages, which comprise one of the fastest growing categories of U.S. exports to Mexico. On a per capita basis, Mexicans consume almost as much non-alcoholic beverages in volume as U.S. consumers. There are major markets in Mexico for used equipment and parts from the United States. Two key sectors are used automobile parts and systems and used office equipment.

> Mexicans have a stronger taste threshold than Americans when it comes to food and beverages. There are certain levels at which Mexicans will simply stop purchasing product, no matter how low the price, if it doesn't agree with their taste buds. By contrast, Americans will consume a lower range of foodstuffs and beverages as long as the price is comparably cheaper.

Rincón & Associates
6060 N. Central Expressway, Suite 670
Dallas, TX 75206
U.S.A.
Telephone: 214-750-0102
Fax: 214-750-1015
E-mail: info@rinconassoc.com
Website: http://www.rinconassoc.com

Who should I contact for marketing research?

The U.S. Department of Commerce can conduct customized sales surveys for American firms at a subsidized price.

Contact the Commerce Department by e-mail via the website noted above. The full address of the Commerce Department's office in Mexico City is provided in Appendix II. The U.S. embassy in Mexico City can refer companies to private market research firms active in the country, as well as to major international consulting and law firms that also conduct market research. One company very active in the Mexican market is McKinsey and Company which you can contact on the World Wide Web via their website at

http://www.mckinsey.com.

HOW TO BRING A PRODUCT TO THE MARKET

This chapter describes the steps entailed in bringing your product to market in Mexico. Not every product will work the same on its way to the Mexican consumer, but the generalized pathway and procedures described here should illustrate the fundamentals of distribution in the country. The place to begin is to describe the path a foreign import must take to enter the market, so we have provided a step-by-step approach to market penetration for a sample product. We then turn to an overview of relevant government regulations and options for distributing goods in Mexico. We weigh the options of establishing a network of independent sales agents and working with a Mexican wholesaler. We also discuss franchising as an alternative route to capturing the Mexican market. Finally, this chapter addresses the nuts and bolts of Mexican Customs for the time when you are ready to bring products across the border.

What route must an imported product follow to enter the market?

Penetrating the Mexican market requires attention to detail and investments of time to develop relationships with Mexican business partners and customers. In the following list, we have provided some recommended steps for penetrating Mexico for the first time with a new product. For illustrative purposes, we will assume the product is a CD-ROM.

1. As a first step, visit a customs broker in the United States to inquire whether an import license will be needed to sell the product in Mexico.

   Confirm the *Normas Oficial Mexicanas* (NOMs), or Official Mexican Standards, requirements for the product to be accepted in the Mexican market. More information regarding specific NOMs and their applicable products can be acquired from the *Dirección General de Normas* (DGN), the Directorate General of Standards. They are at:

   Puente de Tecamachalco No. 6
   Col. Lamas de Tecamachalco, Sec. Fuentes
   53950 Naucalpan, Edo. De Méx., México
   Tel: (52) (5) 520-8493, 520-8494
   Fax: (52) (5) 540-5153

2. You will then need to submit a sample of the CD-ROM to an authorized testing lab in Mexico or an affiliate in the United States. Often Underwriters Laboratories (UL) can fulfill this role. More information on appropriate testing labs in Mexico can be obtained from SECOFI's Directorate General of Foreign Trade Services.

   Dirección General de Servicios del Comercio Exterior
   Secretaría de Comercio y Fomento Industrial (SECOFI)
   Calle Alfonso Reyes No. 30
   Col. Condesa
   06140 México, DF, México
   Tel: (52) (5) 211-0036, 286-1757, 286-1823, 286-1461
   Fax: (52) (5) 224-3000, 286-0804, 286-1551, 286-1543

   It will take about one month to obtain approval for your product.

   You will receive a certificate which you will supply to your Customs broker so he/she can bring the product into the country legally.

3. The next challenge is to distribute the product in Mexico. Start by soliciting an existing distributor of retail CDs rather than establishing your own at the outset. Start with the large chains, including the American retail giants such as

Wal-Mart and Price Club which are already set up in Mexico. These outlets have been hit hard by the peso devaluation and might be willing to take on a new product.

4. If you see some success, the final step is to set up your own distribution network.

If you are in the sales business, you will need a special import registration number to do business in Mexico. If you are a company which imports and exports, sources in Mexico report that this registration number will be given to you on the same day or the day after you apply for it. But if you are a company which just wants to import and sell in Mexico, you will have to wait for a month or a month and a half. Keep this fact in mind when you register your business.

What import/export regulations must you be aware of?

The best way to familiarize yourself with detailed import and export regulations for Mexico is through NAFTA Facts Service. This fax-on-demand service provides access to a wide range of easy-to-follow documents that guide you through shipping, labeling, and other relevant regulations. The NAFTA Facts fax number is (202) 482-4464. For more information or help in using the service, call the Office of the NAFTA at (202) 482-0300. Many of the topics discussed below will refer to specific NAFTA Facts documents that contain more detailed information.

The basic documents needed to comply with import/export regulations for Mexico are summarized in NAFTA FACTS document 8401. Among these are specific labeling requirements that depend on the type of product being shipped to Mexico. A summary of Mexican labeling requirements is in NAFTA FACTS document 1602.

Mexico regulates products in a number of areas for health and safety reasons; examples could include hazardous materials, pharmaceuticals, some food items, and medical equipment. Exporters should work closely with their importers and

Mexican customs brokers to determine if their products are subject to such restrictions. These regulations regarding health and safety are classified under the catch-all term "NOM," or "Official Mexican Standards." (NOM is an abbreviation of the Spanish *Normas Oficial Mexicanas.*) A product which is subject to the mandatory NOM regulations cannot be imported into Mexico unless its compliance has been certified. To research the NOM requirements for a specific product exporters should employ the NAFTA FACTS fax service. Request NAFTA FACTS document 1102 for additional information regarding Mexican NOMs.

Mexico has a particular set of regulations that govern the import of pharmaceutical products. Specific information is in NAFTA FACTS document 8406.

What does Mexico's goods distribution system look like?

Mexico's goods distribution system mirrors that of most countries. Goods are purchased directly by Mexican-owned end-users and retailers or distributed wholesale through networks of agents and distributors. For new foreign products, trade shows and exhibitions are often the first step towards establishing a distribution system in the country. Trade shows in Mexico City, Monterrey and Guadalajara draw a variety of brokers and agents looking to represent foreign goods, particularly in key manufacturing sectors that are sourcing equipment and parts from foreign producers. A next step would be to directly link with a Mexican wholesaler. For consumer goods, many companies may prefer to engage in direct marketing. Mexico's retail sector is still dominated by small companies, although a number of larger chain stores have achieved success in the country. Included in this category are selected foreign-owned discount stores.

Note that the Mexican government is a major purchaser of goods and services throughout the country. Every year the Mexican government purchases more than 15 percent of the country's total imports, although this number includes purchases by major state-owned monopolies. For almost any intermediate product a qualified sales broker should have experience in bidding on procurement contracts let by the

Mexican government. Often contracts are granted through a bidding process that allows each potential supplier to submit an offer to the relevant government agency.

How can a foreign company operate its own distribution network in Mexico?

The most effective way to develop a distribution network in Mexico is through the creation of a cadre of independent sales agents. These agents, who often specialize in specific states or regions of Mexico, will operate on an exclusive basis with your company. Sales agents will call on potential customers and solicit sales. However, your own marketing staff will be responsible for consummating the deal. Another important element in an effective distribution system is a qualified shipping agent who should be familiar with the process of clearing goods through Mexican Customs and delivering goods on a timely basis to their end destination within Mexico.

Over time increased sales may require the establishment of one or more local representative offices in various parts of Mexico. Obviously this will be in regions of strongest sales, but many companies find they can establish a sales office in Mexico City while servicing other parts of Mexico using independent agents. In addition, many U.S. firms find it most effective to use U.S.-based personnel to service customers on the U.S.-Mexican border. Even after establishing a local representative office, assume that your sales staff will continue to be almost exclusively Mexican.

FRANCHISING

Franchising has emerged as an extraordinarily effective way to penetrate the Mexican market and establish an effective sales and distribution system. Well-known brands and efficient services born in America are selling well to Mexico's urban class. Radio Shack, Dunkin' Donuts, Mailbox, Etc.—all have achieved high visibility in Mexico's most populous cities in this way.

Despite the effects of the recent Mexican recession, franchises in Mexico have expanded significantly over the last five years. They have been able to use economies of scale, incorporate chain-wide pricing strategies, and export their concepts and products abroad to insulate themselves from changes in the Mexican economy. More importantly, many franchises with affiliations to U.S. firms—such as Subway, Ceiling Doctor, Midas and Blockbuster—have reached a fixed exchange rate agreement with their master franchises north of the border to protect them from currency risks.

Specialized franchises that are responsive to changes in Mexican culture and consumption habits are realizing extraordinary successes. For example, Guadalajara-based *Diversiones Moy* operates a 75-store chain of gaming arcades throughout the country, and is now expanding to other parts of Latin America. Entertainment-related franchises such as Diversiones, Discovery Zone and the entertainment-oriented restaurant-bar Freedom have reported some of the most notable success stories in Mexico. Other industrial sectors enjoying similar successes are bottled water outlets and car service centers, such as Sir Speedy and Precision Tune.

What are the characteristics of the country's retail sector? Can foreigners open retail outlets?

Mexico's retail sector is divided between formal and informal (or underground) segments. It is estimated that approximately 8 million Mexicans work in the latter. There is no definitive estimate of its value, although estimates range between 20% to 40% of the total value of the formal sector. Also, it is clear that the underground economy is currently growing faster than the formal sector.

Mexico's formal retail sector consists of pockets of major retail centers in Mexico's largest cities. Commercial real estate for retail operations is often at a premium, because the major retail *grupos* will all concentrate their stores in the same areas. A few discount chains of retail outlets have grown to national prominence; however, most retail systems are regional. Often suppliers are capable only of servicing retail

centers in a particular region, and lack the capacity to distribute goods to the stores of a single customer throughout the country. Privatization of Mexico's warehousing system should help to enhance the efficiency of the retail sector.

Foreign companies can directly open retail outlets, although many foreign companies who operate in retail have preferred to use a franchise model to grow their businesses. One exception is the growth of foreign discount chains such as Wal-Mart, which have enjoyed notable success in communities at the U.S.-Mexican border.

Another marketing tool with significant potential for small business is direct marketing. While the Mexican postal service is spotty at best, direct-mail services are less costly in Mexico than in the United States. A few American marketing companies have conducted direct-mail campaigns for Mexican companies, and have enjoyed promising results. In one example a mailing of 8,000 pieces received a 10% response rate, an extraordinary result by industry standards.

Experts in this field caution that many existing mailing lists on the market for Mexico are weak and outdated. Companies considering direct-marketing campaigns are encouraged to build their own lists using specific corporate and industry directories and the memberships of selected trade associations.

How does the foreigner locate an appropriate wholesaler?

Foreign companies seeking to market light industrial and consumer goods may prefer to work on a non-exclusive arrangement with a local distributor or wholesaler. Many major distributors operate throughout Mexico, while those more specialized have state or regional market territories.

Two easy sources of distributors are the U.S. Foreign and Commercial Service and the U.S. Trade Center. The Foreign and Commercial Service operates an Agent/Distributor location service at local offices throughout the United States. It will work with country officers in Washington D.C. and local representatives in Mexico to locate a distributor for your product or service.

For a U.S. Foreign Commercial Service Office in your area, contact the Trade Information Center in Washington D.C. at 1-800-USA-TRADE. You can also interface directly with the Commercial Service in Mexico at its offices in Mexico City. Contact either by phone or fax:

Tel: (52) (5) 211-0042
Fax: (52) (5) 207-8938

or send an e-mail through its World Wide Web site at:

http://uscommerce.org.mx.

The U.S. Trade Center operates a service that secures local representatives and distributors for your products. The U.S. Center sponsors three annual general trade shows in Monterrey, Mexico City, and Guadalajara, respectively. A recent show in Mexico City drew over 1,100 visitors and featured 50 exhibitors. The Center advertises the shows through the business press and via telemarketing. The Center can help you do your homework before entering Mexico by supplying you with briefing materials describing Mexico's economy, standards, finance, and offering its representative finding service which will generate five potential distributors for your product. The Center's clientele has plummeted in number since the peso crisis; the agency is currently operating at one-third utilization, says Trade Center Director Robert Miller, compared to 1994. There has been an upward trend in early 1997, however, says Miller, as more companies make their way back into the market.

Contact the Trade Center at:

U.S. Trade Center Mexico
Liverpool 31
Col. Juarez
06600 Mexico, D.F., Mexico
Tel: (52) (5) 591-0155
Fax: (52) (5) 566-1115

The Trade Center also sponsors a trade show for local representatives in Mexico called RepCom. Over 3,000 independent agents and distributors attend this annual event.

Another good source of leads is the American Chamber of Commerce in Mexico. The Chamber is discussed in greater detail in Chapter 13.

Are there problems in dealing with Mexican Customs?

All paperwork should be prepared in advance to expedite the process of clearing Mexican customs. Typically all duties, fees and the VAT will be paid at the time of clearance. After confirming that the paperwork is correct and that the appropriate fees have been paid, Mexican Customs will clear the declaration of value, or *pedimento de importación,* and stamp it *pagado* (paid). Depending on the product and the pace of the day at the Mexican port of entry, your goods may be flagged for inspection. The inspection process is straightforward and should take about three hours.

If your goods need to be unloaded and transshipped to a Mexican shipping firm, Mexican Customs will typically give you fifteen days to get this done. After that time, your goods may be transferred to a private bonded warehouse.

Potential problems with Mexican customs can best be avoided by developing close working relationships with an experienced American freight forwarder and Mexican Customs broker, or *agente aduanal.*

A good first step for finding a high-quality *agente aduanal* is to contact the Mexican Customs Broker Association.

> Asociación de Agentes Aduanales
> Xola 1707-A
> México, DF, Mexico
> Tel: (52) (5) 530-6804

Or contact your local freight forwarder to make the appropriate arrangements with a preferred Mexican partner.

ADVERTISING TO MEXICANS:
THE MEDIA, RATES,
AND TABOOS

This chapter introduces the world of Mexican advertising and media to the foreign businessperson. Here we include a brief survey of your advertising media options, including radio, newspapers, and television. We also consider the merits of launching a full-scale advertising campaign versus on-the-ground efforts such as sales calls and presentations at trade shows. The chapter discusses advertising in Mexico in the context of a business culture that esteems personal and family ties over cold sales pitches via the media sphere. Businesses may find that working directly with sales agents and customers may produce a more effective return on investment than advertising blitzes. In addition, businesses may be able to save a tremendous amount of time and money on developing a local advertising campaign by first attending an appropriate trade show. Finally, the chapter provides referrals for finding an advertising agency in Mexico that can help you to promote a product or service.

How are products and services promoted in Mexico?

Products and services are promoted in Mexico via advertising, word-of-mouth, and cooperative relationships between companies and institutions. The importance of family in Mexican culture translates into business relationships. Often suppliers and customers are part of an extended family network, and frequently entrepreneurship in Mexico is tied to a

family business wanting to start a new enterprise to advance its business goals. For foreign companies, products and services are typically promoted via trade shows, government trade delegations and promotional services and advertising. Occasionally firms will produce small gift items such as pens or calendars to promote their products. The most frequent way to promote an industrial or manufacturing product is through regular sales calls, presentations, and demonstrations, often in conjunction with a Mexican sales agent.

What are the various modes of advertising in Mexico?

NEWSPAPERS

Mexico has a number of daily newspapers that originate from Mexico City and from other major cities: Excelsior, El Universal, El Sol de Mexico, and La Prensa.

There are approximately 15 Spanish-language dailies that are widely known, if not widely read, by the Mexican population. These papers have varying degrees of credibility and varying levels of dependence on subsidies and advertising sponsored by the government. The Mexican press has a tradition of *gacetillas,* pre-written articles that are actually paid advertisements but placed and published as articles. Some papers, such as La Jornada, will use different fonts or italics to distinguish *gacetillas* from legitimate articles. For many newspapers, *gacetillas* represent their primary source of income and they cannot survive without them.

Many of Mexico's newspapers have very limited readership. Only one, La Prensa, is estimated to have a circulation in excess of 100,000. For this reason, many companies do not bother with newspaper advertising.

In addition to pre-written *gacetillas,* reporters will also accept payments from companies or government agencies. Many are per article, although well-known reporters may also receive a bonus from relevant ministries or agencies in return for favorable coverage. It is not unknown for reporters to actually approach companies with an offer to write a flattering story in exchange for adequate compensation.

Given the financial dependence of individuals and newspapers on government support, it is not surprising that Mexican press coverage of the government and the ruling PRI party is often less than critical. The Mexican government typically does not have to exercise direct censorship of the press; instead many papers commit self-censorship to avoid financial and political pressures.

There are, moreover, two additional ways in which further pressure can be applied on the print media by the Mexican government. One is through the physical availability of newsprint. The government owns the only reliable source of paper in the country, the company PIPSA. Second, the ruling PRI party controls the distribution of newspapers throughout the country by its ties to affiliated unions.

TELEVISION

Television in Mexico is dominated by Televisa, a company that was privatized a few years ago and was formerly the state-run television monopoly. Televisa, which controls 90 percent of the country's television market, and its owners are closely linked to the ruling PRI party and the Mexican government. It broadcasts seven networks to nearly 10 million Mexican households that receive television. In addition, there are a variety of cable systems and satellite networks operating in the country. Certain areas also receive network broadcasts from the United States.

RADIO

Mexico has nearly 1,000 radio stations, most of which provide commercial broadcasts. Needless to say, the vast majority of broadcasts are in Spanish, although English-language broadcasts are appearing with increasing frequency. The estimated audience for Mexican radio broadcasts is 25 million radios.

What forms of advertising are available and at what rates?

A full listing of media outlets (both print and broadcast) that offer advertising in Mexico is published in the quarterly directory *Radio and T.V.* published by:

Medios Publicatarios Mexicanos, S.A. de C.V.
Avda. México 99-303
Col. Hipodromo Condesa
06170 México, DF, México
Tel: (52) (5) 574-2604, 574-2858
Fax: (52) (5) 574-2668

Companies seeking assistance in developing and placing
advertising in Mexico can hire a Mexican or international
advertising agency. An excellent source of agencies is the
country's Advertising Agency Association:

Asociacion Mexicana de Agencias de Publicidad
Plaza Carlos J. Finlay 6, Piso 4
06500 Mexico, DF
Tel: (52) (5) 535-0439
Fax: (52) (5) 592-7139

Should a company begin promotion of its products and services at a trade show in Mexico?

Absolutely. Trade shows are important in Mexico for both
importers and exporters. The U.S. Trade Center (see Chapter
7) regularly offers trade shows designed to allow American
manufacturers to exhibit their products to potential Mexican
buyers. Other trade events are sponsored in Mexico by the
U.S. Commercial Service in Mexico City. The opportunities
available through trade shows in Mexico are discussed in
more detail in Chapter 13.

Are foreign companies well-advised to handle their own advertising or hire a local advertising company?

Many experts argue that the best way to promote your service is through Mexican intermediaries. While this may
include an advertising agency, it may also be comprised of a
network of independent agents. Rather than publish slick-
looking brochures or run advertisements, many companies
find that the best way to announce the services or products
of their firm is to visit with each major company involved in
their subsector and forge personal relationships.

THE PAPERWORK:
BANKING, INSURANCE, TARIFFS AND TAXES

A business venture will not see the light of day without the necessary financing. Finding money to borrow in Mexico is virtually impossible, but there are domestic sources of financing you can try. In addition, there are a few alternatives in the States that can supplement your personal capital or money raised in Mexico. This chapter will acquaint you with Mexico's banking system and various sources of start-up investments, export financing and working capital. It also discusses the art of money management in Mexico, and suggests how to balance your capital holdings in dollars and pesos to minimize exposure to currency risks. In addition, this chapter briefly reviews the function of insurance in Mexico, and provides alternatives for insuring your business, your goods and your car while in the country. Finally, we explain the ins and outs of tariffs, fees and taxes for goods imported into Mexico. Exporters will need to familiarize themselves with these details, even though they will often be handled by your Mexican shipping agent.

One golden rule we found: don't try to avoid the formalities or be tempted to circumvent them by attempting to "grease" the wheels of the system. Do it by the book and enjoy full nights of sleep.

BANKING

How is Mexico's banking system set up to serve foreign companies?

Mexico's banking system has suffered from nationalization and re-privatization in the 1980s and ongoing swings in the fortunes of the Mexican economy. The financial crisis of late 1994-1995 was particularly hard on Mexican banks, which were saddled with huge portfolios of bad or defaulted loans after the devaluation of the peso. Mexico's leading banks are known as the *bancas de primer plano,* or "first tier banks." These companies operate branches throughout Mexico and offer a full range of commercial banking services. The four largest are Banamex, Bancomer, Banca Serfin and Multibanco Comermex. These banks are probably the most reputable in terms of dealing with foreign companies, although multinational firms can expect to invest a significant portion of time in developing working relationships with Mexican banking partners.

Traditionally Citibank was the only foreign bank allowed to operate in Mexico. Under the provisions of the NAFTA, commercial banking services have been opened for participation by foreign firms, and many foreign banks are ultimately expected to enter the Mexican marketplace. Several foreign banks were poised to enter Mexico on the eve of the 1994-1995 economic crisis, however most pulled back and are just now re-exploring their Mexican options.

In addition to commercial banks, Mexico maintains a series of development banks designed to provide financial support for economic development activities in the country. The most important of these entities for foreign companies is the *Banco Nacional de Comercio Exterior,* or Bancomext, which is Mexico's foreign trade bank. It provides financing for Mexican exports, as well as for special approved imports and selected export development projects. Typically Bancomext serves as a financial support system for small- and medium-sized Mexican producers

seeking to export their products abroad. Bancomext can be beneficial to American importers who require a letter of credit from their Mexican suppliers; it maintains lines of credit with many foreign banks, and can often help to expedite the importation of key Mexican trade goods into the United States.

The main Bancomext office is at:

Banco Nacional de Comercio Exterior (Bancomext)
Camino Santa Teresa No. 1679, Piso 12 Ala Norte
Col. Jardines de Pedregal
01900 México, DF
Tel: (52) (5) 652-4022, 227-9000 x3394, 568-2122
Fax: (52) (5) 652-7255, 652-4235

Can I obtain a business loan for starting my business in Mexico?

Yes, depending on the needs of your business activities. For a start-up company in Mexico, raising the necessary equity capital to launch the business can be difficult. You will face many of the same barriers to financing that confront entrepreneurs in the United States, but without the public financing options such as the Small Business Administration. Commercial banks in the United States will attach a significant risk premium to any loan made to start a business in Mexico, because of the implied risk associated with the Mexican currency. Avoid the trap of holding a business loan with payments due in dollars if you are going to be selling products or services priced in pesos.

In Mexico, commercial credit is available but very expensive. Most banks will expect you to borrow at least half a million U.S. dollars worth of pesos. Effective interest rates will range from 20 to 40 percent, an extremely high cost of capital compared to U.S. financing. The best way to finance a business in Mexico is to raise venture or business angel capital. Keep your reserves in dollars and try to limit your working capital exposure as much as possible. For certain types of businesses, particularly ventures that are producing products for

export, you may be able to raise capital through the Mexican development banks. Bancomext offers a variety of financing packages for export-oriented and import substitution ventures.

Should my business be conducted in pesos, dollars, or both?

As a foreign company it is almost inevitable that your business will be conducted in both dollars and pesos. In many cases companies will prefer to leave reserve capital in accounts denominated in dollars to limit currency risk. In Mexico your working capital loans may be denominated in pesos, and certainly your accounts receivable and accounts payable with Mexican customers and suppliers will be in pesos. On the other hand, you may have outstanding contracts with foreign suppliers or customers where the business transactions are denominated in dollars. In border cities such as Tijuana and Cuidad Juarez, businesses may find that many products and services are priced in pesos but are informally tied to the value of the dollar. The reality is that large segments of these regional economies are "dollarized."

What is the best method for transferring money between the U.S. and Mexico?

The most common way to transfer funds is between your commercial banks in the U.S. and Mexico. For regular currency transfers you may be able to negotiate a wholesale exchange rate but the realized savings will be minimal. Note that there are no regulations on the transfer of funds in and out of Mexico. No approvals are required and there are no government controls on the flight of investment capital. For small amounts foreigners have ready access to ATM machines in major Mexican cities that will allow you to withdraw cash from a commercial bank account in the U.S. using common debit systems (e.g. Star, Cirrus) or against a major credit card. You can also transfer funds via wire transfer using American Express Moneygrams or Western Union. Both companies have outlets in many parts of Mexico.

INSURANCE

How does insurance operate in Mexico?

Like many other financial services, the insurance industry was essentially closed to foreign investment prior to the 1990s. Under the provisions of the NAFTA, foreign firms will be able to acquire up to 100 percent ownership in Mexican insurance companies after the year 2000. However, regulations will continue to limit the percentage market share any foreign-invested firm may hold in the Mexican insurance market. Under the NAFTA no foreign-invested firm will be allowed to hold in excess of 1.5 percent market share for the total Mexican insurance market, including all major product categories such as life, health and property and casualty insurance. Currently the few foreign insurance companies operating in Mexico are minority partners in joint ventures with Mexican insurance firms.

A quick note for business travelers: As residents of U.S. border cities well know, almost no automobile insurance policies in the United States cover damages experienced in Mexico. Business travelers taking a car into Mexican border cities or beyond need to purchase supplemental Mexican insurance coverage. A good insurance option for driving in Mexico is the American Automobile Association.

How are goods exported to Mexico insured?

Exporters should secure insurance for goods they are shipping to Mexico. Under current Mexican law this coverage must be purchased from a Mexican insurance company. One of the strongest business opportunities under the NAFTA anticipated by American financial service firms is to capture a share of this market. The exporter should obtain coverage against damage until the goods pass into the care of the importer. Note that at that point the foreign company can secure supplemental coverage from a foreign insurance firm.

Exporters can find an insurance agent in Mexico through the Insurance and Guarantee Agents of Mexico Association.

Associación Mexicana de Agentes de Seguros y Fianzas
Florencia No. 18, Piso 1
Col. Juárez
06600 México, DF
Tel: (52) (5) 511-3118, 511-5937
Fax: (52) (5) 533-4983

Alternatively, insurance can often be arranged through the *agente aduanal,* your Mexican shipping agent. Agentes aduanales are discussed in greater detail in Section III of this book.

TARIFFS AND TAXES

What duties and taxes must be paid for bringing imported products into Mexico from the States and elsewhere?

Tariffs are assessed on goods entering Mexico where they clear Mexican customs. Goods are classified for the purposes of assessing tariffs using the universal Harmonized Commodity Description and Coding System. Approximately 85% of the product categories are subject to duties that are assessed on the freight-on-board (FOB) value of the products as specified on the commercial invoice. Tariffs typically range from 5 to 20 percent, with the highest tariffs being assessed on finished goods headed for the consumer market.

The declared value of goods will be accepted providing the invoice is certified by an industry association or chamber of commerce in the originating country. Typically an importer will be required to post a bond or other guarantee of payment with the *Secretaría de Hacienda y Crédito Público* (Hacienda). Often this process will be conducted by a Mexican shipping agent, or *agente aduanal,* that has been contracted by the exporter in the United States or other foreign country.

Note that the above process does not apply to inputs imported into Mexico for use in maquiladora manufacturing. Under regulations established by SECOFI, maquiladoras can import

raw materials and other inputs duty-free as long as most of the finished goods are re-exported outside of Mexico.

Goods imported into Mexico are also subject to a customs processing fee assessed at 8 percent of the declared FOB value of the imported goods and due at the time of entry. In addition, most Mexican imports are subject to a value-added tax (VAT) of 10 percent assessed on the total declared value of the goods (FOB), plus the amount of the applied tariff and the customs processing fee.

INTERVIEW WITH LIC. ROLANDO GARCÍA TREVIÑO
Director General of GT and Asociados in Mexico City

Mr. García graduated from the technical college in Monterrey in 1971 and then began working for various Customs brokers, transportation firms, and other companies involved in U.S.-Mexico trading. He had already been long-oriented to international business because he was raised in the border region. "People didn't know [how to conduct trade then]. They used to bring merchandise to the border and would have no license to import it."

García perceived an opportunity and started making calls at Mexican and American companies located in Mexico (including General Electric), which wanted to purchase products from the United States and needed assistance in doing so. Mr. García then offered his company's services to the supplying companies on the U.S. side to help them deal with Mexico's import regulations, freight forwarding, and Mexican standards (NOMS).

Mr. García's tactical approach was to visit with the export departments of American firms and hear them out about their wishes and problems in dealing with the Mexican market. With a full understanding of a company's experience in the country, García would then present his proposal for how his company could help. Sometimes such help meant forming a full-fledged export management arm of the company aimed at the Mexican market; in other instances, the company only needed assistance in a single area, for example, in understanding import quotas.

Were these American companies fairly knowledgeable and adept at this time, or pretty naive about exporting to Mexico?

Each company would have a person who handled exporting but who often wouldn't know everything related to Mexico specifically.

How did the import-export environment change with NAFTA?

The economic crisis in Mexico has forced many companies to try to sell to foreign markets. Before NAFTA the Mexican economy was rather closed; now Mexican companies are looking to export to other countries to earn foreign exchange because the peso market has been crippled by the devaluation.

> Rolando tells the story of a Mexican manufacturing company in Monterrey. Its strategy was to import materials duty-free and manufacture them into finished product. But in order to obtain the duty-free status the company would have to export 20 percent of its total production. The Mexican CEO said he wasn't sure he would be able to do that. Rolando encouraged him to try because only through exporting would the company have a chance to survive the 1994 economic crisis.

But I empathize with the CEO's fear, because if he doesn't comply with the government's policy of selling 20 percent overseas in order to obtain the preferential treatment, he may be penalized.

If you go to the authorities and say, "Hey, I'm sorry, I wasn't able to meet the requirement, but I'm trying and though I didn't make it this year, next year I will," the authorities will hear you. The government is trying to encourage export-led growth in Mexico as in Korea and Japan and so on, so the mentality is like the father to his son. When you have a son who wants to try something new and doesn't succeed the first time, he's given another chance. Try again. It's more or less the same.

The maquiladora sector of the Mexican economy is thriving; are there shortcomings to the typical maquila?

I have two experiences dealing with maquiladoras. In one of them, the American partner manufactures in Mexico using

97

cheap labor, and then imports it into the United States before sending it on to markets in South America. I asked, "Why do you do that?" If it sent the products from Mexico with a certificate of origin from Mexico, no duty would be owed, or at least less duty because of Mexico's free trade agreements with, for example, Argentina, Colombia and others, members of Mercosur.

And it took your company to figure this out for the American maquila owner?

Yes . . . . You know, we have not had that much good experience with American companies. We work with companies all over the world but we've had some problems with American firms because, generally speaking, before an American company comes to Mexico it has already hired an American lawyer and an American accountant to represent its interests in Mexico. And both of them usually have a corresponding office in Mexico.

That's what the guidebooks say to do—hire a lawyer and accountant to negotiate a deal in Mexico.

Right; and that's good enough. As long as that law firm and accounting firm specialize in international commerce. But too often, they don't.

Even with an office located here, there is still no real strong expertise about Mexico?

You said it. Here's an example. Part of the maquila program is a set of incentives called PETIC. The typical maquila is an American firm that establishes a company which will export 100 percent of its production back to the States. But in Mexico you have a good market; in Mexico City alone, you have 20 million people. But the maquila isn't looking at that. It doesn't pay attention to the fact that it could grow the maquila into a company that could sell

98

into the Mexican market and also export to other Latin American markets. Why? Because what its law firm usually knows is the maquila program, which provides that after one year the firm can sell 50 percent of what it sold in its first year of operation. With PETIC, you have to export 30 percent of production; the rest you can sell in Mexico or elsewhere as you wish. (Duties would apply to the import of materials for the non-export production only.) The situation is even better in the case of strategic industries. If you are setting up in Mexico to build auto parts, for example, you can expect to pay no duties at all on imports of materials. Strategic industries are those for which Mexican imports are heavy, including production machinery and some consumer products like toys and bicycles. But you must go and find out to realize these benefits. Besides that, you can use your company in Mexico to import from, say, South America and find additional benefits.

If you want to sell to Mexico, when and where will you have to interface with government entities? And is the process transparent?

The government has created a one-stop service for those wanting to sell in Mexico, especially for small companies. Previously the task of just forming a corporation meant, first, getting a name permit, then visiting the notary, and so on . . . the ordeal involved going to 20 or so different offices. It would take about two months just to register the company and get started. In the United States you can incorporate in a couple of days. Now you can do the same in Mexico—at least for a small company—in 2-3 days. So the streamlining is a reality.

What are some important rules to follow in approaching Mexico to do business?

Don't view Mexico only as a source of cheap labor for the production of goods to be sold in the United States. The

99

Mexican market itself is worthy in size and scope and should warrant your company's attention. In fact, the Mexican market can easily come to represent 10-20 percent of your company's U.S. sales, a handsome revenue stream especially during downtimes.

Second, large institutions in Mexico, including Pemex, purchase large quantities of specialized goods from foreign suppliers; yet a common requirement is that the supplier maintain an office and/or service presence in the country. After-sales service, in fact, is often more important than price in the buying decision. The hit-and-run approach will not address the needs of the large-scale Mexican purchaser. Hence, a longer-term perspective on how your company is to engage with Mexico may be needed.

Is the bureaucracy becoming more transparent or more messy?

This is how I would answer this question. If you are in the sales business, you will need a special import registration number. If you are a company which imports and exports, this registration number will be given to you on the same day or the day after you apply for it. But if you are a company which just wants to import and sell in Mexico, you will have to wait for a month or a month and a half.

Because the government is not trying to encourage direct importing, but wants to generate foreign exchange through exporting?

Right.

So if an American company attempts, say, to purchase an old steel mill in Mexico with the aim to upgrade it and sell all of the production into the Mexican market, there may be delays—as opposed to the foreigner who approaches the Mexicans with a plan to sell some of

the production in Mexico and some to other parts of the world.

You are reading it right.

So you have to tailor your proposal to Mexico's investment priorities; what are these priorities in your mind?

Acquire technology. Create jobs. Sell outside Mexico. For maquiladoras, in which the American side brings in material and ships it into the States without any technology transfer or market creation outside Mexico, the government of Mexico is encouraging joint ventures. It is willing to trade access to the Mexican market for access to technology and to the know-how of selling to other markets, which American and Japanese and European firms possess. The main problem in Mexico is that companies here don't have access to credit. They don't have access to cheap money. On the other hand, the U.S. comes in offering its technology and working capital. It's going to show us how to produce a product, and loan the money to get started, and tell us who we can sell to.

How do you best promote your service in Mexico?

The best way to promote your service is through the intermediary. In our case, that's the transportation company or the Customs broker that engages with the companies who are buying and selling and experiencing problems. When a problem blows up, they ask the intermediary what to do. Hopefully, the intermediary refers your company.

Rather than publish slick-looking brochures or run advertisements, Rolando found that the best way to announce the services of his firm was to visit with each and every company involved in cross-border trade and to forge relationships. During the past 20 years the company has, on occasion, sent out promotional materials to its list of 5,000

101

potential clients to solicit inquiries from companies which might be experiencing problems in selling to Mexico. Unfortunately, the response rate to these mailings has been dismal; that leaves referral as the primary mode by which the company wins its customers. Moreover, the best sales tool is the company's list of past clients, which includes the likes of General Electric.

Is there a Mexican mentality that differs from that in the States?

In Mexico one might ask first "how much can I lose?" instead of "how much can I earn?" The American is motivated at the outset by how much a deal can earn him; I will be asking how much can I lose by getting involved in it.

INTERVIEW WITH DAVID HOSTLER
Computer Consultant for Seguros Banamext Aegon

David Hostler was trained in international business at Thunderbird, the American Graduate School of International Management in Arizona, from which he graduated in 1975. For the past six years, he has been engaged in international computer consulting projects; given his fluency in Spanish, Mexico was the logical place to begin his foreign endeavors. In his most recent project, which took seven months, his consulting company, Aerolyte International, was subcontracted to set up a computer system and train Mexican personnel for an insurance company joint venture in Mexico City.

Tell me about the project you just finished working on in Mexico City.

The project was to install a mainframe computer system for Seguros Banamext Aegon. Aegon is the Dutch insurer, one of the largest in the world, and with Banamext it put together a joint venture, of which Banamext owns 52 percent and Aegon 48 percent. It has been very exciting seeing the mix of people from Aegon, from Banamext, and from the consulting company I worked for, coming together to install a mainframe insurance package with auxilliary feeds to the work stations. The total cost of the project was in the millions of dollars.

And your role was to consult on ...

What technology to install, how to install it, actually installing, and changing the programs to fit...for example, one thing we had to cope with was Mexico's use of the European date format. The program we were installing had never had to deal with that, and of course many of the transactions are driven by date. I worked in Mexico City for seven months, my first long stint working in the country.

*Was the relationship between the Dutch company peo-
ple and the Mexican side a smooth one, or were there
cultural hurdles that had to be surmounted?*

One thing we noticed was that even though people on
both sides were speaking in English, they didn't always
understand each other. This was partly because for a
Mexican it is impolite to say "No"; a Mexican will skirt
around while actually saying "No," but some people who
don't have the experience will not understand replies like,
"We just can't do it that way," or whatever.

*So all of the communication between the partners
was done in English?*

There was no person on the Aegon side at the management level who spoke Spanish.

It seems that would have been nice to have.

Yes, it *would* have been. I would be standing there looking totally aghast at some of the things I would be hearing
said between the parties. I found myself having to interpret
the English to my boss many times, telling her, "I know
that's what they said, but this is what they are saying."

*Did you find differences in training people in Mexico
in comparison with training people in the United
States?*

Yes. The procedures for working with mainframe comput-
ing were largely foreign to the Mexicans. This was the first
time many of them had worked in an insurance shop or
with this type of system. And trying to instill certain methods and procedures, especially regarding production problems, was very difficult. Especially when there are many
projects underway at once, there seems to be a very
sequential type of tendency in the worker. This is ingrained
by the educational system. You do one thing and finish it,

and when you're done you move on to the next thing. When you have three or four things going at once, it becomes difficult for them to abandon the sequential approach and to multitask.

What was your working schedule?

We worked from nine until two. The cigarette people would take breaks but normally the other people would not. After lunch we would come back and work from four until seven. And I thought that people would pretty much fade out in the afternoon. Some of the Americans had a lot of trouble with that because we're accustomed to getting off at five or four-thirty by going into work early in the morning. And we were discouraged from working over-time late in the evening to get a certain problem dealt with.

One thing that really shows the office hierarchy is the *abrazos,* the hugs. By the way a Mexican hugs you can tell where you stand with him. If you get three pats on the back, that's pretty warm, and you're in pretty good. Less than that the warmth factor diminishes. Sometimes you get a wet-fish handshake, which is not a good sign. These greeting rituals define which person is more important than others. It's definitely a more tactile experience in Mexico, and if you can get in an abrazo once in a while it helps a lot. We started out with the handshake and got into the abrazos more as time went on. However, we never got into the kissing greeting between male and female, and between female and female, which is natural to them.

The guidebooks to Mexican culture always portray the Mexicans as perceiving time differently from mericans, as being less obedient to a schedule or deadlines. Was this your experience?

We had a teacher come in from Washington, D.C. to conduct a software training class, and I told him to figure that

people would show up exactly fifteen minutes late. The class was at 9 and I told him they would show up at 9:15. However, it started raining that day so I refigured 9:30 A.M. Sure enough, they showed up at 9:30. Those are the things that happen.

Was management in the joint venture tolerant of the tardiness or did it try to enforce a more rigid schedule?

It was tolerant. In Mexico City, the numbers on your license plate determine whether you may drive on certain days. That was used as an excuse for being late, because people had to rearrange their transportation.

The Mexicans are really underestimated for their dedication. They work hard; it's just that sometimes—because of that sequential thinking—it seems that they didn't always work that smart. As if wearing blinders, they will focus in on one thing.

Did you find that there was a certain degree of nepotism in the hiring practices in the company?

I was in a special situation because this was a start-up of an insurance company. But there were many people who worked in our computer center who had husbands or wives who worked for Banamex. And there was some old-boy network stuff where a manager would "bring in his own people."

Did you find that skilled people in Mexico are in good supply? And how do you find them?

No. It seemed that anybody who had decent mainframe, programming, and insurance skills who walked through the door had a really good shot at getting hired if there was an opening. There were very few people with these skills. Also, you may find a person who, for example, knows Cobalt Basic programming language, but who has

very little concept of designing a product in reality, as opposed to only understanding the theoretical. Among the people we were finding, there were few hands-on software building skills.

If you really needed to find someone with these skills in Mexico, how would you go about it?

Go to Monterrey, because of the technical school there. While there is a branch of the school in Mexico City, there is a higher skill level in Monterrey and the people you find are more likely to have worked in the United States or have knowledge of how things are done in the United States...and you don't have to pay them as much. If you're going to develop a piece of software in Mexico, I'd do it in Monterrey.

What did you enjoy most about living and working in Mexico City for seven months?

One of the things I enjoyed most and where I developed many contacts was the Toastmasters group that I joined in Mexico City. We met on the first and third Fridays of the month, and it was very exciting. There were generals there, corporate heads, lawyers—just a very good networking situation. I had already been a part of Toastmasters in Arlington, Texas, which is a bilingual Toastmasters and I sought out its counterpart in Mexico through the Internet. I called ahead of time and the group said, "Yeah, come on down." I ended up joining the club and giving several speeches and one time even won the improvisational speech contest in Spanish.

David Hostler's current project is designing and programming commercial websites for clients in Mexico.

Amway Corporation has spread its direct selling network to include over 40 countries around the world. The company has penetrated emerging markets as rapidly as any, and at a rate of 4-5 new market entries per year since coming to Mexico in 1990. Since that time, Amway has achieved excellent results there and remains positive about the future.

"This last period in Mexico has been bumpy for us," says Dick DeVoss, president of the company, "but we remain bullish on Mexico and feel it will continue to be a very strong lead market for us in Central America and potentially South America." In this conversation, Mr. DeVoss provides an overview of how his company's direct selling network took root and blossomed South of the border.

How did Amway Corporation become involved in Mexico?

Mexico was obviously very logical for us because we were already operating at that time in Guatamala and Panama. So we had Mexico somewhat surrounded. There was substantial interest in Mexico because of the size of the market and because of the relative success other direct selling companies had reported to enjoy in Mexico. However, we were put off until 1990 by regulations which precluded controlling foreign ownership and made importation difficult, so we were a little late in the game.

So Amway's competition had already gone into Mexico and formed partnerships?

Yes, many had formed partnerships but, unfortunately that was a model which in our particular line of business we're not comfortable with unless there exists some really extraordinary circumstances. We have done very few partnerships and those we did do, we control as opposed to the converse, which is to assume a minority position.

So we started to focus on Mexico in 1989. The changes made then plus the economic changes started to indicate some economic stability in the marketplace, and these were encouragements to us too. As is typical for us, after we do our market research, we will send staff into the market to meet with legal, fiscal, and tax council and technical regulatory advisors about legal requirements, fiscal obligations, tax law, and product registration processes. We'll also investigate the market—shop the market a bit, and see what's available. We'll talk through distribution issues. And assuming all those check out, we begin by assembling a team that will analyze what it would take to put together all of the pieces and introduce Amway products to the market. Over the past five years, we've averaged about four new market entries a year, so we have this process very well developed.

With Mexico, was there anything that was entirely unexpected, or did it fall into the normal challenge of entering a new market?

After the ownership issue was cleared up, we had some hurdles with product registration. Registration was required for all imported products; it took from four to nine months to complete the product registration process, which made things tight in terms of scheduling. Other companies should plan on spending a little more time on this; at least, this was our experience.

That was all in 1989 and we opened in June of 1990 in Monterrey. Our research took place all over the country, looking at the major cities primarily, and we evaluated various locations for our headquarters and decided on Monterrey. That's also where our major warehousing operation is located. From a transportation standpoint, Monterrey seemed to work out better for us, as well as quality of life for our staff and the relative ease of access for people coming in from the U.S.

109

How many Amway people were relocated to Mexico during this stage?

Off the top of my head, I think we had about four or five expats. We opened with 14 products and recruited more than 25,000 distributors in the first month of the operation which is an excellent opening for us.

Was network marketing well received in Mexico, and was this due to anything special about Mexican culture?

It really was. The Amway business is focused on relationships; the strength of relationships is critical both in the product selling process and in the recruiting process for new distributors. In Mexico, as well as most of Latin America, the family is very much the center of the society. So the strong family in Mexico was a very important value in terms of expanding our selling method. And it's not surprising when you're dealing with person-to-person selling, if someone is happy about a product or finds something that they enjoy—that they're confident about and know its value—they naturally will tend to communicate that to those they associate with and care about, which will be family.

Who is the typical distributor for Amway in Mexico; mainly housewives with families or some other profile?

The normal presumption is that Amway distributors are mostly housewives but our distributor profile is really a "slice of life." We tend to skew slightly toward women on average, but not a lot. While many direct selling companies focus on women and they are eighty to ninety percent of their sales force, we encourage husband and wife teams in our business, and we saw those same results in Mexico too. Because Amway was perceived as an opportunity and not a job, we probably skewed a little bit younger than we do

110

in other markets, but the average Amway distributor in Mexico was middle to lower-middle class, looking for an opportunity, somewhere in their twenties to early thirties.

Did you focus on Monterrey first, or launch in other cities as well?

We opened with four distribution centers: Monterrey, Mexico City, Guadalajara, and Tijuana.

Do you manufacture the products and ship to Mexico, or produce products in Mexico?

All the products were manufactured in the U.S. and shipped to Mexico, with the exception of sales promotion literature, which is printed in Mexico, and our durable goods catalog, which also is sourced locally.

What kind of products were included in the original basket of 14 products offered in Mexico, and did the set of products differ from what you may have offered in another country besides Mexico?

In terms of the initial launch, the products were pretty much standard. We tend to launch in two different categories, a selection of home care as well as personal care products. We came with our laundry detergent, our all-purpose cleaner, a hand dishwashing cleaner, a spray cleaner, and automobile polish. On the personal care side, we came with a shampoo and a couple of cologne items. We've expanded that now to include cosmetics, clothing care, food supplements (including vitamins and nutritious foods), and our catalog of about 70 consumer durable goods.

What have been the best selling items?

Interestingly, our best-selling items are toothpaste, laundry detergent for machine washing, and food supplements.

111

How does Amway project its corporate culture into the Mexico operation, or is the operation run solely by Mexican locals at this time?

Our general manager is a South American native. Our remaining staff is all Mexican and doing a fine job.

However, this is an area where companies doing business in Mexico need to be particularly mindful, as in some other countries, there are certain practices in the marketplace that could be customary but may be outside of what's normal for your organization. So you need to be very clear with your people, especially your management staff, about what is acceptable and what is unacceptable in terms of your own culture and how you operate. Even the little things, like expenses—What are acceptable versus unacceptable expense categories, and what is the process for documenting expenses?

Does Amway have some way of making clear its standards of business ethics in Mexico?

Absolutely. We do that aggressively in our training for employees. We bring our senior staff up to our United States headquarters and review those issues and processes. We obviously have regular audits; we've found that sending audit teams into Mexico is very helpful. Not just to try to "catch" people, but to find out where there may be misunderstandings and to ensure that we are effectively training and preparing people who work with us in Mexico.

Did Amway find that in Mexico, certain unorthodox methods of doing business were more or less profound than in other emerging world markets?

There was probably a little more confusion in Mexico just because there have been so many economic changes and

112

there may have been some practices previously in the market driven by previous factors, such as high tax rates, and other things that are just holdover practices. And I think that situation is going to improve as opposed to get worse.

Any specific areas where Amway had to deal with such practices?

We had to deal with the issue of appropriate business expenses. When we did some audits, we discovered that there were some expenses that were being run through that were not appropriate. And we were told, "well, at my old company, that was something that was quite acceptable." And we said, "well, that's not the standard by which we operate, and here are the rules and here are the requirements." We had to manage that one carefully.

We had another issue with the disposition of capital assets. In our case, this issue related to the disposition of company automobiles and how that is properly handled on an arm's length basis to ensure that the company is appropriately compensated for the vehicle.

It wasn't that there was necessarily anything inappropriate, as there is a process that needs to be followed to be sure it does not have the appearance of or the reality, frankly, of an inside deal.

BUYING
FROM MEXICO

"There is no aspect of life in Mexico where the personal does not transcend everything else."

Jake Lustig
*General Director of Reunion Mezcal Company Inc.
and Compañía de Mezcal Reunión, SA de CV, in Oaxaca*

*"Mexico is a country where you need to get everything in writing. Everything.
You don't leave anything to interpretation."*

Mary Bragg
Owner of Pancho's in Cabo San Lucas

Chapter 10

V

WHAT'S MADE IN MEXICO:
AND THAT YOU CAN SELL
AT HOME

The grand challenge of buying from Mexico is finding products there which will have a market in the States. This is easier said than done. It involves both careful research regarding product demand and evaluation of the quality and capacity of potential Mexican suppliers. This chapter provides a road map for the process, by reviewing the advantages and disadvantages of importing from Mexico and listing major product categories and specific opportunities for Mexican goods. The statistics regarding the volume and character of Mexican imports listed in this chapter are drawn from Mexican government data. Our recommendations for specific importing opportunities come from a variety of sources: trade periodicals, interviews, online international business forums and Mexican trade associations. The chapter also makes some comments about the quality and dependability of Mexican suppliers. We note that sources of goods from Mexico can be improved over time with close personal attention from the foreign buyer.

What are the key benefits and most salient problems in sourcing products from Mexico?

The key benefits to sourcing products in Mexico can be summarized as follows:

1. *Proximity.* Mexico's proximity to the United States can substantially reduce transportation costs for importers. In comparison to other low-wage countries, Mexico represents a significant opportunity for manufacturers to source products and transport them to the United States using a high-quality system of highways and surface roads.

2. *Relatively cheap labor.* While Mexico's average wage cannot be compared to truly low-wage export platforms such as southern China and Vietnam, its wage structure offers significant advantages for the production of goods using low-cost but reasonably skilled labor.

3. *Pre-established network of high-quality input suppliers.* In certain industries, such as automobiles and metal products, Mexico has a system in place that can support foreign firms assembling products for export.

Major complaints regarding goods sourced in Mexico include:

1. *Unreliability.* Mexican manufacturers won't always stick to a schedule for the completion or delivery of contracted goods.

2. *Illogical trans-shipment requirements.* American regulations limiting the operations of Mexican trucking in the United States often require goods to be transported from Mexico to the U.S. side of the border, and then reloaded onto a U.S. vehicle for transportation to the final destination. Some of these problems can be circumvented by using sea transport to bring the goods directly to a major U.S. port. Also, under the NAFTA the parties are supposed to negotiate agreements that will expand the freedom of Mexican trucking firms to operate in the United States.

3. *Irregular quality.* It can be very difficult to perform on-site quality checks of goods manufactured in Mexico. This process is even more complicated if your company uses Total Quality Management (TQM) and statistical measures to assess quality.

Do many American companies currently source products from Mexico?

Various American firms are currently relying upon Mexican partners to supply inputs and final goods for distribution in the United States. Key sectors with significant numbers of goods imported from Mexico are auto parts, mineral products, specialized food and beverage products, electronics, and apparel.

The largest sources of imports from Mexico are maquiladora manufacturing operations along the U.S.-Mexico border. The stereotypical maquiladora is a massive electronics or auto parts plant owned by a multinational corporation such as Ford or Sony. However, many medium-sized U.S. companies have profitably established maquiladoras to assemble goods that are imported duty-free for sale in the United States. In addition, many maquiladoras are looking for business partners who can help to use excess capacity and distribute their products in various U.S. markets.

What specific sorts of products does Mexico offer to the American importer?

Mexico's exports have grown more competitive over the last few years. For example, in 1995 Mexico achieved a trade surplus of $7.4 billion, a significant turnaround from its 1994 deficit of $18.46 billion. Its total exports for 1995 were valued at almost $80 billion, a 31.5% increase over the previous year. Mexico achieved its strongest export gains in non-petroleum-related manufacturing (up 47.3%), agricultural products (up 50.2%), and products from mining and other extractive industries (a 52.8 % increase).

Through November of 1996 Mexico's exports were up over 1995, to $87.5 billion (the latest figures for which data are available). Of this amount, $26 billion was in consumer goods, $46.5 billion in intermediate goods and $14.75 billion in capital goods.

Mexico's top manufacturing exports by sector for Jan.–Nov., 1996 are illustrated on the next page.

Sector	$ (millions)
Metal Products Machinery & Equipment	$50,722
Textiles, Apparel, & Leather Industry	$5,817
Chemical, Rubber and Plastic	$5,804
Basic Metal Industries	$4,379
Food, Beverages, & Tobacco	$2,699
Non-Metallic Mineral Products	$1,572
Other Manufacturing Industries	$1,296
Paper, Printing and Publishing	$797
Manufacture of Wood	$793

Source: *Secretaría de Hacienda y Crédito Público, Banco de México and INEGI, SECOFI.*

For the full year of 1995, the top 15 specific export product categories were as follows:

➤ Petroleum Products

➤ Automobiles

➤ Automobile Motors

➤ Fresh Vegetables

➤ Automobile Parts

➤ Machinery Parts

➤ Computer Equipment

➤ Coffee

➤ Cattle

➤ Pig Iron

➤ Glass and Related Products

➤ Steel Tubing

➤ Plastics and Synthetic Resins

➤ Silver Ingots

➤ Steel Plates and Sheets

These items represent the core strength of Mexico's export sector. Petroleum products, including oil and natural gas, account for approximately 25% of the value of all Mexican exports. This is down significantly from the mid-1970s, when oil accounted for over two-thirds of all Mexican exports.

Based on interviews and personal experience, we believe exciting opportunities exist for U.S. importers with the following Mexican products:

➤ Fresh vegetables and fruit, particularly tropical fruits and wine grapes

➤ Furniture, particularly handcrafted furniture targeted at upper-middle income U.S. consumers

➤ Handicrafts targeted at U.S. Hispanic market segments, particularly items tied to festivals and holidays

➤ Pre-mixed ingredients for traditional foods such as *mole poblano* and *pipian*

➤ Fresh-frozen seafood, either line-caught, net-caught or reared via aquaculture

➤ Mexican beers, notably regional beers that are bottled in allotments that qualify as "micro-brews" in the United States. Particularly strong potential for the East Coast of the United States

➤ Silver jewelry

➤ Cardboard and packaging papers

➤ Sports apparel

Between 1982 and 1990 Mexico's manufacturing exports grew almost 500 percent, representing the commitment of the Salinas administration to an Asian-style, export-led model of economic development.

Key manufacturing products for export are metal products, machinery and equipment, as well as chemicals and food, beverages and tobacco. Other key sectors include woodworking products and plastics and rubber products. In the

future, the integration of Mexico into the other economies of North America is expected to enhance export opportunities in metal products, chemicals and mining.

What level of quality and dependability can be expected from a Mexican company?

As noted earlier, the quality and dependability of goods sourced from Mexico can be widely varied. This is perhaps the strongest argument for sourcing products from companies along the Mexican side of the U.S.-Mexican border. The border cities have strong commercial cultures that stress quality and reliability. In addition, the extensive presence of multinational investments in maquiladoras contributes to a more professional business culture. However, the cost advantages of the border may be less explicit. Most analysts agree that NAFTA is going to drive up wages at the border, as investment increases in the Mexican interior and maquiladoras have to offer incentives to retain their workforce. However, if quality is key to your importing strategy, the border remains your best bet.

The next line of defense in the quality battle is the individual reputation of your supplier. Even if you are satisfied with its provided samples, place a small order to test its quality before committing to a long-term relationship. A good indicator of reliability is the educational background of the owner or key managers of the Mexican business. Many managers who have received post-graduate business training in the United States have absorbed critical lessons regarding quality and will help to ensure the ongoing reliability of your products.

Be sure to visit your supplier continually in Mexico. Don't rely on his or her traveling to the United States. Repeat visits will allow first-hand inspection of facilities and equipment. More importantly, you will be able to develop a personal relationship with the managers of the company. These personal bonds will be critical when you need that rush shipment down the road.

Chapter 11

V

THE MEXICAN SUPPLIER:
FINDING ONE, KEEPING ONE, RETRAINING ONE

Whether you want to import wheel bearings or folk art from Mexico, your basic challenge will be the same: finding a supplier you can work with and count on to perform on time and at a standard level of quality. The capacity of Mexican suppliers to meet this challenge varies from region to region and industry to industry. In this chapter we provide some guidelines for working with a Mexican supplier. The goal is to get the supplier to achieve, and then maintain, a desired degree of quality in the product. Ideally one would like a supplier to be consistently improving quality levels, as well as expanding capacity and becoming more flexible to meet your performance requirements. Here, you will find recommendations for doing this using private, nonprofit and government resources. We also offer a list of tips for qualifying a potential supplier before signing a long-term contract. Ultimately, one should motivate the supply company to upgrade its technology in order to expand and enhance the product line. So we close by making some suggestions about how to improve the quality and productivity of your Mexican partner.

Where is industry located in Mexico? Where are the hot spots for manufacturing?

The two major locations for manufacturing in Mexico are the central industrial states grouped around Mexico City and at

123

the U.S.-Mexican border. Most goods manufactured at the border are *maquiladora* assembly operations that rely upon inputs temporarily imported from the United States. The maquiladoras and NAFTA have made Mexico a world center for the production of consumer electronics, particularly televisions, VCRs and computer monitors. For example, Tijuana is now the largest producer of televisions in the world.

Mexico's industrial heartland includes the metropolitan area of Mexico City (including the Federal District), the state of Mexico, and the surrounding states of Morelos, Tlaxcala, and Hidalgo. Other key industries are grouped in densely populated urban areas such as Guadalajara, Orizaba, and Puebla.

Mexico's main manufacturing industries are steel, food processing, petroleum refining, the manufacture of petrochemicals, synthetic fibers, textiles, fertilizers, paper, pharmaceuticals, and automobile assembly.

How do you quickly locate an appropriate product and supplier in Mexico?

To find a high-quality supplier of products from Mexico, we recommend a four-step process of investigation and research.

First, start with the **Office of the NAFTA**. Contact its trade representatives in Washington D.C. at (202) 482-0300 and specify the types of products you are seeking. It should directly investigate suppliers, and should also put you in contact with U.S. trade representatives at the U.S. Foreign and Commercial Service office in Mexico City. You will be able to get an electronic mail address for a specific trade officer who specializes in the product area(s) you are seeking. Managing this process by e-mail is fast and essentially free.

Second, purchase or subscribe to the **National Trade Data Bank** (NTDB), a trade database published monthly by the Department of Commerce's International Trade Administration. You can also access the NTDB for a subscription fee via the World Wide Web. The address and website for the NTDB is listed below. It provides access to a Foreign Traders Index that describes agents and suppliers of products from around

TRADE GROUPS AND ASSOCIATIONS:
WHICH SHOULD YOU JOIN?

In the United States, memberships in trade or business associations offer many advantages such as opportunities for networking, continuing education, and career advancement. The same holds true for Mexico. In fact, memberships in trade associations may be even more critical in Mexico, where the value of personal relationships in business is absolutely critical. In Mexico current information regarding business deals, tenders, available new products and job opportunities is not always published in a timely manner. A trade association can provide a vehicle for staying current with the business climate. In addition, in a culture where "connections" within an industrial sector can mean the difference between success and failure, trade associations provide essential networking opportunities and forums for deepening business relationships into friendships. In this chapter, you will learn about the most important trade associations in Mexico for foreign businesspersons, the descriptions of the most important of these, and referrals for more information.

What benefits accrue from membership in a trade association in Mexico?

Trade associations in Mexico provide critical networking opportunities for American businesspersons. While Spanish will be the *lingua franca* of most trade association meetings,

many company representatives will be able to speak English. Take plenty of business cards in English and Spanish. Businesspersons should look for Mexican affiliates of their own trade associations in the U.S.

What are the most prominent business associations in Mexico?

The most important business association for U.S. businesspersons in Mexico is the American Chamber of Commerce. The Chamber boasts over 2,500 member companies, and actually has more Mexican company members than American. A nonprofit organization that promotes U.S. trade and investment with Mexico, its members represent 85 percent of U.S. direct investment in that country.

The Chamber publishes one of the country's leading English-language business publications, *Business Mexico,* as well as various studies, directories and business manuals. In addition, the Chamber maintains an InfoCenter that assists American businesses in finding answers about questions concerning commerce in Mexico. It also helps its members to secure or renew business visas. Note that since the implementation of NAFTA Mexican immigration officials are much more attentive to regulations that require foreigners conducting business in Mexico to hold an authorized business visa.

For information on joining the Chamber, contact its Membership Services department in Mexico City at:

Tel: (525) 724-3800 ext. 3222
Fax: (525) 724-3824 or 703-2911

Or contact the office by e-mail at:
amchammx@amcham.com.mx

The American Chamber also operates satellite offices in Guadalajara and Monterrey.

What foreign chambers and trade associations are most active in the country?

The American Chamber is the most active chamber of commerce in Mexico. U.S. businesspersons can also mortgage the value of their local chamber of commerce by drawing on the resources of the Association of American Chambers of Commerce in Latin America (AACCLA). Its offices are in Washington D.C. but it has a strong network of contacts in Mexico, and can be reached at:

> Association of American Chambers of Commerce in Latin America
> (AACCLA)
> 1615 H St., N.W.
> Washington, D.C. 20062-2000
> Tel: (202) 463-5485/5609
> Fax: (202) 463-3114
> Contact: Andrew Howell, Executive Director

Another active American organization in Mexico City is the United States Hispanic Chamber of Commerce *(Camara de Comercio Hispana de Los Estados Unidos)*.

> Camara de Comercio Hispana de Los Estados Unidos
> Lic. Lorenzo Lopez, Director of International Affairs
> Balderas 144, Piso 3
> Col. Centro
> 06079 Mexico, D.F.
> Tel: (52) (5) 709-2281
> Fax: (52) (5) 709-1177

A useful binational organization for Northern Mexico is the National Council for Foreign Trade, or Consejo Nacional de Comercio Exterior (CONACEX). This voluntary business organization has its origins in Monterrey, although it now has six regional chapters and influences national policymaking. The organization is primarily composed of importers and exporters.

> National Council for Foreign Trade
> Circuito Cronistas 190
> Cuidad Satelite
> 53100 Naucalpan de Juarez
> Edo. de Mexico
> Tel: (52) (5) 562-9948
> Fax: (52) (5) 562-9948

Mexico has a wide variety of industry-specific trade associations as well. If you are establishing a registered, foreign-owned business in Mexico, membership in these organizations will be *de rigeur.* The American Chamber and the International Trade Administration can help refer you to the appropriate trade association for your business. In a joint venture, your partner probably belongs already to the appropriate associations. If you have long-term plans for expansion in Mexico, you may wish to join the group directly. Otherwise, you should be able to attend events and network as the guest of your partner firm.

In addition, many trade associations in the United States have affiliate relations with the appropriate trade association in Mexico.

How are these groups viewed by the Mexican business community?

Useful but not essential. Definitely place the most emphasis on the American Chamber of Commerce. One-to-one relationships with individual companies and their representatives are more important for business success in Mexico. Lobbying is critical for Mexican firms and the Mexican government. Mexican companies and government agencies employ some of the most aggressive and savvy lobbyists in Washington, and most Mexican leaders see developing and maintaining relations with the U.S. government as far more critical to long-term business success than deepening relationships with U.S. business associations.

There is a separate issue to be concerned with if you are doing business at the U.S.-Mexico border. These border communities have highly developed business and civic associations with strong ties to the United States. In particular, the Border Trade Alliance is a critical forum for public education, lobbying and binational communication on border issues. Also, many maquiladoras belong to regional maquiladora associations that have considerable clout in regional policy-making. Many exercise considerable authority because of the existing and potential investment committments by their multinational parent corporations.

Border Trade Alliance
P.O. Box 53999, MS-8612
Phoenix, AZ 85072-3999
Tel: 602-250-2113
Fax: 602-520-3360

What are the benefits of attending a Mexican trade fair?

Trade shows can provide an invaluable opportunity for networking with Mexican businesspersons, for securing sales representatives, and for finding suppliers. There are now several hundred established trade fairs in Mexico. Surprisingly Mexico City is not the largest venue for these shows in the country; perhaps a third are held at Expo Guadalajara, which is Mexico's largest trade show facility. A similar number are held each year in Monterrey at Cintermex. There are several in Mexico City, including Exhibimex, the Palacio Mundial de las Ferias and the World Trade Center.

U.S. exporters seeking to develop markets in Mexico may welcome the hospitable reception at the U.S. Trade Center, a facility that hosts roughly a dozen major trade shows each year for U.S. manufacturers. The facilities there include four exhibit halls, seminar and meeting rooms, and simultaneous translation systems. The Center also provides a network of bilingual Trade Aides to assist exhibitors and attendees at trade shows.

The Center has extensive experience in working with American companies new to Mexico, and can help make the transition to the Mexican market as easy as possible. The Trade Center can also organize and host trade events in Monterrey and Guadalajara for companies seeking wider exposure in the Mexican market.

U.S. Trade Center Mexico
Liverpool 31
Col. Juarez
06600 Mexico, D.F., Mexico
Tel: (52) (5) 591-0155
Fax: (52) (5) 566-1115

U.S. Mailing address:

> U.S. Trade Center Mexico
> P.O. Box 3087
> Laredo, TX
> 78044-3087

How do I prepare to participate in a trade fair?

You should start by identifying and writing for more information regarding those trade shows you might wish to attend. For a list of upcoming trade shows in Mexico, we recommend that businesses contact:

> Trade Commission of Mexico
> World Trade Center
> 350 Figuero St., Ste. 296
> Los Angeles, CA 90071
> Tel: (213) 628-1220
> Fax: (213) 628-8966

The Trade Commission provides a 24-hour Fax Information Service that offers detailed descriptions of upcoming trade events. You can contact this service and request information using your fax machine, presuming it has a handset or speaker that allows you to listen to the instructions.

> Tel/Fax: (213) 628-8966

Another good source of information is the U.S. Trade Center's office in Laredo, Texas (address listed above).

U.S. companies seeking to participate in Mexican exhibitions and trade fairs should keep in mind that trade events in Mexico are less structured than equivalent exhibitions in the United States, Japan, or Western Europe. Be ready for the paperwork involved in bringing samples, equipment and other materials into Mexico as temporary imports. Consider renting exhibit equipment such as booths, televisions and VCRs in Mexico rather than transporting them from the U.S.

There may not be a cadre of laborers ready to help you assemble your booth at the exhibit hall. Ask if such support is available, or if it can be arranged for a supplemental fee. Otherwise,

you may wish to hire your own temporary workers to erect and strike your exhibit.

For printed materials, you may wish to rely on branch offices of reputable U.S. companies like Kinkos and have your printing completed in Mexico.

All measurements in Mexico, including booth sizes, are metric. This may provide an additional incentive to rent a booth in Mexico rather than importing your own.

TRADE SHOW TIPS

Here are ten practical tips for achieving success at a Mexican trade fair.

1. Choose the right fair. Make sure the attendees represent the types of products or services you are seeking.

2. Blend. Wear comfortable but businesslike clothes. Have plenty of business cards prepared with the information printed in Spanish on one side and English on the other.

3. Have an early evening's destination planned for further conversation with your strongest new contacts. A comfortable nearby hotel bar is a good option.

4. Take breaks. Be aware in advance if the weather is warm and the trade show site is not air-conditioned.

5. Think about long-term relationships. Take liberal notes on the broad range of business interests expressed by new contacts. Keep their cards around, even if they don't immediately have the product or service you're seeking.

6. Don't neglect the trade fair's organizers and sponsoring trade associations. Stop by their booths and pick up membership information.

7. If you're still working on your Spanish, arrange for an interpreter to meet you at the fair for part of the day. Introduce yourself and offer your card, then summon your

interpreter to assist with the conversation. Don't have your interpreter introduce you.

Consider using a Trade Aide if you are attending a U.S. Trade Center-organized trade fair. These Center staff members will conduct background research on the exhibitors and key contacts prior to the fair, and then will serve as your guides for the event. In this case, it is perfectly acceptable to have the Aide introduce you.

8. Find out in advance who is exhibiting. Make sure these ex-hibitors fit your business goals. If you want to import products into the U.S., make sure you're not attending a trade fair full of exhibits by foreign companies seeking to sell to the local market.

9. Follow-up promptly. Send out follow-up faxes and letters within a week of returning from the fair. Try not to rely on the post mail to send follow-up letters. Faxing is better, or consider DHL if the letter is to an important new contact.

10. Mark down all salient information regarding new contacts on the back of their business cards. Do it right after you meet them; don't wait until a break or the end of the business day.

PROFILES

For the past ten years, Ginger Blossom has owned the Ginger Blossom Gift Shop outside Chicago, for which she does her own importing, much of it from Mexico. The imported products originate from four different continents and are generally folk art with an emphasis on textiles and floor coverings. Ginger is on the road about four months out of the year searching for items that promise to sell in America, arranging with artisans in villages in Turkey, Morocco, Chile, Peru, Argentina, and Mexico. On average she ventures deep into Mexico six times a year importing folk art and textiles. This includes rugs woven by Zapotec Indians of Oaxaca, Mayan-style textiles from Chiapas, handicrafts made by Tarahumara Indians such as drums and pine bark animals, Casa Grande pottery from Chihuahua, dance masks from Guerrero, and Seri Indian ironwood. She doesn't know whether it's because people are suddenly discovering her store or because her two wholesale accounts are on the increase, but Mexican folk art is hot at the moment, prompting Ms. Blossom to take more and more trips to Mexico. As she says, "Mexican goods have always done pretty well, but at the moment they're doing very well."

How do you find these products in the first place?

Part of it is that I have a fairly decent library on folk art so I glean some of the sources of the items from there. For some I do go down to Mexico and look around. For others I might also look in stores in areas that are a little more trend-setting than Richmond, Illinois and see what they're carrying, and see if I can find out where it came from.

Do you advertise your store or publish a website?

I don't have a website. I do advertise locally but it's mostly word-of-mouth. I also belong to the Fair Trade Federation in Barre, Massachusetts, which is a watchdog for conscientious consumerism to avoid sweatshop situations. Anyone who does importing tries to abide by Fair Trade Federation guidelines which say, first, that we will pay a fair market price for products that are produced in ecologically sound ways, so that the producers can live with dignity. Second, we will not exploit child labor. We try to put something back into the village rather than just take out. We try to eliminate many of the middle men so that if the price has to go up, the money goes back to the producer.

After you have found something you want to import, you go back to the village to talk to suppliers. Can you stay in communication with them or must you return to see them in person every time you want to place an order?

Yes. However, I think I'm rather atypical in that I try to buy things from the people who actually make them. I'm working in primitive areas, remote areas with less infrastructure than mainstream Mexico. For example, in one town of 10,000 people I think there are only three phone lines, and it's a six-month wait to get a phone line. And a lot of people don't have bank accounts so it's a problem sending them a check. Often there's no such thing as money transfers because you need a bank account to do that.

So you arrive in the village and contract with them, or just buy what they have and come back in three months for more?

It depends. Let's use weavings as an example. Usually there is one weaver who is outstanding, who produces more

143

complicated designs and expects orders, so I'll leave a small order with him and tell him I'll be back in three months. For others, I'll just leave a general guideline of what colors I like. Or, if it is a special order, I'll ask the supplier to send it to me, but not every weaver can do that because it might involve going to the city and working with papers, and so on.

How do you ship? Do you bring stuff back in your own vehicle?

No. Most of the things are air-freighted out. I have found that air freight is relatively economical if you're going with large enough quantities. Some things, because of the nature of what they are, I have to bring back up in my van. There's only one trip that I drive on; most of the trips I fly.

Is there any hassle with Customs, and what are the duties on this kind of stuff?

Because these are cottage industry goods with the proper stamp from Mexico so certifying, the duty is five percent or less. Is there a hassle with Customs? Always. It's endless. On the Mexican side and the United States side. Part of it is getting the proper papers to export from Mexico; you need a licensed producer because the Mexican government wants to take its percentage from the person who is producing. But with small cottage industries, 95 percent of them don't have the proper stamp or aren't registered. Thus you have to find someone who does have a register who is willing to have the person put their goods on their stamp, and then you pay a percentage for that. Yes, the Mexican government puts up hurdles, but so does the U.S. government; it's endless. You never know what the problems are going to be. It's always something new.

So you often have to wait a while until your products get through?

No, because if you wait a long time you'll be paying storage, so you need to resolve the problem in a hurry. It's

always frantic. For example, my very latest problem was that my crate was shipped to Houston, Texas as its port of entry. The Mexicans had made the crate out of wood that had bark on it; the inspecting agent didn't like it and claimed that he had told my shipper before that he couldn't do that. Of course, he hadn't told the shipper, he had told whomever on this end was receiving the product, and that person didn't take the time to inform the shipper in Mexico that you can't do that. Thus, my crates would either have to be inspected for bugs and be sent off for four days, or I could send the crates back to Mexico, or I could have the crates destroyed and, to ensure against possible contamination, pay to have the debris properly disposed of and the goods recrated in Houston, Texas. That's just one of many horror stories. There's always something. Always.

What about quality? Do you find that on the first order the quality will be there, and then on the next, the quality will drop?

Quality varies. This is why I don't mail a letter down saying, "Send up 10 rugs." It's a gamble. They may send the crooked rug or the rugs that don't sell or the rugs that were made by the weavers on an off day. But if you go down and pick the selection, then you're doing the quality control yourself. On a special order sometimes it's unbelievable how they hit a color on the head so well, it's amazing. On others, you don't even recognize what you ordered because they have changed it so much.

What Mexican items seem to move best in the Chicago area at the moment?

At the moment, I would say Tarahumara handicrafts.

Do your customers know who the Tarahumara Indians are, or is it the item itself?

No, they don't. It's the item itself.

145

"You have to just relax and take one day at a time," Carolyn Majors says, and then tells you the story about the roadblocks in rebel-controlled jungle country in Chiapas. Ms. Majors is the owner of Major Trading Company located in Fallbrook, California. She is in her third year of business importing folk arts from Mexico for sale in the southern California area. Ms. Majors had thought about getting into the import business long before NAFTA; her husband, Dave, has lived and worked in southern Mexico and has been bringing arts and craft items home for years. Carolyn's experience in Mexico goes way back. As Carolyn describes it, she "always had a connection with Mexico," from her childhood when a Mexican girl lived with the family to participate on Mayan archeology digs with Dave in Chiapas before she and Dave were married.

Where do you find Mexican folk art, and how do you find it?

The products I import from Mexico come from all over the country. Once a year I drive my van through Mexico visiting small towns and Indian villages looking for just the right item that will find a market in California. The buying expeditions begin in places like Guanajuato, the state of Mexico, Oaxaca, and end up in Chiapas in the deep South where I make my way to remote Indian villages. The items I find include weavings, pottery, and folk crafts. With no communication links in place in some of these places, my system is to place orders while there and return in five months to pick up the production. In Chiapas, I deal with Indian communities, each with their own leader and language dialect, like those of the Miztec, Lacadon, Zacathancas. Each village is self-governed.

What types of items are most popular with your customers?

Oaxaca wood animals, which are actually small works of art, and for which I am always looking for new artists. They start as low as $8 and go as high as $500. Black pottery is another hot item. Jewelry, including silver, charms, glass beads, and milagros. Jaguar figurines from Chiapas sell well too, and the polished floral pottery from Guanahuato which sells for between $7 and $95.

What is the hardest part about importing folk art from remote parts of Mexico?

Getting introduced to the right artists. I benefited from a close relationship with a Mexican woman who stayed with us in our home; I taught her how to drive. She introduced me to a village maestro and helped me to inquire about obtaining local artworks. Each village tends to specialize in one craft or another, like crude pottery in a village called Amatenango del Valle where women are the potters and ceramics are fired on the street using sand and clay. I made many contacts there.

Keeping up a level of quality is another big problem. The more I buy the more the local artist makes and the more demand there is for the product as it becomes more popular. Then the competition comes in and the Indians also figure a way to sell to tourists. The result is that inevitably the quality goes down. The artist might also become sick, but as is often the case, he begins to use his new money to buy liquor, fiestas. Alcoholism is in the culture.

How do you deal with that?

Working with women is a good strategy. They're crafty, smart, and more responsible.

How do you place orders with Indian artisans in remote villages?

Some Indian villages have a store that will have a phone. You can call the store and indicate the name of the artist

you want to speak with; someone from the store will go into the village and find that person. I then call back in 20 minutes and the person will have come to the store to receive the phone call.

Once you have found a product and an artist, how do you transport the goods to the States?

Recently, we put in place a friend in San Cristobal de las Casas to help store items there, and then drive the goods from there to the border at San Diego. We make 2-3 deliveries from Mexico and Guatamala each year.

Do you have to pay duties on items such as these?

At the border, I bring the goods across as personal items and not for resale. Using Dave and my friend in San Cristobal we can bring in three van loads and pay only about $400 in duties for each load. In fact, Customs duties on arts and crafts from Mexico—in part due to NAFTA— have been reduced to only 5 percent.

Who makes up your market for Mexican folk art in California?

I started with just selling to friends. Now I also sell to a retail gift shop in Fallbrook called Greenstone Court, and out of my home as well, by appointment only. The business is small but I can sell all that I can import and I intend on wholesaling in the near future. Although I see plenty of demand for the products, the hitch is how to increase production while maintaining a high level of quality. That's why I continue to sell mainly from my home by appointment, because increasing production is so difficult given the problems of communication and quality control.

Is it dangerous for you traveling in rebel-held areas of Chiapas?

You have to go with the flow. It's not uncommon to come upon an impromtu road block. These are set up by so-called campasino organizations which block off the road with rope and rocks, forcing you to stop. They extort 10-20 pesos from each car and they're polite about it. In other cases, the roadblocks are set up to stop traffic going in both directions and no one is allowed to go through at all, perhaps for the entire weekend. In this case, you have to walk through and leave your truck. It might be a walk of a mile or more, but there are little boys with wagons who will carry your things for a few pesos, and there are taxis and combis waiting on the other side to accept a fee to transport you to the next town. The last time this happened we had to have a friend go and fetch my truck the next day.

How long do the road blocks remain?

You never know. And there's a challenge around every corner, though I have experienced no real threat to my safety and I go to areas where tourists never go.

Photographs and Captions

All photographs by Christopher Engholm (co-author)

1.

New Year revelers arrive in Mexico City's central Zocalo. Will President Zedillo's reforms sustain economic recovery or is Mexico's middle class to see yet harder times?

2.

Called "The Angel," the Monument to Independence was a gift from France and celebrates Mexico's independence from Spanish colonial rule in 1810.

3.

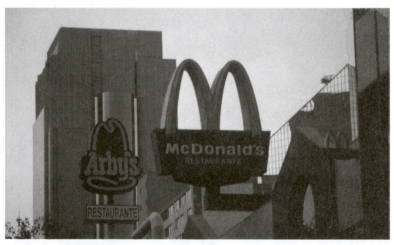

A new breed of monument on the Mexico City skyline. Over the last several years many foreign fast food chains have successfully penetrated the Mexican market, often via franchising to Mexican entrepreneurs.

4.

A billboard jests that even the Aztec sun and moon thirst for Coke. Unlike most Americans, who develop a consistent taste for either Coke or Diet Coke, most Mexican cola drinkers will alternate back and forth between the two beverages on a regular basis.

5.

The new World Trade Center looms above the David Siquieros Museum, honoring one of the country's greatest artists.

6.

Masks of Carlos Salinas Gotari, Mexico's former President who now lives in exile in Ireland. Mexico's next round of elections will likely focus on the slow pace of investigation into the complex financial dealings of the Salinas family.

7.

To augment her family's income, a young girl wipes windshields under the facade of the Banco de Mexico. Such sights are common in a country where there is pronounced income inequality. Over 40 percent of the country's national income is earned by the top 10 percent of the population.

8.

An increasing number of foreign logos crowd the horizon in Mexico City.

9.

Lunch break (siesta) means a leisurely meal and perhaps a nap between 2:30 P.M. and 6:00 P.M. The long luncheon meal, or la comida, is the major meal of the day.

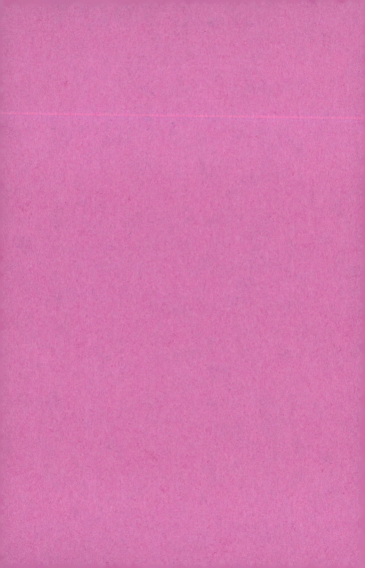

HOLD FORM

Date: 10/13/98

Name: Keith Perkins

Phone: X 3142

Book Title: Doing Business in Mexico

Date Notified: 10/13/98

(Phone) Mail Other   left message

Initials: MWL

Comments:

10.

Rebel Zapatistas offer Supercommandante paraphernalia in Mexico City's Zocalo. Members of the Zapatista leadership of the southern state of Chiapas have become media icons in a country that prizes its revolutionary history.

11.

Government manipulation of media continues but news sources have diversified. Foreign readers need to distinguish between legitimate newspaper stories and stories that are essentially paid advertisements for local companies.

12.

The lottery has captivated Mexicans for years; now legalized gambling may be approved by the Senate. Gambling is expected to spark a new boom in tourism, and local officials dream of a mini-Las Vegas in Cozumel and Cabo San Lucas.

13.

Anything to make ends meet, a teenager in Veracruz ignites a mouthful of gasoline in hopes of impressing rush hour commuters.

14.

Green VW Beetle taxis, with passenger seat removed, are the ubiquitous mode of city travel. Be sure to confirm with a driver that the meter is working before entering a taxi. If the claim is that it's broken, bargain the fare in advance.

15.

Students take notes on Diego Rivera's sprawling *The Struggle for Independence*. Diego Rivera is one of Mexico's leading artists and his murals are revered throughout the country.

16.

The *Monumento a los Niños Héroes* honors six young army cadets who battled until death against invading American troops on September 13, 1847. The veracity of the story has been questioned by some scholars, but the role of the story in forming Mexican identity is unquestionable.

17.

Crime in the city means armed guards at every chic shop in the Zona Rosa, Mexico City's equivalent to Fifth Avenue or Rodeo Drive.

18.

A movie poster for the Hollywood movie *101 Dalmations*. American cultural products are an important component of U.S. exports to Mexico, and recently the country has emerged as a preferred shooting location for major Hollywood films such as *Romeo and Juliet* and *Titanic*.

19.

Some like it hot—a method for the distribution of pizza appropriate for Mexico City's traffic congestion.

20.

Three boys perform in traffic, offering a rendition of former President Salinas as a *chupacabras*—a mythic blood-sucking creature believed to have alien origins—though most would call him worse. Salinas once sought the post of head of the World Trade Organization after his Presidency; today he hopes to avoid returning to Mexico for trial.

PART IV

MANUFACTURING
AND INVESTING

"The so-called Mexico 12 [billionaires] are not to be thought of as so many corrupt captains of industry taking advantage of the system. In fact, they know the way of doing business during this geological era of Mexican history. They're shrewd. They're good. They are not corrupt; they are industrialists. And there are roughly 100 such tycoons in Mexico, and many more minor ones, who can be considered as potential partners by major American companies."

Valente Souza
*Consultant in Energy and Environment with Booz,
Allen & Hamilton
in Mexico City*

Chapter 14

∀

STRATEGIES FOR INVESTORS:
FROM CAPITAL MARKETS TO ECO-TOURISM

You might be surprised to learn that foreign investment in Mexico, despite a downturn just after the peso crisis of 1994, has rebounded dramatically through 1997. In other words, the opportunity to make money in Mexico appears to be as attractive as ever. Most foreign investment entering the country originates in the United States and is aimed at a few key sectors such as electronics and automobiles, but emerging areas of opportunity exist, even for the small corporate investor and the individual investor looking to diversify his or her portfolio. In this chapter, we review opportunities for direct equity investments in Mexico, as well as making investments in Mexican securities. We'll look at regulations limiting certain types of foreign investment in Mexico and hypothesize regarding a few selected investment opportunities. We'll also look specifically at investing in Mexican real estate. Subsequent chapters in this section will deal more specifically with the logistics of placing your money in Mexico.

Which commercial sectors in Mexico have been targets for foreign investment?

Evaluating foreign investment in Mexico requires you to distinguish between financial and nonfinancial foreign investment. A significant percentage of investments in Mexico each

year is devoted to investments in short-term bonds denominated in foreign currency issued by the Mexican government. In addition, there is significant direct foreign investment in the Mexican stock market.

Non-financial direct foreign investment is concentrated in industry, including industrial manfacturing, services, and retail commerce. Other areas receiving direct foreign investments include extractive industries such as mining and agriculture.

Direct foreign investments in Mexico are guided by the Mexican foreign investment law, which has been in effect since 1994. Under these statutes, investments in various sectors are permitted by foreign investors or reserved exclusively to Mexican firms and/or the Mexican state. For those sectors in which foreign investment is permitted, the law limits or permits various levels of foreign equity ownership. Generally speaking, commercial sectors that welcome foreign investment either allow up to 25 percent, up to 30 percent, up to 49 percent, or up to 100 percent foreign ownership.

For illustrative purposes, major commercial sectors receiving significant foreign investment in each of these categories are summarized below.

➤ 25% or less: internal domestic air transportation and specialized air transportation

➤ 30% or less: securities firms, stock exchange service firms, nation-wide commercial banks

➤ 49% or less: insurance companies, leasing companies, manufacturing of firearms, cable television, freshwater and coastal fishing, commercial port management, domestic shipping

➤ up to 100%: international shipping, private education, credit information services, legal services, cellular telephone services, petroleum drilling, petroleum pipeline construction, mining activities.

It is worth noting that under the provisions of the NAFTA, many of the restrictions on equity ownwership of financial services firms are expected to be phased out by the year 2000.

If one were to invest $250,000 in Mexico, what would be the most profitable opportunities? How about $1,000,000?

Let's assume you are going to make a direct equity investment in Mexico, rather than investing in the Mexican stock market. As a venture capital or "business angel" investor in Mexico, you would be best advised to enter as a minority partner providing foreign capital for a business venture whose success was nearly guaranteed by current or pending regulatory regimes. A few examples are noted below.

TEQUILA

Mexican tequila producers are experiencing a boom as tequila is becoming a more fashionable drink in the United States and Europe. Moreover, Mexico recently scored a coup with the European Union by persuading that body to designate the name "tequila" as unique to alchohol produced in Mexico. This regulation is similar to the French claim that the only true champagne is made in France. As a result, Mexico has cut the legs out from underneath its primary tequila competitors in Spain and Portugal. This provides an exciting opportunity for direct equity investments in tequila manufacturing operations in Southern Mexico. This may also offer an enhanced opportunity for U.S. exporters who can source tequila in Mexico and ship it using lower freight costs from American ports.

CASINOS

A number of factors, including the Mexican economic crisis, extensive Caribbean competition for tourist dollars, and the advent of the NAFTA, have combined to renew Mexican interest in legalizing casino gambling. A study commissioned by the Mexican government concluded that the legalization of casino gambling in Mexico could generate billions of dollars in public and private revenue. The study, conducted by Harrah's Entertainment of Memphis, Tennessee, concluded that casinos operating in 10 key Mexican cities, most seaside resorts and border cities such as Tijuana, could generate $2.3 billion a year in new tourist dollars and 24,000 new jobs. The

study also projected some $740 million in tax revenue for Mexico by the fifth year of operation. Many prognosticators expect that casino gambling will be legalized in Mexico in 1997. Every major casino company in the U.S. will go to Mexico if gambling is legalized; however, a savvy investor could tie up key sites in major tourist destinations such as Cancun, Ixtapa, or Cabo San Lucas in anticipation of this event.

What types of foreign ventures are allowed, and what types are prohibited?

Major commercial sectors that welcome foreign investment are noted above. For more detailed information on sectors looking for foreign investors and specific industry and regional regulations, contact the Mexican desk officer at the U.S. Department of Commerce or the Office of the NAFTA.

The following selected commercial sectors are reserved for Mexican resident nationals or the Mexican state:

1. petroleum and other hydrocarbon extraction
2. basic petrochemicals
3. satellite communications
4. nuclear energy
5. retail distribution of gasoline
6. radio broadcasting
7. credit unions

Note that President Zedillo has publicly stated that he will seek changes in Mexican law to allow foreign ownership of satellite communications companies. Also, the law allows joint ventures in satellite-based commercial broadcasts such as DirectTV-style television. It only precludes two-way communications systems.

Is real estate investment a good bet?

Real estate investment in Mexico is a very risky venture. The volatility of the Mexican economy and the peso makes placing dollars in peso-denominated land ventures a questionable

enterprise. The absence of a secondary mortage finance market in Mexico makes the development of residential real estate for Mexican consumers particularly risky. Real estate in Mexico is primarily a cash-only transaction; it will be several years before a full scale real estate financing system for the development and construction of property emerges in the country.

Now that these caveats have been stated, there are a few key opportunities that should be considered by foreign investors interested in penetrating Mexico's real estate sector. Long-term trends in Mexico and the United States suggest that condominiums and houses in the major Mexican coastal resorts will be in increasingly high demand. As described in Section V of this book, the major demographic characteristics of the U.S. population will drive a significant number of U.S. residents to retire in Mexico in the coming years. Thus time-share and full acquisition of properties in Cancun, Cabo San Lucas or the Mexican (Pacific) Riviera are probably safe bets.

The continuing migration of global firms to Mexico is also creating exciting opportunities in commercial real estate, particularly at the U.S.-Mexico border. However, in many border cities commercial real estate is almost completely controlled by a few well-connected families who own major industrial parks. Key opportunities will lie in portions of central Mexico where clusters of foreign firms congregate as part of key industries such as automobile manufacturing and elelectronics. Savvy foreign investors with long investment horizons may be interested in working with Mexican real estate brokers to tie up these key sites in central Mexico in anticipation of companies expanding or attracting their suppliers from other parts of the world.

Is it possible for the individual foreign investor to play Mexico's capital markets?

Absolutely. The *Bolsa Mexicana de Valores* is one of the world's leading stock exchanges. It is also one of the most volatile. The Mexican stock exchange is highly dependent on the economic planning activities of the Mexican federal gov-

ernment and the ruling PRI party. Mexican equity markets are inextricably tied to Mexican debt, particularly short-term, foreign-denominated debt instruments that are frequently issued by the Mexican government to raise foreign exchange from the world's capital markets. The economic crisis in 1995 was largely attributable to the Mexican government's high debt ratio, and the subsequent devaluation of the peso had the effect of scaring large volumes of foreign capital from the country, including its equity markets.

Foreign investors need to go into Mexico with their eyes wide open. As part of a balanced emerging markets portfolio, selected Mexican equities make sense for a medium-risk investor. High-risk investors can earn significant returns by closely following the moves of the Mexican central government and swapping their Mexican portfolio between equity and debt. For long-term investors, key high-quality and diversified companies such as *Grupo Pulsar* and *Grupo Televisa* are the Mexican blue chips.

A number of Mexican stocks also trade on foreign stock exchanges as American Depository Receipts, or ADRs. Mexican ADRs trade in the U.S. over-the-counter market and on the New York Stock Exchange. Mexican firms also issue restricted shares of stock in the U.S., primarily to institutional investors.

One interesting long-term trend regarding Mexico and Latin America is that their economic and political crises rarely coincide. A number of smart mutual fund companies have established Latin American funds that achieve strong returns by anticipating and avoiding various bumps in the road to long-term economic development in these countries.

A good source of intelligence on the Mexican stock market is *El Financiero,* a daily Spanish-language financial paper published in Mexico City that is Mexico's closest equivalent to *The Wall Street Journal. El Financiero* also publishes a weekly summary edition in English called *El Financiero Internacional.* You can obtain subscription information for each version at the following contacts:

El Financiero
Grupo Editorial SEFI
Lago Bolsena 176
11320 México, DF
Tel: (52) (5) 254-6299
Fax: (52) (5) 255-1881

El Financiero Internacional
2300 S. Broadway
Los Angeles, CA 90007
Tel: (213) 747-7547
Fax: (213) 747-2489

Another strong source of English-language market intelligence is *Mexico Business*. which is a leading English-language monthly magazine covering business and finance in Mexico. Sample articles and subscription information are available via its website at:

http://www.mexicobusiness.com.

You can also subscribe to its free weekly e-mail newsletter at

Insider@mexicobusiness.com

LAWS GOVERNING INVESTMENT IN MEXICO

Mexico's legal atmosphere changed markedly with the NAFTA. Today there is a new transparency and a centralization of information regarding laws governing foreign investment in Mexico. The online resources available also make the jobs of documenting an investment deal and contract writing less expensive and time consuming. For all the improvement, however, there are still aspects of Mexico's commercial legal system that make deal-making in Mexico different from that in the United States or Canada. In this chapter we provide an overview of how Mexico regulates foreign investment, including regulating agencies, corporate taxation, and requirements regarding exports of manufactured products. In addition, the chapter discusses joint venture law, and notes how joint ventures in Mexico are dissimilar from those in other emerging markets. We also describe the basic differences between business contracts in Mexico and those in the United States and other industrialized countries. A separate discussion reviews the role of commercial arbitration in Mexico and lays out the options for a foreign company that comes into dispute with a Mexican partner. Finally, we provide references for businesspersons and lawyers that want to conduct more detailed research on the Mexican commercial code.

How does the Mexican government regulate foreign-invested companies?

The National Foreign Investment Commission (FIC), or Comisión Nacional de Inversión Extranjera, is responsible for overseeing foreign investment in Mexico and for approving certain investment projects. It is managed by SECOFI (Secretaría de Comercio y Fomento Industrial), although it includes participation by other cabinet-level agencies of the Mexican government.

Prior to the new investment law of 1993 the FIC was responsible for directly approving investments in excess of U.S. $100 million. While the new law did not comment on this threshold, the FIC can issue supplemental guidelines that may raise or lower this number. In addition, investment projects in certain sectors may require FIC approval even if the amount of the proposed investment is less. The FIC is responsible for acting on a formal application within 45 days of its submittal. After this point the investment is automatically approved.

Whether or not an investment project requires FIC approval, all businesses that are partially owned by foreign interests must register with the National Registry of Foreign Investment *(Registro Nacional de Inversión Extranjera)* within 40 days from the date of the investment. Note that these reports are not available to the public.

What is the corporate tax rate for foreign ventures?

Mexico's tax system has three components—the income tax, the value-added tax and the asset tax. Corporations will be subject to all three of these taxes at the federal level. There are few state or local taxes, besides those on real estate acquisition and limited property taxes. The Mexican federal tax system is regulated and overseen by the Ministry of Finance and Public Credit *(Secretaria de Hacienda y Crédito Público)* or "Hacienda."

Mexico's corporate income tax is assessed against gross revenues less deductible expenses. In Mexico one can be taxed on inflationary gains, and inflationary losses are deductible. The income tax due can be credited against assessed asset taxes. In most cases the income tax due will be equal to or

greater than applicable asset taxes, and no additional tax will be assessed. The V.A.T. in Mexico is assessed on selling price of the company's goods, rights or services, less taxes paid on purchases. The general V.A.T. rate is 10 percent.

Taxes in Mexico coincide with the calendar year. Within three months of the end of the calendar year every Mexican company must file a corporate income tax return that displays its tax liability.

In addition to the taxes noted above, companies must make contributions to the Mexican social security program on behalf of their employees. Social security in Mexico represents a broad range of programs, including health care, disability and unemployment insurance and pension plans. Contributions to this program are shared by the employer and employee, and are calculated using the employee's daily wages. Currently the combined assessment is approximately 17 percent of income, with the employer contributing the greater part (75 percent) of that amount.

Employers are also required to pay into Mexico's National Housing Fund at a rate of approximately 5 percent of salaries. Contributions to the social security program and the housing fund are capped at a multiple of the national minimum wage. As a result there are ceilings to the contributions that prevent employers from bearing extraordinary costs based on the salaries of their top managers.

Does the government require foreign ventures to export production or utilize local supplies?

One of the effects of the NAFTA has been to reduce certain performance requirements on direct foreign investment in Mexico. Foreign corporations in many sectors are now no longer required to export a certain percentage of their production or rely primarily on local suppliers. The exception to this rule is the maquiladora program, in which foreign companies with manufacturing facilities in Mexico are allowed to import inputs duty-free with the understanding that the resulting products will be exported from Mexico. Under the

maquila law Mexican suppliers to the maquiladoras have been viewed by the Mexican government as exporters, and thus have not been subject to the country's value-added tax. Thus, while not required by law, many Mexican suppliers can serve as competitive suppliers to the maquiladoras because of this tax incentive.

Under the NAFTA, requirements that a significant percentage of goods manufactured by maquiladoras be exported are slowly being phased out. The NAFTA schedule provides for a rising percentage of production by a maquila to be sold on the domestic market each year.

What other salient laws concerning your venture should you be aware of?

One approach to avoid the stipulations of the Mexican foreign investment law is a joint venture agreement, or *asociación en partipación* (A. en P.) This contractual relationship represents a vague middle-ground in foreign investment statutes. Typically a joint venture is entered into for short-term, cooperative projects between Mexican and foreign partners. Under the law a joint venture is not a new separate entity and is not subject to limitations on foreign investment. However, some legal experts argue that such entities can be considered a foreign investment if the foreign partner collects 49% or more of the venture's profits and/or exerts primary managerial control. A local legal professional should be consulted before entering in an A. en P. if the foreign party is doing business in a sensitive sector typically reserved for Mexican companies. Most experts recommend that such entities should be registered with the FIC even if a formal application is not submitted for approval.

Under Mexican law, investments made by a foreign national with permanent resident status *(immigrado)* are typically treated in the same manner as investments by Mexican citizens. In sensitive areas, however, this designation can be overridden by the appropriate agency.

How are commercial disputes settled between Mexican and foreign companies?

Informal arbitration and mediation are the preferred methods for resolving disputes between foreign companies and their Mexican business partners. A lawsuit brought against a business party in Mexico is likely to be lengthy and very costly for the filing company. Mexican law tends to favor the defendant in commercial cases, and there are many ways for a Mexican company to delay the suit at little expense. By contrast, the foreign company often has to hire expensive lawyers with Mexican legal expertise and keep them on the case until the dispute is resolved.

Formal arbitration via "alternative dispute resolution," or ADR, is a relatively new concept in Mexico. Such formal actions will likely be perceived in the same manner as a lawsuit, and the resulting delays can still be costly for a foreign company. There is a formal arbitration procedure for dispute resolution under the provisions of the NAFTA, and a broad commercial dispute resolution system is currently being developed in Mexico by BancoMex, the Mexican foreign trade bank. More information regarding these processes is on the World Wide Web at the Office of the NAFTA's website at

> http://iepnt1.itaiep.doc.gov/nafta/nafta2.htm.

Where can you research Mexico's investment laws?

Good summaries of Mexican investment laws are available on SimPex, the website operated by BancoMex, at *http://mexico.businessline.gob.mx*. Detailed descriptions of many aspects of Mexican investment law are also available via the Office of the NAFTA at the site listed above. Another good source is the Mexico Business and Trade Forum on Compuserve.

Many international law and accounting firms publish general summaries of Mexico's investment laws. We would recommend Baker and McKenzie (law) and Price Waterhouse (accounting). Often these publications are available at the business libraries of major universities.

An excellent source of regular updates on Mexican investment and commercial law is the National Law Center for Inter-American Free Trade in Tucson, Arizona. The Center is a non-profit research organization that conducts studies of the legal framework for Mexico and the NAFTA region. It also publishes *Novades,* a monthly newsletter that provides breaking news on Mexican commercial and investment laws and the Center's activities.

You can contact the National Law Center for Inter-American Free Trade at:

111 S. Church Ave., Suite 200
Tucson, AZ 85701-1602
Tel: 1-520-622-1200
Fax: 1-520-622-0957
E-mail: natlaw@natlaw.com

The Center's website provides a menu of its publications, back issues of the newsletter and a set of links to NAFTA-related sites on the Internet. The website is available at:

http://www.natlaw.com

What do Mexican business contracts look like?

Traditionally Mexican business contracts have been short and lacked many business details. This reflected a business culture that emphasized personal relationships and trust over suspicion. Now they have become more complicated and detailed, particularly those with foreign business entities. However, they retain several basic differences from those typically signed in the United States.

The major characteristics of business contracts in Mexico are summarized below.

1. The Mexican law of contracts is contained principally either in the Civil Code for the Mexican location where it is entered into, or where one of the parties is located (e.g. Michoacan), whichever law the parties choose in negotiations.

The U.S. party usually wants U.S. (e.g., CA state law) to apply; the Mexican party generally wants the Federal District code, to which all the other Civil Codes of the Mexican states are similar.

2. Mexican lawyers still prefer short contracts. American lawyers tend to like long and detailed documents. This is likely to become an early matter for negotiation.

3. Some Mexican contracts have very special rules. For example, any land transaction (mortgages, etc.) must be executed before a Notary Public who in Mexico is a lawyer with advanced training, not a certified secretary as in the United States. Other Mexican contracts may require special provisions (e.g., an option, which requires a time limit and/or a pledge. The pledgee cannot hold the pledge; it must be held by a third party.)

4. The provisions of the Civil Code are supplemented by the Commercial Code. There are special commercial provisions for contracts on mortgages covering land as well as personal property (e.g., working capital loans), plus a notary.

5. Some common American (U.S.) contract provisions are non-enforceable in Mexico (for example, a promise to vote stock in a particular direction).

In practice the foreigner, who often has the bargaining power by bringing investment capital to Mexico, will impose a draft contract on the Mexican partner. Even when the contract needs a special Mexican form, it may include detailed American clauses to satisfy U.S. law.

ORGANIZING FOR VENTURE START-UP:
STEP-BY-STEP

Like other countries in the emerging market world, Mexico has realized that its bureaucracy is its own worst enemy in its bid to attract foreign investment. It was once said that 25 separate offices needed to be visited just to register a new business in the country, but now the process has fortunately been streamlined. However, the logistics of getting your business from the point of feasibility study to storefront will still require much jumping through hoops and dodging of potholes. In this chapter, you'll learn the nuts and bolts of starting a business in Mexico, from registration to incorporation to regulatory compliance. We talk about the different options for forming a corporation or starting a joint venture in Mexico, and provide general contact information for the necessary Mexican government offices that will (hopefully) usher you through the process. We also discuss the different routes you will take if you are starting a standard Mexican company or a maquiladora that will concentrate on manufacturing for export.

What sort of licenses and permits are needed to open a business in Mexico?

The first step to starting a business in Mexico is to register with the National Registry of Foreign Investment (see page 171). In addition, any entity conducting commercial activity in

Mexico must register with the National Commercial Registry, which is maintained by SECOFI.

Typically a foreign company will prefer to start a new Mexican corporation as its vehicle for entering the Mexican marketplace. This will expedite government approval (where necessary) for the business. It also limits the foreign company's exposure by not assuming the potential tax liabilities of an existing corporation. A corporation (S.A. or S.A. de C.V.) is typically preferred to a limited partnership or general partnership.

A quick note on acronyms. Mexican company names are typically followed by the suffix S.A. or S.A. de C.V.

➤ S.A. *Sociedad Anónima*. Equivalent to "incorporated." Often used as a suffix for a company's name. Typically S.A. is used by companies that sell shares of stock, i.e. corporations.

➤ S.A. de C.V. *Sociedad Anónima de Capital Variable*. A suffix similar to S.A. Applied to very large companies.

Foreign companies must acquire permission from the Ministry of Foreign Affairs *(Secretaría de Relaciones Exteriores)*; the address is noted on page 179. In addition, as noted above, some forms of investment ventures may require the approval of the Foreign Investment Commission (FIC). Establishing a Mexican subsidiary corporation is routine in most cases, and should take two to four weeks if no approval is required by the FIC.

Major corporations are likely to hire an attorney or consultant familiar with Mexican business practices to start their business entity. For small businesses, the fastest way to navigate this process is to order the publication "NAFTA Investment," which is available free of charge from the Office of the U.S. Trade Representative.

Office of the U.S. Trade Representative
600 17th Street NW
Washington, D.C. 20506
Tel: 1-202-395-3204

After receiving this useful guidebook, contact the Trade Information Center at the U.S. Department of Commerce at 1-800-USA-TRADE for information regarding the specific type of business you want to start in Mexico.

Further support can be obtained from these key Mexican agencies:

Secretaría de Comercio y Fomento Industrial (SECOFI)
Calle Alfonso Reyes No. 30
Col. Condesa
06140 México, DF, México
Tel: (52) (5) 211-0036, 286-1757, 286-1823, 286-1461
Fax: (52) (5) 224-3000, 286-0804, 286-1551, 286-1543

Secretaría de Relaciones Exteriores (SRE)
Secretariat of Foreign Affairs
Ricardo Flores Magón No. 1, Piso 19
Col. Juárez
06696 México, DF
Tel: (52) (5) 277-5470, 782-3312, 782-3660, 782-4144
Fax: (52) (5) 254-5549, 254-7285, 782-3511

Can a foreigner open a solely owned business?

A foreign company can operate a solely owned business in Mexico in a wide range of industrial, commercial and service sectors. A few sectors that permit 100 percent foreign ownership were described in Chapter 14. Under the provisions of the NAFTA, a few additional sectors will be opened for foreign ownership over the next several years. The fastest way to confirm that your planned business can operate in Mexico under your sole ownership is to contact the Commercial Service at the U.S. Embassy in Mexico. Its telephone number is (52) (5) 211-0042, or send an e-mail via its website at

http://uscommerce.org.mx.

What issues need to be considered in deciding where to locate a factory in Mexico?

Site selection managers weighing alternative investment locations in Mexico need to consider issues of cost, labor avail-

ability, access to transporation and supporting infrastructure. Often the first question to be addressed is whether to locate a factory at the U.S.-Mexican border or within the Mexican interior. Each option offers its own advantages. Border sites provide easy access to the U.S. consumer market, including a strong local market composed of distribution outlets and shoppers from both sides of the border. Access to U.S. transporation infrastructure in the form of roads, trains and ports may reduce shipping costs. Also, border plants may allow selected managers to live on the U.S. side of the border.

Sites in the Mexican interior offer lower labor costs, and, in some cases, limited tax incentives for foreign investments. Certain interior regions also offer access to clusters of supplier firms in key industries, including automobiles, electronics and garment production. Interior locations will experience lower rates of labor turnover because the working population is much less transitory. Businesses seeking to target Mexico's expanding consumer class should consider investment locations in the suburbs that surround such major metropolitan areas as Mexico City, Monterrey, and Guadalajara.

When is a border maquiladora best?

Weighing the option of a maquiladora pits the percentage of your sales that are going into the United States against the transportation costs of getting the product there. Recall that under revisions to the maquiladora law, maquiladoras can be established in the Mexican interior, as long as duties are paid on the inputs used for products to be sold in Mexico. But until the export requirements are completely phased out under NAFTA, most maquiladoras will continue to be located at the border to minimize transportation costs.

A hidden advantage to border maquiladoras is their proximity to vibrant U.S. border communities such as San Diego, Sonora, AZ, and El Paso and Brownsville, TX. These cities offer strong local consumer markets for products, as well as residential real estate for managers and supporting business services.

Part of the maquila program rests in a set of incentives called *Programa de Impotación Temporal para Producir Artículos de Exportación, or PITEX*. The typical maquila is an American firm that establishes a company which will export 100 percent of its production back to the States. But Mexico also offers a strong market for many products. In Mexico City alone, you have 20 million people. Many foreign firms with maquiladora operations don't pay attention to the fact that they could grow the maquila into a company that could sell into the Mexican market and also export to other Latin American markets. With PITEX, maquiladoras can sell up to 30 percent of their production locally, or export via a port different from the port of entry. Again, duties apply to the import of materials for the non-export production only. The situation is even better in the case of strategic industries. If you are setting up in Mexico to build auto parts, for example, you can expect to pay no duties at all on imports of materials. Strategic industries are those for which Mexican imports are heavy, including production machinery and some consumer products like toys and bicycles. But you must go and find out to realize these benefits. In addition, one can use the company in Mexico to import from other regions, such as South America, to enjoy additional benefits.

What entities will be involved in the approval and operations of a foreign project?

As noted above, the major entity involved in approving major foreign projects in Mexico is the Foreign Investment Commission. Foreign investors should understand that, while the FIC is administered by SECOFI, it is a consortium of a number of cabinet-level agencies, each of which may have specific concerns or authority depending on the investment project. The advantage of the FIC is that it provides a central clearinghouse for airing these issues, rather than forcing a foreign company to deal with a number of different entities.

Companies wishing to start a maquiladora in Mexico will be subject to a slightly different path in getting their project

approved. As with any company, the entity must first be approved by the Secretariat of Foreign Relations (SRE). Because SECOFI takes primary responsibility for overseeing the maquiladora program and approving new maquilas, a new maquila must register with its National Foreign Investment Registry. Maquiladoras are subject to closer scrutiny from the Secretariat of Social Development (SEDESOL) regarding environmental compliance. The Secretariat of Labor will oversee the facility's labor relations. In addition, the maquiladora will likely have extensive relationships with Mexican Customs and its parent agency, the Secretariat of Finance and Public Credit, as it develops systems for quickly moving its inputs and final products in and out of the country. Note that rather than dealing with the main federal offices of each of these agencies in Mexico City, the maquiladora management will likely work with local or regional offices that have been established at strategic locations throughout Mexico to support this program.

What are the regulatory steps in getting a project approved in Mexico?

Foreign projects in Mexico are typically approved prior to the incorporation of a Mexican company.

Most foreign projects in Mexico are subject to approval via SECOFI without having to pass the muster of the Foreign Investment Commission. Under Mexican investment law dating from 1989, a foreign investment project in Mexico that is valued at less than U.S. $100 million will be approved without formal review by the FIC if it meets the following criteria:

➤ The foreign company is investing paid-in capital from abroad equal to at least 20 percent of the total fixed assets of the investment at the beginning of operations.

➤ The investment project is located outside of the main commercial areas of Mexico City, Monterrey, and Guadalajara.

➤ The investment complies with relevant laws regarding environmental regulations and technology transfer.

➤ The project creates new Mexican jobs and has a plan for worker training.

➤ During the first three years of the project, the net influx of foreign capital will equal or exceed the flow of capital out of the country.

If the proposed project does not meet one of these requirements, the company (and its partner(s), if applicable) will need to prepare a formal application for submission to the Foreign Investment Commission. SECOFI's Directorate General of Foreign Trade Services can assist with this process. If the project is approved, the company will then need to register with the National Foreign Investment Registry.

Chapter 17

ᐁ

FINDING THE PERFECT PARTNER:
THE IMPORTANCE OF THE RELATIONSHIP

Before the passage of NAFTA the foreign business person/ owner was often required to have a Mexican co-owner. With the implementation of the free-trade agreement this requirement has been dropped for many industrial and commercial sectors, encouraging foreign businesses to go it alone. However, foreign companies need to understand the potential benefits of bringing in a Mexico partner, as well as the attendant costs. In a business culture that strongly esteems close, personal connections and familial ties, business partnerships with Mexican firms can be a key to success for many foreign companies. In addition, foreign firms must know how to find the right partner in this corporate landscape. In this chapter we review the advantages of partnering with Mexican firms and make recommendations for finding and qualifying potential corporate partners. The chapter also discusses how small steps and personal gestures can help to build a long-term, trust-based business relationship in Mexico.

Do I need, or should I have, a Mexican business partner?

With the passage of the NAFTA, some experts now argue that it is less important to partner with a Mexican firm when investing in Mexico. The NAFTA has served to make investment processes more transparent and has streamlined the

process for starting and operating a business. An entrepreneurial American starting a small restaurant, real estate service firm, art gallery, or any other small business, can feel particularly confident in beginning a business in Mexico without having a Mexican partner.

However, for larger enterprises and investments serious consideration of the merits of a Mexican partner is still warranted. Despite the transparency of Mexican regulations, many major sectors in Mexico are dominated by a network of firms with long-standing ties to the Mexican government and the ruling PRI party. It is not wise for an American company to charge into the Mexican business landscape without understanding the complex relationships that exist between the major "Grupos" and the ruling families that control them. Here a Mexican partner is critical to help you navigate the business terrain in Mexico City, Monterrey, Guadalajara and other major business centers.

How do you find an appropriate business partner?

Methods for finding a business partner will depend on the type of business you want to operate in Mexico. For companies with clear-cut business plans, listings of Mexican companies seeking foreign investment partners are readily accessible via the Internet. The SIMPEX site operated by BancoMex contains a thorough directory of Mexican companies seeking foreign partnerships, including descriptions of specific business projects and the amount of required investment capital. SIMPEX can be reached on the World Wide Web at

http://mexico.businessline.gob.mx

Companies can also find potential business partners by working with the U.S. Commercial Service in Mexico City. For a small fee the Commercial Service will task its market research analysts to seek Mexican investment projects or Mexican companies that relate to your business interests.

The American Chamber of Commerce in Mexico is a third source. This is a particularly appropriate option for companies that are committed to Mexico but who are still exploring

potential business ideas. For other companies that are still weighing the option of involvement in Mexico a good first step is to contact the closest Mexican government consulate in the United States.

Larger companies with more extensive market research and strategic planning budgets can tap into the wealth of international consultants and multinational law and accounting firms that are happy to play matchmaker for a stiff hourly billing rate. U.S. companies should be very exacting and demanding when working with multinational business service firms; many experienced Mexico hands argue that these firms often do not possess the strong internal Mexican networks that one could access through a Mexican law firm.

How can you conduct due diligence on a prospective partner before tying the knot?

Snapshot approaches to due diligence are not possible in Mexico. The country lacks a commercial credit market, and quick background checks on a company are not possible. For a small fee the U.S. Commercial Service in Mexico City will run one on a potential Mexican partner. This effort is probably worth the minimal investment. More broadly speaking, a foreign company should investigate the family, business, and political ties of a potential business partner before launching a major cooperative project. Mexican law firms, as well as asking around through major trade and industry associations, are other good options for conducting this process.

How can a foreigner best build (and maintain) trust-based relations with a Mexican counterpart?

Socialize, socialize, socialize. Mexicans do business with their friends—it's that simple. It is important that you create opportunities where you are forced to place trust in your partners. Similarly, let them know whenever you are required to "bend" the rules as a token of your friendship. To solidify your business relationships consider giving small gifts or inviting your associates to a dinner or reception. And absolutely

accept an invitation to someone's home. Make sure you review Section V for more detailed comments on these issues.

More specifically, you should socialize at the same social or business level. For example, if you're an entrepreneur or small business owner, socialize with other entrepreneurs and the owners of small businesses, including your suppliers and customers. Don't worry if you're not being invited to elite gatherings. If you are part of a larger company, socialize with your equivalents—CEO to CEO, executive to executive, and staff to staff.

To make a strong impression quickly at the beginning of the relationship, display extraordinary etiquette in your relations with your business partners. For example:

➤ Use ultrapolite language in your conversations.

➤ Respect formality (use *"usted"* rather than *"tu"*).

➤ Take every opportunity to enhance the informal relationship.

➤ Personalize gifts whenever you can.

➤ Wait for client to hang up phone first.

➤ When acting as a host, take an active role and pay constant attention to your guests' needs.

Over time any foreign company that invests in Mexico will be expected to make larger contributions to the community. Efforts to improve community well-being will help to solidify relationships with your business partners, as well as with government representatives, labor groups, suppliers and customers. Participate in community fundraisers and festivals. If you are a resident expatriate manager you must develop relationships with the community, not just with the individuals you deal with on a day-to-day basis.

One last simple warning. While 90 percent of the population is Catholic, many elites, at some point or another, will also consult shamans to gain insight into the mystical unknown, and especially as a way to choose a course of action in busi-

ness. Raul Salinas hired them. And recently fired Attorney General Lozano consulted a diviner. Be warned that before signing a contract your Mexican partner may venture to the Mexico City suburb of Ixtapalopa to consult a mystic about your venture.

THE PEOPLE FACTOR:
TIPS FOR MANAGING
IN MEXICO

In contrast to the corporate culture of *El Norte,* the Mexican work-place puts absolute priority on the value of human relations. Managing workers in Mexico is about helping people, publicly esteeming them when they succeed and privately cautioning them when they need to make improvements. The manager must also make sure that each person feels like a part of the greater whole. With this in mind, it isn't surprising that the Americans to whom we spoke about running a business in Mexico were unanimous in feeling that learning to find good people and building strong relationships were the primary challenges faced by managers. The purpose of this chapter is to answer some essential questions about managing Mexican employees. We also intend to blast some intransigent myths concerning the productivity of the Mexican worker. This chapter briefly reviews the labor market in Mexico and estimates the costs and skill levels of available employees. It then turns to the core question of managing on the shop floor, including building teamwork and retraining workers to take on new or expanded tasks.

What effect has economic reform had on the typical Mexican worker, and working conditions?

While overall economic reform has expanded opportunities in Mexico, the crisis of late 1994-1995 had substantial effects

on Mexican households. Many have still not recovered their purchasing power of the early 1990s. Mexican wages have not come close to keeping pace with the rate of inflation between 1995 and 1997. On the other hand, the decline in wages has only enhanced Mexico's competitive position as an export platform vis-a-vis the economies of East and Southeast Asia. But basic working conditions in Mexico have been relatively unaffected by the recent economic crisis. Real threats to Mexican workers lie not on the factory floor but in living conditions in neighborhoods surrounding many Mexican factories.

How productive is the Mexican worker?

Mexico's strength is in a competitively priced workforce and rising manufacturing output. Its labor force is basically one-third semi-skilled or skilled and two-thirds unskilled. As manufacturing output has risen, demand for skilled and semi-skilled labor has risen accordingly. However, Mexico has been adding workers to its workforce because of a demographic bulge in the population, which continues its labor surplus.

Individual worker productivity varies widely throughout Mexico. In key industrial clusters the country has developed a level of labor productivity that compares favorably with many industrialized countries. However, significant segments of the economy are comprised of inefficient workers laboring in subsidized industries. Recently the Mexican government has been active in raising the level of productivity of the Mexican workforce. In addition to government-sponsored training and reinvestment programs, it has taken a unique approach to managing labor productivity. Under Mexican law, strikes must be approved by the government. Through a close informal relationship between Federal Labor Arbitration and Conciliation Board (JFCA) and labor unions dominated by the PRI, the government sets and evaluates productivity goals in manufacturing operations that are subject to strike threats. As long as these goals are achieved, strikes are not likely to be authorized by the JFCA. In addition, the government is also encouraging firms to negotiate

contracts with labor unions based on the achievement of productivity targets.

Are Mexicans willing to work for a foreign business?

Yes, if you pay them what they're worth and offer opportunities for advancement and upgrading their skills. This is particularly true for managers and engineers. Companies should develop aggressive recruitment plans that include private insurance benefits, opportunities for travel abroad, and continuing education programs in the United States.

In many border communities, Mexican workers are at a premium due to the influx of maquiladora operations. In cities such as Tijuana there is essentially no unemployment, and companies often provide supplemental incentives to attract the best employees. Many Mexican workers will look at secondary working conditions when choosing an employer: the availability of a cafeteria, recreational facilities, and the plant's proximity to their neighborhood.

What will you have to pay Mexican workers?

Compensation packages tend to run around 40% of U.S. equivalents in technical fields, with the possibility of a maximum year-end bonus of 25% of the annual salary. These numbers may be higher in Mexico City and in border cities where Mexican managers are at a premium.

Do not disrupt your compensation scheme unnecessarily. Discourage your U.S.-based employees from bring up the topic of compensation. Resentment may ensue because of the inevitable disparity. However, the disparity may not be as great as it appears at first glance, because of the lower cost of living in Mexico and the higher level of government benefits.

Private benefits of any kind are not common, so whatever you offer in terms of private health care, especially for families, will be cherished. Note some American health insurance plans now offer cross-border products that would allow your employees to seek health care on either side of the border.

Can skilled workers and managers be easily recruited?
Can you advertise for workers, and where?

Skilled workers and managers must be recruited from other companies, often from other foreign operations, or directly from colleges and technical schools. Try interfacing with the alumni associations of major Mexican universities to find unusually qualified employees. A good source of manager employees is the chemical engineering schools, which have traditionally been a breeding ground for top Mexican managers across all sectors of industry. For technical managers, try the top city of Monterrey.

You can advertise employment opportunities in Mexican newspapers, but few workers use this route to find employment. Most job opportunities for managers and executives come from referrals using personal networks of co-workers, families and friends. If you want to advertise, consider placing an ad in an English-language newspaper. Many young Mexican professionals read these papers regularly and may respond to attractive opportunities.

For recruiting front-line workers for a manufacturing operation, you will work directly with a labor confederation or labor union. Membership in unions varies widely in different parts of Mexico; however, many workers are enjoined by informal labor confederations. During the site selection process foreign companies should use their contacts with Mexican trade and industry associations to identify appropriate labor leaders for meetings and preliminary discussions. In fact, the American Chamber of Commerce in Mexico has a labor relations committee that can assist U.S. firms seeking workers for the first time.

Note that resumes can be far more detailed in Mexico than in the United States. Often they will include personal information that would be unexpected or illegal in the U.S. Unusual characteristics often noted on Mexican resumes include: religion, civil status (married, etc.), age, sex, height, weight, citizenship, names of father and mother, occupation, elementary school attended and detailed references. Even mid-career professionals can have resumes that run 5-6 pages.

What worker rights—including minimum wage—are guaranteed by Mexico's labor laws? Are Mexican workers unionized, and are they strike-prone?

The Mexican minimum wage is a hotly debated topic. Unlike the United States, where a relatively small percentage of the population earns the minimum wage, estimates are that between 20 and 50 percent of Mexicans are at that salary level. In reality, there are a series of minimum wages set up for different parts of the country and different industries. The minimum has been raised repeatedly in the 1990s, but it has not come close to keeping pace with increases in the inflation rate.

As noted previously, unionization in Mexico varies in different parts of the country. About 80 percent of all Mexican union workers belong to one of nine major unions that operate throughout the country. The balance are typically members of a single firm union. The largest union in Mexico is the powerful *Confederación de Trabajadores Mexicanos (CTM)*, the Confederation of Mexican Workers, which is closely tied to the PRI and has approximately 6 million members. Strikes in Mexico are rare, although unions will often file their intention to strike with the JFCA as part of an increasingly open process of collective bargaining. The Mexican government is closely involved in all aspects of labor relations, so rarely do they deteriorate seriously without the involvement of the Secretariat of Labor.

THE ART OF MANAGING PEOPLE IN MEXICO

What are the key areas of difference in managerial style between American and Mexican firms?

Mexicans are still used to a traditional top-down approach to management. While this is changing in some more progressive companies, most Mexican firms are rooted in a culture of rigid hierarchies and clearly defined responsibilities. Foreign companies trying to implement contemporary American man-

agement models that stress teamwork and quality circles may find fierce resistance from local employees.

A key issue for success in managing in Mexico is flexibility. Recognizing cultural norms, particularly the importance of holidays and festivals, is essential. Flexibility and cultural sensitivity should be rooted in the specific local customs and norms of your manufacturing site. Be ready to accept a local holiday even if it is not observed in Mexico City.

Many Mexican companies take a more embracing or paternalistic approach in their relations with their employees. This often means providing services that are not traditionally considered the responsibility of employers in the United States. For example, many Mexican employees will expect the company to provide transportation to the work site. This is often accomplished by subcontracting privately owned buses to travel through the neighborhoods of the employees and gather the workers each morning. Many firms provide cafeterias and feed their employees lunch each day. These provisions are particularly important at the U.S.-Mexico border, where the influx of workers has far exceeded the capacity of the supporting infrastructure. Private companies must provide transportation for their employees because public transportation systems are inadequate or nonexistent.

When managing people in Mexico, what approach should be used?

Managing Mexicans requires flexibility, patience and cultural sensitivity. Below we have listed more specific suggestions in the several areas of management:

A. TEAMWORK

Teamwork is still a foreign concept in Mexico. For management success, there must be a clear "carrot" or set of incentives for the individual.

However, here are a few tips for American managers to successfully build and manage teams in a cooperative U.S.-Mexican business venture.

Make your American team members learn Spanish. It is likely your Mexican team members will speak some English. Asking the Americans to learn rudimentary Spanish helps to bring the team members to the table with equal status.

Make frequent contact with Mexican team members. This builds the relationship, particularly those between the team members and their superior, such as the team leader. Requests by Mexican team members for more contact does not imply a need for greater supervision, but rather is due to their desire to deepen the relationship.

Prepare to be treated with unusual respect and authority. Mexican team members will likely extend to you the same respect they grant to superiors and elders in Mexico. Be prepared to accept deference, even if it makes you uncomfortable at first.

Define team members' roles clearly. Avoid the emphasis on cross-disciplinary collaboration and shared responsibility that dominates much of contemporary management theory in the United States. Spend time defining each member's role and responsibilities; then create processes that encourage collaboration.

Design follow-up and documentation processes. Be very explicit about what processes need to be documented, and the when, where and how of the documentation. Don't assume such procedures should be obvious. Use documentation and follow-up tasks by managers as a way to encourage more personal contact with team members.

Create team-oriented leisure activities. Let team members socialize between and after work hours. Remember, Mexicans work to live, they don't live to work.

B. Generating Self-Discipline and Responsibility

One way to create self-discipline is to structure tasks so that employees continually experience increasing successes. This is not babying your employees, it is introducing them to a foreign business culture.

1. Explain one-on-one to the person what the work is and why it is important.

2. Ask for input from the person.

3. Tell other people publicly you are glad that the person is going to do "X."

4. Create benchmarks designed to steer the employee, not to demean or police anyone's behavior.

5. Acknowledge success immediately and publicly.

6. Assign something harder and give an excuse for being unable to watch so closely.

Acknowledge past successes, repeat the process, and be sure to say "I specifically chose you because . . . ." You can find ways to elevate the individual as part of your one-to-one management efforts.

C. RAISING MORALE

Set team goals and recognize completion with an event (perhaps a party). Make small improvements to the working conditions, even if they seem insignificant. (Get Mexican management approval beforehand if necessary.) For example, implement a Friday casual day (very unusual in Mexico). Employees will still be bragging to their friends four months later about their "progressive workplace."

D. PUNCTUALITY

Many experts on managing in Mexico suggest you pick other battles if your employees are accomplishing the work. If not, the problem must be addressed. Start by scheduling important events, meetings, etc. early in the morning or just after lunch. One effective way, legal in Mexico, but nasty, is to make an example out of someone and dismiss him or her. However, there are so many other ways to increase productivity that we recommend not trying to alter strong cultural perceptions such as time. Extreme abuse is rare, and that can be dealt with directly.

E. PROJECT ORGANIZATION

Successful project managers in Mexico must create clearly defined roles and responsibilities; you also need rewards and

consequences. Mexican employees are very used to top-down authority, so if authority overlaps, you must define both who will be in charge of resolving the dispute and the guidelines for its resolution.

F. Meeting Deadlines

Mexican employees generally seem to understand the necessity of deadlines. In the first case of an employee failing to meet one, explain its importance and the consequences, and then threaten with mild shame. ("WE really don't want to me the ones to hold up this project, do we?" "People will not look good on us if we do." "I'd rather try to get it in early and . . .")

G. Retraining People

This can be sticky and is, even in the language, *estar* ("to be" origin, occupation, i.e. more permanent). One's occupation is considered part of one's very nature. In the United States persons may legitimately declare a different occupation on their IRS forms for eight years running. By contrast, Mexicans rarely change. Retooling even an educated person still carries some of this stigma, so managers are advised to proceed with caution. Be sure the person is capable of learning the new position. Also, guarantee for yourself that the person will do the new job once it is learned and not just revert to the old work plan. Again make sure the role and its importance are clear and always train with large quantities of hands-on exercises and simulations.

H. Promoting People

If you find a good worker with vision, do everything you can to keep him or her. Beware of the tendency in foreign manufacturing operations in Mexico to have way too many managers in the enterprise. Recognize and reward great employees, for they are essential and truly outstanding ones are at a premium. Keep them moving in the organization, but expose them to many things so they don't become ingrown in their ideas or concentrated on one area of manufacturing or distribution.

What issues affect women working in Mexico, particularly those serving in managerial positions?

Traditionally Mexico has been an extremely patriarchal, even sexist, society. Today problems of sexism in the workplace vary based on the size of the organization and the level of the work unit within the company. Recent observers have commented that women executives in Mexico are "holding their own" more effectively than in the past, and are subject to less harrassment from their male counterparts. Many contemporary Mexican professional women have struck an effective balance between their feminine persona, which has always been highly valued in Mexican society, and a more gender-neutral role that is equivalent to modern sex relations in the U.S.

Is it a good idea to enlist a local Mexican manager to run the business?

Whether or not a local Mexican manager is tapped to run a local operation, Mexican management must be employed in senior supervisory positions and must be included in major decision-making processes. It is essential for managing employee relations and negotiations with local unions and trade associations. For small-scale manufacturing operations, foreign companies may be comfortable hiring local Mexican managers to run the operation alone. For larger manufacturing ventures, the management team may be comprised of native managers and expatriates working together. This is particularly true when U.S. technology is being transferred to a new Mexican operation. Here the team may consist of a senior American manager, bilingual and with experience managing in Mexico, and two executives, a U.S.-trained technical executive and a native Mexican executive who concentrates on human resources.

Consider large-scale maquiladora operations on the U.S.-Mexican border as a good source of high-quality Mexican managers. Many mid-level executives at these enterprises have extensive experience and technical training from leading Mexican universities. Most do not hail from the border region and are often looking for opportunities for management positions in firms located in other parts of Mexico.

INTERVIEW WITH JAKE LUSTIG
Producer of Fine Mezcal in Oaxaca

Jake Lustig is big, blonde, and speaks Mexican Spanish like a native. Born in 1972 in California, he is the son of a radical-leftist academic father and a chef-entrepreneur mother. When his parents split up early in his life, his father became his primary caretaker.

Jake's father, a founder of the "free speech movement," traveled from campus to campus on yearly contracts without tenure or permanent dwelling place. For Jake, that meant a succession of poor dwellings in low income neighborhoods, often among Hispanics of Mexican descent or citizenship. "There probably are not more than four non-Hispanic names in my address book, aside from business contacts," Jake says.

When he was old enough to travel, Jake shuttled between California and Mexico, where his mother was living. Summers and vacations were spent south of the border and when he was in community college he spent half his time in Mexico. His professors at the University of California were generous with his "field study" credits, as he continued to educate himself in Mexican history and culture by reading the original documents, in the archives, in Spanish. By the time he graduated, "I didn't have any choice. Really, I didn't choose Mexico, it chose me."

Jake spent two years working for a California liquor importer/wholesaler who was interested in contacting Oaxaca mezcal manufacturers for possible export arrangements. During that time he got to know all the significant producers. When his boss decided against buying from small producers in favor of mass production, he and Jake parted company. He then spent a year selling his idea to investors and learning all the export and import laws, tax regulations and customs procedures. Then he came back to Oaxaca to pursue his own vision.

199

The result is that Jake Lustig is the General Director of both the Reunion Mezcal Company Inc. and Compañía de Mezcal Reunión, SA de CV in Oaxaca. The first imports, and the second exports, Don Amado brand Mezcal, a high-quality 80-proof distillation of hand-picked Agave grown in Oaxaca state. Presented in hand-blown glass bottles in small quantities, Don Amado is aimed at the "cognac crowd" of mezcal drinkers.

Each company is a 50/50 joint venture between a Mexican company—in the form of a Mexican entrepreneur who provided the initial investment capital and who is otherwise uninvolved in the day-to-day operations—and an American company which, in turn, is 15 percent owned by providers of services for the venture's startup.

After all the time you spent in Mexico, what could have surprised you?

My biggest surprise was how difficult it is to get folks to generalize: to be able to take the lessons learned from one experience and apply them to another. One problem is that there isn't a period of general study. Mexicans go from Secondaria (our Junior High) to Preparatoria (our High School) to trade school. They call it University, but in fact all training is for a specific postgraduate skill: attorney, teacher, electrician, whatever. So a student of law, for example, is never required to take a course in history or philosophy or psychology, because in a sense the phase we would call undergraduate education is skipped. Added to this problem is that the Mexican schools do not encourage original thinking or analytical thinking. Students are never asked "what did you think of this book?"; they are told what the professor thinks of it, and are expected to learn from that. Further, they are required to memorize a great deal of material and spit it back out when test time comes around. So they never learn to think for themselves.

Would you say it is easier to fail in business in Mexico than the United States, or harder to fail?

It's easier to fail, if you're talking about the rate of failures versus successes. It takes a lot of determination to come down here to start a business. You have to be better prepared, more knowledgeable, more committed. Lots of folks in the U.S. go into business because they find themselves out of work and can't find a job they want. They really don't have a vision for themselves, and aren't prepared. Whether or not they succeed is most often a matter of luck. People who want to come down here face much tougher circumstances: language, customs, food, the very colors people paint their walls, all are different. So they may fail, but probably less from lack of preparation than from plain bad luck.

What strengths did you bring with you when you came to Oaxaca to do business?

I'm young and, or maybe therefore, I am a very adaptable person. That is, I don't have a lot of "shouldn't" or "unacceptable" or "immoral" in my makeup. I think a lot of older folks have too many preconceived notions about how things ought to be. I'm looser than that. That is not to say that I don't demand excellent work of myself and others. I'm just not judgemental about other people's customs and behavior.

Can you give me an example of what you mean?

Sure. For example, I don't mind accompanying some important officials to a sleazy down-and-out cantina full of drunks and bar girls and drinking until four in the morning. In fact, if that is what they want to do, I will do it even more ostentatiously than they do. The idea is to get what I want. If I was uptight about the macho behavior of the

average Mexican male, it would have cost me another hundred thousand dollars to get my operation going. If it was up to me, I might prefer to do away with some of these oppressive and regressive customs, but since it is not up to me I do not make judgments.

Wait a minute. We are talking about corruption here, right? What you are saying is that, unlike back home, official government business is best conducted outside the office.

First, I don't believe for a minute that similar things don't happen at home. Otherwise what are those three-martini lunches about? So I'm not talking about a different set of office morals. I'm talking about a different kind of social morality.

Second, just because you pay someone a bribe doesn't necessarily mean you get to break the law or violate the regulations. It's different here, in that civil servants don't earn enough to feed their families. So they take bribes, but only, for example, to find time for you today rather than next week. Maybe someone you pay will reveal all the regulations to you right away, rather than forcing you through your hoops one visit at a time. No one will turn you down merely because you do not pay. Being polite and patient, the average person won't come right out and say "give me x-amount and I'll help you." He or she will stall, hoping that eventually you will figure it out for yourself. If you haven't figured it out within a reasonable amount of time, you'll probably get it anyway.

I can't emphasize this enough: in a poor country like Mexico, the people you deal with *need* the money. So even when a friend does something for me, I give him money. Not because I need to pay him for his friendship, but because he is my friend and he has provided me with an opportunity to help him and his family. In the U.S., friends are expected to help for free. Not in Mexico.

But some people refuse money, preferring that you owe them a favor. What about that kind of "friendship?"

The other day I got a ticket for a moving violation and went to someone I know very high in the state traffic police. He took the ticket from me and tore it up. No money changed hands. One day I will drop by and bring him a sample of our mezcal. One friendly gesture for another.

So what you are saying is that official relationships are also personal?

Just like in the States. My mother once said "it's a combination of the grace and the grease." The trick is to fine-tune the two, to get the balance right.

If personal relationships are important in official dealings, they must be even more important in dealing with suppliers, service people, and workers.

Absolutely. In fact, there is no aspect of life in Mexico where the personal does not transcend everything else.

How easy was it to adjust to working with Mexican, as opposed to U.S. workers?

I have worked alongside Mexican workers all my working life. I grew up in the restaurant business in California, and that means with Mexican workers. I have also been a manager, supervising mostly Mexican workers. Santa Cruz County, where I live in the United States, is 48% Hispanic. Mexico is my element.

How did you find your workers?

When I was growing up, I visited my mother here often. At that time my current associate was taxi driving, and we became friends. He took me into his home, and I became part of his family. Like every Oaxacan I know who does business, I looked first to my (adopted) family. Nominally,

he works for me, but really he functions as my partner in all other senses. He has my complete trust and he operates as the buck-stopper when I am gone. His wife is my chief bottler. Her assistant is his cousin. His niece is the bookkeeper, his cousin is the receptionist, his brother is the treasurer, our major producer is a cousin, and his mother owns the building where our factory is located. Then there are another twenty-five or so extended family members who get called on now and then for special jobs.

It seems to me you are a special case. You had this extensive network of contacts before you even knew that you wanted to do business in Mexico. What about the person who comes down here not knowing anybody? How does that person find workers?

First of all, you should never do business without a Mexican partner. That doesn't mean an equal partner, but it does mean that the first person to look for is someone who will operate your business with the care he would give his or her own. And of course you want that person to have the capacity to do the work well.

There is only one way to find that person: get to know everyone who is already involved in that industry. Because you don't want to spend a lot of time reinventing the wheel, not when there are already huge families relating to your chosen subject. So what must be done is to come down and start investigating the industry. Everyone in that line of endeavor will know who is the best, and eventually you will meet that person. From then on it is a matter of finding a fit. It may not be with the very best, but it will be with someone useful.

Wait a minute. You are telling me that people who are already in business will willingly help a potential competitor to go into business against them. Why would they do that?

Good question, and it goes to the heart of what I would contend is the difference between people coming from U.S. culture, and people in Mexico. Where the U.S. attitude is very competitive, the Mexican attitude is more cooperative. Where a U.S. businessman might say "good, he doesn't know anything, if I keep him ignorant he will fail and I will not lose market share," the Mexican will say "there is room for everyone, provided they do not give the industry a bad name. Therefore I will help him so that he doesn't really screw up and hurt the industry."

In Mezcal, for example, everyone wants the product itself to have a good name. If I go into business and turn out some bad batches, the reputation of the product suffers, and everyone suffers because of that. This doesn't mean that people don't keep certain proprietary information secret, but it does mean that if someone says "sure, buy that stuff" or "so-and-so is a good workman" you can believe it.

If you don't think this is true, go to any municipal market. You will see stall after stall selling the same stuff, and even on slow days there is little unfriendliness between individual stall holders. And it comes from this idea that "el postre es bastante grande" (the cake is large); there is always room for one more.

In my own case, this principle has been absolutely essential to whatever success I may have had or will have. Finding producers is just one example. My producers are "small," and I found them by being referred from one producer to another. If they had taken the attitude that most U.S. businesses take, they would not have been as helpful because they would have been afraid of "losing business to the competition."

So you are telling me that you would extend the same helping hand to the next newcomer, even though it might mean serious competition?

205

I am telling you that I already have. There is another Yankee in the area who bottles Mezcal, and we share information all the time. We have managed to save each other an enormous amount of money and trouble. It works.

Can you envision a day when the demand for mezcal will grow so large that the small growers will be squeezed out by big growers using mass production methods?

I don't see why it should play out any different than it did with tequila. Tequila is just another name for mezcal, you know. It is a particular type of mezcal, but they both come from the maguey plant. Tequila is a mezcal from the tequila region of Jalisco.

When the government decided to make a project out of tequila, it encouraged large-scale bottling. Large scale bottlers sell a kind of "varietal," a blend of product from a large number of suppliers. Because there is no "extra value" to anonymously produced varietals, the per-liter price is as low as it can get. Because there is so little money in each liter produced, the pressure is on the grower to produce more liters. This means putting more time into the production process, and therefore less time into selecting the raw materials. This means that when sugarcane is considerably cheaper than maguey, you put as much sugar cane in as the regulations allow: 49%.

As it turned out, not every producer was willing to do that. A few continued to make it the old fashioned way because they found that more satisfying. After a while, as more and more scotch and brandy drinkers began to look for a less caloric, lighter liquor, the good tequila started coming into demand. While admittedly small in unit sales, top shelf tequila is now the single fastest-growing segment in the liquor market. As a result, more growers and processors are discovering that there is money in making fewer units of a higher-priced product. The same thing will happen here.

206

Should a firm get involved, and grow with Mexico, or wait until the atmosphere is more "modern?"

That depends on the firm, and how much they are willing to accommodate the culture that exists here. If you wait until Mexico is "safe" for conventional U.S. business attitudes, you could be waiting until your beard is long and grey. On the other hand, if you are not prepared to swim in the stream that is present day Mexico, perhaps you ought to wait awhile. Personally, I think that there is no way to tell anyone else what the answer will be. You can always dip your big toe in the water and see if the temperature seems inviting.

What's the cost of doing business in Mexico, and how much of that cost will be in unexpected expenses?

Don't do business here if you are not prepared for the unexpected. This is, after all, a foreign culture. Why would you expect yourself to anticipate every twist and turn? But I will tell you my expectations: it costs as much to do business in Mexico as it does in the U.S.—if you expect to do business in the same way. That's why business partners and personal contacts are so necessary. Unless you are coming down to run a maquiladora type of plant, where people are just dispensable and interchangeable production cogs, don't be lured by the promises of low-cost, compliant peasant labor.

But isn't labor really cheap here?

Labor is undeniably cheaper in Mexico, but my experience is that good labor costs a premium wage. And benefits are very substantial here, about 35% of salary. Now you can certainly hire workers for an hourly or a piecework wage, and not pay benefits. But the other side of that coin is turnover, which is fine for the maquiladoras, but not for "niche" businesses like mine that rely on consistency and

207

quality to sell the product. It's maybe okay for building a road, but not for hydrating a batch of mezcal, for example. So while it is cheaper than in the States, labor still represents a major expenditure of funds in my business. And in any business that uses "white collar" workers, where benefits and decent wages (by Mexican standards) are expected.

You are located in Oaxaca, which is a relatively isolated place, a long way south of our border. What future do you see for your area of Mexico?

Plans are underway which will make Oaxaca a more prominent industrial center in the near future. There already is a superhighway that connects Oaxaca to Mexico City, cutting the travelling time by half, to 4.5 hours. Construction has already begun on another superhighway connecting Oaxaca to the Pacific Ocean port of Salina Cruz, cutting the time for that trip down to four hours. With a major seaport so close, Oaxaca will definitely move up in the world. Under programs initiated by the last President, three duty-free industrial parks are already located in the central valleys of Oaxaca. These are modern facilities, with technical advisors available to help small startups to grow. A major coffee exporter, a mango cannery, and a large plywood plant are already in place, to name just a few.

How do you quickly locate an appropriate product and supplier in Mexico?

"Quickly" is an illusion. I generally can locate what I need "quickly" because I have done all my homework, hired the right people, made the right contacts and speak the language. I ask my competitors, my "family," and my employees.

How do you ship your product, and why?

Because it is still a little isolated, Oaxaca is a hard place to ship out of—or into, for that matter. We would probably

drive our shipments to Puebla or Mexico City to be shipped, except that we buy some of our supplies in Guadalajara, Jalisco. Presently, we find it more efficient to drive the load to Guadalajara and drop it at a freight forwarder there. They take care of moving it to Tijuana and then across the border. Then we pick up our supplies on the way back home. There is no sane way for us to move an alcohol product across the border by ourselves. The cross-border freight forwarders are absolutely worth the money they charge.

How do you raise the quality and reliability of the product you sell?

Money and leadership. As I said earlier, when it comes to getting employees to think for themselves and analyze things, you are going to be swimming against the tide. So you have to teach them what you want them to learn, and the best way to teach is by demonstrating. Everyone has more respect for someone who can do what they want you to do, as opposed to someone who just comes in and gives orders. People who expect their orders to be instantly obeyed just because they are the boss, either give orders that the workers want to hear, or fail to truly accomplish what they set out to do. I give my workers cash rewards for suggesting better ways to do things. I give them more if the idea gets used. This lets them know that I am serious about the value of their contributions. I work alongside my workers. There isn't anything that I ask them to do that they have not seen me do myself. I go over the books in minute detail, as I do everything else. They all know that I check everything, and that I know everything that goes on. And they know that I do so not because I am trying to catch them or because I do not respect them, but because I am concerned for our enterprise—because I want to make a better living for all of us.

Interview with Susana Trilling

Owner of Seasons of My Heart Cooking School in Oaxaca

Susana Trilling started working in the food business in Philadelphia in her teens; apprenticeship has always been her favorite way of learning, whether about food, business, or people. "I would walk into a restaurant I had heard of," recalls Ms. Trilling, " and whose cuisine I was interested in, and order a meal. If I was truly impressed, I would ask the chef to take me on for a week or two without pay."

By the time Susana was 30, she had two successful New York City restaurants (one which was a renowned Cajun bistro), a catering service serving the wealthy, and offers to develop more restaurants for significant sums of money.

But she decided to sell her interest in the Cajun restaurant, and with a catering service running itself, she took a vacation to Brazil before signing a new restaurant development contract. There, she had a life-changing experience: "I was sitting in this beautiful old church, and suddenly everything seemed very clear to me. I could literally see myself walking the concrete path of New York money and cachet. I could also see myself walking a path through a village."

Two years later, having opened a restaurant in Australia as a watering hole for competitors in the America's Cup yacht race, and sustaining a stint of deep meditation in Thailand, Susana returned briefly to the U.S., and then traveled on to Mexico. She has been in Mexico now for eight years.

At first, she tried farming with her husband, a Dutch expatriate. When she came to Oaxaca, Mexico she knew almost no Spanish. She learned it in the village, little by little, "just like a child learns." The farming was too physically difficult, and she was getting interested in cooking again. She started a pizza stand in the village with a friend.

All through this period, Susana haunted the markets, from the small weekly retail market of San Pablo Etla to the giant wholesale vortex in Oaxaca city's Centro de Abastos, learning and making friends. There were, she discovered, seven

basic *moles* made in the kitchens of Oaxaca. (MO-lay, a sauce, takes its name from the Nahuatl Indian word "moli," meaning mixture or concoction.) She was determined to make them all.

She wrote a major article on her discoveries for *Chili Pepper* magazine and two things happened: she was rediscovered by her old fans, and she started getting requests for modest exports of local peppers. Through friends, she then began to teach classes in International Cuisine to Oaxacan women, borrowing a kitchen and dining room from a friend in the city. Her teaching method mirrored her learning method: she apprenticed them in producing, and then consuming, a meal. Susana's *Seasons of My Heart Cooking School* grew out of that experience.

As word of her prowess spread to the expatriate community, a demand grew for classes in English, emphasizing traditional Oaxacan cooking. At the same time, people "in the business" contacted her and asked if she would be willing to hold "master classes" in Oaxacan cooking, both in Oaxaca and in the U.S. Travel booking agencies began arranging tours based on her classes. She published a small book, *My Search for the Seventh Mole,* which she is now expanding.

Our conversations took place first at the Casa Colonial hotel and later at her home/school, Rancho Aurora, a fieldstone and adobe farmhouse designed and built by her husband, Eric Ulrich. Her kitchen, and the dining room, take up most of the ground floor, with tall windows providing a commanding view of the valley in which they live and work.

What strengths did you bring with you to Mexico, which helped you develop your business?

First, I was willing to learn the language, understanding that unless you speak Spanish you never get below the surface of things, and that not knowing the language traps you in a client/buyer reality. Second, I had a willingness

to deal directly with people, to tell them clearly what I was feeling and seeing. I don't mean that you need to be judgmental, but you know what you expect, and you should say so when you don't get it.

Certainly, joy of learning [is important], but also a desire to teach. Since I know how I want things to be, it is my responsibility to make sure that the people I work with know *how* to produce what I want. It doesn't help them to know *what* it is I want, if they don't know how to make it happen.

Also, I'm adaptable. When I can't have what I want, I look around and see what I can use. I don't give up trying to get what I want, but I build what I can in the meantime. This is especially useful here in Mexico where not only local customs and culture, but a whole national gestalt, are foreign to us Yankees.

And most important are a sense of humor and a lot of patience. Tons of patience.

What would you consider essential for being successful doing business in Mexico?

Business here is very personal. I take the time to establish a personal relationship with each and every one of my suppliers. Your suppliers are as interested in getting to know about you as you are about them. I'm not talking about fiscal stuff here, where before someone will do business with you they have to check your credit rating. I'm talking about getting to know you personally.

Most of my regular suppliers have visited here. It happens like this: I order some peppers, let's say, and the supplier says he will bring them out on Sunday, since that is the only day he can get away. Now I know that Sunday is also the only day he gets to spend with his family, so I say okay, and bring your family. Because that mixing together of family is a real bonding event that raises the level of the concern we have for each other in our business dealings.

Also, I accept the phenomenon known as "Mexican time"—that things are going to take longer than you hope they will, so you might as well plan for delays right from the start. That includes things that happen to me, that on occasion prevent me from delivering on time. The river floods unexpectedly, for instance, and the drive time to town doubles.

With all your experience here, do you harbor any complaints about the way Mexicans operate?

People here do not understand service. I don't mean that there aren't plenty of attentive waiters. I mean that the average person who goes to someone for a product or a service accepts delivery of inferior merchandise or results. And they don't demand better. They just accept it; it's just the way things are.

For instance, I hired a roofer to fix the leaks in our roof. He came out and took a look, and we negotiated a price. I asked him how long his work would be guaranteed. He replied that he gave no guarantee. I asked, but what if it rains the next day and the roof leaks? He said, "well, you will just have to pay me to do it again." Eventually, Eric had to do the work himself.

How much of a problem is corruption and bribery for your business?

Actually, I have never had to pay a bribe. I do pay commissions to people who find me students, but bribes, no. Corruption, on the other hand, is a serious problem, not for me as a business person but for me as a resident. Funds for road improvements and bridge repairs disappearing——that kind of thing.

On a business level it is important to know the laws—and when and how it is okay to go around the law. You must always remember that everything—everything—is nego-

tiable. That doesn't mean that everyone can buy their way out of everything, but it goes back to the fact that [in Mexico], mutual satisfaction is an important part of life.

How do you find workers, and how do you train them?

I hire by word of mouth. Someone who is working for me says "I have a brother/cousin/neighbor who is a good worker. He/she is out of work. Could you talk to him/her?" I interview the person, to get a sense of strengths and weaknesses. If I make a hire, I make it clear that there will be a probationary period during which we will discover if it is a good idea for us to work together. I do this because it is harder to fire people here than it is in the States.

The best workers are often the ones who have gone North to work. Not just to the U.S., but also to places like Monterrey, Saltillo, and Mexico City. There is a different attitude toward work up there, an emphasis on technical training and scheduling. People who return from the North are more disciplined. However, that doesn't mean they are more honest, more personally dependable, or more eager to learn. It's a balance.

In my case, I have been fortunate because I have been able, as an employer and a neighbor and a friend, to make a difference for the better in the lives of a few families.

What is the most difficult aspect of the business to manage?

Quality control. In the food business, particularly when you are out to build a following around a particular taste—a unique vision brought to the table—consistency is essential. You make it very clear that you want the best. Cheapest often doesn't make it. For example, we buy from a pepper supplier who delivers a clean product. No dirt, no sticks, no fillers. We pay a little more, but we know that what we get is ready to use. Second, you need suppliers

214

who are themselves well enough supplied so that you can continue to get what you need when you need it. I'm talking about wholesalers here. Third, you deal as much as you can with the same people.

Would you advise others to invest in Mexico now, or to wait until the economy fully recovers and the political scene is more stable?

I think that if you wait, you will lose your edge. The longer you wait, the more likely that someone else will already be here doing what you want to do. Also, there will probably be more regulations, more taxes. Provided a person is prepared to undergo a different experience than in the U.S., and has the personal characteristics to adapt to Mexico and Mexican ways, I would advise people to get their butts down here and get to work.

On balance, has your experience in Mexico met your expectations?

I came to Mexico to find my spiritual roots. One set of grandparents were Mexican by birth. I went back into business because of a love of food and cooking, and because I needed to contribute financially to our household. In the process, I found a home, a village, a community, and work that is rewarding and profitable.

The previous two interviews were conducted by Stan Gotlieb in Oaxaca.

INTERVIEW WITH DR. MARC ERHLICH
American Psychologist Working in Mexico City

Dr. Marc Ehrlich moved to Mexico City from the United States when his wife asked him if he would like to live in Mexico "tampico," meaning for a short time. That was 16 years ago. Since then, he has run a psychology practice in Mexico City serving both the Mexican and the foreign business communities.

In fact, his extensive work with expats has resulted in a book called *The Challenge of Working and Living in Mexico,* as well as a corporate seminar which he conducts for companies wishing to orient executives and staff for working in the country. The book explores the problems and hurdles of crossing culture and workplace differences from a decidedly psychological perspective, which we feel is an important and helpful approach for anyone preparing to work or live in Mexico. In his seminar, Erhlich uses personality typing to profile what characteristics in people will make it easy or difficult for them to relocate to Mexico. His fundamental thesis is that culture shock is really "personality" shock. By using the profiling system, Erhlich can identity where an individual expat will likely encounter problems both in the Mexican workplace and in his family life. The seminar program—which he runs for groups of 8-10 mostly American couples—became popular and profitable until the market cooled off with the devaluation of the peso in 1994. Since then, Erhlich has concentrated on his practice and on marketing his book, which was published by a local publisher in Mexico City.

What is your background and what type of work are you doing in Mexico?

I am a clinical psychologist who dedicates much professional time to the practice of psychotherapy. I also run team building seminars for companies, both multinational and

national. Helping the foreign executive integrate into the Mexican work environment is one of my specialty areas.

Mexican managerial style is said to be "patriarchal": does this hold true today in your opinion, and what does this mean for the American coming in to form a joint venture and/or co-manage a firm?

It's a definite problem which I found within Mexican organizations which are usually quite top-heavy. Many are also not public-minded. They come out of family-owned business where there is a hierarchy which one has to respect. More important though, I found that at some levels within the Mexican organization the mentality of personal ambition was lacking; the belief that the amount one does and the amount one achieves will result in personal advancement was simply not there. There is the sense that most of these levels are quite stratified, whereas in an American company everybody is more open-minded and entitled to every position.

In the U.S. workers tend to exhibit "loyalty" to their team; in Mexico, to an individual superior. In Mexico, do we continue to see one-person rule, and what implications does this have for the American manager?

When the Mexicans have to, they will feel loyalty to their peer group, and when they have to, they'll feel respect and obedience—though not necessarily loyalty—to an abstract organization. From my experience, the most important thing for the Mexican is what's best for him personally. Maybe with some work and training, there could be the notion of giving over to an organization, but I'm not convinced this is a major part of the Mexican personality, whereas in most Anglos there is a very strong notion of loyalty to group.

What advice do you give to an American manager coming in who has to deal with that type of mentality?

First, that he doesn't try to throw around his credentials. That he doesn't think that technology is going to win over the Mexicans, and they're going to fall on the floor and be grateful for this great white technocrat who is coming in. It's better for him to put away his strategies for operating procedure as written up in the manuals, and wait and see exactly how things are done here. The problem right now with these managers is that they have a lot of pressure from the home office to get results very quickly, which shakes things up and pushes them to the point where they're not taking the time to read between the lines to see where the loyalties are and the connections are. And to see that there are personal benefits in that. Anglo-American managers often come in and feel that Mexicans are going to fall down on their faces and let the system work. Meanwhile, the Mexicans are accustomed to a philosophy that says what really works is what you can get done without going through the system. What they don't want to do is go through that system because it is just filled with bureaucracy and corruption. It is not something that is revered as it is in the States.

Do you find that many American managers and executives in Mexico are uncomfortable in doing business in rather unorthodox ways?

Exactly. Many Americans come to Mexico with a very strong work ethic. But the impetus to follow a policy or system in Mexico just does not exist. In fact, allegiance to the system is seen as somewhat of a stumbling block.

Would the American therefore be much more legalistic?

Absolutely. Over and over again I hear the Americans say, "that's just not the way it's done." And I ask them where

they get that idea from; they say "because we have a manual, we have objectives, and we have procedures, and they do work here." And so rather than question the procedures and the manuals, they begin to criticize the Mexicans for either not being serious enough, or honest enough, or responsible enough. The Mexican, in the face of such things, reacts by closing down.

In your counseling of foreign expats living and working in Mexico, do you find that they experience psychological reactions to this kind of difference in the work environment?

Everybody has psychological reactions. What I emphasize in my book and seminars, is that what we're dealing with is less culture shock but personality shock. For instance, the American comes down to Mexico with a certain type of self-esteem because the system has worked, and the procedures have worked; but in Mexico, he finds that putting into the system is not going to advance him. There's a loss of translation, so to speak. That creates what I see as depression or anxiety, which either might be dealt with through anger or withdrawal. Also, the spouse finds herself emerged in an environment where she—in most cases it's "she"—has less access to her own sense of independence. Especially with the latest crime wave and all the stories about Mexico, a lot of these women are afraid to drive, or don't drive by themselves, or have to be driven by chauffeurs. Rather than seeing that as freeing up of their time, many women see it as a total inactivity. Unfortunately, many of them fall into depression.

Do you mean by "withdrawal" that the foreigner is suddenly socializing with only other foreigners from their own company?

Either that, or not socializing at all. Another thing I am seeing is that the tension is often transferred to the children.

219

The parents get dependent on the children having school problems, and while they talk about all the problems the kids are having, there might be pressure on the marriage. One ends up doing a lot of crisis intervention, without calling it that, but that's actually what it is.

Each one of us comes to Mexico within a developmental stage, and given that particular stage, the threat of living in Mexico is going to affect us differently psychologically, or affect us according to where we are psychologically. So, depending on whether a person is 10, 20, or 30 years old, each expat will respond differently.

Give me the psychological profile of the person a company would want to send to Mexico.

The first thing is that the person wants to come. Second requirement is a sense of adventure. Third is an already learned humility . . . an awareness that the way he or she does things is not the only way, and that what has to change are habits, structure, the way of doing business, of relating to others. At least people have to be open to adding on to their personalities rather than just doing it their own way. Then also they have to learn how to speak Spanish.

Learning the language is absolutely essential?

That's a priority. One of the biggest complaints I heard from the Mexican counterparts is these American guys come to the meeting and expect everybody to speak English. I mean, what's that all about? The Mexican would respond very well to the American who makes the effort to speak Spanish even with mistakes; that's better than just expecting everyone to speak English, which puts many Mexicans at a disadvantage.

INTERVIEW WITH DR. MARC ERHLICH *(cont'd)*

Is it not true, though, that most elite Mexicans with whom Americans deal will speak English?

They could, but you see there's a certain resentment about it. There are some upper-level executives that would look forward to speaking English because they like to show off their skills. But the American has to make the effort to show that one can juggle with Spanish; if the Mexican chooses to speak English, then the meeting can be conducted in English. There's a difference between allowing the person to choose to speak English and insisting that he do so.

Mexicans are stereotyped as not always being obliged to hold to their stated commitments; is this a myth or a discernible reality?

Absolute reality. With the Mexican, a commitment is less a commitment to act than it is with the Anglos, who think a commitment is something agreed to. So for the Mexican to say "I'll be there at 10:30" means that "I'm going to do the best I can to get there at 10:30, but if I get there at 11:30, please understand that life is difficult and that I might not get there anyway." So when people here tell me they'll be somewhere at 10:30, I don't take them seriously. I don't base my day upon what they tell me. I just ask myself, how long am I actually going to wait before I start to do other things, leave, or start badgering him? Anglos come in with this concrete notion that one plus one equals two. Someone tells you to be there at 10:30, you're going to be there at 10:25. There are some Mexicans who are very punctual, so you have to learn to identify them. This perhaps comes from the fact that every government that has come into power in Mexico has issued this wonderful Five-Year Plan, and Mexicans have become somewhat jaded by what is said, and what is actually done.

One hears the phrase, "Somos Mexicanos," we're all Mexicans, but on the other hand, one's class position (and for that matter, skin color) seem critical to a person's chance of success in Mexican society. What's going on here? Is Mexico in reality an extremely stratified and hierarchical culture, or do Mexicans truly see themselves in group terms, as the saying above would indicate?

It's a very stratified society. You can tell this by simply going to a house and witnessing the difference between the maids and the gardener, chauffeur, the plumber, the electrician, and the family members, the neighbors around the corner.

How is one's status assessed in Mexico? For example, by one's family name, company affiliation, school attended, title, etc.?

Education, culture, socio-economic status, access to luxuries, profession and job. You can always find out a person's status by asking what his or her profession is. The bottom rung of society is occupied by the bricklayers and construction workers, and from there you climb all the way up to licenciado, or Phd. It also comes down to where the person lives, the neighborhood, which will give you an idea of the socio-economic category. Family name is important to a very small percentage of the population; there may be a hundred family names that represent "old money," and there are last names that indicate to you "new money." Old money is better than new money.

The Mexican workplace appears to be extraordinarily sexist, both in excluding women from decision making and in the treatment of women as sexual objects. Would you agree with this or have things changed?

The problem of a sexist attitude varies according to the level within the organization. At mid-management and above, women have a considerably easier time being treated as equals. Line workers tend to be more "macho" and, consequently, more inclined to be condescending and sexist. Executive women lately seem to be holding their own and finding it somewhat easier to break the glass barrier. Mexican female executives tend to be more comfortable relying on their femininity while performing their professional duties. The female executives that I have met strike me as being able to find a comfortable balance between being a woman within a patriarchal society and maintaining their professional image.

Dr. Marc Ehrlich can be reached at:

MEHRLICH@iserve.net.mx.

His website URL is:

http://www.netimagemx.com/mexico

LIVING AND
WORKING
IN MEXICO

Chapter 19

V

WORKING (AND RETIRING) IN MEXICO AS AN EXPAT

Perhaps no place on earth is more alluring as a place of retirement for Americans than Mexico. By most estimates, in the neighborhood of 500,000 Americans make their homes in Mexico, with the majority having chosen to retire there. But many of these admit they "failed" at retiring in Mexico, and found themselves so enamored with the available business opportunities that they have started new enterprises late in life, some with astounding success. Many younger expatriates have come to Mexico to live in order to escape the impersonal, fast-paced character of the American workplace. Others have come for the natural beauty and because the cost of living in Mexico is roughly one-third of that in the States. Our intention here is to both excite you with the benefits of working and living in Mexico and also to give you a healthy dose of realism about the potential challenges and hidden drawbacks of relocating there. The chapter covers where people retire in Mexico and what options exist for purchasing retirement real estate. It estimates the costs of retirement and describes both the benefits and hassles that come with life south of the border. It also provides some additional sources of information, including names of real estate agents and opportunities to tour the country's retirement havens prior to making any long-term commitments to Mexico.

What are the advantages of living or retiring in Mexico?

Retiring in Mexico is an increasingly realistic option for many Americans. The main advantages are the country's mild climate and low cost of living. Many American retirees find that after selling a home in the U.S. they can afford a larger home in Mexico, as well as servants and other amenities that would not be possible in the United States.

How many Americans live in Mexico, and where are their enclaves?

An estimated 300,000 American retirees call Mexico home for at least part of the year, and builders anticipate a wave of baby boomers will rapidly expand that number. Part of the trend driving Americans to retire in Mexico is the sheer size of the retirement population in the United States. Over the long-term, the requirements of retiring baby boomers are expected to reshape American concepts of retirement living. Spacious and modern apartments, houses and nursing home beds for 73 million senior citizens will be required by the year 2035. With the number of Americans age 65 and older expected to more than double, the attention of hotel companies, real estate developers and nursing home operators has increasingly turned to providing a sort of "starter home" for the newly retired. It is estimated that by 2030, 20 to 25 percent of the U.S. population will be over 65.

The greatest concentration of retirees is in the central state of Jalisco. The Lake Chapala region near Guadalajara has approximately 15,000 retired Americans, estimated to be the largest population of retirees outside the U.S. Additional pockets of retirees are clustered around resort retirement developments on the Mexican Coast. Major resort areas include Cabo San Lucas in Baja California, Cancun and Cozumel on the Yucatan Peninsula, and Mazatlan, Puerta Vallarta and Acapulco on the Pacific Ocean, often referred to as the "Mexican Riviera."

Is the country safe for an American living and working there?

Safety conditions for American retirees and expatriates are similar to those for short-term business travelers. Certainly one is very safe in coastal resort developments and major American retirement enclaves in Central Mexico. In Mexico City and other major cities, American expatriates face the same situation as Mexican citizens. Typically, upper-middle and upper-class neighborhoods are safe, particularly since Mexican police forces have implemented a variety of "community policing" systems.

Note that while kidnapping is a relatively common crime targeting Mexico's upper classes, kidnapping of expatriates is almost unknown. The high-profile case of a Japanese executive who was kidnapped in Tijuana in 1996 was the first known incident of this kind. It is very unlikely that kidnappers would target American residents living in Mexico, because to do so would be to invite the involvement of American law enforcement.

In what sectors of the economy are Americans working in Mexico?

Americans are working as expatriate salaried employees, freelancers, and entrepreneurs in a wide range of industries and professions in Mexico such as:

Maquiladora manufacturing, particularly in automobiles, auto components, electronics, electronic components, and furniture.

- ➤ Petrochemicals
- ➤ Real estate development
- ➤ Tourism
- ➤ Professional services
- ➤ Food and beverage production

➤ Importing manufacturing equipment

➤ Foreign language instruction

What is the cost of living in Mexico?

Within the major resort developments such as Mazatlan, Cozumel, and Cabo San Lucas, daily living expenses are roughly equivalent to those of similar retirement communities in the United States. Outside of the major resort developments, living costs are about U.S. $18,000 a year (paid at least in part in pesos), including flights home, a maid and a gardener, and membership in a country club.

Living costs for expatriates in attractive communities of Mexico City are significantly higher. To live comfortably there in a gated neighborhood costs about $4,000 per month, everything included. The rent for a three-bedroom apartment in a gated community with a car port or garage runs about $1,500.

What documentation will you need to work and live in the country?

It is relatively simple for most Americans to live on the other side of the border. Most retirees live in Mexico on tourist visas which require you to leave Mexico every six months. A new six-month tourist visa is issued upon your return. You can also obtain a permanent resident designation, although the cost in legal fees may exceed $1,200. Note that you will need to become a permanent resident if you want to start a business after retiring to Mexico.

Potential retirees should also know that Medicare will not cover health care treatment costs outside of the United States. American retirees can purchase into the Mexican state health care system for approximately $270 a year. This program provides care through a designated family doctor and at specific public clinics and hospitals, and also covers all prescriptions.

How does an expat go about renting or purchasing a house in Mexico?

Many of Mexico's best properties can be reviewed and purchased through U.S.-headquartered real estate agencies. The largest U.S. real estate company in Mexico is Century 21, with some 100 offices in 45 cities.

Tel: 1-714-553-2100 (U.S.)
(5) 202-6777 (Mexico)

Another good source for upscale properties is Grupo Situr.

Tel: 1-602-553-0533

Can foreigners purchase residential real estate property in Mexico? What does land cost?

Generally speaking, there are two categories of real estate available in Mexico. One is the resort condo or villa, priced in dollars, which is often part of a larger retirement community development. Such properties offer amenities including golf courses, restaurants, boutiques, cable TV, cleaning services, nursing care, and for coastal developments, a marina. In recent years, thousands of such units have been built in new resorts on both the Atlantic and Pacific coasts. The biggest are in Cabo San Lucas, Puerto Vallarta, Cancun, Cozumel and Mazatlan.

These properties have been encouraged by changes in Mexican law that have permitted foreigners to buy, sell, rent, lease and transfer property in coastal areas. Foreigners are forbidden to buy Mexican land within 50 miles of the ocean, so the Mexican government in 1972 set up the *fideicomisos* system whereby foreigners could lease land close to the ocean for up to 30 years and then build. The system requires the involvement of a fiduciary institution such as a bank, which acts as a go-between to hold the land lease in trust. The costs to maintain these renewable trusts is about U.S. $350 per year. Key to the success of these communities is the ease for Americans to purchase and finance. The major development companies, such as Grupo Situr and Koll International, will arrange bank trusts that are necessary for non-Mexicans to own land on the coast.

Cost of properties in the coastal resort and retirement developments varies widely based on the type of property, location, and services provided. However, typically such units will run between U.S. $50 to $120 a square foot. Real estate in most of the newer resort areas is priced in dollars, not pesos. All financing for such properties will be carried in dollars.

Outside of the major resorts, homes are priced in pesos, not dollars, and there are significant cost savings for retirees. An attractive, three-bedroom house will cost the equivalent of about U.S. $100,000.

Mexican banking regulations prohibit banks from offering a dollar-denominated checking account. As a result, Americans living in Mexico generally keep most of their assets in the U.S. and maintain small peso savings accounts in Mexico.

Almost all American retirees who purchase homes priced in pesos pay cash up front. Mexican mortgages carry an average 25 to 30 percent annual interest rate, and Mexican law precludes American banks from underwriting peso-denominated mortgages.

Experts on the subject of retiring in Mexico recommend that retirees rent for six to eight months before purchasing a home. This allows you to acclimate yourself to the country and test the proposition of permanent retirement outside of the United States. Some retirees prefer to split the difference by purchasing a home in Mexico and a condominium in the United States.

What will you have to pay in income taxes?

Permanent residents of Mexico are subject to Mexican income taxes on their worldwide income, regardless of nationality. The tax rate ranges from three to 35 percent. Residents will be granted a foreign tax credit on taxes paid for their foreign-source income. Non-residents are taxed only on their Mexican-source income. If you are a short-term expatriate, you will not be taxed on a salary paid by a non-resident employer provided you spend 183 or more days

(consecutive or non-consecutive) out of the country. You will be considered a resident once you have established a home in Mexico unless you spend 183 or more days (consecutive or non-consecutive) in another country and claim residence for tax purposes in another country.

Where can you find out more about the details and legalities of taking up residence in Mexico?

Several companies conduct tours of retirement communities in Mexico for U.S. citizens who are considering retirement south of the border. We recommend South of the Border Enterprises, a Petaluma, Calif.-based company that operates eight tours a year for clients who want a guided introduction to Mexico's culture and retirement opportunities. Their phone number is (707) 765-4573.

For more information on taxation and legal details for permanent residents, we recommend requesting the free tax guides available from major accounting firms such as Price Waterhouse or Ernst and Young.

Price Waterhouse maintains offices in several major Mexican cities, including Mexico City, Monterrey, Tijuana and Guadalajara. Its main office is in Mexico City at:

Tel: (52) (5) 722-1700
Fax: (52) (5) 286-6248

You can also request tax guides through its local offices in your own city.

COMMUNICATING AND NEGOTIATING:
WHERE YES MEANS MAYBE AND MAYBE MEANS NO

No one is on completely solid ground in understanding how people in a given country communicate with one another and with foreigners, let alone how "they" negotiate business deals. This is dangerous territory at best. Yet we would be remiss if we didn't share with you who are rooted in cultures north of the border what we have discovered about how the "typical" Mexican might behave when communicating. We think it's even more important to try to predict what to expect when hashing out a business deal. In this chapter we try to cover the essentials of blunder prevention and the most adhered-to rules of negotiating in the country. As part of this conversation we go into some detail regarding the art of being interpreted in Spanish and make the strong recommendation that you learn Spanish as quickly as possible. We hope such information keeps you in good form and well-prepared for the art of the Mexican deal.

Do I need to speak Spanish in order to do business in Mexico?

While most Mexicans conducting business with the U.S. can speak English, the assumption that they should speak English recalls older paternalistic attitudes and can be irritating to Mexicans because its exclusive use communicates a lack of respect. To be perceived as a serious player in the Mexican

market, one should learn to speak Spanish. In the interim, practice with an interpreter and engage the services of a high-quality translation service.

Spanish-language courses are widely available at community colleges and continuing education programs throughout the United States. One can also take crash courses through Berlitz and other regional language schools. A more attractive option for executives committed to developing extensive Spanish capabilities is to combine a vacation in Mexico with study at a high-quality, short-term language school available in many Mexican cities such as Oaxaca or Morelia.

What are the secrets of being interpreted well?

Your interpreter, should you need one, will need to be a true assistant, with professional expertise in the area to be discussed. Many companies offer interpreting services in Mexico but you have to shop around for exactly the right person. The *Mexico City News* is a starting place to find advertisements posted by interpreting and translation companies. A competent company should supply you with an interpreter who will be thoroughly bilingual, dress smart, understand the business you are involved with, and be able to impart to you insights about how the negotiations are progressing after each meeting.

Using an interpreter can be a challenging experience for a businessperson in a strange country for the first time. Key to being translated well is to take personal responsibility for it, rather than simply relying on your interpreter. Here are some simple tips and tricks.

➤ Limit your sentences to seven to 15 words. If you're working from a script, such as a speech or welcoming address, tightly edit your text to conform to this rule.

➤ Be redundant. State the same concept a few ways in the course of your communication. This is especially important for the key points you want to make in your address.

➤ Find and work frequently with a single good interpreter. If you hire a quality interpreter in Mexico City, it will probably be worth your investment to have that person travel with you throughout the country. It is difficult to ask several interpreters to each scale the same learning curve as they master your accent and speech patterns.

➤ Rehearse major presentations. This is particularly important for marketers who have developed complex presentations prior to departing for Mexico. Rehearse, and make sure your interpreter is comfortable with the text and with any audio-visual or multimedia aids to be used as part of the presentation.

➤ Do not speak until your interpreter has finished speaking. During a negotiation, don't interrupt the interpreter, even if you are angry or strongly disagree with what has been said by your potential business partner.

➤ When you are using an interpreter, look at the person you're speaking to, rather than directly at the interpreter.

➤ During serious business negotiations, bring your own interpreter, even if your counterparts volunteer to provide one. Also, consider bringing a Native Spanish speaker to major negotiations even if you are extremely comfortable with your own level of Spanish.

Do Mexicans communicate in ways different from the typical Anglo-American?

Following are some tips for understanding Mexicans when speaking to them directly. They assume you have an interpreter or are reading a translated document, although they are also applicable if you are speaking/reading Spanish.

➤ It takes about 25 percent more words to express the same idea in Spanish as in English. This means that business communications are typically lengthier and more formal.

➤ Because Mexicans esteem relationships, communications tend to be filled with niceties and relationship-building

phrases. Thus introductions, as well as business letters and memos, may start with relatively long personal greetings.

➤ Mexicans customize the relative formality of their language according to the age or status of the person they are addressing.

➤ Mexicans often speak metaphorically and use lots of vernacular sayings, even in the business world. The use of *la picardia*—little jokes, comical anecdotes or funny sayings—and double entendres is common. They are used frequently between men to build trust and add enjoyment to the relationship. These word games tend to disappear when Mexicans have to use English.

Mexican businesspersons occasionally feel that Americans have perfected the art of "all work and no play." In the process, it seems they have lost the art of conversation. It continues to flourish in urban Mexico, however, and as a foreign businessperson in the country, you should keep your conversational blades sharpened.

Another key issue is the art of nonverbal communication. Women greet each other and men with whom they are familiar with a handshake and a peck on the cheek. Hugs are common among friends. Proximity is closer. Eye contact is more direct.

One quick example of a nonverbal communication tool: The pinky touching a tooth and twisted slightly is used to indicate that a person spoken about is *colmillo,* that is, savvy, with all the necessary skill to screw anyone in any deal. *Colmillo* is defined as "fang." The gesture is to screw a finger into a tooth at the side of the mouth.

Emblematic of the fact that Mexico is a who-you-know society, people carry their address books with them at all times. At a social event you won't see people exchanging business cards as often as exchanging phone numbers and jotting them down in their pocket address books; hence, a small leather one crammed with contacts is an essential accessory.

What about making yourself understood when the language being spoken by both sides is English?

All parties must realize that the use of English is a communication tool. It is not an attempt for domination by one culture. Rather it is the deck we are often dealt from, because it is so universally taught.

Neither is English a game. Business meetings are, believe it or not, for communication, not for people to practice or show off their dominance of a language. Indeed, many people consider themselves to be better at English than they really are.

Build confidence wherever possible. The receiver most likely feels alien by listening to English; keep the communication going.

What if both parties are speaking Spanish (without an interpreter)?

The number one hindrance to communication is pronunciation. There are people who have taken an untold number of classes in Spanish who know the language well, yet are not understood because of their pronunciation. The fix for this is to learn (relearn) the alphabet from a native speaker. Unlike English, all the sounds are there (except dipthongs). Remember, to speak a foreign language, you must perceive and make sounds that sound weird to you.

Another related situation is the use of Tex-Mex phraseology. Tex-Mex Spanish *(pocho)* contains many Anglicisms and many words held over from the 16th Century. The reaction by Mexicans to these words is the creation of an image similar to that of the U.S. "country bumpkin" or "bubba" image. Avoid lapsing into the English equivalents of words because they "sound similar."

Also, remember these quick tips:

➤ Include listening checks, but don't insult by constantly saying "do you follow me?"

> ➤ Using a person's name is very important; use it as a way of solicting feedback. Make sure to use it positively wherever possible, never negatively.

> ➤ Minimize use of set jokes; humor is important, but set jokes are often not understood which can be a blow to the confidence of the listener or can be misinterpreted.

What gestures might be offensive to a Mexican person?

Mexicans tend to be much more expressive and expansive in their use of hand gestures than Americans. Be ready for broad sweeping motions and extensive gesticulation. Note that a number of gestures in Mexico carry connotations unknown in the United States. For example, making a circle with the thumb and index finger as a way of saying "o.k." is an extremely offensive gesture in Mexico.

Don't point with your index finger; use your whole hand. When paying for something, place the cash or credit card in the receiver's hands; don't put it on the counter. In Mexico men will cross their legs at the knee, rather than resting one ankle on the other knee and thigh.

How do the Mexicans negotiate—what is their bargaining style—and how should the foreigner respond?

Bargaining and negotiations in a Mexican business setting will be relatively formal. Lay out clearly who will be attending the negotiations, what their positions and titles are, and what the specific issues are to be discussed. Make sure to reach consensus regarding these issues prior to arriving at the initial negotiation session.

A hard-nosed, point-by-point style of negotiating will not succeed in Mexico. Negotiations should seek to achieve the most mutually beneficial agreement possible. It should reflect not only a new commercial relationship but a new social relationship between the parties. Also, an excessively aggressive posture in a negotiation may spark an ugly streak of machis-

mo in your counterparts that could disrupt the session. However, Mexicans will expect to bargain *(regatear)* over some specific points. This process is an interactive experience, an enjoyable give-and-take that is as much a test of social skills as a debate over business details.

Be conscious of differences in business philosophies. Many times U.S. businesspersons expect closure from a discussion or meeting. In Mexico, meetings are often showcases, summits for niceties that may be perceived as conclusions or finalities by U.S. participants. The Mexican participant knows key issues will be decided by higher-ups one on one or unilaterally in any case. Be aware that nice platitudes do not equal a "yes."

Where will negotiations be—in an office, meeting room, or a restaurant?

Negotiations will typically take place at a restaurant, hotel conference room, or other "neutral" territory. Rarely will a Mexican company conduct extensive negotiations at its own place of business. A useful method for balancing the power relationship prior to the start of negotiations is to select a meeting location, and then ask your counterparts to make the actual arrangements. This grants some control without making your potential partners, suppliers or customers your "hosts" for the negotiation session.

Who will be the players in a typical negotiation in Mexico?

Typically lower-level executives will arrive earlier (but not early) to a negotiation session, along with assistants, secretaries, and interpreters. A senior executive with more assistants will arrive later, in order to make an impressive entrance into the negotiation scene. Small talk and pleasant conversation will be conducted for an extended period before the discussion shifts to more substantive matters.

What role do lawyers play in negotiating a deal?

An extensive role for the rule of law, particularly commercial law, is still a relatively new concept in Mexico. It is possible that attorneys may attend negotiating sessions. Certainly for large-scale investment contracts an attorney will be present, and for many business deals an attorney will be reviewing the final contract before it is signed. Nevertheless, most Mexican executives will value the word of their business partners and the strength of their social relationship over the legal clauses of a contract. It is worthwhile to engage a local firm to review major contracts prior to their signing, but American businesspersons should understand that launching legal action for redress under Mexican commercial law will be an extensive and time-consuming undertaking.

Certainly one should feel free to bring an attorney to negotiating sessions, but such a person should be introduced as simply part of your team rather than as an adversary or third-party. Avoid uncomfortable situations in which negotiations are brought to an abrupt halt so that you may "consult with your attorney." Most American executives negotiate with their lawyers at their side. Hence, Mexican executives tend to bring in their lawyers as well when engaging with a foreign firm.

What role does an accountant play in Mexican business?

Accountants act in Mexico to manage companies' complex relationships with the byzantine Mexican federal tax code. Mexico City and other major Mexican cities are home to a variety of high-quality local accounting firms that have affiliate relationships with one of the major multinational accounting companies. In addition, the easing of restrictions on the practice of international business service firms in Mexico has allowed international accounting companies such as Ernst and Young, Price Waterhouse and Arthur Andersen to enter the Mexican market directly. These firms not only provide

direct accounting services for multinational companies, but have also established successful roles as brokers, dealmakers and sources of networking for companies seeking to enter the Mexican market.

How should the foreigner deal with a request for a bribe or illegal commission?

Under the Foreign Anti-Corrupt Practices Act, an American businessperson can be held criminally liable for offering bribes, payoffs or kickbacks to public officials in a foreign country. In addition, you can also be held liable for paying an illegal bribe or commission to a private company that acts as a dealer or broker for a Mexican purchaser. Our advice is to not make that initial payment. Word will spread and you will find yourself frequently being asked for new or additional contributions. The exception to this rule, as noted previously in this book, is small-scale bribery by local customs, law enforcement or immigration officials in more rural areas. In major business environments, the answer should be no.

Having stated this, the fact is that corruption is still part of the Mexican business climate. One advantage of hiring local managers, subcontractors and brokers is that often they will budget these unavoidable "hits" as part of their cost for doing business. If such payments must be made, better that they appear on your books as part of someone's salary or hourly fee rather than as unexplained business expenses. Make it clear to your Mexican employees or subs that you don't approve, and, more important, that you don't want to know about it.

ESSENTIAL ETIQUETTE AND PROTOCOL

Remember the nightmare kids often have of arriving at school having forgotten to wear clothes? Its international business equivalent is the more plausible adult possibility of committing a vile faux pas in the presence of one's foreign hosts. Nobody wants to enter an emerging country with his pants down, and this chapter intends to prevent you from doing so in Mexico. Here we review essential etiquette and protocol when entering into business relationships with Mexicans. The advice is compact but covers the social gamut from business cards to attire to entertaining. We spend some time talking about the ritual of being invited to a Mexican's home, an important step forward in a business relationship. We also discuss the routine and hazards of drinking socially in Mexico, often an awesome challenge for foreign guests. In addition, we discuss the role of gift-giving in Mexican society and make some suggestions for readers who may wish to give a gift to a Mexican and/or his family.

How should a foreigner greet a Mexican business person? Are business cards required?

Greet a Mexican businessperson, male or female, with a firm handshake. If you are familiar with the women you will also receive a kiss on the cheek.

Get your business cards printed with English on one side and Spanish on the other. Ensure proper translation for your title and any signifying initials attached to your name. Titles are important, although remember that there are many "fake" doctors, and relatively few real medical doctors.

TITLES:

    DR.

    LIC.

    ING. (ENGINEER)

    ARQ. (ARCHITECT)

You'll need to check the veracity of titles in Mexico, but be polite about it as many of them are faux titles.

What is appropriate business attire for doing business in Mexico?

Upper-middle-class Mexicans from the major cities will wear formal business attire to most meetings. This extends to early evening social occasions that also have a business function. In hot weather or in more informal settings, men may appear without a tie; however, don't assume Mexican businessmen won't wear one.

Businesspersons from North America should match this custom by wearing formal business attire to meetings. Dark, conservative, masculine clothes are more appropriate for businessmen than flashier, more colorful suits, jackets and ties.

In smaller towns and rural areas business attire is much less formal. A button-down shirt with a sportcoat and no tie is acceptable for businessmen. This should also be the attire of choice if you are going on a site visit to a rural area or are being taken on a visit to a tourist attraction such as a Mayan ruin.

Businesswomen from the United States should also favor conservative clothes complemented by jewelry, makeup and heels.

Perhaps status, and the attention to it, marks Mexican business style as much as anything else. While the typical American

adopts a modest profile, downplays the role of status, and emphasizes the equality of the sides, the Mexican will often turn business into a game of status. Appearance and apparel matter, and so most Mexican business people you deal with will wear suits. They wear Rolexes. Gucci. Brand names are critical.

A Mexican will judge the status of another by jewelry, mastery of English, and by proficiency in French, which is highly valued at the moment both for status and for use as a "private language" among friends. English proficiency remains a top priority among Mexico's urban young people.

How are you expected to entertain Mexican business people?

The most common way to entertain businesspersons in Mexico will be to invite them to a restaurant for the main meal of the day, the *comida,* an extended lunch that occurs between 1:00 and 4:00 P.M. Choose a restaurant recommended by a friend, the concierge, or by your guest. Meals are social occasions so you will not discuss business in any substantive way. Even though you are host, expect your guest to argue vigorously with you over the check. Resist gently but firmly.

Alternatively, host a cocktail party at your hotel for the representatives of the company or companies you are involved with in Mexico. Arrange for plenty of finger foods as well as a full bar, and don't invite your guests' spouses. Such business functions are a single affair.

If you are hosting a delegation of Mexican businesspersons in the United States, we strongly encourage you to invite them to dinner at your home. Schedule the meal around their customs, starting at around 9:00 P.M. (eat a snack in advance of their arrival). Exposure to your family and home is a critical tool for cementing a profitable, long-term relationship with a Mexican business partner.

What are the most important points of dining etiquette in Mexico? And is it appropriate to talk business over a meal?

Certain Mexican foods will be served family-style with several rounds of tortillas to be shared by all parties. Help yourself and dig in.

In smaller towns and rural areas many restaurants, particularly the most popular ones, will not have the time or staff to clean tables exhaustively after each group has left. Don't be concerned if your table retains some residual evidence of previous diners.

Keep in mind that no matter how nice the restaurant, all food comes from the same markets. The ice is not sterilized and the lettuce is not purified just because the restaurant is air-conditioned and the tables have cloth napkins.

It is considered rude to refuse an offered item or dish. On the other hand, it is acceptable to pick at an item. You don't have to clean your plate. If you must refuse something completely, blame it on "doctor's orders." Don't make explicit reference to Mexico and its potential effect on your digestive system.

As noted above, meals are not the place to discuss substantive business. Use this time to learn more about your potential partner. Ask about his family, his family's history, Mexican history, art and literature and other sites that should be visited on a future trip. Avoid discussions of Mexican politics, particularly the rather tortured relationships at the top of the Mexican political hierarchy. Absolutely do not discuss narcotics trafficking and its expanding role in Mexican society. By contrast, expect to be quizzed closely on American views towards Mexico, Mexican immigrants, and specific American laws that target Mexicans and Mexican-Americans, such as California's Proposition 187.

Do the Mexicans drink alcohol as part of business entertaining?

Drinking is a near essential skill for doing business successfully in Mexico. Even if you are not a drinker, being able to build relationships in a drinking setting will help to ensure your Mexican business success. Note that while Mexicans are heavy social drinkers, they disapprove of excessive public

drunkenness. Don't start to drink heavily and then refuse when someone offers to buy you a drink. Drink slowly and pace yourself. Know your limits and don't exceed them while you're with a Mexican business partner.

If you don't drink, apologize at the beginning of the meal or cocktail. Blame your abstinence on your doctor, because medical advice is an acceptable excuse for not indulging.

A few tips and tricks for negotiating booze south of the border:

➤ Beer is available everywhere in Mexico, and may be the beverage of choice for foreign businesspersons who don't wish to match their Mexican counterpart shot for shot. In addition to beer, several imported wines and liquors are available, as well as homegrown Mexican specialties such as *tequila, pulque, Mezcal,* and *Kahlua.*

➤ Mexicans may drink heavily in bars, cantinas and at private parties, but public drunkenness is frowned upon.

➤ Distinguish between *vino* (liquor, such as *tequila*) and *vino de uva* (grape wine). Also, while *vino blanco* technically means "white wine," it is commonly understood to refer to any sort of clear liquor. Order *vino de uva* and then specify *blanco* or *rojo.* Also, be aware that in some parts of Mexico, particularly in Monterrey, men who drink white wine are often perceived as being homosexual.

➤ You may wish to buy alcohol as a present to take to a private party or dinner at a person's home. A small bottle of high-quality tequila or brandy is very appropriate. Look for *Herradura* tequila or *Don Pedro Reserva Especial* brandy. Liquor can be purchased at liquor stores (*licorerías* or *vinos y licores*) and supermarkets.

➤ A well-known ritual among male Mexican society is the *borrachera,* a bout of binge drinking that may last more than one night. Beware of being pulled into a serious *borrachera* if you're not a drinker. The risk of this happening is rather small unless you have developed a long-term, close relationship with a Mexican business partner.

BECOME AN INSTANT EXPERT IN TEQUILA

To master tequila is to be able to express knowledge and appreciation for the national drink of Mexico. Developing a taste for straight tequila, not just margaritas, is a helpful business skill, and one of the more enjoyable continuing education projects you may ever undertake.

To understand tequila, memorize these basic facts:

- Tequila is a type of Mezcal.

- Mezcal is a liquor distilled from maguey, a fruit plant that is a member of the agave family. There are many species of agave. It is not a cactus but a family separate from cacti.

- True tequila is distilled only from Agave tequiliani, also known as Weber's maguey, the blue agave, or Mezcal azul.

- Mezcal is made from a variety of types of maguey plants.

- The center of Mezcal production is Oaxaca. The town of Tequila is the center of tequila production in Mexico.

- The most common brands in Mexico are the same brands you see in U.S. liquor stores, José Cuervo and Sauza.

- Mezcal is typically less lethal than tequila.

- Aged tequila assumes a gold or amber color and is referred to as *anejo* or *reposado*.

Should a foreign visitor bring gifts for a Mexican business partner? Are there taboo gifts?

Gifts should not be offered on a first visit or to a businessperson with whom you do not have a prior relationship. They are used in Mexican culture to cement relationships, not to form them. Note that a relationship means a face-to-face relationship. You are not close friends with a Mexican even if you have spoken on the phone a dozen times. When you have visited Mexico, spent extensive time with the person in and out of the office, met the family—then you may consider it a close business relationship.

If you want to give a gift to a Mexican businessperson with whom you've developed a close relationship, consider small,

high-quality imported items such as cigarettes and cigars, liquor, gold pen-and-pencil sets, and electronic organizers. Avoid giving silver, such as silver jewelry. Silver is abundant in Mexico and silver jewelry is often considered a tourist item. For the family, consider electronic or brand-name toys for your friend's children. Don't give gifts to your friend's wife.

If you have extensive dealings with a secretary or administrative assistant, a small bottle of American perfume is appropriate. For that matter, also concentrate significant attention on the secretaries of your business partners. Businesspersons (which often means businessmen) in Mexico spend much more time out of the office than their American counterparts. They attend long meals at restaurants, visit friends, or go home in the middle of the day to see their families. Pagers and cellular phones have exploded in Mexico, but they are often ignored or turned off by their users. All of these facts mean that you may spend a significant amount of time talking with a business partner's secretary or assistant while he or she tries to run down the boss for you. Reward all this effort with attention, lavish praise to the boss openly, and, over time, small gifts.

Business Holidays

The following list reviews the major holidays observed in Mexico.

New Year's Day	January 1
Constitution Day	February 5
Benito Juarez's Birthday	March 21
Good Friday and Easter	Late March or April
Labor Day	May 1
Battle of Puebla Day (Cinco de Mayo)	May 5
Declaration of Independence Day	September 15
Independence Day	September 16

Day of the Race (Columbus Day)	October 12
All Saints/All Souls Day	November 1-2
Anniversary of the Mexican Revolution	November 20
Day of Our Lady of Guadalupe	December 12
Christmas	December 25

Most government agencies, banks and many businesses are closed on the holidays noted above. In addition, business slows down considerably and many Mexicans take extended vacations around Christmas/New Year's and the week before Easter Sunday.

What should you be aware of before visiting a Mexican person at home?

Invitations to a Mexican's home should be prized as evidence that you are viewed as a valuable associate. Most likely you will be invited to dinner. Wear business attire unless specifically told otherwise and arrive 30 minutes to an hour after the stated time. You may bring a gift or gifts as it seems appropriate. (See the discussion of gift-giving above.) If this is your second or third trip to the country and you anticipate that you may be invited to an associate's home, consider bringing a bottle of good red California wine with you for a gift.

After arriving you may be taken on a tour of the home. Express admiration for the house and its furnishings, although avoid noting too much enthusiasm for any one item. Mexican traditions of gift-giving are so strong that if you compliment a particular piece of pottery excessively, your host may feel obligated to give it to you. To refuse would be an even worse offense, so be cautious. Taste and compliment each dish with gusto. You will not be allowed to help in any way, no matter how poor the home or informal the setting. Offer to leave about a half hour after the meal. You will be encouraged to linger and can do so for as long as the atmosphere seems comfortable.

Chapter 22

V

HELPING MEXICO:
WHAT CAN ONE PERSON DO?

The United States and Canada are home to many of the world's leading individual philanthropists and charitable foundations, while Mexico is a place where the work of the non-profit organizations is often sorely needed. This match between supply and demand makes the nonprofit sector one of the strongest and most rewarding forums for partnerships between the United States and Mexico. Today collaborative projects of every sort are underway in Mexico, set up by people with a sense of mission about helping the country. Non-profit organizations in Mexico have targeted economic development, health care, housing and wildlife preservation as priority areas for their charitable efforts. In the pages that follow you will find out more about non-profit activities in Mexico and how you can be a part of philanthropy south of the border. Included in the discussion is an overview of how you can form a tax-exempt non-profit organization in Mexico to engage in charitable work.

What kinds of philanthropic work are being done by foreigners in Mexico?

Today there is a wide array of active non-profit and non-governmental organizations active in Mexico. Many are subsidiaries of multinational non-profits. In addition, there are a number of high-quality U.S. non-profit organizations that

work throughout the country. In Mexico they work in almost every social sphere imaginable. Major efforts are underway in health, education, housing and economic development, including microenterprise lending and Grameen Bank-style peer lending networks.

Several human rights organizations are active in the southern states of Chiapas, Oaxaca and Quintana Roo, where they work with indigenous peoples who are often at odds with local representatives of the Mexican government. There are also a number of active environmental organizations in Southern Mexico, which concentrate on the preservation of rainforest habitat and the protection of natural resources from excessive development. Many of these organizations coordinate environmental, human rights and economic development activities by combining environmental activism with enterprises that encourage sustainable development. Their efforts have helped to foster Mexico's growing ecotourism industry. Environmental organizations in Mexico also concentrate efforts on the preservation of marine resources in the country's territorial waters, including delicate coral reef ecosystems in the Gulf of Mexico and gray whale birthing waters off the Baja California peninsula.

What foreign-based humanitarian organizations have a strong presence in Mexico?

Several international organizations are active in Mexico, many with U.S. headquarters or branches. Among the most active are Project Concern International, Accion International and the Red Cross. Many of these work closely with local Mexican non-government organizations, including community membership organizations, or *communitarias.* These groups are particularly active in the poor *colonias* that surround many of Mexico's most rapidly urbanizing cities and in rural villages throughout the country. A relatively recent focus of concern has been the new colonias around the outskirts of the cities growing along the U.S.-Mexico border. The increase in maquiladora manufacturing has drawn migrant workers from throughout Mexico to the border, where they have swamped

the supporting infrastructures of the border cities. Many of these workers live in squatter dwellings in the colonias and lack access to water, sewage disposal, and basic health care.

Several U.S.-based non-profit organizations have become involved in organizing *colonia* communities and in providing community lending programs to encourage microenterprise development and self-help housing systems. Among the most successful of these efforts have been innovative housing programs started by the Cooperative Housing Fund and Esperanza International. These non-profits rely upon cash donations and volunteer-labor to construct self-help housing along patterns similar to those developed by Habitat for Humanity.

Charitable activities by non-profit organizations in Mexico receive significant support from major U.S. foundations such as the Ford Foundation, the Mott Foundation, and the Inter-American Foundation. Efforts along the border are also supported by active bi-national community foundations.

Further support for non-profit activities in Mexico is available from multinational agencies created as part of side agreements to the NAFTA:

➤ the North American Development Bank (NADBank), a bi-national lending agency whose main purpose is to finance border environmental infrastructure;

➤ the Border Environment Cooperation Commission (BECC), to assist communities in developing environmental infrastructure projects and certify them for funding by NADBank;

➤ the Border Environmental Cooperation Fund, which provides direct charitable support for environmental and sustainable development projects.

What projects designed to improve Mexico's environment are underway?

The most notable efforts to preserve and improve the environment in Mexico are located in the southernmost states and at the U.S.-Mexico border.

In the states of Oaxaca, Chiapas and Quintana Roo a vigorous coalition of local, national and international organizations is involved in a multi-pronged effort to preserve tropical habitats and species from development interests. Efforts to preserve rainforest and coral reef habitats in Southern Mexico are focused on two areas. First, environmental organizations are trying to limit the development of mineral resources in Southern Mexico and to encourage less invasive mining techniques for those projects already underway. There are similar efforts to limit development of new petroleum resources in areas that might disrupt sensitive marine ecosystems. Non-governmental organizations are also lobbying to prevent the wholesale exploitation of hardwood trees in Southern Mexico, which to date have been relatively undisturbed.

Second, non-profits are trying to encourage the indigenous peoples of Southern Mexico to adopt agricultural practices that limit damage to the natural environment and provide opportunities for sustainable economic development. Part of this effort includes the introduction of renewable species cultivation.

On the U.S.-Mexico border, environmental organizations are working to limit environmental damage from manufacturing and the rapid urbanization of many of the border cities. In Cuidad Juarez, non-profits are introducing new methods of housing construction to reduce the air pollution associated with brick-making kilns that are fired by tires, scrap paper and other harmful trash scrounged as fuel. In Tijuana, non-profit organizations have worked with local government to support the construction of a bi-national sewage treatment plant to prevent the runoff of raw sewage into the Tijuana River and the Pacific Ocean.

What are the salient laws and regulations governing non-profit projects in the country?

The not-for-profit corporation in Mexico is generally governed by the Mexican Civil Law rather than the Commercial Law. Requirements for establishing a non-profit are detailed

under articles 2670 to 2687 of the Civil Code, under a series of headings called *Asociaciones Civiles* (A.C.). Non-profit organizations must be set up before a Notary Public (or Corredor Publico). The Asociacion Civil is typically used as a legal vehicle for neighborhood associations, museums and charities. The name of the organization is approved by the Mexican government, but the Asociacion does not need to present its charter. Like a commercial corporation Asociacion Civil has a specified lifetime and must to be registered under the public registry. Unlike a public corporation you cannot transfer its membership.

If a private corporation borrows money, the lender cannot go against the partners. However, in an Asociacion Civil, the members are personally liable for debts incurred by the Asociacion. For this reason they are often used for coopera-tive credit and peer lending projects that rely on group "shame" as an incentive for the repayment of loans.

There are few laws at the federal level that govern non-prof-it organizations. Most work typically done by non-profits in other countries is conducted by the Mexican government, political parties or affiliates of the Catholic Church.

The Mexican government requires that non-profit organiza-tions submit to annual audit for tax purposes; however, this information is not made available to the public.

What Mexican governmental agencies are normally involved in setting up a non-profit project?

Typically asociacions maintain their revenue streams through tax-deductible donations. For a non-profit to obtain registration as a tax-exempt Asociacion Civil it must register with Hacienda.

For foreign entities to establish a non-profit in Mexico, the first step is to know what kind of Asociacion you need. You start by drafting the by-laws with a lawyer or Notary who will pre-pare the *Escritura* and then apply to *Relaciones Exteriores* to set up the Asociacion and confirm a Charter. Next, one must prepare the documents for tax exception from Hacienda.

Mexico does not have a single government agency that oversees the receipt and distribution of foreign charitable aid. In 1995 the Mexican government established an office within the Interior Ministry to oversee the work of non-profit agencies in the country. The resulting Office of Support for Civil Organizations is supposed to coordinate the activities of non-profits in Mexico. However, the office is still relatively small and is somewhat understaffed.

What are the first steps to follow in starting a non-profit venture in Mexico?

For the sake of clarity, it is important to distinguish between two types of organizations: grassroots and non-profit or non-governmental. Grassroots organizations are typically composed of community members who volunteer their time while participating in the group. These have legal status under Mexican law (as "asociacion civil," meaning they have a reliable accounting system, organizational stability, etc.). However, they usually do not receive direct philanthropic support from international funding sources.

By contrast, NGOs typically receive support from national and international sources of charity and have paid staffs. NGOs may provide direct social services, work in community development with grassroots organizations, or combine both activities. Some are limited solely to a policy or advocacy role. Many NGOs work with local community residents through a "promoter" or *promotora* program, in which local residents are hired on a part-time basis to conduct public education, provide services or help to further organize the community.

Any non-profit venture in Mexico will need to secure local community support to achieve any sort of success. Often the best way to do this is to begin by working with existing NGOs and seek introduction to their network of grassroots organizations. Even if your goal is general environmental preservation or wildlife conservation, you must work with the indigenous peoples to realize your goals.

Ideally, you will be approaching your project with a new source of funding for charitable efforts in Mexico. Use your funding to initiate a collaborative pilot project with a local NGO. After documenting its outcomes, you can then turn to national and international sources of matching funds to expand your project.

PROFILES

Don Merwin, with co-author John Howell, is the author and publisher of *Choose Mexico,* one of the first books to help people settle down South of the border to live and retire. The first edition appeared in 1985, and since then the book has sold over 180,000 copies, and has become the impetus for Mr. Merwin and his wife to start their successful Oakland-based publishing house, Gateway Books. When we spoke with Don, he and his wife had recently returned from Mexico after they had conducted research for the next edition of *Choose Mexico.* They had spoken to numerous American expats, many of whom they were able to locate through the World Wide Web. Their story is not so much about business success in Mexico but, as Don describes it, one about the phenomenon of Mexico and the country's attractiveness to American retirees.

How did you get involved in Mexico and how did you get involved in publishing?

In 1983, my wife and I lived in San Miguel de Allende and during that time we observed a very happy and vibrant group of Americans and Canadians living there, and realized there was no book that we knew of about living in Mexico. I had been writing on and off throughout my career, and while I was there I met John Howell, another writer from the Bay area. We spent a fair amount of time in Mexico and eventually combined forces to write the book when we got back. We wrote an outline and a couple of chapters and mailed it out to something like 80 mainstream publishers, and got back a lot of very nice and respected rejection letters.

However, my wife had a background in publishing, and she and I decided to bite the bullet and self-publish the

258

book, as well as seek out other manuscripts for publication. We published *Choose Mexico* about three weeks before the earthquake in Mexico City in 1985; people said "too bad, your book was stillborn." But the book went on to eventually sell 180,000 copies through our mail-order catalog and book stores. I don't think any other book about retiring in Mexico has sold anywhere near that number. We have now published about 30 books all together, most aimed at the over-50 crowd.

Do you know how many Americans are currently living in Mexico?

Nobody has ever accurately pinned the number down. Our estimate is between 100,000 and 150,000. The problem with all the published figures is that they rely on Social Security checks sent to Mexico from the United States, many of which are actually being sent to Mexican nationals. Moreover, many Americans receive their checks via bank transfers within the States.

Where are American and Canadian expats living in Mexico?

The concentrations of expats are in the Guadalajara area of Chapala and Ajijic. There's another concentration just below San Diego and in Baja California.

Of the Americans living in Mexico, are most retirees?

Yes, the majority of them are, except for those who are stationed there by multinational firms. The bulk are of retirement age.

Is the cost of living significantly lower in Mexico, or do you find that there are add-ons that equalize the difference between living in Mexico and living in the States or Canada?

The cost of living in Mexico is very significantly lower. And it's about half what it was before the devaluation of the peso.

So if one wanted to live in San Miguel de Allende fairly comfortably in a two-bedroom apartment, what would the cost be?

Somewhere between $600 and $800 a month. That would include everything: rent, food, health insurance, though it may not include a car. But the bus system is quite well developed so you can get by.

In other words, a Social Security check would get you by there?

Yep.

What type of visa does one need to live in Mexico?

All you need to live in Mexico is a tourist card. The problem is that it has to be renewed every six months, which you have to do by returning to the border, though it can be done on the same day you arrive. There are two forms of resident status: FM3 and FM2. These require less frequent renewals, the import of household goods duty-free, and so on. After five years, a person can obtain FM2 status which guarantees all of the rights afforded to the Mexican citizen.

What are some of the problems for expats living in Mexico? For example, crime and safety?

Safety is not an issue compared to living in the United States. One real issue is staying healthy, which means not drinking tap water and only drinking bottled water. There was a time not long ago when expats found it difficult to find basic goods, including such items as toothpaste, but now consumer goods are easily purchased since Wal-Mart

260

has opened stores there. And there is comfort for expats in having access to imported goods as well.

Did the expats you spoke to experience a high level of culture shock after moving to Mexico?

Mexico is totally different culturally from the United States. Many people are bothered by the visible poverty. This isn't the case in a city like Puebla but it is in other places. Also, someone trying to accomplish something, like building a house for example, will learn that there is less urgency in Mexico. Moreover, people there tend to define politeness by not telling you what you don't want to hear. Expats often view this behavior as dishonesty.

Do you find that most expats who take the plunge and move to Mexico stay there indefinitely?

Not all, by any means. I have known people who, for a variety of reasons, have returned to the United States after several years, but innumerable Americans have stayed on. A certain amount of attrition is due to people making the move without sufficient exploration in Mexico beforehand. And, of course, the language barrier is a serious one. I think many Americans who have moved there, and tourists as well, expect that the Mexicans will all speak English. But once you get outside the resort areas, few Mexicans do.

Do most of the Americans living in Mexico speak Spanish?

Most Americans there can speak Spanish at some level, but I have met very few people who have made the effort to attain real fluency, even though there are plenty of language schools, American-sponsored programs, and libraries.

Do the Americans living in Mexico tend to socialize among themselves or do they mix with the Mexican population?

261

In places where there are large concentrations of Americans there is an enclave mentality and little socialization with the Mexicans. But I have met Americans living in Guadalajara on blocks where few other foreigners live who socialize with the locals as well. In places like Oaxaca, where there is a smaller number of Americans, the involvement with the locals is higher.

Do foreigners rent or buy homes in Mexico?

They are renting and they are buying property. Some are even building new homes. Many developers are going in nowadays.

Do you see more young people moving to Mexico to live as so-called "lone eagles?"

Yes, more are moving there as a function of earlier retirement in the States. Also, many young people who do not fit into the classical mode have moved there to pursue their creative interests, set up small businesses such as restaurants, buy and sell real estate, trade in handicrafts, and work with information.

What are some tips for people considering a move to Mexico to live?

Remember that Mexico is not for everybody. The culture is different and you need to be willing to adapt. We like to say: "You need to try it before you buy it." People call us and ask us to recommend a real estate agent in Mexico because they want to move there. We admonish them to go and spend time there first.

Don Merwin's company, Gateway Publishing, is at

http://www.hway.net/gateway

INTERVIEW WITH STEPHEN C. CONWAY
Mexico Real Estate Expert and Mortgage Loan Broker

For those of us who travel in Mexico, the scenario is all too common. After basking on a *playa* for a few days while nursing icy Corona beers, we hear that little voice in our heads start to ask: "I wonder if I could afford to live down here part of the year? Wow . . . that would really make it . . ." The fantasy then confronts the logistics: "How do I get a mortgage in Mexico?" and "Can a foreigner own beachfront property in Acapulco?" and "If I bought a condo, could I rent it out to friends to pay the mortgage?" and so on, until the dream goes up in a flame of complications.

Stephen Conway, who had studied political science in college and had earned a Masters degree, began his interest in Mexico after he had become frustrated working for the Canadian government, despite a six-figure salary. He began traveling to Mexico on an annual basis as a tourist to places such as Cabo San Lucas and the Yucatan. Soon, he started to think about buying property. He found out, however, that realtors in Mexico are not licensed as they are in Canada and the United States, and are sometimes disreputable. He discovered that real estate investments in Mexico are largely unsecured. So he halted plans to buy there.

During this initial research, however, he found that there was no one available in the United States or Canada to help him in his endeavor to research the real estate market in Mexico. So he became involved in a mortgage company in Canada to represent people like himself who wanted to purchase property south of the border. Within time, he would write a book about the real estate market in Mexico which he self-published in mid-1996. He is currently distributing it in Mexico, Canada, and the United States and promoting it via radio talk shows and a website. The title of the book is *Mexican Real Estate: A Reference Guide for Investors*. He can assist anyone interested in buying residential, as opposed to commercial property, south of the border.

What restrictions exist for foreigners wanting to buy land in Mexico?

Article 27 in the Mexican Constitution is where the applicable land laws are outlined. In short, a foreigner cannot own land in Mexico within 100 kilometers from a border or 50 kilometers from the Mexican coastline. You can obtain land in these restricted areas, but actual title is held by a bank and the individual has beneficial rights, including the right to sell such rights to the land. So-called trusts are set up in these cases, last 50 years, and are renewable for another 50 years. Article 27 also contains a clause, which requires foreigners to consider themselves Mexican citizens in regard to owning land in the country and to understand that all land in the restricted areas belongs to the Mexican government.

Outside the restricted areas, foreigners can own land outright and in perpetuity, just as in the United States and Canada.

How does one obtain a mortgage to purchase property in Mexico?

Traditionally, American banks would not lend on real estate in Mexico because no title was taken and there was no avenue for foreclosure in the country. It was impossible to secure property for collateral. Indeed, Mexican banks wouldn't lend either, because they lacked the funds and had experienced no tradition of mortgage loan financing. However, in the last two months things have begun to change. There are now four outfits which will loan on residential property purchases. One is Collateral Mortgage in Alabama, which will lend up to 70 percent of the appraised trust amount on 15-year loans at a rate of 15 percent above the prevailing interest rate. Two of the others are Inland Mortgage in Indiana and American Equities in Vancouver, Washington. These companies secure the loans with a promissory agreement with the individual purchaser to reclaim the rights to the land in the case of default.

What is the step-by-step process a person must go through to purchase property in Mexico?

The first step is to contact a number of realtors in Mexico and see their lists. The offer to purchase is followed by the drawing up of a trust document. It takes about a month for the property to be transferred. You'll need to get a notary, rather than a lawyer, to carry forward the paperwork. There are four types of power of attorney to choose from in putting in place a notary as your proxy.

What are the possible hitches to buying property in Mexico?

First of all, realtors are not licensed and they are not obligated to make full disclosures about the possible defects in a property. Another is that there is a 2 percent acquisition tax. You'll also have to pay a fee for a certificate guaranteeing that there are no liens against the property. One thing that people don't realize after purchasing a property is that there will be added approximately $20,000 in fees and taxes.

What are the hot real estate spots, including resorts, that are coming on line at present in Mexico?

Currently, there is a bill before the Mexican Congress that would legalize gambling in Puerto Vallarta and Cabo San Lucas, which will increase property values by 30 percent. MGM has already bought in Cabo San Lucas. The expat hot spots are still San Miguel de Allende and Chapala, south of Guadalajara. Although the peso devaluation of 1994 did not affect prices in the resort areas, residential real estate prices in these areas are down by 40 percent, and there are some fantastic values.

Stephen C. Conway can be reached at:
sconway@awinc.com

INTERVIEW WITH RON MADER
Environmental Business Writer and Web Publisher

We met Ron Mader on the Internet, where he maintains a near ubiquitous presence. Mr. Mader is a well-respected environmental writer who publishes Eco-Travels in Latin America, a highly acclaimed website that's home to the largest database of information related to environmental tourism in Latin America. (You'll find the URL on page 272.) Even Mexico's Ministry of Tourism admits that his library of links to Mexico-related sources is the most comprehensive in the world. We spoke to Mr. Mader about the environmental market in Mexico, and the emergence of eco-tourism in the country. We should also mention that he is the author of a forthcoming guidebook to eco-touring South of the border, titled *Mexico: A Natural Destination,* published by John Muir.

First, what is your professional background?

I worked in Mexico City for *The News* until 1993 when I went up to Austin, Texas to write about environmental border issues. As I produced more articles, I published them online on my website, which widened my audience and led to more contacts and more stories. But every magazine and newspaper that I wrote for folded and went under last year. I feel the mass folding of publications related to the environmental market in Mexico was due to a sudden loss of confidence on the part of potential American investors in the market.

You mean they folded in the aftermath of the peso crisis?

It's interesting. I think the environmental market was oversold. And I think that was a problem [exacerbated] by the U.S. Department of Commerce. It was caused by the publications I was working for, who made it sound as if all of these environmental contracts were on the table and all the business was easy to get.

The publications made, say, World Bank-funded contracts sound easy to win for American companies?

The World Bank or, for example, the state of Mexico has a $40 million water treatment contract up for bid. Or a waste treatment facility for a hydroelectric plant. Or consulting fees, et cetera, and that was just not the case. When Mexico did, in fact, grant a contract, and pay for the contract, years would go well. So the businesses who were doing well continued to do well, and the folks who came into the market because of all the hype were let down.

You know, I wonder why we have a U.S. Department of Commerce. It's not its job to be the cheerleader making lies about Mexico. This is something I feel very strongly about. If we were to have said, "here's the situation and here are the obstacles," we would have prepared people to accept the situation on a more realistic basis and the companies would have stayed on. What indeed happened is that we went on promising people high interest rates, great returns, saying "how could you not go into environmental business in Mexico since the country has to invest $400 million a year and it's just begging for your contracts." I wish it were an isolated case, but over and over we heard that kind of garbage.

Was this part of the cheerleading for NAFTA in general on the part of the U.S. government?

Well, yeah, but it continued for two years after NAFTA, and there's a lot of cheerleading for these issues and for business there by people who don't live in Mexico, or if they do, they live in Mexico City and they don't understand the regional complexities. It was just big business leading on economic cheerleading that went on until the collapse of the peso caught everybody.

If you're an environmental company in the United States now, what would you say are the opportunities in Mexico's environmental market? Are there any?

There is a tremendous opportunity in Mexico, but it requires that you commit yourself and your company's resources to a longer-term approach. It requires that you place yourself in Mexico, or, if not physically present, that you have a joint partner. The biggest problem with the American approach you've heard before: "You go in, you shake hands, you make a deal, you get out." And that just didn't work at all. If you look at the environmental market, there are various projects coming for water treatment, hazardous waste, urbanization. But having a good track record may not be enough for your company to succeed in the market. You have to express a greater interest in Mexico for a longer term.

Besides the need to take a longer term view, what are some of the specific obstacles American environmental companies can expect to run into in Mexico?

The problem I hear about over and over again has to do with payment. How are payments made? Under what conditions, and what time frame? A lot of smaller companies have been burned by this, and I think this is one reason they now resist involvement in Mexico. It's really a problem with the government. For example, the city of Mexico, which granted a big contract to Radian Corporation, maker of air quality monitoring equipment, reneged on payment. What are you going to do to get your money out of the government of Mexico City?

Are bribery and corruption obstacles in the environmental business?

The answer is yes, and there are some cases I know of, though those are pretty isolated. I'd say the bigger obsta-

cle in doing environmental business in Mexico is just a lack of information. You can't call it bribery, and "corruption" is too strong a word, but the informal release of contracts is often made to friends or acquaintances of certain companies in a certain sector, and then it will be made public with only one week response time allowed. Now that's a big problem. That's not necessarily corruption, but it is questionable. And I think that sort of thing takes place in other sectors as well.

But beyond that, there is simply a lack of public information: Which project is a priority? What are the funds available? Are there matching funds or not? There is no bulletin board or a central area where you can go to find out about a project or engage in matchmaking. [Projects appear to be based on] spontaneous matchmaking sessions and longer-termed relationships that have evolved.

So if I were to research the environmental market in Mexico, where would I start, or is such information even available?

The best source of information was a very good magazine that went under, *Mexican Environmental Business.*

Okay, what environmental agencies or ministries in Mexico would one visit to obtain such information?

There is a variety. From Hacienda. From the Environmental Secretariat, and within that, its big budgetary office would be the National Commission for Water. You would also want to visit the Technology and Investment Department within the Environmental Secretariat. There are scattered agencies and it's very difficult to get that information.

What about gathering information at the Department of Commerce office in Mexico City?

I would say be wary. It's not that what it says will be out-right lies, but it is promoting something: a better future for Mexico, but too often with its head in the clouds, while business has to struggle with this information gap.

My favorite source of information right now is the magazine *Business Mexico,* as well as *El Financiero International.* These are the two must-reads.

What about consultants? Are there experts in the environmental field you can call upon, perhaps a person associated with a large American consulting firm with an office in Mexico?

There are various consultants, but there's no way I'd trust them. I would say the best information comes from the government, and then the question becomes how to get that information. The consultants use it for what they offer, so there's nothing there I would recommend.

What is the status of the eco-tourism business in Mexico? Has it been hit by the peso crisis like other markets?

The peso crisis has been a bonanza for American tourists. There's been a tremendous explosion in alternative tourism in Mexico. People have done the beaches, they've done the mega-resorts, and now they're looking for something else. One of the biggest components of tourism in the United States is nature-based travel—going to the national parks, wildlife reserves, and such. I would say this year was really a watershed for Mexico in terms of exploring eco-tourism and environmental tourism. There was a memorandum signed between the tourist industry and the environmental secretariat in 1995, and in 1996 they started putting it into order. In 1997, an international conference took place on my website involving the heads of these two institutions as they're trying to blend conservation—and

270

funding for nature conservation—with tourism. In so many ways, this is more of a boxing match than any type of hand shaking, because they're coming at it from two different viewpoints.

My favorite metaphor is that eco-tourism is like a canyon or an abyss, with conservationists on one side and tourist folk on the other. Because for the most part, tourism does not respect the environment—it fills in the mangroves with golf courses, it dynamites places for beaches, et cetera. The conservationists, for the most part, don't like people, let alone tourists. So what have we created: eco-tourism, and it's a true Frankenstein's monster.

What good is eco-tourism bringing to Mexico?

It's calling for a new understanding. I mean there's nothing wrong with multiple use of protected areas; if they are not being harmed, then fine. Eco-tourism allows for education. It allows for revenues. And it allows for local economic development. So all the money is not going into just Mexico City, Guadalajara, and Monterrey. It's going into a small town called Cuatro Ciénegas in Coahuila, or it's going into some cabins outside of Monterrey to take care of a reforesting project. The government's not going to do that. In 1975, there were 800,000 hectares that were burnt in a massive forest fire in Nuevo León, and a couple of folks there with a project are starting to reforest, one tree at a time, but they've planted 400,000 trees in the last ten years. On the coast of Nayarit, there's another interesting private project called El Custodio de las Tortugas. Without that budget they couldn't patrol the beach where the turtles are poached. The project entails actually patrolling this beach three times a night.

There are numerous interesting eco-projects already underway in Mexico. Moreover, the government entities of the environmental secretariat and the ministry of tourism

271

are meeting and pounding out how Mexico is going to proceed in this area. The market demand for eco-tours continues to develop. More people are asking for information about conservation and tourism; they aren't asking just about whale watching, but also how their visit can ensure that these whales will continue to be able to breed off Baja California. So there is an emergence of enviromental consciousness in the country.

For a complete list of environment-related projects in Mexico, see Ron Mader's website, at:

http://www.txinfinet.com/mader/ecotravel/ecotravel.com

APPENDIX I
TRAVELERS' INFORMATION

PREPARING FOR YOUR TRIP

An excellent source of information for an independent or small business traveler is a fax service operated by the Mexican Government Tourism Office. The 24-hour service, called Fax Me Mexico, provides information on hotels, restaurants, history and culture. It offers briefings on more than 20 cities and regions throughout the country. Start by requesting the directory of documents available; then specify additional documents in subsequent phone calls. Note that you have to dial from the same phone that you want to receive the fax on, and it needs to be a touch-tone phone. Its fax-info number is (541) 385-9282.

CHANGING MONEY

Business travelers can change their dollars into *pesos* at a variety of locations in Mexico. Cash and travelers checks can be exchanged at Mexican banks and money exchange houses *(casa de cambio),* as well as at many hotels, restaurants and shops. Banks typically provide the best exchange rates. However, occasionally one can persuade a shopkeeper who is looking for your business to give you a better rate. The most common banks are BancoMex and Bancomer. There is also a bank at the Mexico City airport that gives excellent rates and is open at all times.

PAYMENT

Credit cards are widely accepted in Mexico. Look for the tell-tale stickers at hotels, banks, restaurants and department stores, or ask whether the establishment accepts an American *tarjeta de crédito.* Many major banks will give you a cash advance on your credit card. This may save you credit card processing charges at individual stores, and will offer the best dollar/peso exchange rate. Cash advances will be paid in pesos.

Bartering is common in marketplaces and smaller shops. We would echo Carl Franz's advice to "bargain gently." Despite Mexico's

economic recovery, the devaluation hurt many poor Mexicans
severely and a few cents difference in the price of a souvenir hand-
icraft can be significant to a family.

ENGLISH-LANGUAGE NEWSPAPERS

The leading English-language newspaper in Mexico is *The Mexico-
City News,* which is available in most major cities throughout the
country. Readable newspapers published in Mexico in English
include the *Mexico City Times, Twenty-first Century* (published in
Guadalajara), and *El Financiero,* published daily in Spanish and
weekly in English, and considered the best for economic and business news.

TEMPORARY OFFICES

Several companies in Mexico City offer temporary executive suites
to foreign companies. One of the advantages of renting such an
office is that it will come with a private phone. Otherwise one may
wait several months before being able to get a private line installed.

The following companies offer private offices and dedicated
phone lines to foreign executives, as well as answering services,
word processing, conference rooms and fax services.

HEADQUARTERS COMPANIES
Presidente Masaryk 61-20
Tel: (52) (5) 203-1749
Fax: (52) (5) 531-9659

Servicios Ejecutivos Mexicanos
Avenida Insurgentes Sur 2388
Tel: (52) (5) 550-4657

Servicios Integrales Ejecutivos
Presidente Masaryk 61
Tel: (52) (5) 203-1740, 203-2178

Mexican offices tend to be fairly modest, making great use of
office cubicle partitions. The head of the department usually has
his or her own office with a door. Security measures are taken to
protect executives, including a guard on the first floor of even small
office buildings who requires all visitors to sign in and present
identification before entering the elevator. Often offices will require
you to buzz an outer door before gaining entry to a reception area.

In light of the high rate of kidnapping of executives, this is a prudent measure.

TRANSLATION SERVICES

The following companies provide English-to-Spanish and Spanish-to-English translation of printed text, as well as personal simultaneous translation, and translation equipment for large meetings and conferences.

Berlitz
Nacional 530 PB, Col. Palanco
Tel: (52) (5) 255-3341
Fax: (52) (5) 255-3817

CITI
Avenida Chapultepec 471
Desp. 403
Tel: (52) (5) 286-9192
Fax: (52) (5) 538-0241

Sittco
Melchor Ocampo 193, Desp. A, Plaza Galerias
Tel: (52) (5) 260-0676

ALTITUDE SICKNESS

Business travelers need to be aware that the cities of Mexico City and Guadalajara rest on the central Mexican plain, over 5,000 feet above sea level. Take it easy your first two days; don't exercise and avoid extended stretches outdoors if the air pollution is noticeably bad. This routine will help you to adjust to the altitude and avoid altitude sickness (shortness of breath, headaches, fatigue, etc.)

DEPARTURES

Business travelers leaving Mexico by plane will be asked to hand in their tourist card and pay a departure tax which should be around U.S. $12.00. Check to see if the tax was included in the cost of your plane ticket. There are no departure fees if you are driving across the border. You may need to show proof of citizenship and your car registration, but most cars are passed through without being asked to stop.

FAXES vs. MAIL

Always fax. The Mexican postal system is notorious. Faxes will be available in most hotels, either at the front desk or in the business center. There are also faxes at many major post offices. Don't send anything by regular post that must reach a destination in a timely manner. As an alternative, use FedEx, DHL or UPS. Each has offices in the major Mexican cities.

HEALTH PREPARATION AND INSURANCE

Business travelers in Mexico can anticipate health problems by preparing a short summary of their health status and requirements. This should include any special needs for emergency treatment. Carry a written health summary that includes a brief medical history, any allergies or hypersensitivities, and the names of any currently prescribed medications. You should also note your blood type, immunization history and any chronic ailments, and provide contact information for your personal physician. Confirm that your health insurance covers treatment in Mexico; even if it does, you will likely have to pay for the treatment upon receipt of care and then apply for reimbursement once you have returned to the United States.

You may wish to consider acquiring supplemental coverage to insure yourself against unusual costs, such as medically required transportation to the States. You can buy expanded overseas health insurance coverage through companies, such as Mutual of Omaha, either directly, at international airports, or through organizations such as the American Automobile Association. Typically these travel insurance plans will provide you with a toll-free number to call if an emergency occurs. If it doesn't work in Mexico, there will be another number provided for making a collect call.

Such supplemental insurance plans will typically cost $2-3 per day of coverage. Deductibles should range between $25—$100.

If you want more specific information regarding health conditions in Mexico, particularly for the southern states, use the State Department's Consular Information Program. Users can receive information from the Program by fax using a fax retrieval service at (202) 647-3000. You can also receive updated information via its website at http://travel.state.gov on the Internet. In addition to providing this information, the Program will be able to recommend specific insurance companies for travelers who want to purchase supplemental coverage in advance of their trip.

Note that individual insurance companies may be able to provide you with a directory of English-speaking doctors in Mexico who accept their health plans.

TIME ZONES

Most of Mexico is on Greenwich Mean Time minus six hours, the equivalent of U.S. Central Standard Time. The far northwest of Mexico is on U.S. Mountain Time (minus seven hours Greenwich Time) and the peninsula of Baja California is on U.S. Pacific Time.

Mexico does shift to daylight savings time, except in Baja California.

ENTERTAINING AND SOCIALIZING

Working hours in Mexico tend to include both work and socializing. Evening soirees are common, even on week nights. And people dress. Educated society in Mexico City is as cosmopolitan as that in Manhattan. Working hours are 9:30 A.M. to 2:00 P.M. and then 6:00 P.M. to 9:30 P.M. Academics tend to work from 9:30 A.M. to 6:00 P.M.

To help you with budgeting, there are price ranges on the menu for one of Mexico City's finest restaurant chains, Sep's—a perfect place to meet business associates for lunch or dinner.

TELEPHONE CALLS

Most public phones now take calling cards instead of coins, but just when you're prepared to find one, you'll come across the other type. Ladatel calling cards are sold in either 20 or 50 peso denominations, and can be found at various stores and restaurants.

To call other cities in Mexico, use the "91" national code and then the number. To call the U.S. and Mexico, dial "95" first and then area code and number. Call collect by dialing "96." To call other countries, dial "98" first.

BUSINESS HOLIDAYS

New Year's Day	January 1
Constitution Day	February 5
Benito Juarez's Birthday	March 21
Good Friday and Easter	Late March or April
Labor Day	May 1
Battle of Puebla Day (Cinco de Mayo)	May 5

Declaration of Independence Day	September 15
Independence Day	September 16
Day of the Race	October 12
(Columbus Day)	
All Saints/All Souls Day	November 1-2
Anniversary of the	
Mexican Revolution	November 20
Day of Our Lady of Guadalupe	December 12
Christmas	December 25

Most government agencies, banks and many businesses are closed on the holidays noted above. In addition, business slows down considerably and many Mexicans take extended vacations around Christmas/New Year's and the week before Easter Sunday.

SMOKING

Cigarette smoke is a constant nuisance and irritant in Mexico City. At the airlines, we were asked about our seat location. "Smoking?" We answered, "Non-smoking." The attendant looked surprised and asked, "Non-smoking?" hinting that most choose the other.

BANKING

Mexico's currency is the peso, and prices are indicated by the "$" sign. The peso is divided into 100 centavos. Coins come in denominations of 10, 20 and 50 centavos and one, two, five, 10 and 20 pesos. Notes come in two, five, 10, 20, 50, 100 and 200 pesos.

You can exchange foreign currency at banks or at exchange houses (casas de cambio). Exchange rates will vary, and often you'll get a better rate if you exchange currency instead of traveler's checks. The exchange rate is particularly poor at hotels. I've found that while the Mexico City airport offers a good return, the Cancun airport offers one of the worst! Be cautious.

You can easily get a cash advance from an ATM machine at one of the major banks. While you will be charged a greater fee from your credit card company, this is relatively hassle free. Make sure you have your access number, because most companies have a policy of not reporting the number over the phone.

APPENDIX II
ADDITIONAL BUSINESS CONTACTS

CONEXION EJECUTIVA

Businesses seeking a general contact resource for business in Mexico could consider Conexion Ejecutiva, which is a print directory with the addresses, telephone and fax numbers of Mexico's corporate and government leaders. Its 4,000 listings include cabinet ministries, the Congress, congressional committees, federal agencies, political parties, state government offices, international organizations, embassies, NAFTA offices, government Internet sites, newspapers, magazines, radio, television and foreign press.

The directory also includes major Mexican and multinational companies, financial institutions, U.S. state trade offices, chambers of industry, nonprofit organizations, law firms, accounting and consulting, advertising and public relations, professional associations, think tanks, labor unions, real estate and useful numbers.

Sample pages and ordering information for Conexion Ejecutiva can be requested from the Mexico City offices of Paradise Publishing, S.R.L de C.V. at (52) (5) 250-3502 or, or by e-mail at paradise@iserve.net.mx. Information is also available through its New York offices at (212) 535-9468 or by fax, (212) 535-9468. A subscription to the directory is U.S. $50.00.

MEXICAN CONSULATES

Here we have provided contact information for various Mexican consulates in the United States. We have also noted selected consulates in other countries that are accessible via the Internet. These offices are useful first-stops for information regarding Mexico's commercial environment. They can often provide referrals to appropriate offices in Mexico City and can facilitate communication with various secretariats and agencies. They will also help in arranging business visas for foreign travelers to Mexico.

UNITED STATES

Albuquerque
Consul General
Carlos Gonzalez
400 Gold S.W., Suite 100
Albuquerque, NM 87102
Tel: (505) 247-2139
Fax: (505) 842-9490

ATLANTA

Consul General
Teodoro Maus
3220 Peachtree Road, N.E.
Atlanta, GA 30305
Tel: (404) 266-1913
Fax: (404) 266-2309

AUSTIN

Roberto Gamboa
Consul General
200 East 6th Street, Suite 200
Austin, TX 78701
Tel: (512) 478-9031
Fax: (512) 478-8008

BOSTON

Consul General
Martha Ortiz
20 Park Plaza, 5th Floor, Suite 506
Boston, MA 02116
Tel: (617) 426-8782
Fax: (617) 695-1957

BROWNSVILLE

Consul General
Juan Carlos Cue Vega
724 Elizabeth
Brownsville, TX 78520
Tel: (210) 542-2051
Fax: (210) 542-7267

CALEXICO

Consul General
Ecce Iei Mendoza Machado
331 West Second Street
Calexico, CA 92231
Tel: (619) 357-3863
Fax: (619) 357-6284

CHICAGO

Consul General
Leonardo French
300 North Michigan Ave, 2nd Floor
Chicago, IL 60601
Tel: (312) 855-0056
Fax: (312) 855-9257

CORPUS CHRISTI

Consul General
Armando Beteta
800 North Shoreline Blvd, Suite 410
N. Corpus Christi, TX 78401
Tel: (512) 882-3375
Fax: (512) 882-9324

DALLAS

Consul General
Julian Adem Diaz
8855 Stemmons Freeway
Dallas, TX 75247
Tel: (214) 630-7341
Fax: (214) 630-3511

DEL RIO

Consul General
Mario Najera
300 East Losoya
Del Rio, TX 78840
Tel: (210) 775-2352
Fax: (210) 774-6497

DENVER

Consul General
Carlos Barros
48 Steele Street
Denver, CO 80206
Tel: (303) 331-1871
Fax: (303) 331-0169
E-mail: mexico@vaultbbs.com
Website: http://www.vaultbbs.com/%7EMexico

DETROIT

Consul General
Vicente Montemayor
600 Renaissance Center, Suite 1510
Detroit, MI 48243
Tel: (313) 567-7709
Fax: (313) 567-6543

EAGLE PASS

Consul General
Javier Aguilar Rangel
140 Adams Street
Eagle Pass, TX 78852
Tel: (210) 773-9255
Fax: (210) 773-9397

EL PASO

Consul General
910 East San Antonio Street
El Paso, TX 79901
Tel: (915) 533-3645
Fax: (915) 532-7163

FRESNO

Consul General
Guillermo Ramos
830 Van Ness Avenue
Fresno, CA 93721
Tel: (209) 233-4219
Fax: (209) 233-5638

HOUSTON

Consul General
Manuel Perez Cardenas
3015 Richmond, Suite 100
Houston, TX 77098
Tel: (713) 524-2300
Fax: (713) 523-6244

LAREDO

Consul General
Luis Humberto Ramirez R.
1612 Farragut Street
Laredo, TX 78040
Tel: (210) 723-6369
Fax: (210) 723-1741

LOS ANGELES

Consul General
Jose Angel Pescador
2401 West 6th Street
Los Angeles, CA 90057
Tel: (213) 351-6800
Fax: (213) 389-6864

MCALLEN

Consul General
Sr. Ortiz Rosas
600 South Brodway Avenue
McAllen, TX 78501
Tel: (210) 686-0243
Fax: (210) 686-4901

MIAMI

Consul General
Luis Ortiz Monasterios Castellanos
1200 N.W. 78th Avenue, Suite 200
Miami, FL 33126
Tel: (305) 716-4977
Fax: (305) 593-2758

MIDLAND

Consul General
Jose Luis Suarez
511 W. Ohio, Suite 121
Midland, TX 79701
Tel: (915) 687-2334
Fax: (915) 687-3952

NOGALES

Consul General
Roberto Rodriguez
486 Grand Avenue and Terminal Street
Nogales, AZ 85621
Tel: (520) 287-2521
Fax: (520) 287-3175

NEW ORLEANS

Consul General
Agustin Garcia Lopez
World Trade Center Building
2 Canal Street, Suite 840
New Orleans, LA 70130
Tel: (504) 522-3698
Fax: (504) 525-2332

NEW YORK

Consul General
Jorge Pinto Mazal
8 East 41st Street
New York, NY 10017
Tel: (212) 689-0465
Fax: (212) 545-8197
E-mail: conmxny@quicklink.com
Website: http://www.quicklink.com/mexic (espanol)
    http://www.quicklink.com:80/mexico/ingles/ing.htm
    (english)

ORLANDO

Consul General
Martin Torres
823 East Colonial Drive
Orlando, FL 32803
Tel: (407) 894-0514
Fax: (407) 895-6140

OXNARD

Consul General
Luz Elena Bueno Zirion
Transportation Center
201 East 4th Street, Room 209
Oxnard, CA 93030
Tel: (805) 484-4684
Fax: (805) 385-3527

PHILADELPHIA

Consul General
Manuel Lombera Lopez Collada
111 South Independence Mall East
Bourse Building, Suite 1010
Philadelphia, PA 19106
Tel: (215) 625-4897
Fax: (215) 923-7281

PHOENIX

Consul General
Luis Cabrera Cuaron
1990 W. Camelback Rd, Suite 110
Phoenix, AZ 015
Tel: (612) 242-7398
Fax: (612) 242-2957

PORTLAND

Consul General
Gustavo Maza
1234 South West Morrison
Portland, OR 97205
Tel: (503) 274-1442
Fax: (503) 274-1540

SACRAMENTO

Consul General
Carolina Zaragoza
716 J Street, 1010 8th Street
Sacramento, CA 95827
Tel: (916) 393-0404
Fax: (916) 363-0625
E-mail: edomcuri@quiknet.com
Website: http://www.quiknet.com/mexico/spanish.html

SALT LAKE CITY

Consul General
Araceli Perez Charles
458 East 200 South
Salt Lake City, Utah 84111
Tel: (801) 521-8502 & 03
Fax: (801) 521-0534

SAN ANTONIO

Consul General
Carlos Manuel Sada
127 Navarro Street
San Antonio, TX 78205
Tel: (210) 227-1085
Fax: (210) 227-1718

SAN BERNARDINO

Consul General
Rosa Curto Perez
532 North D. Street
San Bernardino, CA 92401
Tel: (909) 889-9836 & 37
Fax: (909) 889-8285

SAN DIEGO

Consul General
Luis Herrera-Lasso
1549 India Street
San Diego, CA 92101
Tel: (619) 231-9741
Fax: (619) 231-4802

SAN FRANCISCO

Consul General
Cesar Lajud
870 Market Street, Suite 528
San Francisco, CA 94102
Tel: (415) 392-6576
Fax: (415) 392-3233
E-mail: conmxsf@quicklink.com
Website: http://quicklink.com/consulmex-SF

SAN JOSE

Consul General
Sergio Casanueva
380 North First Street, Suite 102
San Jose, Ca 95112
Tel: (408) 294-1954
Fax: (408) 294-4506

SANTA ANA

Consul General
Ma. Maricela Quijano
282 N. Broadway Street
Santa Ana, CA 92701
Tel: (714) 835-3069
Fax: (714) 835-3472

SEATTLE

Consul General
Hugo Abel Castro
2132 Third Avenue
Seattle, WA 98121
Tel: (206) 441-0552
Fax: (206) 448-4771

TUCSON

Consul General
Marco Antonio Garcia Blanco
553 S. Stone Avenue
Tucson, AZ 85701
Tel: (520) 822-5595
Fax: (520) 822-8959

MONTREAL

Consul General
Celso Humberto Delagado
200 Rue Mansfield, Suite 1015
H3A 2Z7 Montreal, P.Q. Que
Canada
Tel: (514) 288-2502
Fax: (514) 288-8287

OTTAWA

Mexican Embassy
E-mail: nstn0281@fox.nstn.ca
Website: http://www.DocuWeb.ca/Mexico

TORONTO

Consul General
Ramon Gonzalez
199 Bay Street, Suite 4440
Commerce Court West
M5L 1E9 Toronto, Ontario
Canada
Tel: (416) 368-2875
Fax: (416) 368-3478
Website: http://www.quicklink.com/mexico/toronto/
    consulado.htm

VANCOUVER

Consul General
Gabriel Rosales Vega
810-1130 West Pender Street
V6E 4A4 Vancouver, B. C.
Canada
Tel: (604) 684-3547
Fax: (604) 684-2485

AUSTRALIA

Mexican Embassy
Tel: 06 273 3963

GERMANY

Mexican Embassy
Ambassador Juan Jose Bremer
Adenauerallee #100
53113 Bonn Germany
Tel: 228 914 860 / 228 914 8634
Fax: 228 914 8619
E-mail: sreale01@attmail.com
Website: http://www.inf.fu-berlin.de/~mexico

NORWAY

Mexican Embassy
Drammensveien 108B
0244 Oslo Norway
Tel: 47 224 31165
Fax: 47 224 44352
E-mail: mexico@sn.no
Website: http://home.sn.no/~mexico/index.html

ROMANIA

Mexican Embassy
Website: http://www.inf.fu-
berlin.de:80/~mexico/rum/rum1.htm

SOUTH AFRICA

Mexican Embassy
E-mail: clfembmx@iafrica.com
Website: http://www.embamex.org.za

UNITED KINGDOM

Mexican Embassy
Ambassador Andres Rozental
42 Hertford Street
London W1Y7TF
Tel: 171 499 8586, 171 495 4024
Fax: 171 495-4035
E-mail: mexuk@easynet.co.uk

Mexican Consulate
Consul General Jose Hector Ibarra Morales
8 Hal Kin Street
London SW1X 7DW
Tel: 171 235 6393
Fax: 171 235 5480
E-mail: consullondon@easynet.co.uk
Website: http://www.demon.co.uk/mexuk

URUGUAY

Mexican Embassy
E-mail: embmexur@netgate.comintur.com.uy
Website: http://www.rau.edu.uy/embamex

APPENDIX III
MEXICO BUSINESS PUBLICATIONS

The following is a list of mostly English-language publications that focus on Mexican business, compiled by Ron Mader, and is reprinted here with the author's permission. The index is regularly updated at the Mexico: Read All About It Website:

http://www.txinfinet.com/mader/ecotravel/mexico/9995mexpub.html

EL FINANCIERO INTERNATIONAL
Lago Bolsena 176
Col. Anauac
Mexico, D.F. 11320

U.S. Address: 2300 South Broadway
Los Angeles, CA 90007
Phone: 213-747-7547
Fax: 213-747-2489
E-mail: alfonsos@infosel.net.mx

Excellent weekly newspaper; sister publication of the Mexican daily *El Financiero*.

MEXICO WATCH
3201 New Mexico Ave. N.W.
Suite 249
Washington D.C. 20016
Phone: 202-237-0155

Monthly Newsletter.

BUSINESS MEXICO
American Chamber of Commerce——Mexico
Lucerna 78
Col. Juarez
Mexico, D.F. 06600
Phone: (011)(52)(5) 724-3830
E-mail: amchammx@amcham.com.mx

Subscription in Mexico $120 a year; in the U.S. $134; outside of North America U.S. $150.

MEXICO BUSINESS
3033 Chimney Rock
Suite 300
Houston, TX 77056
Phone: 713-266-0861
Fax: 713-266-0980
From Mexico: 95-800-010-2166
E-mail: mailbox@mexicobusiness.com
Web: http://www.mexicobusiness.com/

Subscriptions are $45 in U.S. and Mexico.

MEXICO INVESTMENT UPDATE
Mexican Investment Board
221 East 63rd Street, 2nd Floor
New York, NY 10021
Phone: 212-821-0383, 800-642-2434
Fax: 212-223-6460

Free.

MEXICAN BUSINESS MONTHLY
214 Massachusetts Avenue, N.E.
Washington, DC 20002
Phone: 202-546-4400

MAQUILA
114 South Oregon Street
El Paso, TX 79001
United States
Phone: 915-542-0103

MEXICO CITY NEWS
Balderas 87
Col. Centro
06040 Mexico, D.F.
Phone: (52)(5) 518-5481, (52)(5) 512-1368
E-mail: news@novedades.com
Web: http://www.novedades.com

Daily newspaper; oldest English-language paper in Mexico.

MEXICO CITY TIMES
Avenida Juarez 100
06040 Mexico, DF
Phone: (525) 518-4262
Fax: 518-6639
E-mail: 74052.3051@compuserve.com

Monday-Saturday, English-language newspaper.

TWIN PLANT NEWS
4110 Rio Bravo Drive
Suite 108
El Paso, TX 79902
Phone: 800-880-1123, 915-532-1567
Fax: 915-544-7556

Monthly magazine focusing on the maquiladoras.

LATIN AMERICAN REGIONAL REPORT: MEXICO
Latin American Newsletters
61 Old Street
London EC1V 9HX
England
Phone: (44 17) 251-0012
Fax: 253-8183

The report appears 12 times per year.

LATIN AMERICAN MONITOR: MEXICO
56-60 St. John Street
London EC1M 4DT
England

Mexico is published monthly; subscriptions cost $235 per year.

MEXICO
Economic Intelligence Unit
13 Regent Street
London SW1Y 4LR
Phone: (44 71) 830-1000
Fax: 499-9767

Subscription: 4 issues/year, $350; a progressive discount rate is given on multiple subscriptions.

INDEX

V

A

295